7   Health

The Career Information Center includes:

7 Health

career information center

Sixth Edition

MACMILLAN LIBRARY REFERENCE USA
Simon & Schuster Macmillan
NEW YORK

Prentice Hall International
LONDON   MEXICO CITY   NEW DELHI   SINGAPORE   SYDNEY   TORONTO

Editorial Staff

Editorial Directors, Richard Lidz and Linda Perrin

Project Director, Suzanne J. Murdico

Editorial Assistant, Andrew Scoblionko

Writers, Debra Goldentyer, Bruce Goldstone, William Harless, Jonathan M. Leeds, Nancy J. Nielsen, Judith Peacock, Donna Singer

Copy Editor, Patricia Ciaccio

Photo Research Coordinator, Sara Matthews

Researchers/Bibliographers, Amy B. Lewis, Andrew Scoblionko

Production Supervisors, Amy Davis, William A. Murray

Electronic Production, Lisa Evans-Skopas, Cynthia C. Feldner

Art and Design, Maxson Crandall

Acknowledgments: It would be impossible to acknowledge the many people who gave their help, their time, and their experience to this project. However, we especially want to thank all the people at unions and trade and professional associations for their help in providing information and photographs. We also wish to thank the U.S. Department of Labor, Bureau of Labor Statistics, for their cooperation and for providing up-to-date statistics, salary information, and employment projections for all the job profiles.

Developed and produced by Visual Education Corp.,
Princeton, New Jersey

Macmillan Library Reference USA
Simon & Schuster Macmillan
866 Third Avenue
New York, NY 10022

ISSN 1082-703X

ISBN 0028974727 (set)

ISBN 0028974794 (volume 7)

Printed in the United States of America

printing number
1 2 3 4 5 6 7 8 9 10

This paper meets the requirements of ANSI/NISO Z39.48-1992 (Permanence of Paper).

Career Information Center
Editorial Advisory Board

Contents

Job Summary Chart

Job	Salary	Education/ Training	Employment Outlook	Page
Jobs Requiring No Specialized Training				
Admitting Clerk	Starting—$7 to $8 an hour Average—$8.50 to $9.50 an hour	High school	Very good	39
Ambulance Driver	Starting—$17,500 to $21,000 Average—$25,000	License	Good	40
Dental Assistant	Average—$17,300 to $19,100	High school	Very good	42
Dental Laboratory Technician	Varies—see profile	High school plus training	Fair	43
Dialysis Technician	Starting—$16,500 to $17,800 Average—$18,000 to $22,200	High school	Very good	45
EEG and EKG Technologist	Starting—$15,200 to $19,700 Average—$17,200 to $23,400	High school plus training	Varies— see profile	46
Home Health Aide	Starting—$6.25 an hour Average—$7.50 to $9.25 an hour	None	Excellent	48
Laboratory Animal Care Worker	Starting—$13,000 Average—$15,000 to $18,000	High school	Very good	50
Nurse's Aide and Orderly	Average—$13,800 to $17,900	None	Very good	51
Operating Room Technician	Average—$20,200 to $23,200	Voc/tech school	Excellent	52
Substance Abuse Counselor	Starting—$12,000 to $20,000 Average—$15,000 to $25,000	High school plus training	Excellent	54
Ward Clerk	Varies—see profile	High school	Good	55
Jobs Requiring Some Specialized Training/Experience				
Biomedical Equipment Technician	Average—$20,500 to $24,900	High school plus training	Very good	57
Dental and Medical Secretary	Starting—$15,000 to $17,500 Average—$20,000 to $27,000	High school	Good	58
Dental Hygienist	Average—$610 a week	2-year college; license	Excellent	60
Emergency Medical Technician	Average—$22,800 to $28,000	High school plus training	Very good	61
Hospice Worker	Varies—see profile	Varies—see profile	Varies— see profile	63

Job	Salary	Education/ Training	Employment Outlook	Page
Medical Laboratory Technologist	Starting—$18,200 to $22,600 Average—$24,900 to $36,800	Varies—see profile	Good	98
Medical Physicist	Starting—$30,000 to $41,000 Average—$78,000	Advanced degree	Good	100
Medical Record Administrator	Average—$28,000 to $35,000	College	Excellent	101
Nurse Anesthetist	Average—$66,600	Varies—see profile	Good	103
Nurse-Midwife	Starting—$31,000	College plus training	Good	105
Occupational Therapist	Starting—$28,000 to $32,200 Average—$30,500 to $45,000	Varies—see profile	Excellent	106
Ophthalmologist	Varies—see profile	Varies—see profile	Varies— see profile	108
Optometrist	Starting—$45,000 Average—$75,000	Varies—see profile	Good	110
Osteopathic Physician	Varies—see profile	Varies—see profile	Very good	112
Pharmacist	Varies—see profile	College; license	Very good	114
Pharmacologist	Starting—$24,000 to $35,400	Advanced degree	Good	115
Physical Therapist	Varies—see profile	College; license	Excellent	117
Physician	Varies—see profile	Advanced degree; license	Very good	119
Physician Assistant	Starting—$32,500 Average—$32,500 to $49,800	Varies—see profile	Excellent	121
Podiatrist	Starting—$35,600 Average—$100,300	Advanced degree; license	Very good	122
Prosthetist and Orthotist	Starting—$18,000 to $25,000	Varies—see profile	Excellent	124
Psychiatrist	Average—$110,000	Advanced degree; license	Very good	126
Psychologist	Starting—$30,000 to $34,000 Average—$48,000 to $76,000	Advanced degree	Excellent	127
Recreation Therapist	Varies—see profile	2-year or 4-year college	Very good	129
Registered Nurse	Average—$27,800 to $41,600	High school plus training	Excellent	131
Speech Pathologist and Audiologist	Starting—$28,000 to $29,100 Average—$33,900 to $42,100	Advanced degree	Excellent	133

Foreword

The sixth edition of the *Career Information Center* mirrors the ongoing changes in the job market caused by new technological and economic developments. These developments continue to change what Americans do in the workplace and how they do it. People have a critical need for up-to-date information to help them make career decisions.

The *Career Information Center* is an individualized resource for people of all ages and at all stages of career development. It has been recognized as an excellent reference for librarians, counselors, educators, and other providers of job information. It is ideally suited for use in libraries, career resource centers, and guidance offices, as well as in adult education centers and other facilities where people seek information about job opportunities, careers, and their own potential in the work force.

This sixth edition updates the features that made the earlier editions so useful.

- A Job Summary Chart, a quick reference guide, appears in the front section of each volume to help readers get the basic facts and compare the jobs described in the volume.
- Each volume of the *Career Information Center* begins with an overview of the job market in that field. These "Looking into . . ." sections have been completely revised and updated. They also include new graphs, charts, and boxes providing information such as industry snapshots and the fastest-growing and top-dollar jobs in the field.
- Each volume has a section called "Getting into . . . ," which contains useful information on entering the particular field. It offers self-evaluation and decision-making help; and it relates possible job choices to individual interests, abilities, and work characteristics. There is also practical information on job hunting, using classified ads, preparing resumes, and handling interviews. "Getting into . . ." also includes a section on employee rights.
- Each volume has a listing of all job profiles in the series and the volumes in which they appear, making access to profiles in other volumes easy.
- *Career Information Center* contains more than 648 occupational profiles in which over 3,000 jobs are discussed. Each profile describes work characteristics, education and training requirements, job entry, advancement possibilities and employment outlook, working conditions, and earnings and benefits.
- Job Summary Boxes, provided for each occupational profile, highlight the education or training required, salary range, and employment outlook. High-growth jobs are identified by means of an eye-catching logo.
- Volume 13 has been revised to reflect career concerns of the 1990s and employment trends through the year 2005. This volume includes updated articles on benefits, employment law, health in the workplace, job search strategies, job training, and job opportunities at home. This sixth edition also contains two completely new articles on adjusting to job loss and identifying opportunities for retraining.
- Volume 13 has been expanded with the addition of 35 new occupational profiles. These profiles contain complete, up-to-date descriptions of jobs not discussed in earlier editions of the *Career Information Center*.
- More than 750 photographs appear in the *Career Information Center,* including many new photos. Each profile is illustrated with a photo, providing a visual glimpse of life on the job. Special care has been taken to select photos that give the reader a sense of what it feels like to be in a specific field or job.
- Updated bibliographies in each volume include recommended readings in specific job areas. Additional titles for the vocational counselor are included in Volumes 1 and 13.
- Each volume also contains a comprehensive directory of accredited occupational education and vocational training facilities listed by occupational area and grouped by state. Directory materials are generated from the IPEDS (Integrated Postsecondary Education Data System) database of the U.S. Department of Education.

The *Career Information Center* recognizes the importance not only of job selection, but also of job holding, coping, and applied life skills. No other career information publication deals with work attitudes so comprehensively.

Using the Career Information Center

The *Career Information Center* is designed to meet the needs of many people—students, people just entering or reentering the job market, those dissatisfied with present jobs, those without jobs—anyone of any age who is not sure what to do for a living. The *Career Information Center* is for people who want help in making career choices. It combines the comprehensiveness of an encyclopedia with the format and readability of a magazine. Counselors, librarians, teachers, and other professionals will also find it a useful guidance and reference tool.

The *Career Information Center* is organized by occupational interest area rather than by alphabetical order. Jobs that have something in common are grouped together. In that way people who do not know exactly what job they want can read about a number of related jobs. The *Career Information Center* classifies jobs that have something in common into clusters. The classification system is adapted from the 20-cluster organization used by the U.S. Department of Labor into a more manageable 12-cluster system. Each volume of the *Career Information Center* explores one of these occupational clusters.

To use the *Career Information Center,* first select the volume that treats the occupational area that interests you most. Because there are many ways to group occupations, you may not find a particular job in the volume in which you look for it. In that case, check the central listing of all the profiles, which is located in the front of each volume (1 through 12). This listing will direct you to the number of the volume in which each profile appears. Volume 13 also includes a comprehensive index of all the jobs in the volumes.

After selecting a volume or volumes, investigate the sections that you feel would be most helpful. It isn't necessary to read these volumes from cover to cover. The books are arranged so that you can go directly to the specific information you want. Here is a description of the sections included in each book.

Job Summary Chart—This chart presents in tabular form the basic data from each profile: salary, education and training, employment outlook, and the page on which you can find the job profile.

Looking into . . .—An overview of the occupational cluster, which describes the opportunities, characteristics, and trends in that particular field.

Getting into . . .—A how-to guide designed to help you decide what jobs may be most satisfying to you and what strategies you can use to get the right job. You'll learn, for example, how to write an effective resume, how to complete an application form, what to expect in an interview, how to use networking, and what to do if someone has discriminated against you.

Job Summary Box—This box gives the most important facts about the job: education and training required, salary, and job outlook.

Education and Training indicates whether the job requires no education, high school, college, advanced degree, voc/tech school, license, or training.

Salary Range is given as an approximate yearly wage unless "a week" or "an hour" is noted. These are average salaries that may vary significantly from region to region.

Employment Outlook is based on Bureau of Labor Statistics' projections through the year 2005. The ratings are defined as follows: *poor* means there is a projected employment decrease of 1 percent or more; *fair* means there is a projected employment increase of 0 to 13 percent; *good* means there is a projected employment increase of 14 to 26 percent; *very good* means there is a projected employment increase of 27 to 40 percent; and *excellent* means there is a projected employment increase of 41 percent or more.

Finally, the job outlook is determined by the projected change in employment plus other factors. For example, a job with *excellent* projected employment growth in which many more people are entering the field than there are jobs available will have an outlook that is *good* rather than *excellent*.

For all categories, the phrase "varies—see profile" means the reader must consult the profile for the information, which is too extensive to include in the Job Summary Box.

An eye-catching logo appears in the upper right corner of some Job Summary Boxes to highlight jobs with high growth potential:

Jobs Requiring No Specialized Training, Jobs Requiring Some Specialized Training/Experience, Jobs Requiring Advanced Training/ Experience—These sections, organized by level of training required to get the job, are made up of the occupational profiles for each volume. Each profile explores a number of related jobs and covers seven major points: description of the job, the education and training requirements, ways to get the job, advancement possibilities and employment outlook, the working conditions, the earnings and benefits, and places to go for more information.

Jobs Requiring No Specialized Training includes jobs that require no education or previous work experience beyond high school.

Jobs Requiring Some Specialized Training/Experience includes jobs that require one, two, or three years of vocational training, college, or work experience beyond high school.

Jobs Requiring Advanced Training/Experience includes jobs that require a bachelor's or advanced degree and/or equivalent work experience in that field.

Further Reading and Resources—A selected bibliography that includes the most recent books and audiovisual materials on general career information, how-to books on such topics as resume writing and preparing for tests, useful computer software, and specific references for each volume. In addition, there are special sections of readings for the career counselor in Volumes 1 and 13.

Directory of Institutions Offering Career Training—A listing, organized first by career area, then by state, of the schools that offer occupational training beyond high school. For jobs requiring a bachelor's degree or an advanced degree, check a library for college catalogs and appropriate directories.

Index at end of each volume—This index serves not only to cross-reference all the jobs in the volume but also to show related jobs in the field. For example, under the entry LICENSED PRACTI-CAL NURSE, you will find Home Health Aide, Nurse's Aide and Orderly, and Ward Clerk. In addition, the "profile includes" part of an entry lists other jobs that are mentioned in the profile, in this case Licensed Vocational Nurse and Registered Nurse.

Volume 13, Employment Trends with Master Index—This volume includes several features that will help both the job seeker and the career counselor. A useful correlation guide provides the DOT (*Dictionary of Occupational Titles*) number of each of the job profiles in the *Career Information Center.* There is also a special section on career information for Canada. The updated and revised "Employment Trends" section contains articles on health in the workplace; employment projections through the year 2005; job search strategies; employment trends for women, minorities, immigrants, older workers, and the physically challenged; employment demographics; employment law; benefits programs; training; and employment opportunities at home. This section also contains two completely new articles on adjusting to job loss and identifying opportunities for retraining. All articles have been written by authorities in these fields. The articles provide job seekers and career professionals with an overview of current employment issues, career opportunities, and outlooks. In addition, this volume contains 35 job profiles that are new to this edition of the *Career Information Center.* Finally, there is a master index to all the jobs included in all 13 volumes.

The *Career Information Center,* then, is exactly what it says—a center of the most useful and pertinent information needed to explore and choose from the wide range of job and career possibilities. The *Career Information Center* provides people with a solid foundation of information for getting a satisfying job or rewarding career.

Career Information Center
Occupational Profiles*

Looking into Health

Every day millions of Americans turn to trained health care providers for their medical care. In private medical offices around the nation, physicians—assisted by nurses and aides—treat minor injuries such as sprained ankles and illnesses such as strep throat and childhood mumps, test patients to diagnose their ailments, and screen people for potential problems. They examine pregnant women and provide prenatal care. They also perform checkups for children and adults. For individuals at high risk for certain diseases, they administer immunizations.

In hospitals, a greater variety of health care professionals perform a greater variety of tasks. Medical professionals help individuals who have immediate, severe, or longer-term needs. Emergency room physicians examine and treat people with immediate life-threatening illnesses or who suffer from severe bleeding or injuries. Internists diagnose and treat medical problems and provide medications that pharmacists prepare. Surgeons, with the help of anesthesiologists, nurses, and others, perform surgical operations.

Every day technicians in hospitals conduct X rays, lab analyses, and other diagnostic tests. Hospital nurses check the vital signs of patients, administer medications, and maintain charts on patient progress. Orderlies, nurse's aides, and others tend to the physical needs of patients, bathe them, and deliver their meals. Dietitians and physical, occupational, and other therapists help patients prepare for release from the hospital. Behind the scenes, supervisors, administrators, social workers, accountants, maintenance workers, admissions clerks, patient records clerks, and other staff members keep the hospital running smoothly.

On the road, ambulance drivers rush paramedics and emergency medical technicians to people injured in car accidents, caught in fires, and endangered by other emergencies. These medical workers provide immediate first aid, set fractures, and keep injured or ill people safe until they get to the hospital. In private homes and in residential health care facilities, nurses, aides, and doctors tend to elderly people and people with chronic medical problems.

Keeping Americans healthy requires millions of workers and billions of dollars—and the numbers keep growing. Overall, the health care industry in the United States employs more than 7 million trained workers.

From Magic to Modern Medicine

In ancient times, people knew little about what caused disease or how the human body worked. They concluded that evil spirits or angry gods caused illness. Some of their cures—boring holes in the skull to let out evil spirits, for example—did more harm than good. Nevertheless, ancient people made some important medical discoveries. More than 4,000 years ago, people in Ancient Egypt were already using castor oil to purge the digestive system and tannic acid to treat burns. An Egyptian text written around 2500 B.C. describes how to use compression to stop bleeding.

The man considered to be the founder of modern medicine was a Greek physician named Hippocrates, who lived in the fifth century B.C. Hippocrates and his followers wrote about 70 books describing a new philosophy of medicine, based not on folklore or magic, but on careful observation of patients and detailed records of their symptoms. With this information, physicians could draw accurate conclusions about what caused disease and how it could be treated. This procedure—collecting data and using it to draw conclusions—is the basis of what we call the scientific method.

Hippocrates made two other lasting contributions to medical science. His observations led him to conclude that disease is often the result of diet, climate, occupation, or other environmental factors. Hippocrates also established a standard of conduct for physicians that still guides the medical profession today. These standards are summarized in the Hippocratic oath, which all new physicians are still required to take. The Hippocratic oath includes this vow: "I will practice my profession with conscience and dignity; the health of my patient will be my first consideration."

The Search for Causes

Ideas like those of Hippocrates did not have a widespread impact on medicine until the Renaissance in the 16th century. The Renaissance was a period of intense intellectual awakening and scientific inquiry in all fields, including medicine. The first accurate anatomy text was published in 1543, about the same time that serious research began into the cause of infectious diseases. A century later, the first precise description of blood circulation appeared, along with an explanation of how the lungs work.

Until then, no one had actually proved how disease spread. In the mid-19th century, a series of experiments by Louis Pasteur proved that microorganisms called bacteria can invade the body and cause infection and disease. More important, Pasteur discovered how to prevent this bacterial invasion through immunization. Robert Koch, considered cofounder with Pasteur of the science of bacteriology, identified the specific bacteria that cause tuberculosis and cholera.

The pace of medical progress quickened in the 19th and 20th centuries. In the 1840s, the use of ether as an anesthetic made possible many surgical operations that were previously too painful for patients to bear. The development of X rays in 1895 revolutionized the diagnostic process. Alexander Fleming's 1928 discovery of penicillin, the first antibiotic, was also a landmark achievement. For the first time a drug could kill disease-causing organisms inside the body of a person who was already ill.

In recent years the fight against the deadly AIDS epidemic has been a key focus of public health agencies around the world.

Medical Science and Public Health

By the mid-19th century medical science had proved what Hippocrates suspected: Disease is often caused by an unsafe environment. This knowledge led officials to begin massive programs to improve public health. They drained swamps to eliminate disease-carrying insects, sanitized drinking water supplies, and quarantined people with infectious diseases. They also began programs of education and vaccination, which led to the virtual eradication of diseases such as cholera, typhus, typhoid fever, and yellow fever in the United States.

Today public health agencies continue their work to keep the public safe and well informed. The United States Centers for Disease Control and Prevention (CDC), the World Health Organization (WHO), and other agencies continue to research new ways to prevent the spread of infectious diseases, promote health, and prolong life.

The CDC's mission is to keep track of diseases in the United States and to help control them. Statisticians and lab workers at the agency pay close attention to epidemics, their spread, and their prevention. The role of the WHO is to oversee the public health of all members of the United Nations. The WHO helps governments to promote family planning and to provide their citizens with access to primary health care. It also watches population patterns and funds public health research and development. The WHO employs researchers, primary health care providers, and others who focus on education, food and water supply, sanitation, immunization, and the prevention and control of disease.

Public health agencies also serve as educators, warning people of health hazards such as those posed by smoking, alcohol and drug abuse, occupational hazards, and environmental pollution. In recent years the fight against the deadly AIDS epidemic has been a key focus of public health agencies around the world.

The Technology Revolution

Slowly at first, and then rapidly since the beginning of the 20th century, technology has revolutionized the practice of medicine. The first three high-tech diagnostic tools—X-ray machines, electroencephalographs (EEGs), and electrocardiographs (EKGs or ECGs)—were all developed early in this century. X-ray machines aim X-ray beams at patients' bodies. Since X rays are better absorbed by bone and other dense structures than by soft tissue such as the lungs, their beams cast shadows of varying intensity. These shadows can be captured on X-ray film. Trained physicians and X-ray technicians can read this film to detect bone fractures, as well as to locate unexplained shadows that may be cast by tumors, infections, or foreign objects.

EEGs and EKGs use electrical impulses to diagnose physical problems. By placing electrodes on a patient's scalp or chest, medical personnel can study the pattern of electricity caused by the movement of

nerve impulses within the body. Certain distinct, abnormal patterns of nerve activity are signs of epilepsy, stroke, brain tumors, and heart disorders. Advanced EKG technology combines this analysis with computerized imaging software to construct a three-dimensional model of the heart, showing problem areas.

Computers and the Medical Profession

In recent decades computer technology has continued to have a tremendous impact on medicine.

In recent decades computer technology has continued to have a tremendous impact on medicine. Computerized axial tomography (CAT or CT) scanners, first used in the 1970s, combine X rays with computerized images, giving physicians even greater detailed information about tumors and cysts within the body. Magnetic resonance imaging (MRI) scanners use radio signals to help diagnose disorders in tissues.

More recent types of diagnostic scanners can show the level of cell activity in certain parts of the body. These scanners can help detect cancer cells, since cancer cells generally grow more quickly than normal cells. Positron-emission tomography (PET) scanners can track the presence of a radioactive isotope. Physicians introduce a small amount of that isotope into the patient's body, then use the PET scanner to see where it travels. A high concentration of the isotope indicates cancer cells. PET scanners are used to locate brain tumors, investigate epileptic attacks, and study brain function in various mental illnesses.

Other medical procedures employ sound technology. Ultrasound scanners use sound waves to view conditions within the body, while lithotripsy uses sound waves to break down large gallstones. Another new technology—magnetoencephalography—permits physicians to study the magnetic fields within the brain, providing even greater detail than

EKGs can. With these high-tech tools, and others such as laser surgery and video imaging, physicians are learning more about the body—both its functions and its malfunctions.

Computer technology also helps physicians, technicians, and nurses manage the vast amount of medical information they need to access records, make diagnoses, and decide on treatment plans. Some computer programs permit physicians to input the medical history of a patient along with information on the patient's current symptoms. The program then compares this information against databases of general medical and pharmaceutical information. After analyzing the symptoms, the program suggests several possible diagnoses, ranks their probability, and lists the tests, treatments, and drug therapies appropriate for each. Of course, computer technology cannot replace the role of the physician, but it can save physicians and patients time and money.

Computers can also aid in patient therapy. Besides helping medical personnel design artificial bones and limbs, prosthesis software gives orthopedic surgeons the ability to customize artificial limbs to match patients' individual needs. Computer-embedded prostheses, therapeutic visors, and other space-age technologies all exist today, and they are helping to improve the lives of millions of people.

Computer-assisted training also is a major part of medical school education. Research developed from detailed CAT scans of cadavers, for example, has resulted in detailed computer-based anatomy texts, which give medical students the ability to use computers to study their subjects, in color, from any angle, and with enhanced detail. Interactive diagnostic programs provide students with experience that cannot be found in ordinary textbooks. The programs allow students to practice observing and diagnosing medical problems.

Computers also play an important part in helping nursing staff and records technicians keep patient records up-to-date and accessible at a keystroke.

The People Doing the Work

All the technology available today is useless without trained, educated health care workers. Inside the hospitals, in doctors' offices, and elsewhere, experts with a wide variety of skills provide medical care. Within the broad categories of doctors, nurses, and technicians are scores of specialized occupations.

Physicians

Physicians today make up about 7 percent of the health care work force. Until after World War I, almost all doctors were general practitioners who treated anyone who came to them, young and old alike. These professionals delivered babies, set broken bones, prescribed medicines and other treatments for disease, and comforted the dying.

As medicine became more complex, medical doctors became more specialized. Nearly 90 percent of all physicians in the United States today are specialists. The majority practice near major medical centers in and around large cities. Cardiologists treat heart patients; nephrologists treat individuals with kidney problems; gerontologists work with the elderly; pediatricians specialize in caring for babies and children; hematologists deal with disease of the blood; and dermatologists treat skin disease and skin problems. Occupational medicine physicians study problems caused by the workplace, such as noise-induced hearing loss, multiple chemical sensitivity, and repetitive stress syndrome. Today there are specialists in every field, including gynecology, ophthalmology, urology, neurology, otolaryngology, psychiatry, and dozens of others.

Although for some time now there has been a trend toward specialization, some physicians have recently begun to move back to general practice (often called family practice). Family practice remains a popular choice among medical school students today, even though it is traditionally a lower-paying field. Family physicians often run private practices. They treat minor ailments; teach disease prevention, nutrition, and good health care; and screen for potential problems.

Not all doctors are medical doctors (M.D.s). Osteopathic physicians (D.O.s), for example, receive much the same education and training as M.D.s and employ many standard medical techniques. However, they approach medicine with a different philosophy. Osteopaths take a holistic approach to medicine, looking for a connection between diet, lifestyle, and environmental factors in diagnosis and treatment. Osteopaths generally focus on the impact of the musculoskeletal system on illness and disorders and often use physical manipulation, rather than medicine or surgery, to diagnose and treat problems.

Some health care practitioners have advanced degrees and licenses but are neither M.D.s nor D.O.s. These include chiropractors, who concentrate on skeletal and muscular wellness and treat pain and problems of alignment by manipulating the bones and muscles; optometrists, who prescribe corrective lenses for sight or eye muscle problems; and psychologists, who treat mental problems.

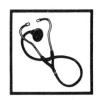

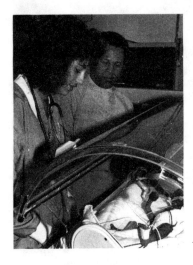

Nurses and Nurse Practitioners

According to some estimates, the current supply of doctors (about 556,000) exceeds the demand throughout much of the country, although many rural areas still suffer a shortage. In stark contrast, nurses have been in short supply for the past several decades, and the demand will continue to grow through the turn of the century. By the late 1980s, the nursing shortage climbed to 20,000 and was deemed so critical that some hospitals were paying signing bonuses of up to $10,000 for each new nurse hired.

One reason for the increased demand is that people are living longer, and they need more nursing care. Also, the level of training required to operate high-tech monitoring and treatment equipment has led many hospitals and other health care facilities to require that nurses have advanced training. Like people in other medical professions, many nurses now specialize, getting additional training beyond their basic four-year degree or diploma. In hospitals and clinics, some nurses work in a particular area of care, such as cardiology, pediatrics, or psychiatry. Others become nurse anesthetists, nurse clinicians, or nurse educators. Nurse-midwives, who are qualified to provide gynecological care and obstetric care, are able to deliver babies when no medical complications are expected.

Nurse practitioners are registered nurses with advanced training. Some practice alongside physicians; others work independently. Nurse practitioners perform many of the same tasks as physicians. Frequently they examine and treat patients in settings where physicians are not readily available.

In the mid-1990s, six of the ten fastest growing occupations have been in health care.

Allied Health Professionals

Changes in technology and payment structures, as well as growth in the demand for health care, have led to an increased need for workers who can provide medical services. In the mid-1990s, six of the ten fastest-growing occupations have been in health care.

Medical assistants work in hospitals and doctors' offices, performing both clinical and administrative work. Physical therapists, occupational therapists, respiratory therapists, recreational therapists, speech pathologists, and other therapists help patients regain or improve their physical skills. Therapy assistants and aides work with therapists and prepare patients for therapy.

Athletic trainers and sports therapists work with athletes and others to keep them physically fit and uninjured. Dietitians and nutritionists, working both inside and outside hospitals, help individuals learn how what they eat can affect their health. Physician assistants, like nurse practitioners, have some (but not all) of the training of medical doctors and may examine patients alongside doctors. Physician assistants may perform laboratory tests and make preliminary diagnoses.

As health care becomes even more dependent on technology, the demand for medical technicians continues to rise. Three of the fastest-

growing occupations are EEG technologists, radiologic technologists, and medical records technicians. Skilled technicians trained to operate dialysis machines are also in demand, as are technicians who operate CAT scanners, MRI scanners, and PET scanners.

Alternative Medicine Professionals

Although many alternative medicine treatments are considered unorthodox, or even worthless, by the medical establishment, an increasing number of people are turning to these methods. In addition, more and more doctors trained in conventional medicine are incorporating these alternatives into their practices. Some health care practitioners even specialize in one area of alternative medicine. For example, herbologists use herbs and other plants to heal and prevent disease. Homeopaths work under the theory that giving an individual a minute amount of a substance that causes a disease can cure or prevent that disease. Acupuncturists insert thin needles into certain parts of the body to ease pain and cure problems. Acupressurists use pressure and touch to help relieve patients' physical problems. These and other alternative healing methods date back centuries.

Beyond the Medical Office and Hospital

Not all health care is delivered in medical offices or in hospitals. Hospitals today have diversified their services to include hospital-run convalescent units, outpatient clinics, rehabilitation centers, and treatment centers for patients suffering from substance abuse.

Ambulatory surgical centers, also known as surgicenters, and freestanding emergency centers, or urgicenters, play an important role in giving individuals greater access to medical care. Low-risk minor surgical procedures such as hernia repairs, tissue biopsies, and some forms of cosmetic surgery are performed in surgicenters. These centers can keep their costs low because they do not need sophisticated backup equipment or provisions for long hospital stays.

Urgicenters operate much like hospital emergency rooms. They are often open seven days a week, 12 to 24 hours a day. Doctors, physician

assistants, and nurse practitioners at urgicenters treat minor problems such as broken bones, sprained ankles, sore throats, stomachaches, and cuts that require stitches. A visit to an urgicenter is usually more expensive than a visit to a doctor's office, but less costly than a visit to a hospital emergency room.

Home-based health care is becoming another alternative to inpatient care as hospitals work to keep costs down by shortening patients' hospital stays. More patients are now sent home still requiring full-time or frequent medical care. Thousands of agencies in this country offer home health care services for the elderly, for people who are recovering after surgery, and for people who are chronically ill. Some of these agencies are hospital based, whereas others are affiliated with community health centers or religious groups. Skilled home health service agencies provide nursing, physical and occupational therapy, and speech therapy. Some agencies also provide support services such as personal care, light housekeeping, meal preparation, and transportation, which enable people to continue living independently despite their health limitations. A great number of elderly people now live on their own, with only occasional care from a physical therapist or aides who can help with chores or physical care.

Individuals who cannot live on their own without frequent medical or nursing care often move into nursing homes, rehabilitation centers, or other long-term care facilities. Here they have 24-hour access to nurses and aides and ready access to physicians. Hospices, which can be either part of residential health care facilities or home based, are for dying individuals who want a comfortable surrounding in which to spend the last days of their lives.

The range of health care delivery options will grow even more diverse in the future, as health care delivery becomes more complex and providers look for new ways to hold down costs. The good news for health care workers is that the development of new health care delivery systems will mean more jobs. From an employment perspective, the health care industry will be a center of growth throughout the rest of the 20th century.

Home-based health care is becoming another alternative to inpatient care as hospitals work to keep costs down by shortening patients' hospital stays.

Health Care Research and Education

A major area of health care is research and education. Health care researchers are constantly working to invent new technologies and improve existing technologies. Researchers and inventors continue to look for technology that will help individuals overcome or compensate for disabilities. Medical researchers, epidemiologists, and pathologists study diseases and seek cures and preventive measures. Geneticists study genes to discover how they may be used to predict or even prevent problems in their patients.

The technologies currently used to diagnose illness are also being used to discover more about the human body and mind. PET scanners, for example, are being used to discover how we learn and retain lan-

Industry Snapshots

Health Care

The future of health care will be decided by the outcome of the debate over how to control costs. Regardless of the decisions made, however, the field will remain one of the strongest growth industries into the 21st century. The increasing prominence of cost-effective alternative delivery care systems, such as home-based health care, will create many jobs.

Hospitals and HMOs

The growing cost of health insurance means that more and more individuals and employers will be turning to alternative health care plans such as HMOs and PPOs. Competition between hospitals and HMOs will lead to widespread restructuring, with large hospital chains and HMOs coming out on top.

Doctors

Most physicians—nearly 90 percent of all physicians in the United States today—are specialists practicing in major medical centers in and around large cities. However, many physicians are returning to family practice. Although there is an overall surplus of doctors, many rural areas still suffer a shortage. As the number of insured people covered by HMOs increases, more and more doctors will work as salaried employees.

Nurses

The rapid growth of home health care and the high demand for nurse practitioners have made the shortage of nurses even more acute. There are currently more than 1.8 million registered nurses in the United States, and the number is expected to increase to more than 2.6 million by the year 2005. The greatest opportunities will be for those nurses trained in high-tech medical specialties.

Allied Health Workers

This field includes some of the fastest-growing occupations in health care, particularly medical technicians. Medical assistants and physical therapists will also be in great demand through the next decade. As health care becomes even more technology intensive, health workers with technical and computer training will continue to be in demand.

guage. They are also an integral part of the study of the causes of hyperactivity. EEG brain wave studies are being used to learn more about depression and other mental problems. Other technologies are being developed that promise to diagnose heart and brain problems before they become acute.

Research into health care policy also is extremely active today. Health economists, for example, advise hospital administrators and public health officials on the financing of health services. Health economists are playing a role in developing health care funding reform measures.

Health educators go to schools, public health clinics, and workplaces to teach people how to care for their own health. They teach about nutrition, exercise, alcoholism, smoking cessation, stress reduction, and ways to avoid sexually transmitted diseases. They also maintain

libraries, serve as information resources for the public, and write articles for popular journals about health care.

Paying for Health Care

While health care technologies and techniques continue to develop, the provision of health care has become increasingly expensive. From the point of view of many Americans, the cost of health care has reached a crisis level. Yet the nation appears to be at odds about how to solve this problem and how health care should be paid for.

The Increasing Cost of Health Care

It now costs nearly $1 trillion annually—more than $3,000 per person—to meet America's health care needs.

Hippocrates could not have imagined the range of medical miracles his philosophy of medicine has made possible: heart transplants, chemotherapy, test-tube babies, artificial hip replacements, and even gene therapy. Today the nation's skilled corps of medical professionals, supported by an army of scientists and a sophisticated array of diagnostic and treatment tools, provide an unprecedented level of health care. However, the cost of this care is unprecedented as well. It now costs nearly $1 trillion annually—more than $3,000 per person—to meet America's health care needs.

Several factors account for the rapid growth of health care costs over the past several decades. First and foremost, Americans are now living longer. Over the years, medical advances have reduced the number of people who die young from diseases such as polio and tuberculosis. Americans take better care of themselves through better nutrition, increased workplace safety, and better preventive care. Longer life expectancy, combined with a lowered birth rate, has driven the median age of the population upward.

The number of expensive treatment and diagnostic options has also increased. Major organ transplants, coronary bypass surgery, and long-term kidney dialysis—all extremely costly procedures—have become commonplace. Technological innovations permit low-birthweight babies and individuals with serious physical impairments (such as accident victims) to survive, although at significant expense. Equipment costs, development costs, and usage costs can be extremely high. Some technologies, such as PET scanners, can cost millions of dollars and are expensive to maintain. Developing, testing, and receiving approval for new drugs can also prove very costly.

Another factor driving up the cost of health care is the growing number of malpractice suits against doctors and other medical professionals. Physicians today pay tens of thousands of dollars each year in malpractice insurance premiums.

Insurance: The Traditional Payment Method

Traditionally, Americans' health care is paid for by medical insurance, which is supplied in all or in part by their employers. Under traditional indemnification insurance, patients receive medical treatment from the

Employment by Occupation, 1992 and 2005 (in thousands)		
Occupation	**1992**	**2005***
Registered Nurse	1,835	2,601
Nurse's Aide/Orderly	1,308	1,903
Physician	519	548
Dentist	183	192
Pharmacist	163	221
Radiologic Technologist	162	264
Dental Hygienist	108	154
Physical Therapist	90	170
Physician Assistant	58	78
Dietitian and Nutritionist	50	63
Chiropractor	46	62

*projected

SOURCE: Bureau of Labor Statistics, *Occupational Projections and Training Data*, 1994.

providers of their choice and send the bills to the insurance companies for payment. Under this system, individuals have no incentive to shop around for bargains, and providers have no incentive to limit costs.

This situation has changed in recent years. As the cost of health care increases, the cost of health care insurance also rises, causing employers to cut back on insurance coverage or to limit the options available to employees. Today, because of less employer coverage and more unemployment, more than 3 million Americans have no coverage for health care and are faced with staggering medical bills when they become sick or injured.

Since the mid-1960s, the federal government has been paying medical costs for two groups that do not generally have employers—the elderly and the poor—through its Medicare and Medicaid plans. These plans help to make sure that everyone has access to health care. Nevertheless, increasing numbers of people are largely or even entirely uninsured and at risk of not getting the care they need in a timely and comprehensive way. Moreover, debates in Congress over how best to reduce the budget may limit the umbrella coverage that currently exists.

Cost-Saving Initiatives
In recent years the nation's health care providers have been under increasing pressure to curb spiraling costs. Hospitals that are part of chains owned by for-profit corporations have also been under pressure to increase profits.

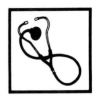

Political leaders, insurance companies, and providers are working together to find a solution to the dilemma of rising health care costs.

As a result, health care providers, economists, and regulators continue to look for new, more cost-effective ways to deliver and pay for health care. Political leaders, insurance companies, and providers are working together to find a solution to the dilemma of rising costs. One approach is to reduce costs through new delivery systems, such as surgicenters. Another is to use less expensive providers, such as nurse practitioners, instead of doctors, whenever feasible.

Other innovations are directed at how health care is paid for. One innovation was the development of diagnostic related groups (DRGs). DRGs were first implemented by the U.S. government in its Medicare system. Under the older system, hospitals had treated Medicare patients and then billed the government. The longer patients stayed in the hospital and the more procedures they underwent, the more the hospital could charge. Under this system, the hospital had no incentive to minimize costs.

The DRG plan, initiated by Congress in 1983, put health economists to work to predetermine how much a hospital should expect to spend for each of nearly 500 categories of illnesses. The government established fees for each illness, based on the average cost of treating it, taking into account the length of a typical hospital stay, the number of diagnostic tests, and the cost of surgery and other procedures. Under this system, hospitals may charge the government only the DRG rate and no more. If the hospital's actual cost of treating a Medicare patient exceeds the set DRG rate, then the hospital loses money. On the other hand, hospitals that find ways to cut the cost of treatment are allowed to keep the overpayment amount.

Top-Dollar Jobs in Health

These are high-paying jobs described in this volume. The figures represent typical salaries or earnings for experienced workers.

$100,000–$200,000	Physician Psychiatrist
$70,000–$125,000	Chiropractor Dentist Ophthalmologist Podiatrist
$40,000–$75,000	Hospital Administrator Medical Physicist Optometrist Psychologist

Summer Jobs in Health

Health Care

Summer internships are available in hospitals and health care agencies. Summer jobs are available for medical and dental assistants, nurse's aides and orderlies, therapy assistants, and laboratory assistants. Contact:
- doctors' and dentists' offices
- hospitals and clinics
- nursing homes
- health care agencies
- camps for the disabled

Sources of Information

American Hospital Association
1 North Franklin
Chicago, IL 60606

National Association of Community Health
  Centers
1330 New Hampshire Avenue, NW, Suite 122
Washington, DC 20036

Related Services

Summer jobs are available in hospitals and nursing homes for catering and housekeeping workers. Clerical workers are needed in hospital admissions and records departments and in doctors' offices. Home health care workers can assist housebound patients. Contact:
- hospitals
- nursing homes
- employment agencies
- social service agencies

Sources of Information

American Health Care Association
1201 L Street, NW
Washington, DC 20005

National Association of Health Unit
  Coordinators
1821 University Avenue, Suite 104
St. Paul, MN 55104

Medical Research

Summer internships are available in universities, research institutes, and hospitals. Summer jobs include those of research assistant, laboratory assistant, and animal care worker. Clerical workers are also needed during summer vacations. Contact:
- research institutions
- hospitals
- medical supply companies
- pharmaceutical companies
- government research agencies

Sources of Information

American Federation for Clinical Research
6900 Grove Road
Thorofare, NJ 08086-9431

Many private insurers have adopted a similar payment system. Because nearly all medical care in this country is paid for by private insurance or the government, this trend has significant implications. Specifically, it means that the control of health care is shifting from health care providers to insurance companies and others who pay for the health care.

More Innovations

While the government took the lead in establishing the DRG system, private insurers and providers have organized two alternative health care plans in their effort to help curtail rising costs. Health maintenance organizations (HMOs) offer medical coverage in a way that is fundamentally different from standard private medical insurance. An HMO is a group of health care providers—including doctors, nurses, and other health care specialists—located at one or more of the HMO's facilities. People join an HMO by paying a fixed monthly fee. When members become ill or need checkups, they visit physicians associated with the HMO, usually at little or no cost to the member. When necessary, HMO physicians refer patients to outside specialists and hospitals. Many employers will pay some or all of the costs for employees who join an HMO because the monthly fees are usually lower than comparable coverage under conventional medical insurance. Under an HMO system, the emphasis is on preventive care. Individuals are encouraged to visit doctors and other providers before their problems become severe.

A variation of the HMO is the preferred provider organization (PPO). A PPO is a network of physicians designated by a particular insurance company to provide medical service. The insurance company offers incentives to its subscribers for choosing a preferred provider. For example, if a patient visits a preferred provider, the insurance company may pay 100 percent of the charges, whereas it may pay only 80 percent of the bill if the patient visits a doctor who is not a member of its designated PPO network.

National Health Care Coverage Debate

Even with these new developments, the cost of health care continues to rise and access remains limited. Many political and business leaders believe the time is ripe for a comprehensive reform of the health care system. Proposals vary, but one of the most frequently suggested alternatives to the current system is an organized delivery system based on managed competition. Under this system, consumers would obtain insurance coverage through large corporations, the federal government, or regional nonprofit health care purchasing collectives sponsored by individual states. These organizations in turn would negotiate insurance contracts with organized delivery systems, such as HMOs, most of which would be run by major insurance companies. Advocates say this plan strikes a balance between free enterprise and government regulation and would provide coverage for everyone. Many oppose such a plan, however, in part out of fear of overregulation. Moreover, the current trend in the federal government is to eliminate government involvement in the private sector.

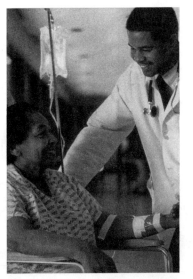

Health Care and Your Future

This volume describes 58 different occupations in a career field that is exciting, stimulating, and rewarding. Only you, by carefully examining each occupation and honestly evaluating your talents and interests, can decide if one is right for you. As you look into the health field, however, remember two key trends.

First, the health care industry as a whole will continue to grow rapidly into the 21st century, creating a wealth of new and diverse opportunities and new jobs. For example, as new technologies develop, opportunities for medical technicians will continue to increase. As new treatment techniques are developed, the need for physical therapists, medical assistants, and other aides and assistants will also increase. Few other industries will offer as many opportunities for employment and advancement.

Second, however, health care providers will find themselves in an increasingly competitive environment in the future. The pressure to keep costs under control may force unprofitable hospitals to close down. Doctors and those in other overstaffed professions will face stiff competition for jobs and slower salary growth. Nurses will see their roles change as they take over more responsibilities from doctors and relinquish some of their traditional duties to aides and other patient care workers. Wise job seekers will monitor these changes and evaluate their impact on employment.

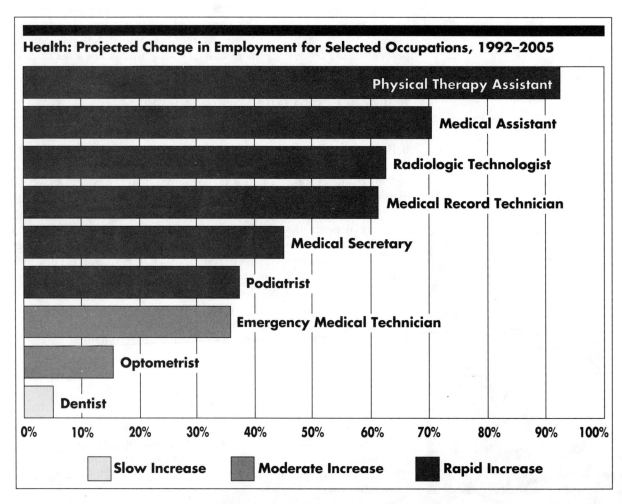

Health: Projected Change in Employment for Selected Occupations, 1992–2005

Getting into Health

Good jobs rarely, if ever, just fall out of the sky. As anybody who has ever been in the job market knows, getting the "right" job takes planning, perseverance, and patience. There are, however, a number of things you can do to make the process easier and more rewarding. This is true whether you are looking for your first job, reentering the labor market, trying to get a new job, or planning a mid-career change.

This essay is designed to serve as your guide to the process of finding a job in the field of health. It starts off with the basics—helping you define your career objectives. Then it takes you through a number of steps that will help you work out a strategy to achieve these goals.

Evaluating Yourself

Most people enjoy doing a job well. Quite apart from any praise from employers or fellow workers, there's an inner satisfaction in knowing that you've taken on a challenge and then succeeded in accomplishing something worthwhile. If you are unhappy or dissatisfied in your job and you are just trying to do enough to get by, you may have a job for which you are not suited. It is also frustrating to do work that is not challenging because you are overqualified for it.

Making a Self-Inventory Chart

Before you make any career decisions, give some thought to your areas of interest and to what you do well. One very useful way of going about this is to compile a brief history of yourself in a self-inventory chart. Such a chart will be helpful when you are deciding what jobs you want to consider. It will also save time when you are writing cover letters and resumes, filling in applications, and preparing for job interviews.

Begin your self-inventory chart by listing all the jobs you have ever had, including summer employment, part-time jobs, volunteer work, and any freelance or short-term assignments you have done. Include the dates of employment, the names and addresses of supervisors, and what you earned. Then add a similar list of your hobbies and other activities, including any special experiences you may have had, such as travel. Next, do the same for your education, listing your schools, major courses of study, grades, any special honors or awards, any courses you particularly enjoyed, and any extracurricular activities in which you were involved.

In determining what you do well and what you enjoy doing, you may find a career pattern beginning to develop. If, however, the picture still lacks detail or focus, try making a list of aptitudes, and then rate yourself *above average, average,* or *below average* for each one. Some of the qualities you might include in your list are administrative, analytic, clerical, creative, language, leadership, managerial, manual, mathematical, social, and verbal abilities. You might also rate your willingness to accept responsibility and your ability to get along with people.

"Evaluating Yourself" will help you take a close look at your interests, skills, and values so that you can make suitable and satisfying career choices.

Compiling a Work Characteristics Checklist

Another way of deciding what kind of work to do is to compile a work characteristics checklist. Go through the questions in the left margin, and then make a list of those work characteristics that are most important to you.

It would be a big mistake to reject a job because it does not meet all your requirements. You have to consider which job characteristics are most important. If the characteristics of a job match most of your preferences, you should give the position serious consideration.

Consulting Counselors

It's important to evaluate yourself and your career options realistically. An experienced career counselor can be of great help in this process. Counselors can give you a series of vocational interest and aptitude tests, and they can review them with you, interpreting and explaining the results.

Vocational testing and counseling can be found in guidance and counseling departments of high schools, vocational schools, and colleges. Some local offices of the state employment services affiliated with the federal employment service offer free counseling.

Consultants and career counseling firms are located in most major cities. The reputation of these services should be checked. (A list of counseling services in your area is available from the American Counseling Association, 5999 Stevenson Avenue, Alexandria, VA 22304. Send a stamped, self-addressed envelope.)

As a rule, counselors will not tell you what to do. They will talk over your options and help you search for conclusions. However, they will leave the final decision up to you. Remember, it's your decision, it's your job, and it's your life.

Evaluating Jobs

After you have taken a good look at what you do well and what you enjoy doing, the next step is to see how different jobs measure up to your abilities and interests. First make a note of all the jobs in this volume that interest you. Then examine the education and training required for these jobs. Decide whether you qualify and, if not, whether it's worth making an effort to get the extra qualifications. If possible, talk with someone who has such a job. Firsthand information can be invaluable. Also look through the appropriate trade and professional journals listed at the end of this essay, and check the section in this volume called "Further Reading and Resources" for books and audio-visual materials that contain more detailed information about the job. In addition, counselors usually have helpful information on careers in health. For more detailed information, you can write to the medical and professional associations listed at the end of each occupational profile.

Once you have found out all you can about a particular job, compare the features of the job with your work characteristics checklist. See how

many characteristics of the job match your work preferences. By following this exercise for all the jobs that appeal to you, you should be able to build up a collection of jobs that match your interests and abilities.

Ways to Find Job Openings

"Ways to Find Job Openings" outlines the methods and techniques you can use to find openings for the kind of work you want to do.

Once you've decided what kind of job suits you, the next step is to look for available positions. Obviously, the more openings you can find, the better your chance of landing a job. Usually, people apply for a number of openings before they are finally accepted.

There are many ways to find out about job openings. This section explores a number of job-hunting techniques and explains how you can follow up on job leads.

Job Finder's Checklist

The following list of job-hunting tips may seem obvious, but getting all the bits and pieces in order beforehand is a great help when you're looking for a job.

Resume. Bring your resume up to date. Assemble a supply of neatly typed copies.

Licenses. Have a copy handy of any professional certificates or licenses that an employer might wish to see to confirm your qualifications.

References. Line up your references. Ask permission of the people whose names you would like to use.

Contacts. Put the word out to everyone you know that you are looking for a job.

Job market. Find out where the jobs are. Make a list of possible employers in your field of interest.

Research. A little homework can go a long way. Find out as much as you can about a job—the field, the company—before applying for the job. A well-informed job applicant is a step ahead.

Organization. Keep a file on your job-hunting campaign with names and dates of employers contacted, ads answered, results, and follow-up.

Appearance. Make sure that the clothes you plan to wear to an interview are neat and clean and help to create a good impression. Business attire, rather than a medical uniform, is appropriate.

Ways to Find Job Openings

Applying in Person

For some jobs, especially beginning positions, your best method may be to apply directly to the company or companies for which you'd like to work. If you are looking for a position as an admitting clerk or ambulance driver, for example, you might make an appointment to see the person responsible for hiring. This is a good method to use for certain kinds of jobs, but applicants for professional or supervisory jobs generally send a letter and resume to the institution or employer first. As a rule, applying in person works best when jobs are plentiful or when an organization is expanding.

Applying in person will allow you to sharpen your interviewing techniques and give you a look at different places of employment. In the long run, however, you will probably get better results with other approaches that require more advance planning.

Phone and Letter Campaigns

To conduct a phone campaign, use the Yellow Pages of your telephone directory to build a list of companies for which you might like to work. Take down their phone numbers, call their personnel departments, and find out whether they have any openings. This technique is not useful in all situations, however. If you're calling from out of town, for example, a phone campaign can become very expensive. You may not be able to make a strong impression by phone. You also will not have a written record of your contacts with potential employers.

Letter-writing campaigns can be very effective if the letters are well thought out and carefully prepared. In the health profession, your letters should be typed. Handwritten letters do not convey a businesslike impression. Most employers will regard form letters or photocopies as indications of lack of interest or motivation.

Besides using the Yellow Pages, you can often get good lists of company addresses in your field of interest by reading the trade and professional publications listed at the end of this essay. Many of the periodicals publish directories or directory issues. Other sources you can use to compile lists of companies are the trade unions and professional organizations listed at the end of each occupational profile in this volume. The reference librarian at your local library can also help you find appropriate directories.

Your letters should be addressed to the personnel or human resources department of the company or health facility. If possible, send it to a specific person. If you don't know who the right person is, try to find the name of the personnel director through the directories in the library. You can also call on the phone and say, "I'm writing to ask about employment at your company. To whom should I address the letter?" If you can't find a name, use a standard salutation. It's a good idea to enclose a resume (described later in this essay) with the letter to give a concise idea of your qualifications and background.

Keep a list of all the people you've written to, along with the date each letter was mailed, or keep a photocopy of each letter. Then you

can follow up, by either a brief note or a phone call, on all those who do not reply within about three weeks.

Help-Wanted Ads

Many people find out about job openings by reading the help-wanted sections of newspapers, trade journals, and professional magazines. Many employers and employment agencies use help-wanted classifieds to advertise available jobs.

Classified ads have their own telegraphic language. Study the box for some common abbreviations. They are usually decodable by common sense, but if one puzzles you, call the newspaper and ask for a translation. The ads tell you how to contact the employers, and they generally state qualifications required. Some give the salary offered. These ads contain a lot of information in a small space. Read them carefully.

As you find openings of interest to you, follow up on each ad by using the method requested. You may be asked to phone or send a resume. Record the date of your follow-up, and if you don't hear from the employer within two or three weeks, place another call or send a polite note asking whether the job is still open. Don't forget to include your phone number and address or box number.

Many help-wanted ads are "blind ads." These ads give a box number but no name, phone number, or address. Employers and employment agencies place these "mystery" ads for a number of reasons. One is to avoid having to reply to all the applicants in whom they are not interested. In other words, it's quite common to hear nothing after answering a blind ad. So don't be discouraged by the lack of response.

Situation-Wanted Ads

Another way of getting the attention of potential employers is with a situation-wanted ad. This can be placed in the classified section of your local newspaper or of a trade journal in your field of interest. Many personnel offices and employment agencies scan these columns when they're looking for new people. The situation-wanted ad is usually most effective for those who have advanced education, training, or experience, since the ad might highlight just the qualifications in which an employer is interested. A situation-wanted ad could also be useful for someone interested in part-time work in the field of home health care, for example.

A situation-wanted ad should be brief, clear, and to the point. Its main purpose is to tell just enough to interest the employer in granting an interview. It should tell exactly what kind of job you want, why you qualify, and whether you are available for full-time or part-time work. Use abbreviations as appropriate.

If you are already employed and do not want it known that you are looking for a new position, you can run a blind ad. A blind ad protects your privacy by listing a box number at the publication to which all replies can be sent. They are then forwarded to you. You need not give your name, address, or phone number in the ad.

Reading the Classifieds

HELP WANTED

BIOMEDICAL TECHNICIAN

Suburban hospital is seeking 2 perm f/t bio-med techs to supervise medical equipment, maintenance program. For further information call 000-0000.
Pine Springs Hospital
Equal Opportunity Employer.

DENTAL ASSISTANT—Fee neg. Chair side & desk work. Exp. pfd. but not nec. Zenith Personnel, 555 Riverview, 000-0000.

LPN—Position avail. all shifts. Must have 6 months exp. and successful completion of formal medication course. Call Joan Philips, 000-0000. Orange County Hospital. Equal Opportunity Employer.

MEDICAL LAB. TECH.

Must have cert. Min. 3 yrs. exp., prefer emerg. lab. exp. Sal. commensurate w/exp. Ask for John, 000-0000.

MEDICAL SECRETARY F/P

Avail. immed. 2 yrs. medical sec. training or equivalent exp. Gd. typ., office skls. WP exp. helpful. Top hosp., sal., gd. bnfts. MEDICAL PLACEMENTS (agency), 000-0000 ext. 24.

ORDERLY

Good oppty for person with 2-3 yrs. exp. & good refs. H.S. grad prfd. Call 000-0000. Equal Opportunity Employer.

PHYSICAL THERAPIST PROGRESSIVE

Rehabilitation center is now accepting applications for registered physical therapists. Responsibilities incl. developmental therapy technique. Avail. Nov. 1. Call for appt. 000-0000.

RESPIRATORY THERAPIST

Afternoon shift. Immediate opening for person with AA degree in respiratory therapy & 6 months experience. Prefer registered therapist. Excellent benefits.
Send resume to OAK PARK HOSPITAL.
Equal Opportunity Employer.

Classified Abbreviations

admin.	administrative, administration
appt.	appointment
avail. immed.	available immediately
bkgd.	background
cert.	certification, certificate
co.	company
col.	college
dept.	department
emerg.	emergency
eves.	evenings
exp.	experience
ext.	phone extension
fee neg.	fee negotiable (fee can be worked out with employer)
f/p., f/pd.	fee paid (agency fee paid by employer)
f/t	full time
gd. bnfts.	good benefits
grad.	graduate
hosp.	hospital
hr.	hour
h.s.	high school
K	thousand
lab.	laboratory
M	thousand
mgr.	manager
min.	minimum
nec.	necessary
neg.	negotiable
oppty.	opportunity
perm.	permanent
pfd.	preferred
p/t	part time
refs.	references
sal.	salary
sec., secy.	secretary
skls.	skills
techs.	technicians
temp.	temporary
trnee.	trainee
typ.	typist, typing
w/	with
WP	word processing
yrs.	years

SITUATION WANTED

DENTAL HYGIENE—Student seeking summer job. 000-0000 Eves.

DENTIST

Trained in American university. Endo & Perio oriented. Seeks to join group practice in downtown area. Call 000-0000.

LPN—12 yrs. exp., hosp. trained. F/t or p/t. Excellent refs. 000-0000.

MEDICAL ASSISTANT—Excellent skills & experience, 000-0000.

MEDICAL RECORD TECHNICIAN

Organized, exp. tech seeks challenging oppty. HS grad w/3 yrs exp county hosp. Knowledge of computer systems. Call 000-0000.

MEDICAL SECY—Excellent skills & experience, 000-0000.

NURSE

Student seeks position in Dr.'s office or home. Also have office exp.
Call 000-0000.

NURSE'S AIDE seeks f/t temp work. Able to work eves. Hosp. & home nursing exp. Good refs. Call 000-0000.

OPTICIAN

Exp. dispensing & shopwork. Superior customer contact, seeks position 3 days a week. Would consider Saturday work, 000-0000.

PHARMACIST

Exp. hosp. dept. supervisor, state registered. Seek hosp. position conducting training programs, upgrading personnel, 000-0000.

RADIOLOGIC TECHNOLOGIST

Career-minded indiv. Grad. AMA approved program w/2 yrs exp. Avail immed, willing to work any shift.
Call 000-0000.

Networking includes talking with friends and acquaintances about jobs in your area of interest.

Networking

A very important source of information about job openings is networking. This means talking with friends and acquaintances about jobs in your area of interest. If you would like to work in dentistry, get in touch with all the people you know who work in dental offices, laboratories, or clinics or who have friends or relatives in the field. It makes sense to use all the contacts you have.

There's nothing wrong with telling everyone who will listen that you are looking for a job—family, friends, counselors, former employers. Get them interested in your efforts, and ask for their help in your search. Don't annoy them; just let them know you're looking. This will multiply your sources of information many times over. Contacts don't have to be high-level executives to be helpful. Sometimes, through a friend, you can find out about a job vacancy before it is advertised. You shouldn't use a contact's name without permission—you may put your informant on the spot with the employer. Don't assume that your friend will go out on a limb by recommending you, either. Once you have received the inside information, rely on your own ability to get the job.

Placement Services

Most vocational schools, high schools, and colleges have a placement or career service. If you are a student or recent graduate, you should definitely check there for job leads. Many employers look first in technical or trade schools and colleges for qualified applicants for certain jobs. Colleges are visited by recruiters looking for people to fill management trainee and other professional positions. These recruiters usually represent large health organizations. Visit your placement office regularly to check the job listings, and watch for scheduled visits by company recruiters.

State Employment Services

Another source of information about job openings is the local office of the state employment service. There are more than 2,700 such offices in the nation, and many employers automatically list job openings at the local office. Whether you're looking for a job in private industry or with the state, these offices, which are affiliated with the federal employment service, are worth visiting.

Notes on Networking

Let people know you're looking. Touch base with friends, acquaintances, teachers, health professionals, former employers—anyone who might know of job openings in your field.

Read newspapers and professional and trade journals for news of developments in your field and for names of people and companies you might contact.

Join professional or trade associations in your field. Contacts you make at meetings could provide valuable job leads. Association newsletters generally carry useful information about people and developments in the field.

Attend classes or seminars. You will meet other people in your field at job-training classes and professional development seminars.

Participate in local support groups such as Women in Business, Job Seekers, Forty Plus, Homemakers Reentering the Job Market, and alumni associations. You can gain information about people and places to contact.

Be on the lookout. Always be prepared to make the most of any opportunity that comes along. Talk with anyone who can provide useful information about your field.

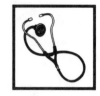

State employment service offices are public agencies that do not charge for their services. They can direct you to special programs run by the government in conjunction with private industry. These programs, such as the Work Incentive Program for families on welfare, are designed to meet special needs. Some, but not all, of these offices offer vocational aptitude and interest tests and can refer interested people to vocational training centers. The state employment service can be a valuable first stop in your search for work, especially if there are special circumstances in your background. For example, if you did not finish high school, if you have had any difficulties with the law, or if you are living in a difficult home environment, your state employment service office is equipped to help you.

Private employment agencies will contact employers who might be interested in you.

Private Employment Agencies

State employment services, though free, are usually very busy. If you are looking for more personal service and want a qualified employment counselor to help you find a job, you might want to approach a private employment agency.

Private employment agencies will help you get a job if they think they can place you. Most of them get paid only if they're successful in finding you a job, so you need to show them that you are a good prospect. These agencies will help you prepare a resume if you need one, and they will contact employers they think might be interested in you.

Private employment agencies are in the business of bringing together people who are looking for jobs and companies that are looking for workers. For some positions, usually middle- and higher-level jobs, the employment agency's fee is often paid by the employer. In such cases, there is no expense to the job seeker. In other cases, you may be required to pay the fee yourself, usually a percentage of your annual salary. Even if you have to pay a fee, it is a worthwhile investment if it leads to a rewarding career. In addition, the fee is tax deductible.

Some agencies may also ask for a small registration fee whether or not you get a job through them. Some agencies may even demand that you pay even though you find one of the jobs they are trying to fill through your other contacts. So be sure to read and understand the fine print of any contract you're about to sign, and ask for a copy to take home. Since the quality of these agencies varies, you should check to see if an agency is a certified member of a state or national association.

Private employment agencies are usually helping many people at one time. They may not have the time to contact you every time they find a job opening. Therefore, you might phone them at reasonable intervals after you've registered.

Computer Placement Services

The latest development in employment services is computer placement. Computer placement services are basically data banks (computerized information files) to which you send your resume or employment profile.

When a company that subscribes to the service has a job to fill, it can call up on its computer a certain combination of qualifications and quickly receive information on the candidate or candidates who fill the bill perfectly. For example, an employer might be looking for a pharmacist who has at least five years of experience, a background in hospital work, and fluency in Spanish and who is willing to relocate. Perhaps in the future everyone will use computer placement services. But for the moment, computer placement is still very limited in scope and number of users.

Civil Service
In your search for work, don't forget that the civil service—federal, state, and local—may have many health jobs. The armed services also train and employ civilians in many fields, including health. Don't neglect these avenues for finding jobs. Civil service positions usually require you to take a civil service examination. Books are available to help you prepare for these exams, and your local civil service office can give you information too.

Unions
In certain areas of health, for example, nursing, unions can be useful as sources of information. If you are a member of a union in your field of interest, you may be able to find out about jobs in the union periodical or from people at the union local.

Temporary Employment
A good way to get a feel for the job market is to work on a temporary basis. There are many agencies that specialize in placing people in short-term jobs in health care. Nurses, nurse's aides, and medical technicians are among the types of workers most in demand. Temporary employment can increase your job skills, your knowledge of a particular field, and your chances of hearing of permanent positions. And, in some cases, a temporary job can lead directly to a permanent position.

"Presenting Yourself on Paper" describes how you can make your written materials—resume, cover letter, application form—work to best advantage to get you a personal interview.

Presenting Yourself on Paper
The first impression you make on an employer is likely to be on paper. Whether in an application form or a letter, you will want to make as good an impression as possible, so that employers will be interested in giving you a personal interview. Your potential employer is likely to equate a neat and clean appearance with good work habits and a sloppy one with bad work habits.

Writing an Effective Resume
When you write to follow up a lead or to ask about job openings, you can do more than just ask for information. You can send information about yourself. The accepted way of doing this is to send a resume with your inquiry letter.

Resume is derived from the French word *résumer,* meaning "to summarize." A resume does just that—briefly outlines your education, work experience, and special abilities and skills. A resume may also be called a curriculum vitae, a personal profile, or a personal data sheet. This summary can act as your introduction by mail, as your calling card if you apply in person, and as a convenient reference for yourself when filling out an application form or when being interviewed.

A resume is a useful tool in applying for almost any job in the field of health. It is valuable, even if you use it only to keep a record of where you have worked, for whom, and the dates of employment. A resume is usually required if you are being considered for higher-level professional and executive jobs. Prepare it carefully. It's well worth the trouble.

The idea of a resume is to capture the interest of potential employers so that they will call you for a personal interview. Because employers are busy people, the resume should be as brief and as neat as possible. But you should include as much relevant information about yourself as you can. This is usually presented under at least two headings: "Education" and "Work Experience." The latter is sometimes called "Employment History." Many people add a third section titled "Special Skills," "Related Experience," or "Personal Qualifications."

If you prepare a self-inventory such as the one described earlier, it will be a useful aid in preparing a resume. Go through your inventory and select the items that show your ability to do the job or jobs in which you are interested. You should plan to highlight these items in your resume. Select only those facts that point out your relevant skills and experiences.

Once you have decided the special points worth mentioning, you can start preparing the resume. At the top, put your name, address, and phone number. After that, it's a question of deciding which items will be most interesting to the employer you plan to contact.

State Your Objective   Some employment counselors advise that you state a job objective or describe briefly the type of position for which you are applying. The job objective usually follows your name and address. Don't be too specific if you plan to use the same resume a number of times. It's better to give a general career goal. Then, in a cover letter, you can be more specific about the position you are seeking in the particular firm you are contacting.

Describe What You've Done   Every interested employer will check your educational background and employment history carefully. It is best to present these sections in order of importance. For instance, if you've held many relevant jobs, you should list your work experience first, followed by your educational background. On the other hand, if you are just out of school with little or no work experience, it's probably best to list your educational background first and then, under employment history, to mention any part-time and summer jobs or volunteer work you've done.

Under educational background, list the schools you have attended in reverse chronological order, starting with your most recent training and ending with the least recent. Employers want to know at a glance your highest qualifications. For each educational experience, include years attended, name and location of the school, and degree or certificate earned, if any. If you have advanced degrees (college and beyond), it isn't necessary to include high school and elementary school education. Don't forget to highlight any special courses you took or awards you won, if they are relevant to the kind of job you are seeking.

Chronological and Functional Resume   Information about your employment history can be presented in two basic ways. The most common format is the chronological resume. In a chronological resume you summarize your work experience year by year. Begin with your current or most recent employment and then work backward. For each job, list the name and location of the company for which you worked, the years you were employed, and the position or positions you held. The order in which you present these facts will depend on what you are trying to emphasize. If you want to call attention to the type or level of job you held, for example, you should put the job title first. But whichever order you choose, be consistent. Summer employment or part-time work should be identified as such. You need to specify months in the dates of employment only if you held a job for less than a year.

The functional resume, on the other hand, emphasizes *what you can do* rather than *what you have done*. It is useful for people who have large gaps in their work history or who have relevant skills that would not be properly highlighted in a chronological listing of jobs. The functional resume concentrates on your qualifications—anything from familiarity with hospital procedures to organizational skills or managerial experience. Specific jobs may be mentioned, but they are not the primary focus of this type of resume.

It is important to include a brief description of the responsibilities you had in each job. This often reveals more about your abilities than the job title. Remember, too, that you do not have to mention the names of supervisors or how much you earned. You can discuss these points during the interview or explain them on an application form.

Explain Special Skills   You may wish to include a third section called "Special Skills," "Related Experience," or "Personal Qualifications." This is useful if there are points you wish to highlight that do not apply directly to educational background or work experience. Be sure these points are relevant to the kind of work you are seeking. This section is most effective if you can mention any special recognition, awards, or other evidence of excellence. It is also useful to mention whether you are willing to relocate or can work unusual hours.

Have References Available   Employers may also wish to know whom they can contact to find out more about you. At the start of your job search, you should ask three or four people if you may use them as references. If you haven't seen these people for a while, you may want

Thomas Goldin
Apartment 11B
25 Hunter Road
City, State 12345

telephone:
(000) 321-7654 home
(000) 321-3333 work

Work Experience

1991 to   Physical Therapist, Pediatric Unit, Midtown General
present   Hospital, City, State

          Conduct in-hospital therapeutic treatment for pediatric
          surgical patients and victims of disabling diseases.
          Provide long-term outpatient care for handicapped
          children. One day a week, provide at-home care for
          housebound patients. Redesigned curriculum for after-
          school play therapy session.

1989 to   Assistant Physical Therapist, Department of Education,
1991   Parkway Hospital, City, State

          Provided information and assistance for orthopedic
          patients and for palsy and stroke patients. Acted as co-
          teacher of classes for the handicapped on mobility and
          returning to work.

Education

1989   Master of Science
          School of Public

          Wrote thesis on d
          victims. Program
          with rotations in
          cardiac unit.

1986   Bachelor of Scien
          Major in Biology

Professional Certification

          Licensed Physical

References Available upor

State your name, address, and telephone
number first.

State job objective or general career goal
in a few words.

List education and work experience in
reverse chronological order, with most
recent item first.

Katrina Perez
30 Richmond Avenue
Town, State 12345
(000) 123-4567

Job Objective Dental assistant in clinic or private office.

Education

1995 to   Diploma, Dental Assistant Program, Charles County
1996   Community College, Town, State

          Program combined classroom instruction with clinical
          experience at Department of Health Dental Services Clinic.
          Clinical experience included performing full series of
          dental X rays.

1991 to   Diploma, Jefferson High School, Town, State
1995
          Participated in Senior Tutors program, assisting grammar
          school children with reading and arithmetic.

Work Experience

Summer,   Receptionist/Clerk Typist, Superior Temporary Personnel
1993 to   Services, City, State
1996
          Completed numerous temporary office assignments for agency
          clients. Duties included greeting visitors, using complex
          telephone systems, typing, ordering office supplies, and
          maintaining records systems. Work required accuracy,
          flexibility, and ability to deal with varied situations.

Summer,   Waitress, Village Chateau Restaurant, Town, State
1992

Professional Certification

          Certificate, Dental Assisting National Board, 1996

References Available upon request.

List your work experience first if it is
more important than your educational
background.

Keep descriptions of your education and
work experience brief.

List special skills and qualifications if
they are relevant to the job.

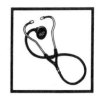

to send them a copy of your resume and let them know what kind of position you're seeking. Your references should be the kind of people your potential employer will respect, and they should be able to comment favorably on your abilities, personality, and work habits. You should indicate whether these people are personal references or former work supervisors. Avoid using relatives. You can list the names and addresses of your references at the end of your resume or in a cover letter. However, it is more usual to state, "References available upon request." Naturally, you should have their names, addresses, and phone numbers ready if you are asked.

Present Yourself Concisely   Tips for making your resume concise include not using complete sentences and omitting unnecessary words. When appropriate, start a sentence with a verb. There is no need to say "I"—that would be both obvious and repetitive.

Present Yourself Well   Employment counselors often recommend that resumes be kept down to one page because employers won't take the time to read many pages. If you've held many positions related to your occupation, by all means go on to the second page, but don't include beginning or irrelevant jobs. If you have a lot of work experience, limit the education section to just the essentials.

You should also concentrate on the appearance of your resume. It should be typed on a good grade of 8½″ × 11″ white bond paper. If you can't type, a professional typist can do it for you for a small charge. Be sure that it is neatly typed with adequate margins. The data should be spaced and indented so that each item stands out. This enables a busy executive or personnel director to see at a glance the facts of greatest interest.

You will probably need many copies of your resume during your job search. Each copy should be as neat and as clear as your original. If possible, input your resume on a computer and print copies on a good-quality printer, such as an inkjet or laser printer. You may want to have your resume reproduced professionally. A photo-offset printer can make several hundred excellent copies for a moderate fee. A photocopying machine may be more economical for smaller quantities.

These suggestions for writing a resume should not be thought of as hard-and-fast rules. Resumes are sometimes adapted to special situations. People with a variety of work experience often prepare several versions of their resume and use the one that's most appropriate when applying for a particular job.

If this is your first resume, show it to someone else, perhaps a guidance counselor, for constructive advice. Above all, remember this cardinal rule when writing your resume: Be truthful, but emphasize your assets. Show the abilities, skills, and specific interests that qualify you for a particular job. But don't go into your weaknesses or doubts about yourself. Do mention any job-related aptitudes that showed up in previous employment or in school. If you feel you have deficiencies in your training, you don't have to mention them in your resume. Don't make up things about yourself; everything that's in your resume can, and sometimes will, be checked.

Writing Application Letters

Often you will be sending your resume through the mail. You should send a cover letter with your resume, whether you are writing to apply for a specific job or just to find out if there are any openings.

A good cover letter should be neat, clear, and brief, with no more than three or four short paragraphs. Since your resume is designed to be used for different job openings, your cover letter should be more specific. Try to get the reader to think of you in terms of a particular job. If at all possible, send the letter to a specific person, either to the personnel director or to the person for whom you would be working. If necessary, call on the phone and ask to whom you should write.

Start your letter by explaining why you are writing. Say that you are inquiring about possible job openings at the company, or that you are responding to an advertisement in a particular publication, or that someone recommended that you should write (use the person's name if you have received permission to do so).

Use your cover letter to call attention to your qualifications.

Let your letter lead into your resume. Use it to call attention to your qualifications. Add information that shows you to be particularly well suited for a specific job. The physical therapist in the sample letter points out that he is interested in program management and in coordination of therapy efforts. These interests fit in well with the position in question. In the second sample letter, the applicant for a dental assistant position mentions that she has experience in the type of dentistry practiced by the prospective employer. She also emphasizes her willingness to work evenings and weekends.

Completing the Application Form

Many companies ask job applicants to fill out an application form. This form usually duplicates much of the information on your resume, but it will probably ask some additional questions as well. Give complete answers to all questions except those that are discriminatory. If a question doesn't apply to you, put a dash next to it.

You may be given the application form when you arrive for an interview, or it may be sent in advance to your home. When filling it out, print neatly in ink or, if it is sent to your home, type the information. Follow the instructions carefully. If the form asks you to put down your last name first, do so.

Usually, the most important sections of a form are the education and work histories. As in your resume, many applications will ask for these in reverse chronological order, with the most recent experience first. But unlike your resume, the application may ask for information about your earnings on previous jobs. It may also ask what rate of pay you are seeking on this job.

Be prepared to answer these and other questions that you have not answered in your resume. Look at the sample application form, and

Apartment 11B
25 Hunter Road
City, State 12345
November 25, 1996

Mr. Mark Strobert
Personnel Department
St. Stephen's Hospital
Route 129
City, State 12345

Dear Mr. Strobert:

I am writing in response to the notice for a Director of
Physical Therapy posted on the employees' bulletin board
at St. Stephen's Hospital. The opening was brought to my
attention by Dr. Kimble (surgery department). I am
interested in taking on responsibility for a physical
therapy program and would like to learn more about the
position.

I understand that the therapy division at St. Stephen's
is structured so that physical, occupational, and speech
therapists consult weekly on each patient. I feel that
this type of coordination is essential, and I would be
eager to take an active role in the system. I have
recently trained two new members of our department at
Midtown General, and as a result, I have become
interested in training and staff supervision.

I enclose my resume and would be free to meet with you
any Wednesday to discuss the position. I would also be
interested in meeting members of the physical therapy
department if convenient.

Very tr

Thom

Thomas

Enclosure

30 Richmond Avenue
Town, State 12345
October 20, 1996

Marcia Sacco, D.M.D.
Franklin Medical Building
Franklin Boulevard
City, State 12345

Dear Dr. Sacco:

Patrick Stone, who has recently joined your office as a
dental assistant, is a former classmate of mine from the
Charles County Dental Assistant Program. He mentioned
that you are looking for a second dental assistant to
work evenings and weekends. I would like to apply for
the position.

During my training, I had the opportunity to participate
in clinical practice on patients of all ages. I
especially enjoyed working with children and adolescents.
I understand that your practice specializes in
orthodontics for young people. This would suit me very
well. Evening and weekend hours would also present no
problem for me.

I enclose my resume, and I can arrange for you to speak
with my references if you would like.

I am available for an interview at your convenience and
can be reached at my home telephone number. I look
forward to hearing from you.

Very truly yours,

Katrina Perez

Katrina Perez

Enclosure

1 Always print neatly in blue or black ink. When completing an application form at home, type it.

2 Read the application carefully *before* you start to fill it out. Follow instructions precisely. Use standard abbreviations.

3 If you aren't applying for a specific job, indicate the general kind of work you're willing to do.

4 You don't have to commit to a specific rate of pay. Write "open" or "negotiable" if you are uncertain.

5 If a question doesn't apply to you, write "NA" (for not applicable) or put a dash through the space.

6 Mention a disability only if you *wish* to.

7 Traffic violations and so on do not belong here. Nor do offenses for which you were charged but not convicted.

8 Take notes along to remind you of school names, addresses, and dates.

9 If you're short on "real" employment, mention jobs such as babysitting, lawn mowing, or any occasional work.

10 Under the heading "Reason for Leaving," a simple answer will do. Avoid saying "better pay"—even if it's so.

11 Indicate only relevant activities or honors.

12 Your references should be people who can be objective about you, such as former employers, teachers and community leaders.

APPLICATION FOR EMPLOYMENT

The Law Prohibits Discrimination Because of Age, Sex, Religion, Race, Color and National Origin

(PLEASE PRINT PLAINLY)

PERSONAL

Name _____
Last   First   Middle Initial   Social Security No. _____   Date: _____

Present address _____
No.   Street   City   State   Zip

How many years have you lived at this address? _____   Telephone No. (____) _____   Area

Previous address _____
No.   Street   City   State   Zip   How long did you live there? _____

Job applied for _____

How did you learn of this opening? _____   Rate of pay expected $_____ per _____

Do you want to work ☐ Full time or ☐ Part time?   Specify days and hours if part time _____

Have you worked for us before? _____

List any friends or relatives working for us _____   If yes, when? _____

If hired, on what date will you be available to start work? _____

If hired, do you have a reliable means of transportation to get to work? _____

Do you have any physical or emotional disabilities that you wish to discuss? _____

Have you ever been <u>convicted</u> of a crime, excluding misdemeanors and summary offenses?
☐ No ☐ Yes
If yes, describe in full _____

PERSON TO BE
Name _____
Address _____

EDUCATION

TYPE OF SCHOOL	NAME AND ADDRESS	How Many Years Attended	Graduated	COURSE OR MAJOR
HIGH SCHOOL				
COLLEGE			☐ Yes ☐ No	
POST GRADUATE			☐ Yes ☐ No	
BUSINESS OR TRADE			☐ Yes ☐ No	
MILITARY OR OTHER			☐ Yes ☐ No	
			☐ Yes ☐ No	

WORK EXPERIENCE (List in order, last or present employer first. Include part-time and summer work.)

DATES FROM	TO	NAME AND ADDRESS OF EMPLOYER	RATE OF PAY START/FINISH	POSITION HELD	REASON FOR LEAVING

ACTIVITIES AND HONORS (List any academic, extracurricular, civic and other achievement you consider significant.)

PERSONAL REFERENCES

NAME AND OCCUPATION	ADDRESS	PHONE NUMBER
1.		
2.		
3.		

PLEASE READ THE FOLLOWING STATEMENTS CAREFULLY AND SIGN BELOW.
The information that I have provided on this application is accurate to the best of my knowledge and subject to validation. I authorize the schools, persons, current employer and other organizations or employers named in this application to provide any relevant information that may be required to arrive at an employment decision.

_____ Signature of Applicant

_____ Date of Signature

make note of the kinds of questions that you are likely to be asked—for example, your Social Security number, the names of previous supervisors, and your work attendance record over the past year or two. If necessary, carry notes on such topics with you to an interview. You have a responsibility to tell prospective employers what they need to know to make an informed decision.

Neatness Counts   Take care to think before you write. Avoid crossing out. An employer's opinion of you may be influenced just by the general appearance of your application. A neat, clearly detailed form may indicate an orderly mind and the ability to think clearly, follow instructions, and organize information. An employer who sees a sloppy, carelessly written application form may conclude that you don't really care about the job, are incapable of working in a structured setting, or cannot express yourself carefully.

Know Your Rights   Under federal and some state laws, an employer cannot demand that you answer any questions about race, color, creed, national origin, ancestry, sex, marital status, age (with certain exceptions), number of dependents, property, car ownership (unless needed for the job), or arrest record. Refer to the box on job discrimination in this essay for more information about your rights.

"Presenting Yourself in an Interview" prepares you for a personal interview, usually an essential step in getting a job.

Presenting Yourself in an Interview

An interview is the climax of your job-hunting efforts. On the basis of this meeting, the prospective employer will decide whether or not to hire you, and you'll decide whether or not you want the job.

Prepare in Advance

There are a number of things you can do to prepare for an interview. To begin with, you might give some more thought to why you want the job and what you have to offer. Then review your resume and any lists you made when you were evaluating yourself, so that you can keep your qualifications firmly in mind.

Try to learn in advance as much as you can about the organization. Check with friends who work there, read company brochures, or devise other information-gathering strategies. Demonstrating some knowledge about the company and what it does will indicate your interest.

Try also to anticipate some of the questions the interviewer may ask and think of how you would answer. For example, you may be asked: Will you work overtime when necessary? Are you ready to go to night school to improve some of your skills? It is also wise to prepare any questions you may have about the company or the position for which you are applying. The more information you have, the better you can evaluate both the firm and the job.

For some occupations, employers may want you to demonstrate your job skills. You may be asked for documents confirming that you are licensed or registered with a professional organization. An applicant for a job as an admitting clerk might be tested on clerical skills.

DO YOU KNOW YOUR RIGHTS?

Job Discrimination—What It Is

Federal and State Law

An employer cannot discriminate against you for any reason other than your ability to do the job. By federal law, an employer cannot discriminate against you because of your race, color, religion, sex, or national origin. The law applies to decisions about hiring, promotion, working conditions, and firing. The law specifically protects workers who are over the age of 40 from discrimination on the basis of age.

The law also protects handicapped workers. Employers must make their workplaces accessible to individuals with disabilities—for example, by making them accessible to wheelchairs or by hiring readers or interpreters for blind or deaf employees.

Federal law offers additional protections to employees who work for the federal government or for employers who contract with the federal government. State law often provides protections also—for instance, by prohibiting discrimination on the basis of marital status, arrest record, political affiliations, or sexual orientation.

Affirmative Action

Affirmative action programs are set up by businesses that want to make a special effort to hire women and members of minority groups. Federal employers and many businesses that have contracts with the federal government are required by law to set up affirmative action programs. Employers with a history of discriminatory practices may also be required to establish affirmative action programs.

Discrimination Against Job Applicants

A job application form or interviewer may ask for information that can be used to discriminate against you illegally. The law prohibits such questions. If you are asked such questions and are turned down for the job, you may be a victim of discrimination. However, under federal law, employers must require you to prove you are an American citizen or have a valid work permit.

Discrimination on the Job

Discrimination on the job is illegal. Being denied a promotion for which you are qualified or being paid less than co-workers are paid for the same job may be forms of illegal discrimination.

Sexual, racial, and religious harassment are forms of discrimination and are prohibited in the workplace. On-the-job harassment includes sexual, racial, or religious jokes or comments. Sexual harassment includes not only requests or demands for sexual favors, but any workplace verbal or physical conduct of a sexual nature.

Job Discrimination—What You Can Do

Contact Federal or State Commissions

If you believe that your employer practices unfair discrimination, you can complain to the state civil rights commission or the federal Equal Employment Opportunity Commission (EEOC). If, after investigating your complaint, the commission finds that there has been unfair discrimination, it will take action against the employer. You may be entitled to the job or promotion you were denied or to reinstatement if you were fired. You may also receive back pay or other financial compensation.

Contact a Private Organization

There are many private organizations that can help you fight job discrimination. For example, the American Civil Liberties Union (ACLU) works to protect all people from infringement on their civil rights. The National Association for the Advancement of Colored People (NAACP), National Organization for Women (NOW), and Native American Rights Fund may negotiate with your employer, sue on your behalf, or start a class action suit—a lawsuit brought on behalf of all individuals in your situation.

What to Do If You Lose Your Job

Being Fired and Being Laid Off
Generally, an employer has the right to fire an employee at any time. In many cases, however, an employer can fire you only if there is good cause, such as your inability to do the job, violation of safety rules, dishonesty, or chronic absenteeism.

Firing an employee because of that employee's race, color, religion, sex, national origin, or age (if the employee is over 40) is illegal. Firing an employee for joining a union or for reporting an employer's violation (called whistle-blowing) is also prohibited. If you believe you have been wrongfully discharged, you should contact the EEOC or the state civil rights commission.

At times, employers may need to let a number of employees go in order to reduce costs. This reduction in staff is called a layoff. Laying off an employee has nothing to do with the employee's job performance. Federal law requires employers who lay off large numbers of employees to give these employees at least two months' notice of the cutback.

Unemployment Compensation
Unemployment insurance is a state-run fund that provides payments to people who lose their jobs through no fault of their own. Not everyone is entitled to unemployment compensation. Those who quit their jobs or who worked only a few months before losing their jobs may not be eligible.

How much money you receive depends on how much you earned at your last job. You may receive unemployment payments for only a limited period of time and only so long as you can prove that you are actively looking for a new position.

Each claim for unemployment compensation is investigated before payments are made.

Should the state unemployment agency decide to deny you compensation, you may ask the agency for instructions on how to appeal that decision.

Other Protections for Employees

Honesty and Drug Testing
Many employers ask job applicants or employees to submit to lie-detector tests or drug tests. Lie-detector tests are permitted in the case of high-security positions, such as police officers. Some states prohibit or restrict the testing of applicants or employees for drug use. Aptitude or personality tests are generally permitted.

Other Federal Laws
The Fair Labor Standards Act prescribes certain minimum wages and rules about working hours and overtime payments. Workers' compensation laws provide payment for injuries that occur in the workplace and wages lost as a result of those injuries.

The Occupational Safety and Health Act sets minimum requirements for workplace safety. Any employee who discovers a workplace hazard should report it to the Occupational Safety and Health Administration (OSHA). The administration will then investigate the claim and may require the employer to correct the problem or pay a fine.

Rights Guaranteed by Contract
Not every employee has a written contract. If you do, however, that contract may grant you additional rights, such as the right to severance pay in the event you are laid off. In addition, employees who are members of a union may have certain rights guaranteed through their union contract.

Make sure you understand any contract before you sign it. Read it thoroughly and ask questions. Checking the details of a contract before signing it may prevent misunderstanding later on.

On the appointed day, dress neatly and in a style appropriate for an interview. When in doubt, it's safer to dress on the conservative side, wearing a tie rather than a turtleneck, or wearing a dress or blouse and skirt rather than jeans and a T-shirt. Be on time. Find out in advance exactly where the company is located and how to get there. Allow for traffic jams, getting lost, looking for a parking spot, and every other possible delay short of a natural disaster.

Maintain a Balance

When your appointment begins, remember that a good interview is largely a matter of balance. Don't undersell yourself by sitting back silently. Don't oversell yourself by proclaiming talents the company will have at its disposal if it is lucky enough to hire you. Answer all questions directly and simply, and let the interviewer take the lead.

Give specific answers. Give an example that demonstrates your diligence rather than saying, "I'm reliable and hardworking." Leave it to the interviewer to conclude that from the example.

It's natural to be nervous before and during a job interview. Try as much as possible to relax and be yourself. You may even find yourself enjoying the conversation. Your chances of being hired and being happy once on the job are better if the employer likes you as you are.

Avoid discussing money until the employer brings it up or until you are offered the job. Employers usually know in advance what they are willing to pay. If you are the one to talk about money, you may be running the risk of setting a price that's either too low or too high.

Be prepared to ask questions. After all, part of the purpose of the interview is for you to evaluate the company while you are being evaluated. Ask about your future with the company. Ask about its training programs and its policy on promotions. But don't force these questions on your interviewer. You will probably be given a fair opportunity to ask them. If not, ask them at the end of the interview.

Don't overstay your welcome. Your interviewer will appreciate your interest in the company but not if it takes too long to express it. Most businesspeople have busy schedules. Again, balance is important.

Don't expect a definite answer at the first interview. Usually, the employer will thank you for coming and say that you'll be notified shortly. Most employers want to see all the applicants before they decide. If the position is offered at the time of the interview, it is perfectly acceptable for you to ask for a little time to think about it. If you are told straight out that you are not suitable, it may hurt your pride, but try to be polite. Say, "I'm sorry, but thank you for taking the time to see me." Don't say, "I wouldn't want to work here anyway." After all, the company may have the right job for you next week.

Follow Up the Interview

If the job sounds interesting and you would like to be considered for it, say so as you leave. Follow up the interview immediately with a brief

Winning the Interview

- Find out all you can about the job and the employer.
- Dress appropriately for the job.
- Show good manners. Be on time. Don't smoke or chew gum.
- Try to be natural. Show self-confidence, but don't put on airs.
- Try to be yourself.
- Be brief and to the point.
- Be prepared to ask questions.
- Leave the subject of salary until the end of the interview.
- Follow up. Write a note to express interest in the job.

thank-you note to the employer for taking the time to see you and for considering your application.

It's a good idea to make some notes and evaluations of the interview while it is still fresh in your mind. Put down the important facts about the job—the duties, salary, promotion prospects, and so on. Also evaluate your own performance in the interview; list the things you wish you had said and things you wish you had not said. These notes will help you make a decision later. They will also serve as good guidelines for future interviews.

Finally, don't hesitate to contact your interviewer if you haven't heard from the company after a week or two (unless you were told it would be longer). A brief note or phone call asking when a decision might be reached will do no harm. It will simply confirm your sincere interest in the job. Your call will remind the interviewer about you and could work to your advantage.

Take Charge

The field of health offers many job opportunities. Job hunting is primarily a matter of organizing a well-thought-out campaign. Scan the classified ads, watch for trends in local industry that might be reported in the news, and check with people you know in the field. Take the initiative. Send out well-crafted resumes and letters. Respond to ads. Finally, in an interview, state your qualifications and experience in a straightforward and confident manner.

Trade and Professional Journals

"Trade and Professional Journals" lists publications of particular use to anyone interested in pursuing a career in engineering, science, and technology.

The following is a list of some of the major journals in health. These journals can keep you up to date with what's happening in all branches of your field of interest. These publications can also lead you to jobs through their own specialized classified advertising sections.

Dentists, Dental Assistants, and Dental Technicians

American Journal of Orthodontics and Dentofacial Orthopedics, 11830 Westline Industrial Drive, St. Louis, MO 63146.

Dental Assistant Journal, 203 North La Salle Street, Suite 1320, Chicago, IL 60601.

Journal of the American Dental Association, 211 East Chicago Avenue, Chicago, IL 60611.

Health Administration and Education

Hospitals and Health Networks, 737 North Michigan Avenue, Suite 700, Chicago, IL 60611.

Medical Assistants, Technicians, and Technologists

Health Technology Trends, ECRI, 5200 Butler Pike, Plymouth Meeting, PA 19462.

Transfusion, 8101 Glenbrook Road, Bethesda, MD 20814.

Nursing

American Journal of Nursing, 555 West 57th Street, New York, NY 10019.

Geriatric Nursing, 11830 Westline Industrial Drive, St. Louis, MO 63146.

Journal of Practical Nursing, 1400 Spring Street, Suite 310, Silver Spring, MD 20910.

The Nurse Practitioner: The American Journal of Primary Health Care, Box 882, Madison Square Station, New York, NY 10159.

Nursing Outlook, 11830 Westline Industrial Drive, St. Louis, MO 63146.

Physicians and Specialized Practitioners

American Family Physician, 8880 Ward Parkway, Kansas City, MO 64114.

American Journal of Psychiatry, 1400 K Street, NW, Washington, DC 20005.

American Journal of Public Health, 1015 Fifteenth Street, NW, Washington, DC 20005.

Anesthesiology, East Washington Square, Philadelphia, PA 19106.

Gerontologist, 1275 K Street, NW, Suite 350, Washington, DC 20005.

JAMA, Journal of the American Medical Association, 515 North State Street, Chicago, IL 60610.

Journal of Nuclear Medicine, 136 Madison Avenue, New York, NY 10016.

Journal of the National Cancer Institute, Membership Services, National Cancer Institute, Building 82, Room 100, Bethesda, MD 20892.

New England Journal of Medicine, 1440 Main Street, Waltham, MA 02254.

Psychology and Mental Health

American Psychologist, American Psychological Association, 750 First Street, NE, Washington, DC 20002.

APA Monitor, American Psychological Association, 750 First Street, NE, Washington, DC 20002.

Community Mental Health Journal, 233 Spring Street, New York, NY 10013.

Psychology Today, Box 55046, Boulder, CO 80322.

Therapists

American Journal of Occupational Therapy, 1383 Piccard Drive, Box 1725, Rockville, MD 20850.

Journal of Rehabilitation, 633 South Washington Street, Alexandria, VA 22314.

Journal of Speech and Hearing Research, 10801 Rockville Pike, Rockville, MD 20852.

Physical Therapy, 1111 North Fairfax Street, Fairfax, VA 22314.

Jobs Requiring No Specialized Training

Admitting Clerk

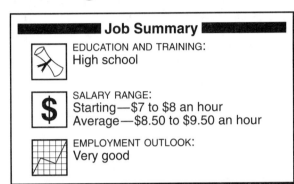

Job Summary

EDUCATION AND TRAINING:
High school

SALARY RANGE:
Starting—$7 to $8 an hour
Average—$8.50 to $9.50 an hour

EMPLOYMENT OUTLOOK:
Very good

Definition and Nature of the Work

Admitting clerks are usually the first employees that patients meet when entering a hospital. Admitting clerks interview new patients and sign them into the hospital. They explain the hospital's rates and policies to patients and to those who bring patients to the hospital. Admitting clerks arrange for new patients to be taken to their rooms. They type the admitting forms and keep careful records for each patient.

Education and Training Requirements

Hospitals prefer applicants who have a high school education. Courses in math, business, and typing are very important. Experience in other clerical jobs is useful. Job applicants who have worked as volunteers in a hospital may also be preferred. Admitting clerks generally learn about the hospital forms and procedures on the job.

Getting the Job

You can apply directly to hospital personnel offices. You can also check want ads in newspapers for job openings. Private employment agencies or your state employment office may list openings.

Advancement Possibilities and Employment Outlook

With further education and experience, admitting clerks can advance to the position of admitting officer. Admitting officers supervise the work of admitting clerks.

The employment outlook is very good through the year 2005 because of increasing demand for health services. The turnover among admitting clerks is high, and many new job openings will be created.

Working Conditions

Admitting clerks come into contact with all types of people. Aside from patients, relatives, and visitors, they deal with doctors, nurses, and other hospital workers. The atmosphere is usually quiet and friendly. At times, however, admitting clerks must deal with patients and relatives who are upset. Admitting clerks need to be tactful when asking personal questions. They should be understanding and able to handle tense situations. Admitting clerks usually work 40 hours a week. Sometimes they work weekends and night shifts. Part-time positions are also generally available.

Earnings and Benefits

Earnings vary depending on location and experience. Currently some beginning clerks start at salaries ranging from $7 to $8 an hour. Admitting officers earn average salaries of $8.50 to $9.50 an hour. Benefits generally include paid vacations and holidays and health insurance.

Where to Go for More Information

American Hospital Association
One North Franklin, Suite 2700
Chicago, IL 60606
(312) 422-3000

National Health Council
1730 M Street, NW, Suite 500
Washington, DC 20036
(202) 785-3910

Ambulance Driver

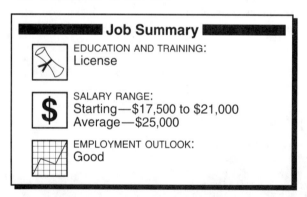

Job Summary

EDUCATION AND TRAINING:
License

SALARY RANGE:
Starting—$17,500 to $21,000
Average—$25,000

EMPLOYMENT OUTLOOK:
Good

Definition and Nature of the Work

Ambulance drivers are often the first members of the medical team to reach patients. They drive vehicles that carry sick people and accident victims to hospitals—people who are too ill or too badly hurt to get to the hospital by themselves. Ambulance drivers work for hospitals and for police, fire, and community first aid squads. They also work for private ambulance companies that provide emergency or invalid carrier service. Invalid carrier service is provided when, for example, a recovering patient is moved from a hospital to a nursing home. In some communities a large percentage of the ambulance drivers are volunteers. Some drivers, however, are salaried.

Ambulance drivers are generally trained as *emergency medical technicians–ambulance*. They are trained to give certain kinds of emergency care, which is called basic life support, when they reach a patient. The best-known emergency medical technicians (EMTs) are called *paramedics*. They are trained to give advanced life support. They work under the direct supervision of medical professionals. When they reach a patient, they notify professionals at the hospital by two-way radio, explain the situation, and carry out the physician's instructions. Paramedics also are trained to carry out a limited number of procedures at their own discretion.

Dispatchers receive calls for ambulance service and relay information to ambulance drivers. The level of training required to become a dispatcher has been raised in recent years. Highly trained dispatchers are called telecommunicators or C-Meds.

Education and Training Requirements

Ambulance drivers must have a driver's license and a good driving record. They must also be trained in emergency medical care. The Department of Transportation has designed a 100-hour program to train emergency medical technicians–ambulance. All states offer this or an equivalent program. Po-

lice, fire, and health departments offer this course. It is also taught in hospitals, medical schools, colleges, and universities.

After taking the course, you can become a Registered EMT–Ambulance by passing a written and a practical exam given by the National Registry of Emergency Medical Technicians.

Training programs for paramedics last from 3 to 5 months. To become registered as an EMT–Paramedic, you must complete the course, have 6 months of field training, and pass a written and a practical exam.

A third type of registration, called EMT–Intermediate, is offered. It is a level above EMT–Ambulance and a step below EMT–Paramedic. Registration is not required to get a job, but registered EMTs may have a better chance of getting higher-paying jobs.

All states have certification requirements, which vary from state to state.

Getting the Job

You can apply directly to your local ambulance service or hospital for a job. If you are in school, ask the placement office for help in finding a job.

Advancement Possibilities and Employment Outlook

Emergency medical technicians can take training courses that lead to higher levels within the job. With further training, some become emergency medical technician–administrators.

The employment outlook is good through the year 2005. An increased demand for medical services will result in some job growth, and emergency medical services are expected to experience average growth. There may be greater competition for EMT jobs. Municipal government and private ambulance services will provide the best opportunities for qualified ambulance drivers.

Working Conditions

Ambulance drivers usually work 40 hours a week. They work irregular hours including nights, weekends, and holidays. Because many ambulance calls involve matters of life and death, drivers work under intense pressure. Ambulance drivers bend and lift and perform other physically strenuous duties. The work is demanding and requires a high degree of commitment.

Earnings and Benefits

Beginning ambulance drivers earn salaries of about $17,500 to $21,000 a year. Experienced ambulance drivers generally earn average annual salaries of $25,000 or more. Benefits usually include paid holidays and vacations, health insurance, and pension plans.

Where to Go for More Information

American Ambulance Association
3800 Auburn Boulevard, Suite C
Sacramento, CA 95821
(916) 483-3827

National Association of Emergency Medical
  Technicians
102 West Leake Street
Clinton, MS 39056
(800) 346-2368

Dental Assistant

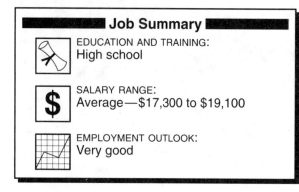

Job Summary

EDUCATION AND TRAINING:
High school

SALARY RANGE:
Average—$17,300 to $19,100

EMPLOYMENT OUTLOOK:
Very good

Definition and Nature of the Work

Dental assistants perform a number of duties in a dentist's office. Many of their tasks are clerical. In addition, they perform chairside duties when patients are in the examination chair. Chairside duties involve direct contact with patients. Dental assistants work under the strict supervision of dentists.

Dental assistants schedule appointments, keep records, receive payments from patients, and order supplies. When patients come to the office, dental assistants locate their medical records for the dentist's use. Dental assistants guide patients to the chair and prepare them for the examination.

Dental assistants often operate X-ray machines. During treatment they hand the dentist the proper materials and tools. They operate the suction hose that keeps the patient's mouth dry so the dentist can work on it. Sometimes dental assistants make an impression of a patient's mouth or teeth. They may also sterilize instruments, develop X rays, and mix compounds for cleaning or filling teeth.

Most dental assistants work in private offices for one or more dentists. Other assistants work in public health departments, clinics, hospitals, and dental schools.

Education and Training Requirements

Dental assistants need a high school diploma. Courses in biology, English, mathematics, bookkeeping, and typing are helpful. Many dental assistants learn their skills on the job.

Many colleges, vocational schools, and schools of dentistry offer courses for dental assistants. These are generally 1- or 2-year programs that lead to a certificate or to an associate degree. Also, the American Dental Association has accredited a correspondence course. Graduates of accredited programs can become Certified Dental Assistants if they pass a test.

Getting the Job

If you go to school to learn to be a dental assistant, the placement office can help you find a job. You can also apply directly to dentists' offices, hospitals, and private clinics. To get a job with the government, apply to take the necessary civil service test. Check with state and private employment agencies. Also check newspaper want ads.

Advancement Possibilities and Employment Outlook

Dental assistants can advance with experience and further training. In a large office they may become supervisors of other assistants. Or they may take courses qualifying them to be dental hygienists or dental laboratory technicians.

The employment outlook is very good through the year 2005. More assistants should be needed as the field of dental care continues to grow. In addition to jobs made available by expansion in the field, more assistants will be needed to replace those who retire. Expanding population, the growing awareness of the importance of dental care, and increasing availability of dental insurance should also add to the demand for dental assistants.

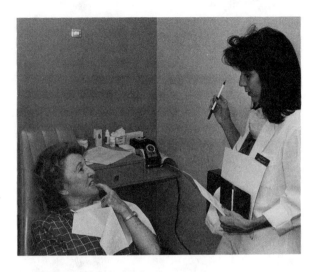

Working Conditions
Most dental offices are comfortable and clean. Dental assistants deal with many kinds of people. They may have to comfort frightened children or calm worried parents. They must also be careful in their work, especially when handling X-ray and dental equipment.

Dental assistants generally work 40 hours a week. Some work part time. Assistants are often expected to work on Saturday.

Earnings and Benefits
Currently dental assistants earn, on the average, between $17,300 and $19,100 a year. Dental assistant trainees earn between $15,000 and $17,000 a year. Those dental assistants employed in the federal government earn, on the average, between $17,000 and $22,000 or more a year. Benefits usually include paid holidays and vacations. Other ben-

efits vary, depending on the employer. Publicly employed dental assistants generally receive the same benefits as other hospital or health agency workers.

Where to Go for More Information
American Dental Assistants Association
203 North LaSalle Street, Suite 1320
Chicago, IL 60601-1210
(312) 541-1550

American Dental Association
211 East Chicago Avenue
Chicago, IL 60611-2678
(312) 440-2500

National Association of Dental Assistants
900 South Washington Street, Suite G13
Falls Church, VA 22046
(703) 237-8616

Dental Laboratory Technician

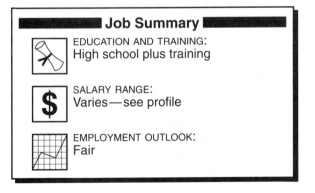

■ Job Summary ■

EDUCATION AND TRAINING:
High school plus training

SALARY RANGE:
Varies—see profile

EMPLOYMENT OUTLOOK:
Fair

Definition and Nature of the Work
Dental laboratory technicians construct and repair dentures (false teeth), bridges, crowns, and other

devices that dentists order for their patients. They work from the dentist's written instructions and from plastic or wax impressions of the patient's mouth.

Dental laboratory technicians work with plaster, wax, ceramics, and plastic, as well as with gold and other metals. They use many different kinds of tools and equipment. They use hand tools for carving and shaping. They use electric drills, presses, lathes, and high-heat furnaces for completing each dental piece.

Some dental laboratory technicians specialize. They may work chiefly on crowns and bridges or with ceramics. Generally these specialists work in large laboratories. Workers in smaller laboratories or in dentists' offices usually do all kinds of dental work.

programs usually last 2 years and are followed by about 3 years of practical experience. Technicians can become Certified Dental Technicians by passing tests given by the National Board for Certification.

Dental laboratory technicians should have good vision and color sense. They also need manual dexterity for handling the tiny pieces of material they use in their work. Because the work demands precision, technicians should have patience and should enjoy detailed work.

Getting the Job

You can apply directly to dentists' offices and laboratories for jobs and training. If you attend school, ask your placement office for help in finding a job. Private and state employment agencies sometimes list openings for dental laboratory technicians. You should also check the want ads in newspapers.

Advancement Possibilities and Employment Outlook

Dental laboratory technicians can advance as they gain experience. They can become experts in a specialized kind of laboratory work. In large laboratories some technicians become managers or supervisors. Some technicians start their own laboratories. To do this they need capital or financing to buy equipment, as well as knowledge about running a business.

Employment opportunities are expected to be fair through the year 2005. Although job opportunities should be favorable, improvements in preventive dental care may somewhat lessen growth in the field.

Education and Training Requirements

You usually need a high school diploma to become a dental laboratory technician. High school courses in art, ceramics, metalwork, and chemistry are helpful. Many technicians are trained on the job or in apprenticeship programs. Dental laboratory trainees work under the supervision of experienced technicians. They start by doing simple jobs, such as mixing plaster and pouring it into molds. Apprentices also get classroom training. The training period generally lasts 3 or 4 years.

An increasing number of technicians are entering formal training programs after high school. These

Working Conditions

Dental laboratories are found mostly in large cities and heavily populated states. Most are very small, but a few employ more than 200 technicians. Technicians usually work 40 hours a week. Those who are self-employed may work longer hours.

Technicians generally work independently. Since each job in a laboratory is different, the work is diverse and interesting. It is not strenuous work, but it does require close attention to detail. Dental laboratories are generally pleasant places in which to work, although there is sometimes pressure when deadlines must be met.

Earnings and Benefits

Salaries vary depending on experience and area of specialization. Trainees in dental laboratories average only slightly above the minimum wage. However, earnings increase greatly with experience. The average salary for experienced technicians is between $24,700 and $30,500 a year.

Benefits usually include paid holidays and vacations, as well as health insurance and pension plans. Self-employed dental laboratory technicians must provide their own benefits.

Where to Go for More Information

American Dental Association
211 East Chicago Avenue
Chicago, IL 60611-2678
(312) 440-2500

National Association of Dental Laboratories
555 East Braddock Road
Alexandria, VA 22314-2106
(703) 683-5263

National Dental Association
5506 Connecticut Avenue, NW, Suite 24
Washington, DC 20015
(202) 244-7555

Dialysis Technician

■ Job Summary ■

EDUCATION AND TRAINING:
High school

SALARY RANGE:
Starting—$16,500 to $17,800
Average—$18,000 to $22,200

EMPLOYMENT OUTLOOK:
Very good

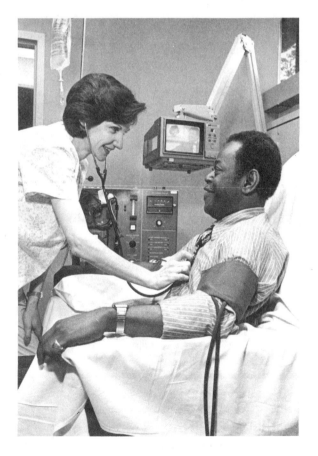

Definition and Nature of the Work

Dialysis technicians work with people who have kidney problems. These technicians, who are sometimes called hemodialysis technicians, operate machines that act as a patient's kidneys. The machines clean poisons out of the blood. Dialysis patients generally use the machine for five to six hours, three times a week. The technicians help the patients get comfortable. They stay with the patients while the machine is working. They must also keep the machine in good working condition.

Most dialysis technicians work in hospitals under the supervision of a head nurse. Others work in dialysis units run by private companies.

Education and Training Requirements

You need a high school diploma to become a dialysis technician. You should also have an interest in caring for people. Courses in science and health are useful, as is volunteer or part-time work in a hospital. Mechanical ability is also important in this job.

Dialysis technicians train on the job. In a hospital they are taught how to operate the machine by a head nurse. Companies that have dialysis units may also offer training.

Getting the Job

You can apply directly to a hospital that has a dialysis unit. You can also apply directly to companies that have dialysis units. In addition, check state and private employment services for job listings and information.

Advancement Possibilities and Employment Outlook

Advancement is possible with education and experience. Technicians working in large dialysis units may become chief technicians. With further training, some dialysis technicians become biomedical equipment technicians.

The employment outlook is very good through the year 2005. The field is growing steadily and there is a need for qualified workers.

Working Conditions

Dialysis technicians work 40 hours a week. Technicians often work with people who need understanding and encouragement. They must be careful workers who can keep calm in a medical emergency.

Earnings and Benefits

Salaries vary with experience. Current average starting salaries for dialysis technicians range from $16,500 to $17,800 a year. Those technicians with more experience can earn between $18,000 and $22,200 a year. Benefits include paid holidays and vacations, sick leave, and health insurance.

Where to Go for More Information

American Hospital Association
One North Franklin, Suite 2700
Chicago, IL 60606
(312) 422-3000

National Health Council
1730 M Street, NW, Suite 500
Washington, DC 20036
(202) 785-3910

National Kidney Foundation
30 East 33rd Street
New York, NY 10016
(212) 889-2210

EEG and EKG Technologist

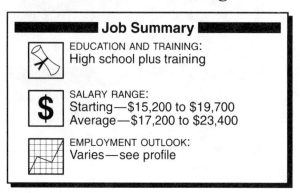

Job Summary

EDUCATION AND TRAINING:
High school plus training

SALARY RANGE:
Starting—$15,200 to $19,700
Average—$17,200 to $23,400

EMPLOYMENT OUTLOOK:
Varies—see profile

Definition and Nature of the Work

Electrocardiograph technologists and electroencephalograph technologists use advanced monitoring equipment to measure two crucial indicators of a person's health—heartbeats and brain waves. Electrocardiograph (EKG) machines record the electrical changes that occur during a heartbeat. The machines print graphs called electrocardiograms (EKGs). Doctors then study the graphs to learn about the condition of their patients' hearts. EKG technologists operate the EKG machines and make sure they are working properly. To take an EKG, an EKG technologist fastens electrodes to the patient's body. The technologist watches the patient during the EKG and prepares the graphs for the doctor.

Electroencephalograph (EEG) machines record brain waves. They print graphs that show electrical charges coming from the brain. These graphs, known as electroencephalograms (EEGs), help doctors learn more about such problems as epilepsy or brain tumors and find out about the damage caused by a stroke. EEG technologists get readable EEGs from patients by explaining the process, insuring that the patient is relaxed, and then placing electrodes shaped like small flat discs on the scalp and fastening them with tape. When the EEG machine is turned on, the electrodes pick up electric impulses from the brain and transmit them to the instrument, which amplifies these impulses. The energy discharge makes a bank of pens trace the patterns of the impulses on a moving strip of graph paper. EEG technologists adjust the instrument and make sure it is working properly. They know how to adjust it so that it produces tracings that accurately reflect brain-wave patterns. They must also understand advanced techniques such as brain-wave mapping, in which a computer translates brain waves into color-coded maps showing variations that occur in the electrical firing of the nerve cells in the brain.

Both EEG and EKG technologists can identify unusual patterns emerging on the graphs. However, they do not interpret EEGs or EKGs or diagnose ailments. They work in hospitals, clinics, doctors' offices, or medical schools.

Education and Training Requirements

You must have a high school diploma for both of these jobs. Most hospitals that employ EKG technicians provide on-the-job training lasting from 1 month to 1 year. Trainees are supervised by a cardiologist or an EKG supervisor. Technical schools and community colleges also offer training programs. Certification is offered by the American Cardiology Technologists Association.

EEG students in a hospital setting enroll in a 1-year program that combines study and clinical practice. The students learn the use of EEG equipment, EEG pattern recognition, and recording techniques. They may enroll in a 2-year college program leading to an associate degree. Courses include anatomy, introduction to electroencephalography, use of equipment, physiology, and routine procedures. Clinical practice includes observation in a neurology ward and EEG laboratories and the testing and care of equipment.

Getting the Job

You can apply directly to hospitals for job openings. If you have some college training, you have an advantage in finding employment. Check with your school placement office. Also check state and private employment services for openings for EKG and EEG technologists. The American Society of Electroneurodiagnostic Technologists has an active placement service for EEG students.

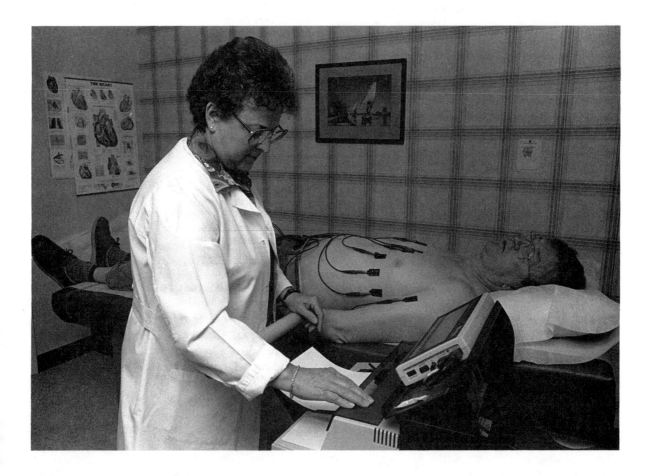

Advancement Possibilities and Employment Outlook

Both these jobs hold good possibilities for advancement. Doctors are using EKGs more frequently as part of routine physical examinations. In large hospitals, EKG technologists can become supervisors of other technologists. As they gain more experience and training, they can move into better-paying jobs as skilled technicians.

The employment outlook for EEG technologists is excellent. Advances in the equipment and use of electroencephalography have made EEGs applicable to a wider range of patients. Certification by the American Board of Registration of Electroencephalographic Technologists may be necessary for supervisory or teaching jobs.

The employment outlook for EKG technologists is fair. New, more efficient equipment will increase productivity. This will keep the field from growing as much as the demand for the service. The best job opportunities will be for those with advanced skills.

Working Conditions

EKG and EEG technologists generally work 40 hours a week. Sometimes they must be on call at nights and on weekends. They usually work in clean, pleasant surroundings and are recognized as an important part of the medical team. They work closely with doctors and nurses, as well as with patients.

Earnings and Benefits

Salaries vary with education and experience. Currently entry-level EKG and EEG technologists earn about $15,200 to $19,700 a year. Registered EKG technologists with some experience earn an average salary of $17,200 a year. Registered EEG technologists earn an average salary of $23,400. Top pay for people with considerable experience averages $28,800. Most employers offer paid vacations, sick leave, pensions, and health insurance.

Where to Go for More Information

EKG Technologists

American Society of Extra-Corporeal Technology
11480 Sunset Hills Road, Suite 210E
Reston, VA 22090
(703) 435-8556

Association for the Advancement of Medical
    Instrumentation
3330 Washington Boulevard, Suite 400
Arlington, VA 22201-4598
(703) 525-4890

National Health Council
1730 M Street, NW, Suite 500
Washington, DC 20036
(202) 785-3910

EEG Technologists

American Electroencephalographic Society
P.O. Box 30
One Regency Drive
Bloomfield, CT 06002
(203) 243-3977

American Medical Electroencephalographic
    Association
850 Elm Grove Road
Elm Grove, WI 53122
(414) 797-7800

American Society of Electroneurodiagnostic
    Technologists
204 West Seventh Street
Carroll, IA 51401-2317
(712) 792-2978

Home Health Aide

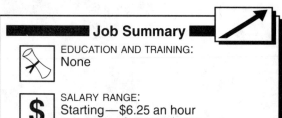

Job Summary

EDUCATION AND TRAINING:
None

SALARY RANGE:
Starting—$6.25 an hour
Average—$7.50 to $9.25 an hour

EMPLOYMENT OUTLOOK:
Excellent

Definition and Nature of the Work

Home health aides provide services in the home for people who cannot care for themselves. They help people who are recovering at home after a hospital stay. They also help people with long-term illnesses or handicaps. Home health aides work for hospitals and health care agencies.

Health aides provide a variety of services for sick people. They give baths and massages and change bandages. Sometimes they help patients to get dressed, do exercises, and get in and out of bed.

Aides see that patients take their medicine, although they cannot prescribe drugs themselves.

Aides often help their patients with household chores. They may change the patient's bed and do some light laundry or cleaning. Sometimes they take patients for walks or rides. They may read to their patients or just keep them company.

In some cases, home health aides instruct patients and their families in health care. For example, they may teach a new mother how to care for her baby. Or they may show parents how to help a handicapped child. Sometimes aides move into the patient's home for a period of time.

Education and Training Requirements

Some employers prefer to hire high school graduates, but a high school diploma is not necessary to enter this field. Volunteer work and part-time or summer jobs in hospitals are good experience. Training courses for home health aides are generally about 2 to 3 weeks long. Hospitals, adult education schools, health departments, and volunteer

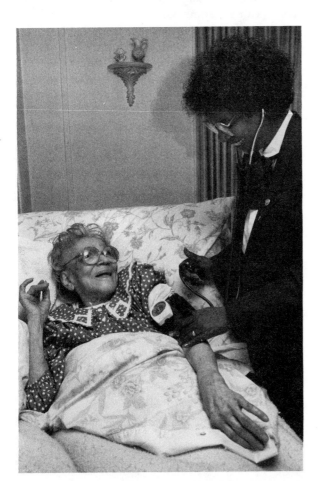

agencies offer these courses. Many home health aides receive on-the-job training under the supervision of a registered nurse. Some states require home health aides to be certified. Home health aides must be in good health. They should also be patient and understanding.

Getting the Job

Apply to local health care agencies or to hospitals for jobs. You can also check the want ads in newspapers. State and private employment agencies may also list openings for home health aides.

Advancement Possibilities and Employment Outlook

With further education, a home health aide can become a teaching health aide or a licensed practical nurse. The employment outlook is excellent through the year 2005. An increase in the elderly population is certain in the years ahead. This should provide many openings in this field and a shortage of workers.

Working Conditions

Home health aides generally work a 40-hour week. They might spend 4 hours at one home in the morning and 4 hours at another in the afternoon. Part-time work is sometimes available. Aides are sometimes needed on weekends and overnight. Aides work with many different kinds of people and in many different kinds of homes.

Earnings and Benefits

Earnings vary depending on experience and location. Current salaries for home health aides range from $7.50 to $9.25 an hour or about $17,000 a year. Benefits generally include paid holidays and vacations and health insurance. Aides also are reimbursed for their travel expenses as they travel from one case to another.

Where to Go for More Information

American Hospital Association
One North Franklin, Suite 2700
Chicago, IL 60606
(312) 422-3000

National HomeCaring Council
513 C Street, NE
Washington, DC 20002
(202) 547-6586

Laboratory Animal Care Worker

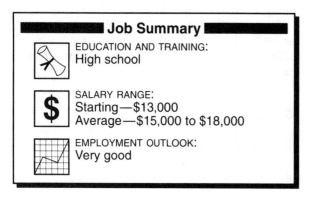

Job Summary

EDUCATION AND TRAINING:
High school

SALARY RANGE:
Starting—$13,000
Average—$15,000 to $18,000

EMPLOYMENT OUTLOOK:
Very good

Definition and Nature of the Work

Laboratory animal care workers take care of animals that are used in scientific research. Laboratory animal care workers include assistant laboratory animal technicians, laboratory animal technicians, and laboratory animal technologists. Scientists do experiments for drug companies, medical schools, and research centers. They use animals to learn about animal and human diseases and treatments. They study small animals to learn about animal behavior and intelligence. Animal care workers help the scientists and carry out their instructions.

Laboratory animal care workers may care for mice, guinea pigs, or rats. Sometimes they work with monkeys, dogs, or even insects or fish. Animal care workers provide food and water for the animals and clean their cages. They check for signs of illness and keep careful records on each animal. They may also order food and supplies for the animals. Sometimes they help scientists or medical doctors to do experiments.

Some laboratory animal care workers are *veterinarian's assistants*. They may give medicine to the animals, treat minor wounds, and prepare animals for surgery.

Education and Training Requirements

A high school education is usually required for unskilled jobs in laboratories. Courses in science are helpful. Some laboratories will give you on-the-job training. You can also take a 2-year program in animal care at a college or technical school. Certification is available from the American Association for Laboratory Animal Science (AALAS), but it is not required for work. There are 3 levels of certification: assistant laboratory animal technician, laboratory animal technician, and laboratory animal technologist. For each level of certification there are age, education, experience, and examination requirements.

Laboratory animal care workers need a knowledge of animals' eating and sleeping habits. They should enjoy working with animals. They must be able to follow directions carefully.

Getting the Job

You can apply directly to medical schools, drug companies, research centers, or animal hospitals. Your school placement office may also have a list of openings. Some laboratories place want ads in the newspapers.

Advancement Possibilities and Employment Outlook

With training and experience, laboratory animal care workers can become supervisors, research assistants, or animal breeders. The employment outlook is very good through the year 2005. Drug companies, medical schools, and research centers are employing increasing numbers of technicians to help them with experiments.

Working Conditions

Laboratory animal care workers usually work 40 hours a week. Sometimes they must work nights and weekends. Working areas are usually well lighted and pleasant. However, animal care workers are exposed to unpleasant smells. They spend most of their time working with animals rather than with people.

Earnings and Benefits

Salaries vary depending on education and experience. Current average starting salaries for laboratory animal care workers are about $13,000 a year. Those with more experience earn, on the average, between $15,000 and $18,000 a year. Benefits include paid holidays and vacations, health insurance, sick leave, and sometimes pension plans and free tuition.

Where to Go for More Information

American Association for Laboratory Animal Science
70 Timber Creek Drive, Suite 5
Cordova, TN 38018
(901) 754-8620

American College of Laboratory Animal Medicine
200 Summerwinds Drive
Cary, NC 27511
(919) 859-5985

Nurse's Aide and Orderly

▅▅▅▅▅ Job Summary ▅▅▅▅▅

EDUCATION AND TRAINING:
None

SALARY RANGE:
Average—$13,800 to $17,900

EMPLOYMENT OUTLOOK:
Very good

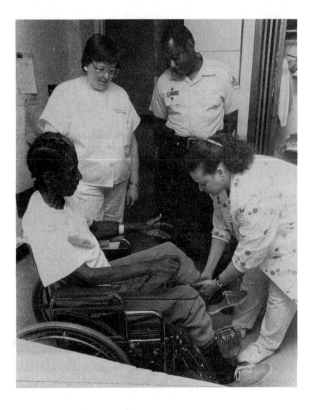

Definition and Nature of the Work

Nurse's aides and orderlies help nurses care for patients. Aides and orderlies generally spend most of their time with patients, helping to keep them comfortable. They carry meal trays to patients, answer call lights when patients signal for help, and help to move patients. Aides and orderlies make beds, give baths and massages, and fill water pitchers and ice bags. They may also take and record temperatures, pulse, and blood pressure. Sometimes aides and orderlies do light cleaning, distribute linens, set up equipment, deliver messages, and assemble meal trays for patients who are on special diets.

Many nurse's aides and orderlies work in hospitals. An increasing number work in nursing homes and long-term care facilities for old people. Some work with psychiatric patients and are called psychiatric aides.

Education and Training Requirements

There are no specific education requirements for these jobs. Aides and orderlies are usually trained on the job under the supervision of a registered nurse or a licensed practical nurse. Training generally lasts from 1 week to 3 months. Some high schools also offer courses that give students credit for on-the-job experience. Volunteer jobs in hospitals are good experience, as are courses in home nursing and first aid.

Getting the Job

Apply directly to the hospitals or nursing homes in which you want to work. You can also check the want ads in newspapers. State and private employment agencies sometimes list openings for nurse's aides and orderlies.

Advancement Possibilities and Employment Outlook

Aides and orderlies can advance with further education. Some train to be licensed practical nurses while working part time as aides or orderlies. Others may learn to operate specialized equipment, such as electrocardiograph machines.

The employment outlook is very good and is expected to continue to expand with the growing demand for health services. The increase in elderly population will contribute to this. Nurse's aides and orderlies will remain an important part of the health care team.

Working Conditions

Nurse's aides and orderlies generally work 40 hours a week. This usually includes some night or weekend work. The surroundings are generally quiet and clean.

Since they deal with sick people, aides and orderlies need to be patient and understanding. They should be healthy and responsible. They should also be able to stay calm in emergencies.

Earnings and Benefits

Salaries vary with experience and place of employment. Salaries for nursing home aides average $11,600 a year. Nurse's aides and orderlies with experience working in hospitals earn an average salary of about $13,800 to $17,900 a year. Benefits usually include paid holidays and vacations and health insurance.

Where to Go for More Information

American Nurses' Association
600 Maryland Avenue, SW
Washington, DC 20024-2571
(202) 554-4444

National League for Nursing
350 Hudson Street
New York, NY 10014
(212) 989-9393

Operating Room Technician

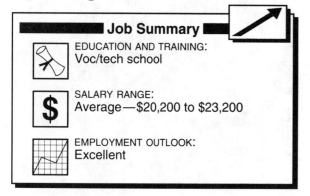

Job Summary

EDUCATION AND TRAINING:
Voc/tech school

SALARY RANGE:
Average—$20,200 to $23,200

EMPLOYMENT OUTLOOK:
Excellent

Definition and Nature of the Work

Operating room technicians are part of the surgical team. They assist the doctors, nurses, and other operating room workers. They help to get patients ready for surgery, clean and set up the surgical equipment, and take the patients to the operating room. Operating room technicians are sometimes called surgical technicians.

Operating room technicians set up the operating room with instruments and supplies. During surgery, they hand instruments and supplies to the proper person. They help keep track of equipment. They may also help to prepare samples of tissues or organs that will be tested in a laboratory. At times they operate some of the machines in the operating room.

After an operation, technicians take patients to the recovery room. They help to clean the operating room and get it ready for the next operation.

Education and Training Requirements

Operating room technicians usually need a high school diploma. Courses in health and science are helpful. Summer or volunteer work in a hospital is also good experience.

Almost all operating room technicians are trained in vocational and technical schools, hospitals, and community colleges. These training programs last

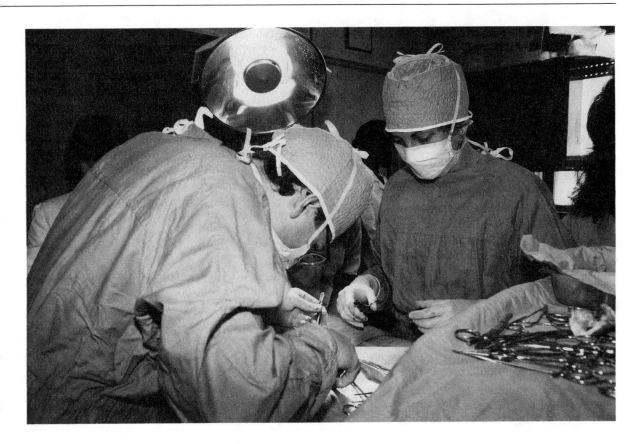

from 9 months to 2 years. Some technicians train on the job in programs lasting from 6 weeks to 1 year. Operating room technicians who pass an exam are certified by the Association of Surgical Technologists. Certification is not required to get a job, but Certified Surgical Technologists generally earn higher salaries.

Getting the Job

You can apply directly to the hospital in which you want to work. Also check job listings at state or private employment offices. The want ads in newspapers sometimes list jobs for operating room technicians.

Advancement Possibilities and Employment Outlook

Operating room technicians can advance to jobs with more responsibility as they gain experience. With further education they can also move into other health care jobs.

The employment outlook is excellent through the year 2005. Growth and aging of the population, advances in surgical techniques, and widespread insurance coverage are expected to increase the number of operations performed. Graduates of postsecondary school training programs will have the best opportunities.

Working Conditions

Operating room technicians generally work 40 hours a week. Sometimes they must be on call for night and weekend work. They work with doctors, nurses, and other hospital workers. Operating rooms are well-lighted, quiet places. Sometimes tense situations arise, however. Operating room technicians need to be careful workers. They must remain calm in emergencies. They should also be in good health.

Earnings and Benefits

Salaries vary depending on education, experience, and location. Currently operating room technicians earn between $20,200 and $23,200 a year. Benefits include paid holidays and vacations, health insurance, and pension plans.

Where to Go for More Information

American Hospital Association
One North Franklin, Suite 2700
Chicago, IL 60606
(312) 422-3000

Association of Surgical Technologists
7108 South Alton Way, Building C
Englewood, CO 80112-2106
(303) 694-9130

National Health Council
1730 M Street, NW, Suite 500
Washington, DC 20036
(202) 785-3910

Substance Abuse Counselor

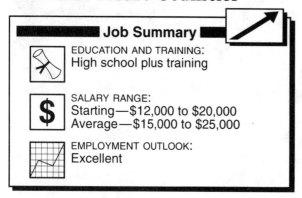

▌▌▌▌▌ Job Summary ▌

EDUCATION AND TRAINING:
High school plus training

$ SALARY RANGE:
Starting—$12,000 to $20,000
Average—$15,000 to $25,000

EMPLOYMENT OUTLOOK:
Excellent

Definition and Nature of the Work

Substance abuse counselors help people who have problems related to alcohol and other drugs. They counsel addicts as well as those who are afraid they might become addicts. They also help former addicts. Sometimes they talk to the families of addicts, too.

Addiction counselors, as they are sometimes called, usually help with practical problems. For example, a counselor might help a former addict find a job. Counselors do not prescribe medicine or provide medical or psychological therapy. Substance abuse counselors are often supervised by doctors, psychologists, or social workers.

Some of these counselors work in halfway houses, where addicts live while they are under treatment. Counselors may also work in outpatient clinics where people come in on a regular basis. Other counselors work in hospitals, treatment centers, or human service agencies. Sometimes these counselors are former substance users themselves. They hold

counseling sessions for one person or for a group of people. At these sessions counselors try to help addicts cope with their problems.

Education and Training Requirements

A high school diploma is usually required for this field of work. Counselors generally are trained on the job. Training programs vary in length from 6 weeks to 2 years. Some colleges also offer training programs for counselors. These programs are usually 2 years long and include courses on the effects of alcohol and other drugs. Students may also learn crisis intervention—a way of handling emergency situations. Emergencies may involve emotional or medical problems. Graduates of these programs usually receive an associate degree. For some positions, a bachelor's degree or higher in sociology, psychology, or a related field may be required.

Getting the Job

You can apply for a job at a halfway house, treatment center, hospital, or clinic that offers substance abuse counseling. Your school placement office may be able to give you job information. Also check state and private employment agencies. Newspaper want ads sometimes list jobs for substance abuse counselors.

Advancement Possibilities and Employment Outlook

Substance abuse counselors who have a high school diploma or an associate degree can advance to the position of director of a halfway house. However, most other advanced jobs in the field of substance abuse, such as rehabilitation counselors or social workers, require at least a bachelor's degree. For other jobs, such as psychologist, the minimum education requirement is a master's degree. The employment outlook is excellent for counselors through the year 2005.

Working Conditions

Most substance abuse counselors work a 40-hour week. Some live in halfway houses. The work can be tense and sometimes frustrating. Counselors work closely with other people and should enjoy helping others.

Earnings and Benefits

Salaries vary depending on education, experience, and level of responsibility. Currently substance abuse counselors entering the field earn between $12,000 and $20,000 a year. Those with a master's degree average $15,000 to $25,000. Benefits usually include paid holidays and vacations, health insurance, and pension plans.

Where to Go for More Information

Alcohol and Drug Problems Association of America
1555 Wilson Boulevard, Suite 300
Arlington, VA 22209-2405
(703) 875-8684

National Association of Alcoholism and Drug Abuse
    Counselors
3717 Columbia Pike, Suite 300
Arlington, VA 22204-4254
(703) 920-4644

Ward Clerk

Job Summary

EDUCATION AND TRAINING:
High school

SALARY RANGE:
Varies—see profile

EMPLOYMENT OUTLOOK:
Good

Definition and Nature of the Work

Ward clerks do clerical work in hospitals. They work at the nurses' station of a hospital ward or nursing unit. Ward clerks usually work under the supervision of a registered nurse. They free nurses to spend more time on patient care.

Ward clerks do most of the paperwork for their nursing unit. They keep records on the patients and on the ward's hospital staff. They may perform other routine clerical duties. Clerks also act as receptionists for their ward. They answer the telephone and direct visitors to patients' rooms. Sometimes ward clerks also do other jobs, such as ordering supplies or taking mail or flowers to patients.

Education and Training Requirements

Most hospitals prefer ward clerks who have a high school diploma. Courses in mathematics and typing and other business subjects are helpful. Volunteer or part-time work in a hospital is also useful experience. Ward clerks are usually trained on the job.

Getting the Job

You can apply directly to the hospital in which you want to work. Also check the want ads of the newspapers for jobs. State and private employment agencies also list openings for ward clerks.

Advancement Possibilities and Employment Outlook

Advancement is possible with further education and experience. Ward clerks can become ward managers, who are in charge of all nonnursing duties in their wards. If they increase their clerical skills, they can become secretaries. Some ward clerks work part time while training to become licensed practical nurses.

The employment outlook is good through the year 2005. Hospitals are using more ward clerks to take care of routine tasks so that nurses are free to perform other duties.

Working Conditions

Ward clerks work 40 hours a week, often on weekends and at night. They usually work in clean and comfortable surroundings. Ward clerks have contact with patients, visitors, doctors, nurses, and other

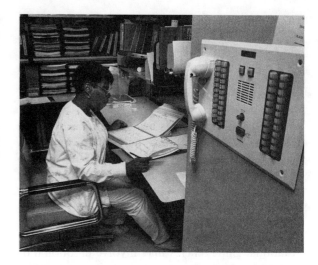

hospital workers. They should enjoy working with people. Ward clerks should also be dependable and careful workers.

Earnings and Benefits

Salaries vary depending on experience, location, and level of responsibility. The salaries of ward clerks range between $12,500 and $23,000 a year, depending on experience. Benefits include paid holidays and vacations, health insurance, and pension plans.

Where to Go for More Information

American Hospital Association
One North Franklin, Suite 2700
Chicago, IL 60606
(312) 422-3000

National Health Council
1730 M Street, NW, Suite 500
Washington, DC 20036
(202) 785-3910

Jobs Requiring Some Specialized Training/ Experience

Biomedical Equipment Technician

Job Summary

EDUCATION AND TRAINING:
High school plus training

SALARY RANGE:
Average—$20,500 to $24,900

EMPLOYMENT OUTLOOK:
Very good

Definition and Nature of the Work
Biomedical equipment technicians are specialists in medical equipment. They maintain instruments, such as heart-lung machines, dialysis machines, and equipment used for measuring blood pressure and brain waves. Unlike electrocardiograph and electroencephalograph technicians, who specialize in one type of equipment, biomedical equipment technicians are familiar with many different kinds of machines. Biomedical equipment technicians work in hospitals and research organizations. They also work for manufacturers' sales and research and development departments. They work under the direction of biomedical engineers.

In hospitals, biomedical equipment technicians may become experts at using certain pieces of equipment. Some technicians work in several departments with many different kinds of equipment. Technicians teach nurses, therapists, and other members of the hospital staff to operate machines. They inspect new equipment to make sure that the machinery received is the same as that which was ordered. They also see that it operates properly.

Technicians make minor repairs on equipment at the hospital. When equipment must be sent back to the maker for major repair, they write an analysis of the problem so the manufacturer can fix and return the equipment quickly. Technicians also maintain detailed records on the use and condition of all equipment.

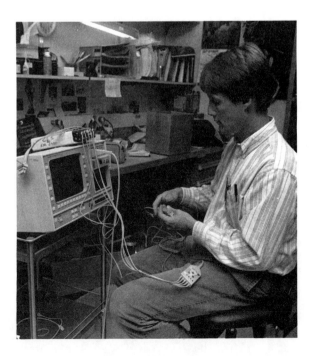

Education and Training Requirements
You need 1 to 3 years of training after high school to become a biomedical equipment technician. Training courses are available at junior and community colleges. These colleges generally work closely with local hospitals and manufacturers. During the training period, students study and learn how to operate many different kinds of medical instruments. Even after they have completed their formal training, technicians must keep up with new developments in the field.

The Association for the Advancement of Medical Instrumentation issues certification for biomedical equipment technicians. In order to qualify, technicians must pass a test given by the association. Many employers prefer to hire technicians who have certification.

Getting the Job

Your school placement office can help you find a job. You can also apply directly to hospitals, biomedical equipment manufacturers, and research organizations. Your state employment office may list openings. Also check newspaper want ads for jobs.

Advancement Possibilities and Employment Outlook

With further education technicians can hold research and teaching positions. To become a biomedical engineer, at least a bachelor's degree and specialized biomedical training are required.

The employment outlook is very good through the year 2005. New jobs are expected to open in the future. Research and development expenditures are expected to increase. The rapid development and wide use of biomedical equipment along with rapid growth in the output of technical products should increase the need for biomedical equipment technicians. The companies that make the equipment have the greatest need for these technicians. Trained workers are also needed in hospitals and research organizations.

Working Conditions

Technicians work with highly trained doctors and engineers. They must be able to communicate their mechanical knowledge to others. Most technicians work in or near large cities where medical facilities and companies are located.

Hours vary for technicians depending on where they work. Hospital technicians generally work 8-hour shifts. They may have to work at night or on weekends. Those employed by research organizations or manufacturing companies usually work regular hours.

Earnings and Benefits

Earnings vary depending on the type of work done and the specific employer. The current average salary for technicians who service equipment is about $20,500 to $24,900 a year. Technicians in advanced positions can make from $30,000 to $35,000 a year. Benefits include paid holidays and vacations, health insurance, and pension plans.

Where to Go for More Information

American Hospital Association
One North Franklin, Suite 2700
Chicago, IL 60606
(312) 422-3000

Association for the Advancement of Medical
    Instrumentation
3330 Washington Boulevard, Suite 400
Arlington, VA 22201-4598
(703) 525-4890

Biomedical Engineering Society
P.O. Box 2399
Culver City, CA 90231
(310) 618-9322

Junior Engineering Technical Society
1420 King Street, Suite 405
Alexandria, VA 22314
(703) 548-5387

National Health Council
1730 M Street, NW, Suite 500
Washington, DC 20036
(202) 785-3910

Dental and Medical Secretary

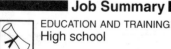 **Job Summary**

EDUCATION AND TRAINING:
High school

SALARY RANGE:
Starting—$15,000 to $17,500
Average—$20,000 to $27,000

EMPLOYMENT OUTLOOK:
Good

Definition and Nature of the Work

Dental secretaries and medical secretaries perform clerical and secretarial duties for dentists and doctors, respectively. They take shorthand, type, and file patients' records. To do their job, they must have an understanding of the procedures and terms that doctors and dentists use. Secretaries may also keep track of patients' payments.

Secretaries sometimes take a patient's medical history before the doctor or dentist sees the patient. Secretaries may also ask what the patient's symptoms are and how long a condition has lasted. If the medical history is completed in advance, doctors can devote their time to treating the patients.

Medical and dental secretaries also arrange appointments for patients. They make sure that people who need immediate care are able to see the doctor or dentist without much delay. When there are emergencies that make the doctor or dentist late, secretaries must tactfully explain the delay to patients who are waiting.

Most secretaries work in the private offices of doctors and dentists. Some work in hospitals and clinics. Secretaries with a knowledge of medical terms are also employed by the medical information and medical emergency departments of large companies. Dental and medical secretaries also work in the research laboratories of drug companies. They work for health organizations and government agencies.

Education and Training Requirements

Most medical and dental secretarial positions require a high school education. Candidates need skills in shorthand, typing, filing, and bookkeeping. Some employers hire secretaries and provide on-the-job training in medical or dental language. However, most employers prefer to hire candidates who have secretarial training. Computer and word processing skills have become increasingly important in this field as part of the secretarial training. Training courses are given in business and vocational schools and in junior and community colleges. Courses last from a few months to 2 years.

Getting the Job

Check with your school placement office. Doctors, dentists, hospitals, and clinics often advertise jobs in local newspapers. For a government job, apply to take the necessary civil service test.

Advancement Possibilities and Employment Outlook

Advancement is possible with further education and experience. Secretaries may go on to become medical or dental assistants or technicians.

The employment outlook is good through the year 2005. As the population grows, doctors and dentists will acquire more patients, and they will need secretaries with some medical knowledge. Also, secretaries will be needed to handle the increase in medical insurance paperwork.

Working Conditions

Medical and dental secretaries work in clean and comfortable offices. Much of their time is spent at a desk. They have a great deal of contact with a variety of people both in person and on the telephone. Sometimes their days are hectic. They must be prepared to move quickly from one situation to another. Medical and dental secretaries must be calm and capable of dealing with all kinds of problems.

Medical and dental secretaries work 35 to 40 hours a week. Because their hours match those of doctors and dentists, many secretaries have some evening and weekend work.

Earnings and Benefits

Salaries vary greatly depending on education, experience, and location. Currently medical and dental secretaries at the entry level earn salaries ranging between $15,000 and $17,500 a year. Those at the intermediate level earn between $20,000 and $27,000 a year. Highly skilled medical and dental secretaries can make up to $36,000 a year. Benefits may include paid vacations, holidays, health insurance, and sick leave.

Where to Go for More Information

American Association of Medical Assistants
20 North Wacker Drive, Number 1575
Chicago, IL 60606
(312) 899-1500

National Health Council
1730 M Street, NW, Suite 500
Washington, DC 20036
(202) 785-3910

Professional Secretaries International
10502 Northwest Ambassador Drive
Kansas City, MO 64153
(816) 891-6600

Dental Hygienist

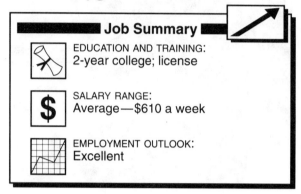

Job Summary

EDUCATION AND TRAINING:
2-year college; license

SALARY RANGE:
Average—$610 a week

EMPLOYMENT OUTLOOK:
Excellent

Definition and Nature of the Work

Dental hygienists are licensed professionals who help dentists provide treatment and care to the mouth, teeth, and gums. State laws limit the duties that hygienists may perform. In some states hygienists can perform some tasks for which dentists have traditionally been responsible. These tasks may include taking dental impressions and administering local anesthetics.

Generally, hygienists keep records of patients' dental histories and take X rays and organize them for the dentist's evaluation. Hygienists may also be responsible for informing the dentist of the condition of a patient's mouth so that the dentist can quickly locate problem areas. In most states hygienists are licensed to remove stains and deposits from the teeth. Cleaning, combined with the application of fluorides to the teeth, helps prevent diseases of the gums and further tooth decay.

Hygienists also teach patients how to prevent dental problems. Patients who do not care for their teeth between visits can undo everything the dentist has accomplished. Therefore, hygienists must emphasize the principles of good nutrition, proper brushing, and the importance of regular checkups.

In small dental offices hygienists may also act as the office assistant or the laboratory technician. They may schedule appointments and do some laboratory work, such as polishing gold inlays and making models from dental impressions. However, not all dental hygienists work in dental offices. There are also job opportunities in clinics and public health agencies.

Education and Training Requirements

To practice, dental hygienists must pass the licensing test in their state. They must also be a graduate of a school of dental hygiene accredited by the Commission on Dental Accreditation. To enter such a school, you must have at least a high school education. To get into some bachelor's degree programs, you must have 2 years of college. Many schools require that you take an aptitude test given by the American Dental Hygienists Association. Two-year associate degree programs qualify you to work in a private office. Four-year bachelor's degree programs qualify you to do research, teach, or work in public or school health programs.

Getting the Job

Your school placement office can help you find a job. Check the want ads in trade and professional journals, as well as in local newspapers. Apply directly to dentists' offices or clinics in which you

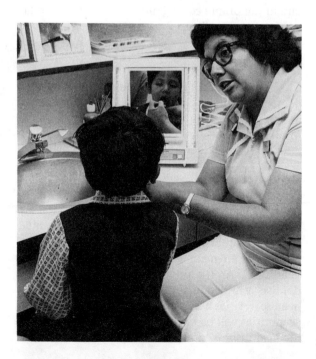

would like to work. If you want to work for a school or public health program, apply to take the necessary civil service test.

Advancement Possibilities and Employment Outlook

Advancement possibilities are best for dental hygienists who work in public, hospital, or school health programs. Those who have a bachelor's or master's degree may take on supervisory or administrative jobs. Hygienists with a master's degree may teach in dental hygiene schools.

The employment outlook is excellent. The total number of jobs in the field is expected to grow through the year 2005. Employment prospects should be favorable as the demand for dental care increases with public awareness of the importance of oral health.

Working Conditions

Most dental hygienists work in dentists' offices. These offices are generally pleasant places in which to work. Dental hygienists work with a small staff and usually enjoy a close relationship with their fellow workers. Hygienists often work with a number of different patients in the course of a day. The work is especially varied in schools and in public health positions.

In general, hygienists work between 35 and 40 hours a week. Part-time employment is also com-

mon. Hygienists who work in dentists' offices may work some evenings and Saturdays. School hygienists work during school hours.

Earnings and Benefits

Salaries vary depending on education, experience, and geographical location. According to the American Dental Association, dental hygienists who work 32 hours a week or more average $610 a week. The average hourly earnings for all hygienists is $18.50. Benefits generally include paid holidays and vacations. Hygienists who work for government health agencies receive the same benefits that other government workers receive.

Where to Go for More Information

American Dental Association
211 East Chicago Avenue
Chicago, IL 60611-2678
(312) 440-2500

American Dental Hygienists Association
444 North Michigan Avenue, Suite 3400
Chicago, IL 60611
(312) 440-8900

National Health Council
1730 M Street, NW, Suite 500
Washington, DC 20036
(202) 785-3910

Emergency Medical Technician

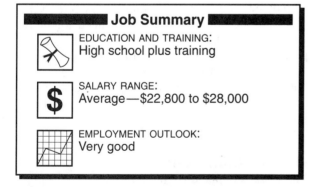

Job Summary

EDUCATION AND TRAINING:
High school plus training

SALARY RANGE:
Average—$22,800 to $28,000

EMPLOYMENT OUTLOOK:
Very good

Definition and Nature of the Work

Emergency medical technicians (EMTs) offer immediate aid to victims of accidents or critical illnesses. They may provide their services at the scene of the crisis, on route to the hospital, or in the

emergency room. Because they are frequently the victim's first source of medical assistance, emergency medical technicians must be able to determine very quickly the nature and extent of the problem and decide how it should be treated. In many cases, they must treat the victim instantly if his or her life is to be saved.

The duties and capabilities of an emergency medical technician depend on the training acquired. However, all technicians are qualified to give cardiopulmonary resuscitation (CPR) to a person suffering cardiac arrest, control the bleeding of an accident victim, and administer oxygen to someone who has stopped breathing. Emergency medical technicians are also trained to deliver babies, subdue people who are displaying violent behavior, treat allergic reactions, apply splints and antishock suits, and treat wounds.

There are four levels of registration for technicians. *Emergency medical technicians–nonambulance* are qualified to give basic emergency care in settings other than ambulances, such as hospitals, nursing homes, and medical facilities. Many are nurses, nurse's aides, or hospital orderlies. *Emergency medical technicians–ambulance* perform basic emergency care and rescue work and operate and maintain ambulances. *Emergency medical technicians–intermediate* have taken additional training courses that enable them to provide more advanced forms of treatment, such as trauma assessment and airway management. *Emergency medical technicians–paramedic* are the most highly trained. They generally work on mobile intensive care units and are in voice contact with a physician. They are authorized to give medication and intravenous fluids under a doctor's guidance. Paramedics are also qualified to use defibrillators on heart attack victims, which involves restoring a regular heartbeat. Emergency medical technicians work for fire and police departments, hospitals, and private and public ambulance services.

Education and Training Requirements

Completion of a standard training program is mandatory for each level of registration. To enter a program, you must have a high school diploma and

a driver's license and be at least 18 years old (21 for the paramedic course). Each state has its own program requirements, but most require nonambulance and ambulance technicians to take approximately 100 hours of classroom training in basic emergency care. Some practical training in an ambulance or emergency room is also required. For instance, ambulance technicians must complete 6 months of ambulance rescue service. Both intermediate and paramedic candidates must have an ambulance technician's training plus 6 months of field experience before they can enter their respective courses. Paramedic training and testing may take more than a year to complete.

Hospitals, police and fire departments, colleges, universities, and medical schools offer EMT courses. Certification involves both written and practical tests. Technicians at all levels must be recertified every 2 years.

Getting the Job

Volunteer technicians are always needed, and this is an excellent way to find out if you are suited to the work. To volunteer, you must take the training courses and pass the tests. For a job, check with your local police or fire department, or apply directly to the first aid squad in your area. You can also apply to hospitals and private ambulance services.

Advancement Possibilities and Employment Outlook

Competent technicians can advance fairly quickly to the paramedic level if they are willing to meet training requirements mandated by their states. The employment outlook is very good through the year 2005. As the population ages, the need for more emergency medical services should increase. Opportunities for paramedics will be best in communities that are just setting up advanced rescue teams. Although job stress and turnover will produce many openings, keen competition is expected for those jobs.

Working Conditions

The work is demanding and unpredictable, requiring physical stamina, manual dexterity, emotional stability, compassion, good judgment, and the ability to react quickly under stressful conditions. Some EMTs work on rotating shifts, working a 24-hour shift for 1 day and then having 2 days off. Others work a single shift each day, totaling anywhere from

40 to more than 55 hours a week. Night and weekend work is often required, and many technicians are on call for emergencies.

Earnings and Benefits

The average salary for EMTs–ambulance is about $22,800 a year. EMTs–intermediate on the average earn about $22,700 a year, and those with extra training or EMTs–paramedic earn about $28,000 a year.

Benefits for EMTs employed by city or local governments include paid vacations and holidays, pension plans, and health insurance. Benefits for EMTs working for private companies vary and may not include pension plans.

Where to Go for More Information

National Association of Emergency Medical
    Technicians
102 West Leake Street
Clinton, MS 39056
(800) 346-2368

National Register of Emergency Medical Technicians
6610 Busch Boulevard
P.O. Box 29233
Columbus, OH 43229
(614) 888-4484

Hospice Worker

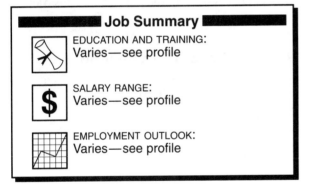

■■■■■ **Job Summary** ■■■■■

EDUCATION AND TRAINING:
Varies—see profile

SALARY RANGE:
Varies—see profile

EMPLOYMENT OUTLOOK:
Varies—see profile

Definition and Nature of the Work

Hospice workers specialize in caring for people who are terminally ill and in helping their families adjust to the loss of a loved one. Most hospice programs offer patients both at-home assistance and residential facilities. Patients remain in their own homes whenever possible. The aim of a hospice program is to make the final weeks or months comfortable for a patient. For many patients, this entails medication to control pain, visits with family and friends, counseling, and assistance with practical matters, such as housekeeping and shopping.

Hospice workers include nurses, doctors, counselors, social workers, clergy, homemakers, and health aides. These professionals work as a team to insure that the physical, emotional, and practical needs of each patient are met and that the family receives comfort and support.

Education and Training Requirements

In addition to the training and education required for the discipline you choose, hospice work calls for specialized instruction in caring for terminally ill patients. Even if you want to work as a volunteer, you generally must participate in training sessions offered by the hospice to become acquainted with the hospice philosophy, the methods of caring for a terminally ill patient, and the emotional effects of the illness on both the patient and the family.

Getting the Job

Volunteer work is an excellent way to break into the field because hospices need people who will donate their time to care for patients either in their homes or at an inpatient facility. This will provide you with training and practical experience.

Advancement Possibilities and Employment Outlook

Volunteer workers can be promoted to paying positions as health aides, but advancement to professional positions will generally depend on level of education. Those who have a degree in social work, nursing, psychology, or medicine should have the best advancement opportunities. They can become directors or coordinators of hospice programs.

The employment picture is uncertain because hospice care remains somewhat controversial since it emphasizes preparing for death rather than sus-

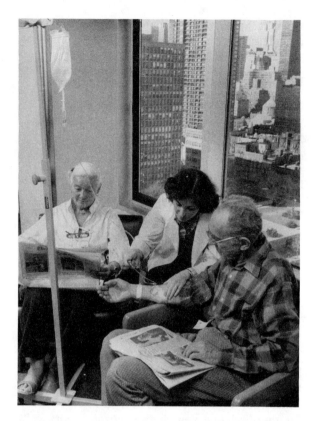

grams are covered by Medicare or Medicaid. The future of hospices will depend on the amount of federal support they receive.

Working Conditions
Hospices are staffed 24 hours a day. Many employees work nights or weekends, remaining on call to patients who are home. The work is emotionally demanding and often very diverse. It requires patience, sensitivity, good judgment, and excellent communication and listening skills.

Earnings and Benefits
Many hospice workers are volunteers and do not receive a salary. Most hospice workers earn salaries similar to those of their counterparts in regular hospitals. Doctors may earn $100,000 a year or more. Nurses earn an average of $22,000 to $40,000 a year, while orderlies earn from $13,800 to $17,900 a year. Benefits for hospice employees usually include paid holidays and vacations, health insurance, and pension plans.

taining life. However, the hospice movement is gaining momentum and is seen by many as a humane and cost-effective way of caring for terminally ill patients. An increasing number of hospice pro-

Where to Go for More Information
National Hospice Organization
1901 North Moore Street, Suite 901
Arlington, VA 22209
(703) 243-5900

Inhalation Therapist

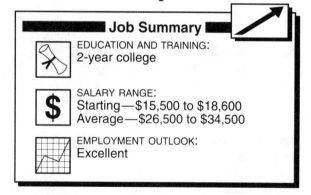

Job Summary

EDUCATION AND TRAINING:
2-year college

SALARY RANGE:
Starting—$15,500 to $18,600
Average—$26,500 to $34,500

EMPLOYMENT OUTLOOK:
Excellent

Definition and Nature of the Work
Inhalation therapists treat patients who have difficulty breathing. They operate such equipment as respirators and oxygen tents. Most inhalation therapists work in hospitals under the supervision of physicians. Inhalation therapists are also called respiratory therapists.

Inhalation therapists often work in emergency situations resulting from injury or illness. They also work in ongoing treatment programs for patients with breathing disorders, such as emphysema.

Inhalation therapists operate machines that provide oxygen. Some kinds of equipment provide medicine in the form of a mist or gas. Usually physicians give inhalation therapists prescriptions stating the medicine and dosage to be given to the patient. It is generally up to the therapist to decide what equipment should be used. Inhalation therapists must be aware of the dangers and hazards involved in each kind of treatment. They observe patients during treatment and report to the doctor any adverse reactions.

In most hospitals inhalation therapists are responsible for having faulty equipment repaired. They may make small repairs themselves. Inhalation therapists are often called on to explain the equipment to nurses. Therapists must also know how to work in a sterilized environment.

Education and Training Requirements

Training programs vary in length from 21 months to 4 years. Technical schools and community and junior colleges offer 2-year programs leading to an associate degree. Four-year colleges offer bachelor's degrees. To get into a training program, you must be a high school graduate with a background in mathematics and science. A good background in English is also helpful because inhalation therapists must keep very detailed records of the treatment they administer.

The National Board for Respiratory Therapy certifies and registers inhalation therapists. To become a Certified Respiratory Therapy Technician (CRTT), you must graduate from a program approved by the Committee on Allied Health Education and Accreditation of the American Medical Association. You must also have 1 year of work experience and pass a written test. To become a Registered Respiratory Therapist (RRT), you must graduate from an approved program, have 62 semester hours of college credit and 1 year of experience, and pass both a written and a practical test. Certification is not needed to get a job. However, it may help you advance.

Getting the Job

Your school placement office may be able to help you find a job. If you receive your training in a hospital, it is likely you will be hired by that hospital. Want ads in trade and professional journals and in newspapers often carry listings for inhalation therapists.

Advancement Possibilities and Employment Outlook

Inhalation therapists may advance to supervisory positions. Those who have advanced degrees may get teaching positions. Advancement depends on training, personal qualifications, and performance.

The employment outlook for inhalation therapists is excellent through the year 2005. The pro-

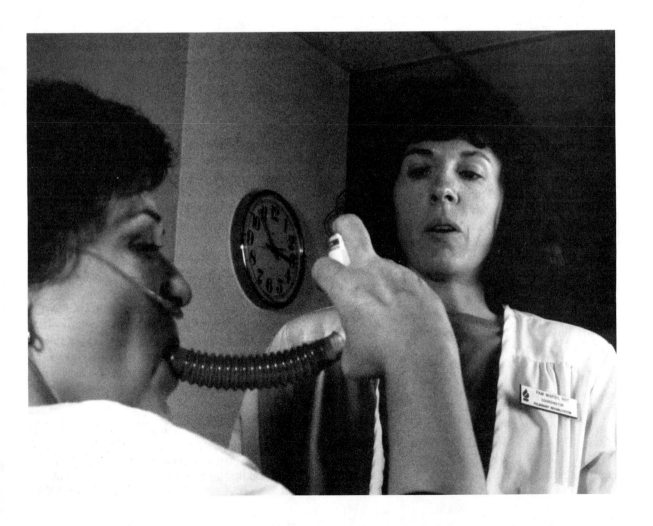

jected growth of the middle-aged and elderly populations is expected to increase the risk of heart disease, and more inhalation therapists will be needed to provide services for these individuals. Also, as respiratory therapists are required to perform a greater variety of duties, this could mean more jobs for inhalation therapists than currently expected.

Working Conditions

Inhalation therapists do most of their work in hospitals. In emergencies they may work in ambulances. However, because most therapy work can be scheduled in advance, inhalation therapists have fairly regular hours.

Therapists generally work 40 hours a week. They may be expected to work some evenings and weekends. Many therapists work part time.

Earnings and Benefits

Salaries vary with education and place of employment. Beginning inhalation therapists earn, on the average, between $15,500 and $18,600 a year. Experienced therapists can make from $26,500 to $34,500 a year. Benefits include paid holidays and vacations, health insurance, and pension plans.

Where to Go for More Information

American Association for Respiratory Care
11030 Ables Lane
Dallas, TX 75229
(214) 243-2272

American Lung Association
1740 Broadway
New York, NY 10019-4374
(212) 315-8700

Licensed Practical Nurse

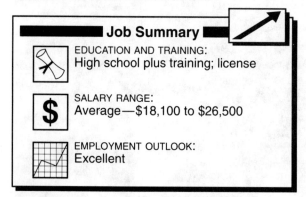

Job Summary

EDUCATION AND TRAINING:
High school plus training; license

SALARY RANGE:
Average—$18,100 to $26,500

EMPLOYMENT OUTLOOK:
Excellent

Definition and Nature of the Work

Licensed practical nurses (LPNs) help physicians and registered nurses (RNs) care for patients. They have the technical knowledge to perform routine nursing duties. This allows doctors and registered nurses to devote their time to patient care that requires specialized knowledge. Most licensed practical nurses work in hospitals, nursing homes, other health care institutions, and private homes. Some are employed in doctors' offices, clinics, and public health agencies. Still others work in large businesses. They care for workers who have accidents or become ill on the job. Licensed practical nurses are also called licensed vocational nurses.

Licensed practical nurses have a great deal of contact with their patients. It is important that nurses keep patients in good spirits. They also take patients' blood pressures, check temperatures, and apply bandages. In some cases, practical nurses may give their patients drugs that doctors have prescribed. Licensed practical nurses watch for changes in their patients' condition. If there is a change, they report it to the doctors immediately.

Licensed practical nurses may work in special units of a hospital. These include cardiac, burn, and maternity units. Here LPNs may be trained to use special equipment and may direct nurse's aides.

Sometimes patients who are recovering from an illness hire licensed practical nurses to work in their homes. Nurses involved in home health care follow doctors' instructions. For example, they may give drugs on schedule or change bandages. In addition, they may take over some homemaking chores.

Education and Training Requirements

Many schools that train licensed practical nurses prefer to admit high school graduates. Admission requirements usually include passing an aptitude test and taking a physical exam.

Training programs currently take 1 year to complete. Junior and community colleges, technical and vocational schools, and hospitals offer these programs. The armed services also offer state-approved courses. However, there is a move to two levels of nursing. Technical nurses, such as LPNs, will be required to have an associate degree. Professional nurses (RNs) will be required to have a bachelor's degree. Those interested in careers in nursing should check current state regulations. All LPNs must be licensed. To qualify for a license, you must complete a state-approved course and pass a written test.

Getting the Job

Your school placement office may be able to help you find a job. You can apply directly to hospitals, clinics, and other institutions in which you would like to work. Check with private employment agencies that specialize in medical job placements. Newspaper want ads often carry listings for licensed practical nurses.

To get a job in home health care, contact local hospitals and clinics. They usually maintain lists of practical nurses. When a patient needs private care, hospitals suggest someone from their lists.

Advancement Possibilities and Employment Outlook

Licensed practical nurses can take extra courses to specialize in one field, such as the care of newborn infants. With further training, they may become registered nurses. However, this training may be extensive.

The employment outlook for licensed practical nurses is excellent. Growth in the number of jobs available will continue. These jobs will be concentrated in clinics, rehabilitation hospitals, and long-term care facilities. There will also be increasing demand for skilled LPNs to work in home health care. There are excellent opportunities for new graduates and experienced workers alike.

Working Conditions

Licensed practical nurses can usually choose where they work, from hospitals to private homes. LPNs must keep an even temper, especially when caring for difficult and unhappy patients. They must stand for long periods and often have to help patients move in bed, stand, or walk. Licensed practical nurses always work under the direction of registered nurses or doctors.

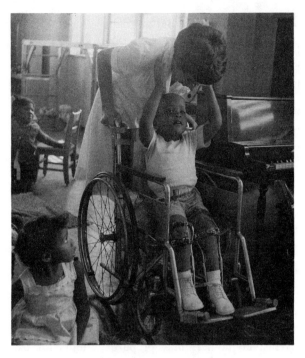

Practical nurses work 40 hours a week. Sometimes they work at night and on weekends. They generally earn premium pay for these shifts. Jobs in private homes often involve longer hours. Each case places different demands on the practical nurse's time.

Earnings and Benefits

Salaries vary with experience and place of employment. Currently most licensed practical nurses working in hospitals earn about $18,100 to $26,500 a year. Nurses who have many years of experience may earn $30,000 or more. In most hospitals salary increases are given at regular intervals. Benefits include paid holidays and vacations, health insurance, and pension plans.

Where to Go for More Information

National Association for Practical Nurse Education
    and Service
1400 Spring Street, Suite 310
Silver Spring, MD 20910
(301) 588-2491

National Federation of Licensed Practical Nurses
1418 Aversboro Road
Garner, NC 27529
(919) 779-0046

National League for Nursing
350 Hudson Street
New York, NY 10014
(212) 989-9393

Medical Assistant

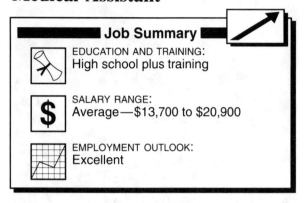

Job Summary

EDUCATION AND TRAINING:
High school plus training

SALARY RANGE:
Average—$13,700 to $20,900

EMPLOYMENT OUTLOOK:
Excellent

Definition and Nature of the Work

Medical assistants aid physicians. They work with patients and perform secretarial duties. Medical assistants work in doctors' offices, hospitals, and medical clinics. The job varies from office to office. Some medical assistants may do laboratory work exclusively; others may prepare patients for examination. Still others may do both.

Most medical assistants work in private offices. There they help doctors examine and treat patients. They check the height, weight, temperature, and blood pressure of each patient. Assistants write down patients' medical histories and run simple laboratory tests. They may answer patients' questions about medicines and treatment at home. Assistants may also give injections, apply bandages, and take X rays. Many assistants take electrocardiograms, which measure the electrical impulses of the heart.

Medical assistants are sometimes in charge of buying and maintaining medical equipment and furniture for the doctor's office. They may also act as office managers. They plan the doctor's schedule, greet patients, file records and correspondence, and type letters and bills. Assistants keep medical records up to date and handle tax and insurance forms. At the doctor's request, they arrange for tests at the laboratory or for a patient's admission to the hospital. In a large group practice or in a hospital clinic, the duties of the medical assistant may be divided among several assistants.

Education and Training Requirements

A high school diploma is required to enter this field. Medical assistants can be trained on the job. Formal training programs, however, are also available. Community colleges offer 2-year programs leading to an associate degree. Vocational schools and business schools offer 1-year programs. More than 220 programs have been approved by either the Com-

mittee on Allied Health Education and Accreditation or the Accrediting Bureau for Health Education Schools.

A medical assistant can become certified by the American Association of Medical Assistants (AAMA). To qualify to take the test for Certified Medical Assistant (CMA), you must have completed an approved course; have a high school diploma or its equivalent, and 1 year of experience; or have 5 years of experience.

Medical assistants can also become Registered Medical Assistants (RMAs). To qualify for this test, you must meet certain education and experience requirements. Certification and registration are not necessary for employment, but they give you professional standing.

Getting the Job

Your high school placement office may be able to help you find a job. State employment offices and private employment agencies that specialize in medical job placements often list job openings. In many communities a local medical assisting association handles job openings throughout the country. Often the local medical society serves as a clear-

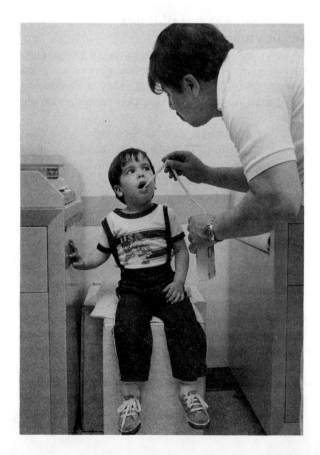

inghouse for employment possibilities in doctors' offices. The want ads in newspapers and professional journals also list openings.

Advancement Possibilities and Employment Outlook

Advancement can come with experience and further training. Additional skills, such as shorthand and the ability to use a transcribing machine, are often useful. These skills make jobs in laboratories, pharmaceutical houses, public health departments, and private industry possible. Medical assistants who show leadership qualities can become supervisors.

The employment outlook for medical assistants is excellent through the year 2005. The best job prospects are for medical assistants with formal training, experience, or both. Medical assistants with word processing and computer skills will have an advantage. The increased needs of an aging population, growth in the number of doctors, more diagnostic testing, and increased volume and complexity of paperwork will cause growth in employment. Many doctors need at least one assistant, and large group practices, clinics, and hospitals need many. The total number of jobs for medical assistants is expected to grow. Also, the high turnover rate among medical assistants creates many openings each year.

Working Conditions

Doctors' offices, hospitals, and clinics are busy and challenging places in which to work. Medical as-

sistants come into contact with all kinds of people. The duties are generally varied. Medical assistants usually work 40 hours a week. Those who work in private offices may work some evenings and Saturdays.

Earnings and Benefits

Earnings depend on training, experience, size of practice, and geographic location. Medical assistants who have an associate degree generally earn more than those who have little or no training. Current average salaries for medical assistants range from $13,700 to $20,900, depending on experience. Benefits generally include paid holidays and vacations. Medical assistants who work for clinics, hospitals, and group practices generally receive health insurance and pension plans.

Where to Go for More Information

American Academy of Physician Assistants
950 North Washington Street
Alexandria, VA 22314
(703) 836-2272

American Association of Medical Assistants
20 North Wacker Drive, Number 1575
Chicago, IL 60606
(312) 899-1500

American Medical Technologists
710 Higgins Road
Park Ridge, IL 60068
(708) 823-5169

Medical Laboratory Worker

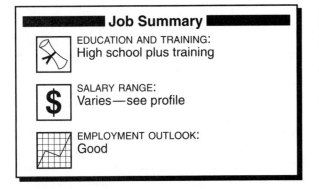

Job Summary

EDUCATION AND TRAINING:
High school plus training

SALARY RANGE:
Varies—see profile

EMPLOYMENT OUTLOOK:
Good

Definition and Nature of the Work

Medical laboratory workers conduct laboratory tests that aid in the diagnosis and treatment of disease. Medical laboratory workers include medical labo-

ratory assistants, medical laboratory technicians, histologic technicians, and cytotechnologists. Medical laboratory workers work under the supervision of medical laboratory technologists and physicians, such as pathologists. Most medical laboratory workers work in hospitals. Some work in research institutes and clinics. Others are employed in commercial medical laboratories that run tests for doctors and hospitals on a fee basis.

Medical laboratory assistants perform routine tasks in the laboratory. For example, they collect examples of blood and urine, label them, and conduct simple tests on them. They sterilize instruments; prepare, stain, and label slides; and keep records of tests. *Medical laboratory technicians* perform tasks that require more technical knowledge than assistants have. Technicians must have two years of train-

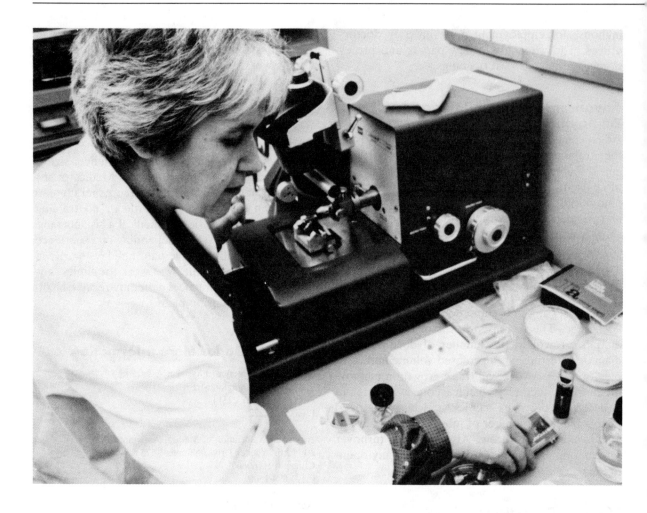

ing after high school, whereas assistants generally need only one. Medical laboratory technicians perform tests involved in blood banking. For example, they may help to determine a donor's blood type. They also perform analyses of blood and urine and tests that require a knowledge of microbiology and chemistry.

Histologic technicians prepare slides of body tissue for examination by medical technologists and pathologists. They freeze tissue so that it can be cut into paper-thin slices. They stain the slides so that the tissue can be seen clearly under a microscope.

Cytotechnologists look for signs of cancer in body cells. Unusual cell formation may be signs of disease. Cytotechnologists look at slides of body tissue through a microscope. They usually work under the supervision of a pathologist.

Education and Training Requirements

You must have a high school diploma or its equivalent to be a medical laboratory worker. High school courses in science and math offer good preparation. You generally need specialized training after high

school. Certification is not required to work. However, it can help you get and advance in a job. Manual dexterity and normal color vision are generally required.

In the past most medical laboratory assistants were trained on the job. However, formal training is now becoming important for new workers. You can attend a 12-month training program in a hospital, vocational school, or community college. The Committee on Allied Health Education and Accreditation has certified training programs for medical laboratory assistants. The programs include classroom instruction, as well as practical experience. Courses for medical laboratory assistants include bacteriology, hematology, urinalysis, blood banking, and serology.

The best way to acquire training as a medical laboratory technician is to take a 2-year accredited training program offered in community and junior colleges, colleges, and universities. The Committee on Allied Health Education and Accreditation has accredited more than 100 of these programs. Several organizations also offer certification for technicians.

In some states technicians must be licensed to work. The requirements vary but usually include a written examination.

Accredited training programs are also available for histologic technicians and for cytotechnologists.

It is very important that medical laboratory workers carefully check into training programs before choosing one. Selecting the right program can help during job hunting because certain areas of medicine have different training requirements.

Getting the Job

Your school placement office can help you find a job. You can also apply directly to hospitals, clinics, laboratories, and research institutions in which you would like to work. Check the want ads of newspapers and professional journals as well.

Advancement Possibilities and Employment Outlook

Additional training is usually required to advance. Medical laboratory assistants may become technicians. Technicians may study to become technologists. A master's degree is generally required for teaching and research positions.

The employment outlook is good through the year 2005. The volume of testing is expected to increase, and clinical laboratories are expected to grow, as the older population grows. The probability of new and more powerful diagnostic tests and research laboratories working to find the cause, treatment, and cure for AIDS (acquired immune deficiency syndrome) also should create jobs.

Working Conditions

Working conditions for medical laboratory workers vary depending on their specialty. However, in all cases the work is very detailed. Medical laboratory assistants sit for much of the day. They rarely have contact with patients. Their tasks are generally routine. Medical laboratory technicians, however, perform a wide range of tests.

Cytotechnologists' work seldom varies from 1 day to the next. They are not closely supervised. Histologic technicians, on the other hand, perform many different tasks. Generally they work under the supervision of several people. Histologic technicians may be under pressure to work quickly. At times, tissue samples of a person who is being operated on are sent to the technicians, and they must prepare the slides immediately.

Medical laboratory workers usually work 40 hours a week. Those who work in hospitals may be required to work some evenings and weekends. Medical laboratory workers may be required to wear uniforms and protective clothing.

Earnings and Benefits

Medical laboratory workers employed by the federal government earn salaries that average between $16,000 and $23,000 a year. Experienced workers may earn salaries that average between $19,100 and $32,900 a year. Benefits generally include paid holidays and vacations. Some workers have pension plans.

Where to Go for More Information

American Medical Technologists
710 Higgins Road
Park Ridge, IL 60068
(708) 823-5169

American Society of Clinical Pathologists
2100 West Harrison Street
Chicago, IL 60612-3798
(312) 738-1336

Medical Record Technician and Clerk

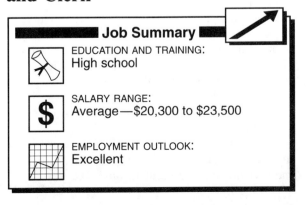

Job Summary

EDUCATION AND TRAINING:
High school

SALARY RANGE:
Average—$20,300 to $23,500

EMPLOYMENT OUTLOOK:
Excellent

Definition and Nature of the Work

Medical record technicians and clerks maintain hospital reports on patients. They keep track of patients' medical histories and charts. They make certain that the medical information is correct and that it is available for use by doctors and nurses. Technicians and clerks work in the record department of hospitals and clinics. Technicians and clerks perform similar duties. However, technicians do work for which specialized knowledge is needed. Clerks do not have this specialized knowledge. In large hospitals technicians and clerks work under the direction of a medical record administrator. In small hospitals and clinics highly experienced technicians may head the medical record department.

Medical record technicians and clerks check each patient's chart before the patient leaves the hospital. They make sure that all necessary information about the patient's illness is on record. These records must be maintained for insurance purposes and in the event the patient returns to the hospital. In addition, technicians and clerks sometimes collect information, such as the kinds of diseases treated in a hospital. The statistics that are gathered from this information can help both doctors and scientists in their research.

Technicians also put medical information into code. This code makes it easier to use the information in the files. Codes also make it easier to cross-index the files. Cross-indexing is a big part of the technicians' job. In a cross-indexed system, information on a particular treatment might be available not only under the name of the patient but also under the name of the disease or under the names of the doctors involved in the case.

Most medical record technicians and clerks work in hospitals, clinics, and nursing homes. In large institutions they may work with computerized record systems. Some government agencies hire people who have experience working with medical records. Health and property-liability insurance companies sometimes need technicians and clerks. These workers help insurance companies collect information to settle medical claims.

Education and Training Requirements

A high school diploma is necessary to be a medical record clerk. Clerks must have basic secretarial skills. They usually receive 1 month of on-the-job training. Completion of a correspondence course in medical transcription offered by the American Medical Record Association is helpful in getting a job.

Medical record technicians need more advanced training. Junior and community colleges offer 2-year training programs that lead to an associate degree. These programs usually include courses in biology, record keeping, and data processing. After training, technicians are eligible to take a test to become an Accredited Record Technician (ART). Although all technicians do not have to be accredited, many hospitals require it, especially for promotion to more responsible jobs.

Getting the Job

If you attend a training program, your school placement office may be able to help you find a job. You can apply directly to hospitals, clinics, and medical centers. Check with private employment agencies and your state employment office for available positions. Newspaper want ads sometimes carry listings for medical record technicians and clerks.

Advancement Possibilities and Employment Outlook

With further education, medical record clerks may become medical record technicians. A few technicians become supervisors. With additional study, a technician can qualify as a medical record administrator. Many hospitals encourage their clerks and technicians to continue their schooling by giving them time off from work to attend classes. Technicians who work for the government may take civil service tests to advance.

The total number of jobs for medical record clerks and technicians is growing rapidly. The employment outlook is excellent through the year 2005.

One of the biggest tasks of the health care industry will be to keep all the medical records necessary for insurance claims, Medicare reimbursement, and legal actions. As the volume of medical records grows, more workers will be needed to keep patients' records up to date.

Working Conditions
The record departments of hospitals are usually pleasant places in which to work. Most technicians and clerks work 40 hours a week. However, as records are needed in hospitals 24 hours a day, there is some night and weekend work. Part-time work is sometimes available.

Earnings and Benefits
Salaries vary depending on geographic location and experience. The average annual salary ranges between $20,300 and $23,500. Medical record tech-

nicians working for the federal government earn an average salary of $22,000 a year. Benefits include paid holidays and vacations, health insurance, and pension plans.

Where to Go for More Information
American Health Information Management
  Association
919 North Michigan Avenue, Suite 1400
Chicago, IL 60611-1683
(312) 787-2672

American Hospital Association
One North Franklin, Suite 2700
Chicago, IL 60606
(312) 422-3000

National Health Council
1730 M Street, NW, Suite 500
Washington, DC 20036
(202) 785-3910

Occupational Therapy Assistant

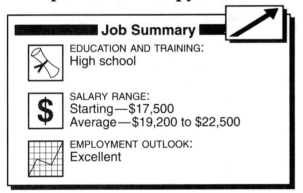

Job Summary

EDUCATION AND TRAINING:
High school

SALARY RANGE:
Starting—$17,500
Average—$19,200 to $22,500

EMPLOYMENT OUTLOOK:
Excellent

Definition and Nature of the Work
Occupational therapy assistants help to teach skills to people who are sick or handicapped. They work under the supervision of occupational therapists. Many occupational therapy assistants work in hospitals. Others work in homes for the aged, clinics, special schools, or occupational workshops.

Assistants may work with paralyzed or crippled people or with people who have just been fitted with an artificial limb. They also work with people who have emotional or mental problems. Assistants may teach patients how to feed and dress themselves. Or they may teach them crafts that will be fun for the patients and will put their minds and

bodies to use. Assistants may also help teach job skills, such as typing or electrical repair, that will help patients to earn a living.

Occupational therapy assistants also order supplies and take care of the equipment used in therapy. They may write reports on the patients and do other paperwork.

Education and Training Requirements
To enter a training program for occupational therapy assistants, you must have a high school diploma or its equivalent. Courses in crafts, health, science, and typing are helpful. Work experience in summer camps or hospitals is useful.

Training for occupational therapy assistants is given in community colleges and vocational and technical schools. Most programs last 2 years and lead to an associate degree. If you graduate from a program approved by the American Occupational Therapy Association and pass a test, you can become a Certified Occupational Therapy Assistant (COTA).

Getting the Job
You can apply directly to hospitals or clinics for a job. Job openings are sometimes listed in news-

paper want ads. School placement offices can also help you to find a job. Also check state and private employment agencies.

Advancement Possibilities and Employment Outlook

In large hospitals and clinics, assistants can become supervisors. With further training and experience, a Certified Occupational Therapy Assistant can become a Registered Occupational Therapist (OTR).

The employment outlook is excellent through the year 2005. Because of a growing public interest in the rehabilitation of disabled people, there will be a demand for rehabilitation services and long-term care. These programs have had great success. Also, there is an anticipated high rate of turnover among occupational therapy assistants, which should result in many openings. The employment outlook is best for graduates of approved programs.

Working Conditions

Occupational therapy assistants usually work 40 hours a week. Some weekend or evening hours may be required. Most occupational workshops are nicely decorated. Assistants should be friendly and understanding. They often work with people who are in pain or who need to be cheered up. Assistants should be good at working with their hands and should enjoy helping others.

Earnings and Benefits

Salaries vary with education and experience. The average starting salary for occupational therapy assistants is about $17,500 a year. Those occupational therapy assistants employed by the federal government earn on the average between $19,200 and $22,500 a year. Benefits include paid holidays and vacations, health insurance, and pension plans.

Where to Go for More Information

The American Occupational Therapy Association
4720 Montgomery Lane
P.O. Box 31220
Bethesda, MD 20824-1220
(301) 948-9626

American Society of Hand Therapists
401 North Michigan Avenue
Chicago, IL 60611
(312) 321-6866

Optician

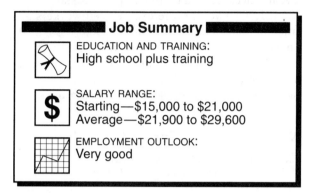

Job Summary

EDUCATION AND TRAINING:
High school plus training

SALARY RANGE:
Starting—$15,000 to $21,000
Average—$21,900 to $29,600

EMPLOYMENT OUTLOOK:
Very good

Definition and Nature of the Work

Opticians fill doctors' prescriptions for eyeglasses. They prepare the lenses by grinding the glass to fit the prescription of each patient. Then they put the lenses into frames. Opticians also make sure that the lenses and frames fit properly.

There are two kinds of opticians: *dispensing opticians,* who are sometimes called prescription opticians or ophthalmic dispensers, and *optical laboratory technicians,* who are also called optical mechanics. Most dispensing opticians work in stores that sell eyeglasses. Optical laboratory technicians generally work in laboratories that fill orders from dispensing opticians. Some retail stores have laboratories on their premises. These stores employ both kinds of opticians. Opticians also work for optometrists and ophthalmologists. Some opticians work for firms that make precision lenses for cameras, microscopes, telescopes, and military equipment.

Dispensing opticians help patients select the size, color, and shape of their frames. They measure each patient's face to decide exactly where the lenses should be placed. They send information on the size, color, shape, and prescription of the lenses to the optical laboratory. When the eyeglasses have been made, the dispensing optician measures and adjusts the glasses for the patient until they fit properly. Dispensing opticians also fit patients for contact lenses. Some specialize in this kind of work.

Optical laboratory technicians actually make the eyeglasses. They receive doctors' prescriptions and the measurements made by dispensing opticians. Technicians use power machines to grind and polish the lenses. In large laboratories they specialize in different parts of the job. *Optical surfacers* take flat pieces of glass and grind them according to prescription. Then they polish the lenses. *Optical finishers,* or bench technicians, cut the lenses so they fit into the frames. Some optical laboratory technicians make contact lenses. *Contact lens techni-*

cians grind pieces of plastic to the right prescription. They use power equipment, such as jewelers' lathes, and also polish by hand. Contact lens technicians generally work in large laboratories. They usually specialize in one phase of the work.

Education and Training Requirements

The training requirements for dispensing opticians and for optical laboratory technicians are similar. Employers generally prefer high school graduates. You should take courses in algebra, geometry, physics, mechanical drawing, and shop.

Most opticians are trained on the job. However, formal training is becoming preferred. On-the-job training generally lasts several years. There are also apprenticeship programs, which usually take 2 to 4 years to complete. Another way to get training is to attend a 2-year college. Two-year programs lead to an associate degree.

Some states require opticians to be licensed. Licensing requirements usually include meeting educational and training standards and passing a written test or a practical test. In some states you must pass both tests.

Getting the Job

Your school placement office can help you find a job. You can apply directly to companies and private dispensing opticians for on-the-job training. In addition, you can apply to companies that operate apprenticeship programs.

Advancement Possibilities and Employment Outlook

Dispensing opticians may advance by becoming the managers of their stores. Some open up their own businesses. Optical laboratory technicians may become supervisors.

The employment outlook for opticians is very good through the year 2005. The anticipated growth of the middle-aged and elderly populations requiring health and vision care will create a need for opticians. Also, as more customers buy contact lenses or more than one pair of glasses, the number of jobs for opticians is expected to increase.

Working Conditions

Dispensing opticians work in clean, quiet offices. Optical laboratory technicians work with power machines. Their work is somewhat dirty, and lab-

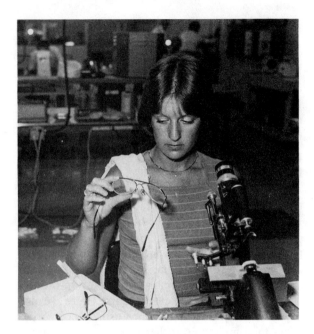

tified opticians earn starting salaries of about $15,000 a year. Licensed and certified opticians start at about $21,000 a year. More experienced workers average annual salaries of about $21,900 to $29,600. Those opticians who own their own shops can expect to earn considerably more. Benefits for salaried opticians generally include paid holidays and vacations, health insurance, and pension plans.

Where to Go for More Information

International Union of Electronic, Electrical, Salaried, Machine, and Furniture Workers
1126 Sixteenth Street, NW
Washington, DC 20036
(202) 296-1200

National Academy of Opticianry
10111 Martin Luther King Jr. Highway, Suite 112
Bowie, MD 20720
(301) 577-4828

Optical Society of America
2010 Massachusetts Avenue, NW
Washington, DC 20036
(202) 223-8130

Opticians Association of America
10341 Democracy Lane, Box 10110
Fairfax, VA 22030-2505
(703) 691-8355

Vision Council of America
1800 North Kent Street
Rosslyn, VA 22209-2152
(703) 243-1508

oratories are generally noisy. All opticians must be precise and exacting. In addition, dispensing opticians must have a talent for sales and enjoy working with people. Opticians generally work 40 hours a week. Dispensing opticians may work some evenings and Saturdays.

Earnings and Benefits

Earnings vary depending on education, experience, and placement of employment. Beginning noncer-

Optometric Assistant

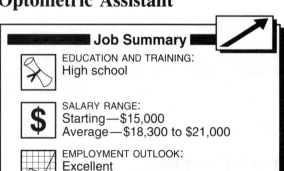

■ Job Summary ■

EDUCATION AND TRAINING:
High school

SALARY RANGE:
Starting—$15,000
Average—$18,300 to $21,000

EMPLOYMENT OUTLOOK:
Excellent

Definition and Nature of the Work

Optometric assistants perform routine tasks in optometrists' offices. Their work enables optometrists to devote their time to patient care that requires specialized training. Optometric assistants do clerical work, such as bookkeeping and scheduling appointments. They also help the optometrist during eye examinations.

Optometrists give their patients eye examinations for vision, color blindness, and eye pressure. When the tests are completed, an optometrist can prescribe the necessary eyeglasses for the patient. Optometric assistants often prepare patients for the tests. They may put drops in patients' eyes or direct and seat patients at eye testing machines.

Assistants may explain eye exercises to patients or teach them how to use contact lenses. In some offices optometric assistants help people choose the frames for their glasses. When the eyeglasses are made, optometric assistants adjust them for a proper fit.

Some assistants work in laboratories that fill prescriptions for eyeglasses. They put lenses into frames or repair broken frames. Most optometric assistants work in private offices. Some work in health clinics or for government agencies. Still others are employed by companies that make optical instruments.

Education and Training Requirements

Optometric assistants should have a high school diploma or its equivalent. Most are trained on the job. Optometrists prefer applicants who are accurate and able to work well with delicate and breakable tools and materials.

There are also formal training programs for this work. Some technical schools, community colleges, and colleges of optometry offer 1-year programs. Training for optometric assistants generally includes secretarial and office skills as well as medical procedures.

Getting the Job

If you attend a training program, your school placement office can give you job information. If you do not have training, contact optometrists in your community and ask about on-the-job training. To get a government job, apply to take the necessary civil service test. State and private employment offices can also provide information about employment opportunities. You should also check the want ads of local newspapers for listings.

Advancement Possibilities and Employment Outlook

An assistant may train with an optometrist who specializes in a field such as contact lenses. Learning a specialty will enable the assistant to get a better-paying job.

The employment outlook is excellent through the year 2005. Job openings will be created by the coverage of eyecare services through public and private insurance programs and the new, more economical eyecare chains. Also, the growth of the older population is certain to assure the need for qualified optometric assistants. Opportunities will be best for persons who have completed a formal training program.

Working Conditions

Most optometric assistants work in modern, well-lighted offices and laboratories. Offices can be very busy at times. However, the work area is usually quiet and clean. Optometric assistants work under the direct supervision of an optometrist. They must enjoy working with people because they have much contact with patients. Work hours vary, but assistants usually work about 40 hours a week. Their workweek may include some evenings and Saturdays. Many optometric assistants work part time.

Earnings and Benefits

Beginning optometric assistants earn a salary of about $15,000 a year. Optometric assistants with experience may average $18,300 to $21,000 a year. Benefits generally include paid holidays and vacations and health insurance.

Where to Go for More Information

American Optometric Association
243 North Lindbergh Boulevard
St. Louis, MO 63141-7881
(314) 991-4100

Orthoptist

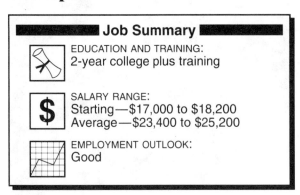

■■■■ **Job Summary** ■■■■

EDUCATION AND TRAINING:
2-year college plus training

SALARY RANGE:
Starting—$17,000 to $18,200
Average—$23,400 to $25,200

EMPLOYMENT OUTLOOK:
Good

Definition and Nature of the Work

Orthoptists work in the field of eye care. They specialize in the treatment of patients who are suffering from problems of muscle imbalance of the eye. The most common of these problems is crossed eyes. Cross-eyed patients do not have binocular vision; that is, both eyes do not work together as they should. Orthoptists use diagnostic instruments and procedures to test patients. They teach them how to strengthen their eye muscles through exercise. Orthoptists work mainly with children because crossed eyes are easier to correct when a patient is young. They teach their patients eye exercises to do at home. They meet regularly with their patients to check their progress. Orthoptists usually work under the supervision of ophthalmologists, who are medical doctors specializing in diseases of the eye. Orthoptists work in hospitals, clinics, private doctors' offices, and medical centers.

Education and Training Requirements

To be trained as an orthoptist, you first need from 2 to 4 years of college. Then you must enroll in a special school that offers courses in orthoptics. These programs usually last about 24 months and include

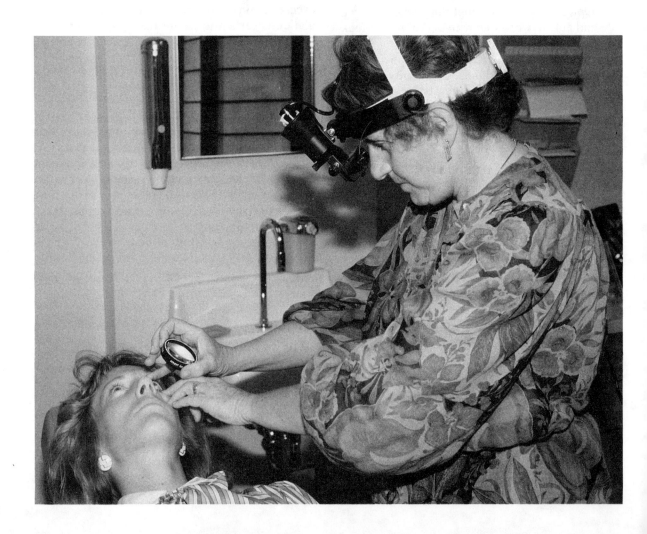

clinical training. You must complete an approved program and pass an exam in order to become a certified orthoptist.

Getting the Job

Your school placement office can help you to find a job as an orthoptist. The American Association of Certified Orthoptists also keeps a file of job openings. Or you can apply directly to an ophthalmologist for employment. Want ads in newspapers may be another source of job information.

Advancement Possibilities and Employment Outlook

Orthoptists are important members of the eye care team. As they gain experience, they often take on more responsibility in the care of patients with crossed eyes and related vision problems. Sometimes they also help in the training of new orthoptists. There are now many more openings than there are qualified orthoptists. The job future also looks promising. More ophthalmologists are making use of the special training of orthoptists.

Working Conditions

As this is a very specialized field, most jobs are located in or around major cities. The offices are generally pleasant places in which to work. Orthoptists work with a variety of people. Usually orthoptists work during ophthalmologists' office hours. This is generally a 40-hour week, which often includes evenings or Saturdays. Part-time work is also sometimes available.

Orthoptists deal with people who have a handicap that can be emotionally upsetting. They should therefore be understanding, enthusiastic, and encouraging with their patients. Orthoptists should be good teachers who can explain eye exercises clearly, especially to children.

Earnings and Benefits

Salaries vary depending on experience, position, and location. Beginning orthoptists earn an average of about $17,000 to $18,200 a year. Experienced orthoptists average about $23,400 to $25,200 a year. Benefits generally include paid holidays and vacations and health insurance.

Where to Go for More Information

American Association of Certified Orthoptists
c/o Pattye Jenkins
Houston Eye Center
2855 Gramercy
Houston, TX 77025
(713) 668-6828

National Health Council
1730 M Street, NW, Suite 500
Washington, DC 20036
(202) 785-3910

Pharmaceutical Detail Representative

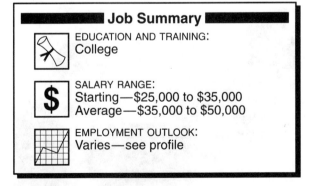

Job Summary

EDUCATION AND TRAINING:
College

SALARY RANGE:
Starting—$25,000 to $35,000
Average—$35,000 to $50,000

EMPLOYMENT OUTLOOK:
Varies—see profile

Definition and Nature of the Work

Pharmaceutical detail representatives are employed by drug companies. They distribute information about their companies' products to physicians, hospital nurses, and medical technicians.

Detail representatives are salespeople, but not in the usual sense. They do not take orders from doctors. They try to persuade doctors to prescribe more of their companies' drugs. Patients then buy the drugs. Most doctors are very busy. Detail representatives usually get to talk to doctors for no more than five or six minutes. In that time they must describe their company's newest products. They outline what a drug is designed to do and how it works. They explain its advantages over older drugs.

Detail representatives must have a basic knowledge of how the human body works. They must also have some understanding of disease and pharmacology. Doctors question detail persons about drugs and their side effects. Detail persons must know which drugs will be of interest to doctors in different specialties.

Detail representatives are assigned territories based on postal ZIP Codes. They make up their own itineraries. They concentrate on the doctors who write the most prescriptions. This information is available from surveys of pharmacists. Detail persons may leave samples of new drugs with doctors. They must keep careful records concerning samples.

Detail representatives must be able to talk clearly and concisely under pressure. They must have pleasant personalities. Building long-lasting relationships with doctors is part of the job. They must be able to accept rejection. About 40 percent of doctors refuse to see detail persons at all. Others will not see them when they are very busy.

Education and Training Requirements

To become a detail person you must have a high school diploma. Most employers prefer to hire college graduates, preferably with a bachelor of science degree. However, 2 years of college should be sufficient to qualify for most jobs. The drug companies provide training. They select trainees on the basis of the trainees' verbal and social skills. The training consists of intensive study followed by supervised field work.

Representatives must keep abreast of current knowledge throughout their careers. They attend regular meetings to get product information. They must maintain a general knowledge of advances in medicine. Correspondence courses are available from the Certified Medical Representatives Institute, which offers certification.

Getting the Job

If you are a college student, ask your college placement office for information about applying to become a pharmaceutical detail representative trainee. Representatives of drug companies may also visit your campus. Otherwise you should write to major drug companies and request interviews. Once you are selected as a trainee, you do not have to look for a job.

Advancement Possibilities and Employment Outlook

Some representatives prefer to stay in the field. Some advance to supervisory and training positions. A few advance to administrative and planning posts. Occasionally a detail person will transfer to another department in the company or go into a related health occupation.

The job outlook for detail persons is fair to good. Some companies are expanding rapidly and will need to hire additional representatives.

Working Conditions

Pharmaceutical detail representatives set their own hours to fit doctors' schedules. The detail representative may have to spend much time traveling. They often have to wait to see doctors despite appointments. The general atmosphere in the drug industry is becoming increasingly competitive. Pharmaceutical detail representatives must be able to cope with stressful situations. These will be caused by competition with other detail representatives for access to doctors during their limited free time.

Earnings and Benefits

Commissions account for a large proportion of earnings for detail representatives. Depending on the company, roughly 10% to 20% of their earnings is derived from commissions based on the drugs ordered by doctors. Beginners' earnings average about $25,000 to $35,000 a year. The average for the occupation is about $35,000 to $50,000 a year. Top earnings are about $60,000 a year. Detail persons receive health insurance, paid vacations, and holidays. They also receive free cars and some travel expenses.

Where to Go for More Information

The Certified Medical Representatives Institute, Inc.
4950 Brambleton Avenue
Roanoke, VA 24018
(703) 989-4596

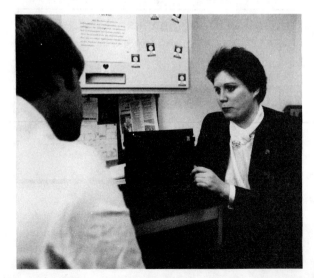

Physical Therapy Assistant

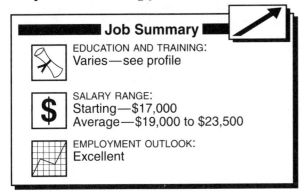

Job Summary

EDUCATION AND TRAINING:
Varies—see profile

SALARY RANGE:
Starting—$17,000
Average—$19,000 to $23,500

EMPLOYMENT OUTLOOK:
Excellent

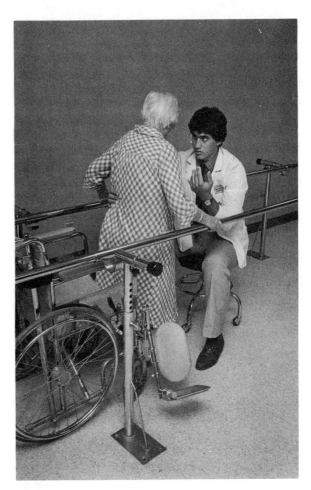

Definition and Nature of the Work

Physical therapy assistants work under the supervision of physical therapists. They use physical means to help people cope with pain and disability caused by disease or injury. Physical therapists and their assistants usually work in hospitals, nursing homes, or clinics. They are part of a health care team that includes doctors, occupational therapists, and social workers.

Physical therapy assistants work with people of all ages. Some work with old people who have trouble moving about. Some work with handicapped children. Others work with people who have lost an arm or a leg, people with arthritis, or people who are paralyzed. Physical therapy assistants use many different types of equipment. They treat patients by using massage, exercise, heat, cold, and light. Assistants help teach patients how to use and care for wheelchairs, braces, and artificial limbs.

Assistants have other duties that give physical therapists more time to put their special training to use. Assistants may do some office work, for example. Or they may get equipment ready for the therapist. They may also help the patient to get ready for therapy.

Education and Training Requirements

If you want to be a physical therapy assistant, a high school diploma or its equivalent is required. You should take courses in mathematics and science in high school. You can also get experience by working part time in a hospital or clinic. Or you can work with handicapped children in summer camps.

Training requirements vary. Most states require that you take an accredited 2-year associate degree program. Many states also require that you be licensed.

Getting the Job

If you receive training, your college placement office can help you to find a job as a physical therapy assistant. You can also apply directly to hospitals or clinics. Another good source of job openings is newspaper want ads.

Advancement Possibilities and Employment Outlook

As physical therapy assistants gain experience, they are often given more responsibility and salary increases. Some assistants continue their education while working and become physical therapists.

The employment outlook for physical therapy assistants is excellent through the year 2005. Opportunities will be best for graduates of accredited training programs. The expansion of rehabilitation services for people with physical disabilities will create many new jobs. The need for physical therapy is expected to grow as the number of people over the age of 75 increases. Advances in rehabilitation medicine and therapeutic techniques are likely to create additional demands.

Working Conditions

Physical therapy assistants usually work in clean, pleasant places. Their patients may sometimes be depressed by their disabilities. Assistants can help them by being cheerful and encouraging. Physical therapy assistants should also be healthy. They should be able to work well with their hands. Most physical therapy assistants work 40 hours a week. Some work part time.

Earnings and Benefits

Salaries vary with experience and place of employment. Beginning physical therapy assistants earn, on the average, about $17,000 a year. Physical ther-

apy assistants employed by the federal government earn between $19,000 and $23,500 a year. Benefits include paid holidays and vacations and health insurance.

Where to Go for More Information

American Physical Therapy Association
1111 North Fairfax Street
Alexandria, VA 22314-1488
(703) 684-2782

National Association of Rehabilitation Instructors
633 South Washington Street
Alexandria, VA 22314
(703) 836-0850

National Rehabilitation Association
633 South Washington Street
Alexandria, VA 22314
(703) 836-0850

Radiologic Technologist

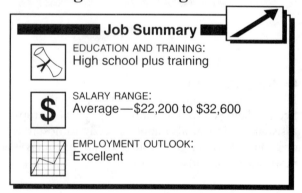

Job Summary

EDUCATION AND TRAINING:
High school plus training

$
SALARY RANGE:
Average—$22,200 to $32,600

EMPLOYMENT OUTLOOK:
Excellent

Definition and Nature of the Work

Radiologic technologists use X rays to help physicians diagnose and treat illness and injury. They usually work under the direction of radiologists, who are medical doctors specializing in X rays. Most radiologic technologists work in hospitals, but some work in medical laboratories, clinics, or doctors' or dentists' offices. Others help to staff mobile X-ray units or work in private industry. Radiologic technologists are usually responsible for writing reports, developing X-ray film, and maintaining their equipment.

There are three types of radiologic technologists. *Diagnostic X-ray technologists* take X rays that help doctors to find tumors, ulcers, broken bones, and other abnormal conditions. Sometimes diagnostic X-ray technologists have patients drink chemical mixtures to make organs show up on X-ray film or on a fluoroscope. *Radiation therapy technologists* help doctors to diagnose and treat disease by exposing certain parts of the patient's body to X rays or other forms of radiation. *Nuclear medicine technologists* help doctors to diagnose and treat disease by using radioactive materials. These radioactive substances are given to patients through the mouth or by injection into the veins. Nuclear medicine technologists use special equipment to trace the progress and concentration of the radioactive materials in various parts of the body.

Education and Training Requirements

You can become a radiologic technologist by enrolling in a 2- to 4-year program in radiography. A high school diploma or its equivalent is needed to enter a program. Hospitals, colleges, medical schools,

a bachelor's degree can become instructors or administrators. Some technologists advance by getting jobs with the manufacturers of X-ray equipment. They may sell or service this equipment.

The employment outlook for the field of radiologic technology is excellent through the year 2005. However, the number of candidates going into the field is also increasing. The best opportunities should be in the South and the Northwest. In the years ahead, a growing number of radiologic technologists will find jobs in offices of physicians, health maintenance organizations, diagnostic imaging centers, and freestanding cancer clinics.

Working Conditions

Radiologic technologists generally work 40 hours a week. Sometimes they must work night and weekend shifts. Part-time work is often available.

Radiologic technologists need manual dexterity and mechanical ability. They come in contact with a wide variety of people and should be sympathetic and friendly. Their working environment is usually clean and pleasant. Technologists should be in good health and must always work carefully to avoid exposing themselves and others to harmful radiation.

and vocational and technical schools offer these programs. The 4-year programs generally lead to a bachelor's degree in radiologic technology. After graduating from an approved program, you can take an exam leading to registration by the American Registry of Radiologic Technologists. With further training and experience, registered technologists can become certified in radiation therapy technology or nuclear medicine technology.

Getting the Job

Many hospitals will hire students that they have helped to train. School placement offices can also help you to find a job. The want ads in newspapers and professional journals are another good source of job leads.

Advancement Possibilities and Employment Outlook

Experienced radiologic technologists can become supervisors of other workers in large X-ray departments. They can also learn to operate other types of hospital equipment. Technologists who have

Earnings and Benefits

Salaries depend on education, experience, and location. Experienced technologists can earn $22,200 to $32,600 a year. Benefits include paid holidays and vacations, health insurance, and pension plans.

Where to Go for More Information

American Association for Women Radiologists
1891 Preston White Drive
Reston, VA 22091
(703) 648-8939

The American Society of Radiologic Technologists
15000 Central Avenue, Southeast
Albuquerque, NM 87123-3917
(505) 298-4500

Radiological Society of North America
2021 Spring Road, Suite 600
Oak Brook, IL 60521
(708) 571-2670

Society of Nuclear Medicine
1850 Samuel Morse Drive
Reston, VA 22090-5316
(703) 708-9000

Jobs Requiring Advanced Training/ Experience

Acupuncturist

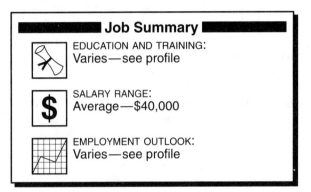

Job Summary

EDUCATION AND TRAINING:
Varies—see profile

SALARY RANGE:
Average—$40,000

EMPLOYMENT OUTLOOK:
Varies—see profile

Definition and Nature of the Work

Acupuncturists practice an Oriental medical therapy. They insert very fine stainless-steel needles into a patient's body at special points. Acupuncturists believe that the body is divided into a number of complicated pathways, or meridians. They contend that energy (or *ch'i*) should flow smoothly along these meridians and that if it does not, ill health will result. They use needles to regulate the flow of energy, which they believe promotes the smooth functioning of hormones, nerves, blood supply, and vital organs. Acupuncture may also be used in place of anesthetics.

Recent medical research has confirmed some of the basic assumptions of acupuncture. It seems that electromagnetic energy flows through the body in patterns like meridians. Stimulation by needles at acupuncture points releases hormones called endorphins in the brain. Endorphins can block pain.

Most people first visit acupuncturists for the treatment of headache pain, asthma, or arthritis. Acupuncturists question their clients about their state of health. They then evaluate pulse rates at 12 different points of the body and make a diagnosis. Taking various factors into account, they decide which size needles to use and where to insert them (there are 365 acupuncture points on the body). Sometimes the needles are rotated. Several sessions may be necessary to achieve the desired result. The treatment is not painful.

Acupuncturists must have sensitive hands. They must be highly accurate; needles inserted incor-

rectly can puncture vital organs. They must sterilize the needles carefully to avoid infection. They need great patience to perfect their skill and must relate well to other people.

Many acupuncturists are qualified in such fields as medicine, nursing, and physical therapy. A number of them offer acupuncture as an additional service while continuing in their original professions.

Education and Training Requirements

Acupuncture is a new profession in this country. Available training varies from apprenticeships to 3-year postgraduate programs. State regulations and minimum training requirements also vary and are subject to change. If you are interested, you must do some research.

First, check whether acupuncture is allowed in the state where you want to live. If it is, find out what minimum training requirements are necessary for obtaining a license. In some states, you must first be an M.D. or a chiropractor. Would you be allowed to establish a private practice, or would you have to work under supervision? A state employment counselor may be able to help you with these questions.

Second, has the profession agreed on minimum training requirements? If not, it might be wisest to aim for a master's of acupuncture (M.Ac.) at a postgraduate school that is accredited by the profession. A background with less training might fall below minimum standards established later. A master's of acupuncture usually consists of 2 years of study plus a year of supervised practice.

Third, at least 5 types of acupuncture are used in this country. A student should be thoroughly grounded in 1 type of acupuncture before learning another. There are about 15 accredited schools; each specializes in 1 type of acupuncture. You must read enough basic material to decide which tradition most appeals to you. Introductory literature and information about schools is available from the National Council of Acupuncture Schools and Colleges.

Finally, you should contact the schools that teach the type of acupuncture that you prefer. Ask for their entry requirements. Most schools will consider only students who have a first degree with certain science and social science courses. Clinical experience with the sick is also required. Midcareer applicants from fields such as nursing usually meet the requirements. High school students can ask for advice on the best preparation.

Getting the Job

Most acupuncturists are self-employed. Only a small percentage are affiliated with hospitals. Until recently, nearly all students in acupuncture schools came from careers in the medical field. Upon graduation, they were advised to continue their previous

work; their acupuncture practices could then be developed very slowly as second jobs; in this way they had time to perfect their skills. Recent graduates lack the experience to work both fast and accurately.

There is still no established route for these graduates to enter practice. A system of associates may be developed; graduates could then spend the first years working with experienced acupuncturists.

Advancement Possibilities and Employment Outlook

Public acceptance of acupuncture is growing rapidly. About two-thirds of the states now regulate acupuncture. Treatments are increasingly covered by insurance. Several joint studies with the medical profession are examining specific uses of acupuncture, such as drug detoxification and control of chronic pain. However, the total number in the profession is still very small. Only about 2,000 physicians and 4,000 nonphysicians have qualified. About 1,000 students are in school.

As with doctors, advancement comes with building a practice. However, most people (and most doctors) know little about acupuncture. The process of building a practice can therefore be very slow.

Working Conditions

Acupuncturists work in comfortable offices that must be kept quiet and clean. They can usually set their own hours. Some work late on certain evenings for the convenience of their patients. A few work in hospitals or clinics.

Earnings and Benefits

Those who have worked in the profession for several years earn an average of about $40,000 a year. Acupuncturists in private practice must provide their own benefits.

Where to Go for More Information

American Academy of Medical Acupuncture
5820 Wilshire Boulevard, Suite 500
Los Angeles, CA 90036
(213) 937-5514

American Acupuncture Association
42-62 Kissena Boulevard
Flushing, NY 11355
(718) 886-4431

AIDS Counselor

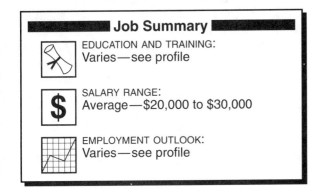

Job Summary

EDUCATION AND TRAINING:
Varies—see profile

SALARY RANGE:
Average—$20,000 to $30,000

EMPLOYMENT OUTLOOK:
Varies—see profile

Definition and Nature of the Work

AIDS (acquired immune deficiency syndrome) is a disorder of the immune system for which there is no cure or vaccine. In the United States, male homosexuals, intravenous drug users, and children born to intravenous drug users are the groups most likely to contract AIDS. AIDS counselors provide support and assistance for those suffering from AIDS. They also provide instructions for AIDS prevention to high-risk groups and information to the general public.

Some AIDS counselors talk to people who are about to have an AIDS test. If the test is positive, they then provide advice and counseling. Others lead individual and family counseling sessions for those who have been diagnosed as having AIDS. Still others lead support groups for patients, those who have lost friends and family to the disease, and those who feel that they are at risk.

One of the jobs of an AIDS counselor is to provide practical advice to people with AIDS on how to cope with their daily lives and the problems they may encounter. This may include finding housing, medical services, and legal advisers.

Volunteers play an important part in assisting organizations that counsel people with AIDS. They may become "buddies," visiting AIDS patients in their homes and assisting with household tasks. Others answer telephone hotlines and give information about AIDS testing and other available help. Many are involved in administrative tasks that help these organizations stay in operation.

AIDS counselors may also spend time writing and talking to the general public. They focus on information about the disease and its prevention. This is done through brochures, discussion groups, and training sessions. They may provide information to employers about AIDS in the workplace.

Education and Training Requirements

Because the AIDS epidemic is a fairly recent development in this country, there is no formal training to become an AIDS counselor. Currently experience is more important than education. The best way to gain this experience is to become a volunteer with an organization that cares for people with AIDS. Most organizations provide initial training for volunteers, and many provide follow-up sessions. Paid positions are usually filled by people with master's degrees in the field of mental health or social work. These people usually have had counseling experience in substance abuse or have worked with people who are at high risk for getting AIDS.

Getting the Job

Organizations that work with people who have AIDS or who are at high risk for the disease rely on volunteers. The best way to get a job in this field is to apply directly to these organizations as a volunteer. Your school placement office may be able to give you information about paid positions. You can also apply to hospitals and hospices in areas where there are large numbers of AIDS patients.

Advancement Possibilities and Employment Outlook

Experienced AIDS counselors with master's degrees can advance to administrative positions. Some may become AIDS educators, writing, organizing, and delivering information to the public. Others become training specialists, designing training programs for volunteers and professionals. Within organizations they may become project coordinators, project directors, or regional directors.

Although the number of AIDS cases will increase steadily in the future, the outlook for paid employment is uncertain. The demand for volunteers will remain high, but paid positions will depend on the level of private and government funding. Job opportunities will be most plentiful for those with master's degrees and experience in a related field.

Working Conditions

AIDS counselors in paid positions usually work a 40-hour week. Some work in clean hospital environments and mental health clinics. Those who work

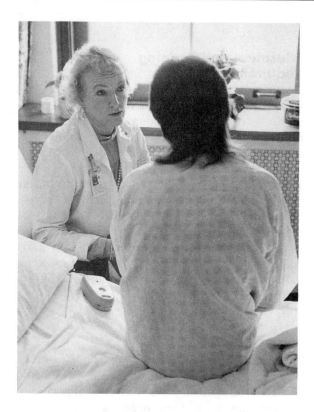

Earnings and Benefits

Many AIDS counselors are volunteers and do not receive a salary. For those in paid positions, salaries are very similar to those of other social workers. Currently social workers with a bachelor's degree earn about $20,000 a year. Those with a master's degree earn about $30,000. Salaries are generally higher for private practitioners, administrators, and researchers.

Benefits for those working for hospitals and public health departments generally include paid vacations and holidays, health insurance, and retirement plans.

Where to Go for More Information

The Academy for Educational Development
1255 Twenty-third Street, NW, Fourth Floor
Washington, DC 20037
(202) 862-1900

American Foundation for AIDS Research
5900 Wilshire Boulevard, 23rd Floor
Los Angeles, CA 90036-5032
(213) 857-5900

American Psychological Association
750 First Street, NE
Washington, DC 20002
(202) 336-5500

American Public Health Association
1015 Fifteenth Street, NW
Washington, DC 20005
(202) 789-5600

CDC National AIDS Clearinghouse
P.O. Box 6003
Rockville, MD 20849-6003
(301) 217-0023

in hospices work in pleasant surroundings. Many volunteers and counselors also visit AIDS patients in their homes, which may be in poor inner-city areas.

People suffering from AIDS are under severe emotional and physical stress. This stress affects their interaction with the AIDS counselor. Therefore, the AIDS counselor must be able to work with people who are very ill and severely depressed due to the effects of the disease.

Art and Music Therapist

Job Summary

EDUCATION AND TRAINING:
Varies—see profile

SALARY RANGE:
Starting—$19,000 to $25,000
Average—$25,600 to $33,500

EMPLOYMENT OUTLOOK:
Very good

Definition and Nature of the Work

Art and music therapists are practicing artists and musicians who combine these talents with professional training in psychology. They devise programs that use their specific artistic talents and health skills to help prevent or alleviate physical, mental, and social problems.

These therapists often work as members of a larger health care team serving a number of patients. Together they discuss their cases and decide on the best form of treatment. Art and music therapists may carry on their work with individuals or in groups.

They work to improve self-confidence and self-control and to relieve depression and anger. Patients are encouraged to deal with these problems by expressing themselves through music and art. For example, with the help of an art therapist, aggressive children may be able to channel their aggression into painting rather than into aggressive behavior. A music therapist may help people who have difficulty in relating to others by having them play and move to music with other people.

Art has proven to be a useful diagnostic tool in mental health evaluation, particularly for children. Art therapists are therefore often involved in diagnosing mental illness. Prevention of mental illness is also an important part of art and music therapy. Therapists work in schools and in centers for elderly people to prevent depression and other problems for those at high risk.

Education and Training Requirements

A good background in art or music is required in order to train as an art or music therapist. To become a certified music therapist, you must complete an accredited 4-year bachelor's degree program in music therapy. Bachelor's degrees in art therapy are also available. However, liberal arts and education majors are acceptable as long as you have taken courses in art and psychology. A master's degree is usually required in order to practice as an art therapist. Students in these programs must complete an internship in order to graduate and receive certification. Those who wish to work in public schools must complete further courses to be eligible for a teaching certificate.

Getting the Job

Your college placement office is probably the best source of job information. Art and music therapists can also apply to state employment offices and federal agencies. Professional organizations, such as the American Art Therapy Association or the National Association for Music Therapy, assist their members in finding positions.

Advancement Possibilities and Employment Outlook

In private practice, music and art therapists can work to expand the number of clients that they see. Those in hospitals and clinics may advance to su-

pervisory positions. Many positions for these therapists are in government-supported institutions. Here advancement is in the form of increases in pay and rank following successful reviews. However, promotion may mean leaving clinical practice and becoming an administrator.

Art and music therapy are growing occupations. More and more hospitals and institutions are employing therapists of all types. Schools and nursing homes are also recognizing the value of art and music as preventive and remedial therapies. The outlook for employment is very good through the year 2005.

Working Conditions

Art and music therapists work in a number of different settings. They work in hospitals and mental health facilities, schools, and private offices. The surroundings are generally cheerful and pleasant. Most therapists work a 40-hour week. Those in private practice may have irregular hours to accommodate their patients' schedules.

Earnings and Benefits

Beginning salaries for art and music therapists with a bachelor's degree are currently between $19,000 and $25,000 a year. Those with a master's degree may earn more. Average salaries are between $25,600 and $33,500 a year. Therapists with a doctoral degree teaching in universities can earn $50,000 a year or more. Benefits usually include paid holidays and vacations, health insurance, and pension

plans. Some therapists receive tuition assistance for further study. Art and music therapists in private practice must provide their own benefits.

Where to Go for More Information

American Art Therapy Association
1202 Allanson Road
Mundelein, IL 60060
(708) 949-6064

National Association for Music Therapy
8455 Colesville Road, Suite 930
Silver Spring, MD 20910-3392
(301) 589-3300

National Association of Schools of Music
11250 Roger Bacon Drive, Suite 21
Reston, VA 22090
(703) 437-0700

Chiropractor

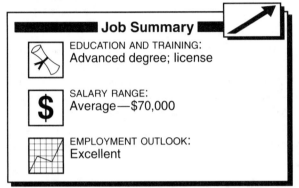

Job Summary

EDUCATION AND TRAINING:
Advanced degree; license

SALARY RANGE:
Average—$70,000

EMPLOYMENT OUTLOOK:
Excellent

Definition and Nature of the Work

Chiropractors practice a special system of health care known as chiropractic. Chiropractic is based on the belief that the nervous system, for the most part, controls physical health. Chiropractors believe that most disorders of the human body can be traced to interference with the nervous system. They treat patients chiefly by manipulating parts of the body, especially the spinal column. The spinal column is important because the spinal cord, an important part of the nervous system, passes through it. Chiropractors try to correct any disorders of the skeleton or spine that may interrupt the flow of nerve impulses to various parts of the body. They do not use drugs or surgery to treat patients.

Chiropractors use a variety of methods to learn about a patient's condition. They ask the patient questions and examine the patient carefully. They usually use their eyes to see and their hands to feel whether body structures are out of place. They often use X rays to get a picture of the patient's bone structure. In addition, chiropractors use laboratory tests, such as urinalysis or blood tests, as well as instruments, such as stethoscopes, to diagnose disorders. Some patients need drugs, surgery, psychiatry, and other types of treatment that chiropractors do not use. Chiropractors refer these patients to physicians who can give them the proper treatment.

Chiropractors use several kinds of treatment. They usually manipulate the affected part of the body. They also treat patients with light, heat, cold, water, exercise, or other forms of physical therapy. In addition, chiropractors often advise their patients about diet and mental outlook to help promote good health.

Most chiropractors have private practices either alone or with other chiropractors. Some teach chiropractic or do research in hospitals, clinics, health agencies, or private industry. Many chiropractors specialize in such areas as athletic injuries, diseases of children or of women, or X-ray diagnoses.

Education and Training Requirements

Students usually need 2 years of college before they can enroll in a special chiropractic college. Courses should include science and other subjects required by the chiropractic college that they want to attend. After completing a 4-year program in a chiropractic college, graduates receive the degree of Doctor of Chiropractic (D.C.). All states require that chiropractors be licensed. Requirements vary, however, from state to state. In all states chiropractors must pass a state board examination. In some states they must also pass a test in basic science.

Getting the Job

Nearly all newly licensed chiropractors enter private practice. Some of them open their own offices right away. Others buy an established practice from a chiropractor who is retiring. Still others join the office of a practicing chiropractor to get experience. Chiropractic colleges can provide information about setting up a practice.

Some chiropractors get salaried jobs. These jobs are usually in clinics, chiropractic colleges, or private industry. Job openings of this kind can be found through the want ads of newspapers or in professional publications.

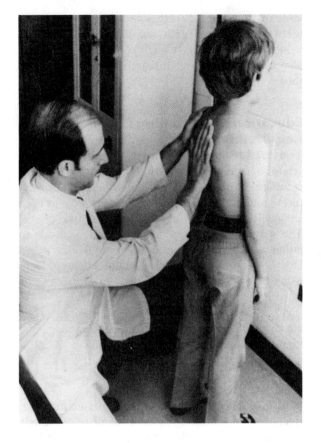

ices. Demand for chiropractors is related to the ability of patients to pay, either directly or through health insurance, and to public acceptance of the profession, which appears to be growing. However, more people are going into this field. There may be competition for jobs in some geographic areas.

Working Conditions

Chiropractors usually work in pleasant offices. If they are in private practice, they can set their own hours. To be successful, they need to have good business sense and self-discipline. They should be able to deal with all kinds of people. Chiropractors must also be able to work well with their hands.

Earnings and Benefits

The earnings of chiropractors vary greatly. Beginning chiropractors who are associates of practicing chiropractors earn approximately $45,000 a year. The average annual salary for an experienced practitioner is about $70,000 after expenses. Some chiropractors can earn over $190,000 a year. As chiropractors are usually self-employed, they must provide their own benefits, such as pension funds and insurance policies.

Advancement Possibilities and Employment Outlook

Chiropractors usually advance by building their practices. The degree of their success depends on their skill and location, as well as other factors. Some chiropractors advance by moving into high-level jobs in teaching, research, or administration.

The employment outlook is excellent through the year 2005 due to growing use of chiropractic serv-

Where to Go for More Information

American Chiropractic Association
1701 Clarendon Boulevard
Arlington, VA 22209
(703) 276-8800

International Chiropractors Association
1110 North Glebe Road, Suite 1000
Arlington, VA 22201
(703) 528-5000

Dentist

▮▮▮▮▮ Job Summary ▮▮▮▮▮

EDUCATION AND TRAINING:
Advanced degree; license

SALARY RANGE:
Average—$90,000

EMPLOYMENT OUTLOOK:
Good

Definition and Nature of the Work

Dentists are health professionals who take care of the teeth, gums, and supporting bones of the mouth. They help their patients to keep their teeth and gums healthy. They also treat diseased teeth and gums. Dentists sometimes detect general diseases of the body that can affect the condition of a patient's mouth.

Most dentists work as general practitioners in their own office or with a group of dentists. They often have dental assistants and dental hygienists

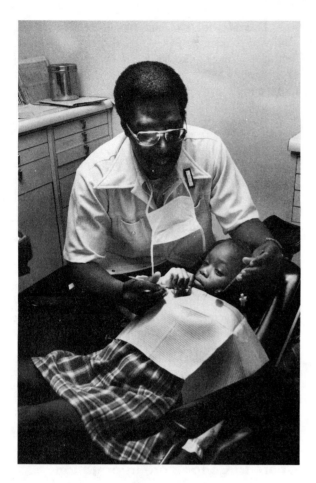

lems of the gums. *Prosthodontists* replace missing teeth with artificial teeth. *Public health dentists* develop care programs. A small percentage of dentists also work in teaching, research, or administration jobs.

Education and Training Requirements

You need from 6 to 8 years of training after high school before you can work as a dentist. You must complete from 2 to 4 years of college before entering a dental college. Most students have at least a bachelor's degree when they begin dental college. The 4-year program at a dental college leads to either a Doctor of Dental Surgery (D.D.S.) or a Doctor of Dental Medicine (D.D.M.) degree. Dentists who decide to specialize need from 2 to 4 years of further training.

All states require dentists to be licensed. They must graduate from an approved dental college and then pass a state board examination.

Getting the Job

Most newly licensed dentists enter private practice. Because it is becoming more difficult to open new practices, many dentists start out by working with a dentist who is already established. Other dentists find salaried positions in hospitals or government agencies. Your dental college placement office can give you information on how to begin a practice.

working for them. Under the dentist's direction these helpers sometimes take X rays, clean patients' teeth, and teach patients how to care for their teeth and gums at home. Dentists may take X rays themselves. They examine patients' mouths for cavities, sores, swelling, or other signs of disease. They may fill cavities, pull teeth that cannot be saved, or replace missing teeth. Dentists use both hand and power tools. They may use a local or general anesthetic to keep patients comfortable during treatment. Some dentists do their own laboratory work. Others send this work out to dental laboratories. Sometimes general practitioners refer patients to specialists.

There are eight areas of specialization for dentists. *Orthodontists* straighten teeth by fitting them with wires or braces. *Oral surgeons* operate on the mouth and jaws. *Endodontists* treat diseases of the soft pulp inside the teeth. *Oral pathologists* diagnose and sometimes treat diseases of the mouth. *Pedodontists* specialize in dentistry for children and teenagers. *Periodontists* are concerned with prob-

Advancement Possibilities and Employment Outlook

Dentists usually advance by building their practices. Some become specialists. Others may go into high-level teaching, research, or administration jobs. The success of preventive dentistry has caused the number of patients with tooth decay to decline sharply. This has caused a current oversupply of dentists. However, the employment outlook is good through the year 2005. The demand for restorative dental health care and the provision of dental insurance are expected to create some new jobs for dentists.

Working Conditions

Dentists must spend long hours on their feet. They must take precautions against infectious diseases and must be able to deal with tense patients. They are rewarded, however, by the prestige of their profession. Because they often have several helpers, dentists must be able to supervise the work of others. They should also have good business sense. They must be responsible and careful professionals who can work well with their hands.

Dentists usually set their own schedules. Many choose to work more than 40 hours a week. These often include some evening and Saturday hours. Some dentists prefer a part-time schedule.

Earnings and Benefits

Earnings for dentists vary widely. They depend on the dentist's experience, skill, and willingness to work long hours. Earnings also depend on location and on the type of practice. Currently the average income for dentists is about $90,000 a year. Dentists who specialize generally earn more than general practitioners.

Since most dentists are self-employed, they must provide their own benefits.

Where to Go for More Information

American Association of Dental Schools
1625 Massachusetts Avenue, NW
Washington, DC 20036-2212
(202) 667-9433

American Dental Association
211 East Chicago Avenue
Chicago, IL 60611-2678
(312) 440-2500

Geriatric Social Worker

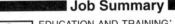

Job Summary

EDUCATION AND TRAINING:
Advanced degree

SALARY RANGE:
Starting—$12,000 to $20,000
Average—$15,000 to $25,000

EMPLOYMENT OUTLOOK:
Very good

Definition and Nature of the Work

Geriatric social workers constitute a special division of social workers. Their concern is the welfare of the elderly. They try to improve the quality of life for senior citizens. They help to alleviate some of the negative aspects of aging and help senior citizens to enjoy happier, more productive lives.

Geriatric social workers are employed in a wide variety of settings and have widely differing duties. Most geriatric social workers specialize in one of three areas. First, the primary function of many geriatric social workers is to assess the needs of senior citizens. These workers are often attached to community organizations, such as family service agencies or day care centers (many of which have outreach programs). The workers may help to decide which senior citizens need home health aides, special transportation, or similar services. With the help of such services, older adults may be able to stay out of nursing homes. Geriatric social workers are trained to recognize normal and abnormal aging patterns. They can suggest when an elderly client needs to see a doctor and can arrange for a visit. They can help a family decide whether it would be best to place the client in an institution.

Second, geriatric social workers help the elderly to deal with their problems. Many older adults are lonely. Social workers encourage clients to participate in group activities. Many workers are skilled in leading these activities or in arranging for others to do so. Some have a background in mental health. They may provide therapy for clients suffering from depression or anxiety (both common conditions among the elderly). Most social workers act as a link between their clients and public and private programs designed for the aging. These programs are numerous and confusing. Social workers help their clients to apply for appropriate services. They help sort out any problems in the delivery of these services. Social workers providing direct services can be found in many types of institutions, including retirement communities, nursing homes, hospitals, and employment programs for older adults.

Finally, a small number of geriatric social workers spend most of their time planning or organizing services for the elderly. Every program or agency has an executive director or the equivalent. Large organizations may have many administrators. State and county long-range-planning bodies have no clients; their function is to estimate future needs and plan how these needs can best be met.

Geriatric social workers must like working with older people and respect them. Strong rapport with the clients is the reward of the occupation. Workers should be emotionally mature, objective, and sensitive. They must also be well organized and keep careful records (which often are required by law).

Education and Training Requirements
Training in social work with a specialty in gerontology is available at associate, bachelor's, and master's degree levels. A postgraduate degree with a specialization in aging is recommended. Some of the better jobs require advanced degrees. Training requirements may vary with geographic region; they tend to be higher in metropolitan versus rural areas. Consult your local guidance counselor.

Getting the Job
Your college placement office may be able to help you find a job. Consult the ads in your local newspapers. You can also contact the organizations providing services for senior citizens in your area and ask for information interviews.

Advancement Possibilities and Employment Outlook
Geriatric social workers can advance to supervisory and administrative positions. The director of a small program may go on to run a larger organization.

The outlook for geriatric social workers is very good. The number of senior citizens is increasing rapidly. The need for geriatric social workers will also rise. However, some cutbacks in government funding may decrease the number of positions available. The best opportunities will be available for those with advanced or specialized training.

Working Conditions
Geriatric social workers are employed in a variety of settings. Their services may be needed at retirement communities, nursing homes, state and government agencies, or hospices. Because the location of employment may differ, the social worker might be providing service in a modern, well-lighted building one day and a poorly maintained inner city setting the next.

Earnings and Benefits
Earnings vary widely. Some of the factors that affect salaries are type of institution, level of training, and region. Beginning salaries are about $12,000 to $20,000 a year. The overall average salary ranges from $15,000 to $25,000 a year. Top salaries range from about $27,000 to $30,000. Those with an advanced degree might earn $36,000 or more in some positions. Benefits usually include medical insurance, life insurance, and paid vacations.

Where to Go for More Information
Association for Gerontology in Higher Education
1001 Connecticut Avenue, NW, Suite 410
Washington, DC 20036-5504
(202) 429-9277

National Association of Social Workers
750 First Street, NE
Washington, DC 20002-4241
(202) 408-8600

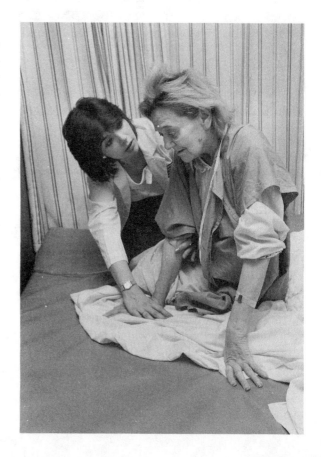

Hospital Administrator

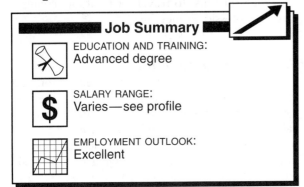

Job Summary

EDUCATION AND TRAINING:
Advanced degree

SALARY RANGE:
Varies—see profile

EMPLOYMENT OUTLOOK:
Excellent

Definition and Nature of the Work

Hospital administrators run today's complex hospitals and clinics. They see to it that every patient receives the best possible care. A hospital often contains more than 30 departments. Large hospitals generally have several administrators, each of whom specializes in one department. Departments run by individual administrators include the X-ray department, patient services, and building maintenance. The department heads organize the everyday activities of their departments. They report regularly to the chief administrator. Chief administrators coordinate the work of all the members of the health care team. They usually report directly to a board of trustees. Chief administrators manage the financial operations at a facility and develop plans for personnel, space, equipment, and supplies. They make sure that long-range plans are carried out.

Hospital administrators perform many varied tasks. Some are responsible for providing hospital workers with continuing education programs. They make sure that the skills of nurses, physicians, and technicians are upgraded regularly. Other hospital administrators develop programs that make the public aware of good health habits. They promote and market the hospital in the community by making sure that people know about the services that the hospital provides. Often they raise funds for the hospital.

Education and Training Requirements

You should begin to plan for a career as a hospital administrator by taking college preparatory courses in high school. You can gain valuable experience by working in a hospital part time or during the summer as a volunteer, aide, or receptionist. You should get a bachelor's degree in liberal arts, business administration, or health. You generally need a master's degree to become a hospital administrator. Most hospitals prefer people with a master's degree in health or hospital administration. You can earn this degree in special 2-year graduate programs that include supervised practical experience. Other hospitals prefer administrators with formal training in a field such as business, social science, or industrial engineering. However, this training must usually be combined with practical experience in the health field. A few specialized hospitals require that their administrators be physicians. These administrators, called physician executives, generally have a master's degree in business administration in addition to their medical training. A doctoral degree in hospital administration is recommended for those students who want to do research or teach in a university or for those who want high-level positions in large health organizations.

Getting the Job

Your college placement office can help you to find a job as a hospital administrator. The want ads in newspapers are also useful. Or you can apply directly for jobs with hospitals, clinics, or health agencies.

Advancement Possibilities and Employment Outlook

Most hospital administrators begin as assistants to experienced administrators. Advancement is based on performance and experience. Those with ability can become senior or chief administrators. Advancement opportunities are especially good at the middle-management level.

The number of hospital administrator positions is expected to increase much faster than the average by the year 2005. The outlook for this field is excellent. There will be competition for jobs, however. Those with advanced degrees will do best. Owing to the aging of the population, there is an increasing emphasis on extended health care facilities and community mental health centers. Qualified administrators will be needed to plan programs for these facilities.

Working Conditions

Although comfortable, hospital offices are hectic places in which to work. Hospital administrators must be calm and able to withstand the pressure and stress of their demanding job. They are often called on to make difficult decisions quickly. They must be able to work well with other hospital workers and with the public. They must be able to take suggestions, as well as to give orders. Hospital administrators usually work more than 40 hours a week. Because hospitals are open around the clock, administrators may be called in to deal with emergencies. They may have to work overtime to solve pressing problems, to travel, or to attend community or professional meetings.

Earnings and Benefits

Salaries vary widely depending on education and experience and on the location and size of the hospital in which the administrators work. Currently salaries for beginning administrators average $32,000 a year in midsize hospitals. Experienced hospital administrators earn salaries ranging from $36,600 to $56,600 in small hospitals to over $166,000 in very large facilities. Benefits include paid holidays and vacations, health insurance, and pension plans.

Where to Go for More Information

American College of Healthcare Executives
One North Franklin, Suite 1700
Chicago, IL 60606
(312) 424-2800

Association of University Programs in Health
    Administration
1911 North Fort Myer Drive, Suite 503
Arlington, VA 22209
(703) 524-5500

Medical Illustrator

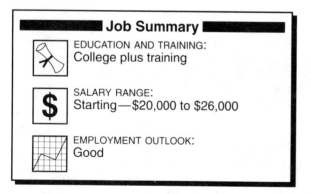

Job Summary

EDUCATION AND TRAINING:
College plus training

SALARY RANGE:
Starting—$20,000 to $26,000

EMPLOYMENT OUTLOOK:
Good

Definition and Nature of the Work

Medical illustrators are artists who work in the field of medicine. They make detailed drawings for textbooks and medical journals that are used by physicians and medical students. Some make graphs or charts for research projects. Medical illustrators also build models of parts of the human body for use in lectures or seminars. They sometimes illustrate the steps that a surgeon uses during an operation or show new ways of operating. They also draw pictures of normal and diseased body conditions. Some medical illustrators help to prepare television programs and films. In some cases they help to create artificial parts, such as ears or eyes, for patients who need them.

The work of medical illustrators is very important to physicians and medical students. Illustrations point out significant details that are difficult to find in the actual body or in photographs of the body. Illustrations often show the relationship of one body structure to another. Such drawings give students a better understanding of how these structures are related than they could get by viewing the structures themselves. Illustrations that simplify body systems and structures can also help medical students to learn about the body before they do laboratory work or treat patients.

Medical illustrators use many techniques and media in their work. Each technique is used to achieve a specific purpose. Illustrators use drawings, paintings, and prints, for example, to simplify and coordinate related information. They create sculptures and models to show a body system in three dimensions. They use cameras to record details in a realistic way. Sometimes they make drawings or models from photographs. Medical illustrators use many different materials, including paint, pencil, ink, charcoal, and chalk. When sculpting or making models, they use clay, wax, plaster, wood, plastic, or metal.

The training of medical illustrators includes both art and science. They are usually taught to work in all branches of medicine. Many specialize, however, in one branch, such as in cardiology, which concerns the heart, or in neurology, which deals with the nervous system.

Some medical illustrators are employed by publishers of medical textbooks. Others work for the publishers of scientific journals. Many are staff members of universities, hospitals, and research institutions. These medical illustrators sometimes teach as well as do illustrations. Some work for museums, drug companies, and commercial art studios. And some medical illustrators work as freelance artists—that is, they are self-employed and receive a fee for each project that they complete.

Education and Training Requirements

Most schools of medical illustration require that students first complete 4 years of college. Requirements vary, but students usually need courses in the biological sciences and in art. Students must also show samples of their art work. The medical illustration training program lasts 2 or 3 years. Students may receive a certificate, an associate degree, a bachelor's degree, or a master's degree after completing the program.

Getting the Job

Your college placement office can help you to find a job as a medical illustrator. Professional associations can give you information about getting a job or finding work as a freelance illustrator. You can also check the want ads in newspapers or apply directly to hospitals, publishers, or drug companies.

Advancement Possibilities and Employment Outlook

Medical illustrators usually advance by improving their skills. They may specialize in one particular field. If they are freelance artists, they can build a reputation that will get them many assignments. Some medical illustrators move into high-level teaching jobs in medical colleges. Medical illustrators who work for publishing companies can direct the art work for a large-scale project, such as a textbook. Those working in hospitals can become senior illustrators and supervise the work of other artists.

The employment outlook is good through the year 2005. Medical illustrators will be needed to help illustrate new developments in medicine. This is a small field, and there may be competition for any openings, however.

Working Conditions

Medical illustrators do much of their work in art studios, laboratories, and offices. These are usually quiet and well-lighted places. Sometimes illustrators must sketch in operating rooms. Although they often work alone, medical illustrators must also be able to cooperate and to work closely with medical staffs, scientists, and publishers. In addition to artistic talent, they need the ability to do exact and detailed work.

Medical illustrators who work for hospitals, universities, and drug or publishing companies generally work 40 hours a week. Freelance illustrators set their own schedules. All medical illustrators face the pressure of meeting deadlines from time to time.

Earnings and Benefits
Earnings vary widely depending on skill, experience, and place of employment. The average start-

ing salary for medical illustrators is between $20,000 and $26,000 a year. Those medical illustrators with more experience earn between $25,000 and $50,000 a year. Benefits for salaried workers include paid holidays and vacations and health insurance. Self-employed illustrators provide their own benefits.

Where to Go for More Information
Association of Medical Illustrators
1819 Peachtree Street, NE, Suite 712
Atlanta, GA 30309-1848
(404) 350-7900

Medical Laboratory Technologist

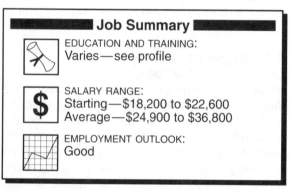

Job Summary

EDUCATION AND TRAINING:
Varies—see profile

SALARY RANGE:
Starting—$18,200 to $22,600
Average—$24,900 to $36,800

EMPLOYMENT OUTLOOK:
Good

Definition and Nature of the Work
Medical laboratory technologists assist doctors and other scientists by performing tests and research in the laboratory. They look for evidence of the presence of illnesses and parasites, identify changes in body chemistry and allergic reactions, and type and cross-match blood. They prepare vaccines and serums. Technologists perform exacting microscopic chemical and bacteriological tests. They also work as supervisors, teachers, and administrators.

Medical laboratory technologists test blood, urine, other body fluids, and tissue samples that doctors send to the laboratory. For example, technologists analyze blood and urine to look for signs of diseases, such as hemophilia or diabetes. They are also responsible for matching blood samples so that pa-

tients are given the correct type of blood during transfusions. Medical laboratory technologists identify parasites and bacteria through their tests. The technologist's work is increasingly important because doctors are depending more on complex tests to diagnose and determine treatment for patients' illnesses.

Technologists may specialize in such areas as blood banking, virology (the study of viruses), cytology (analysis of body cells), and histology (tissue preparation and examination). In large hospitals most technologists specialize in one area. In smaller laboratories they usually perform a variety of duties.

Medical technologists work in large hospital laboratories. They also work in the laboratories of private physicians, in public health laboratories, and in medical research institutes. There are also positions for technologists in colleges and universities, in companies that manufacture drugs and laboratory test equipment, and in the armed services.

Education and Training Requirements
Technologists must train at least 4 years after high school. High school courses in math and science are very helpful. Training after high school includes 3 years of college with emphasis on courses in chemistry, biological sciences, and mathematics. A 12-month clinical training session follows. Hospitals

and schools offer programs accredited by the Committee on Allied Health Education and Accreditation. Many of these programs offer bachelor's degrees.

Recent graduates who pass appropriate examinations can become certified. Several organizations offer this certification. Certification is important for technologists, as it indicates that they have met recognized standards of competence. Some states require that technologists be licensed. Requirements for licensing vary but usually include a written examination.

Many universities offer graduate programs in medical technology and related subjects for technologists who want to do certain types of laboratory work or for those who want to work in teaching, administration, or research.

Getting the Job

The placement office of your school can give you job information. You may find employment where you received your clinical training. Newspaper want ads and medical journals sometimes list openings. It is a good idea to apply directly to hospitals and laboratories. You can also apply for a position with federal, state, and local health departments.

Advancement Possibilities and Employment Outlook

Technologists can advance with further training. They may choose to specialize in one form of laboratory work or do research. Technologists can also advance to positions as teachers or administrators. A master's degree is generally required for these jobs.

The employment outlook is good through the year 2005 because of increased volume of medical testing due to an increase in disease and disability among the older population. New, more powerful and accurate diagnostic tests and advances in biotechnology should create a need for qualified medical technologists. Workers will be needed to fill supervisory positions in all laboratories. However, because of advances in equipment, technicians can now do tests that once required the expertise of a technologist.

Working Conditions

Working conditions for medical technologists are generally pleasant. Most laboratories are clean and well lighted. With careful training and proper handling of materials, technologists can keep hazards

to a minimum. The hours are generally regular and the work steady. There are many opportunities for part-time work. Hospital workers may be on emergency call 24 hours a day at least once a month. Most technologists work a 40-hour week.

Earnings and Benefits

Salaries vary depending on experience, location, and the type of laboratory. Starting salaries for medical laboratory technologists in hospitals and medical centers range from about $18,200 to $22,600 a year. Technologists with more experience earn salaries that average between $24,900 and $36,800 a year. Benefits include paid holidays and vacations and health insurance.

Where to Go for More Information

American Society for Clinical Laboratory Science
7910 Woodmont Avenue, Suite 1301
Bethesda, MD 20814-3015
(301) 657-2768

American Society of Clinical Pathologists
2100 West Harrison Street
Chicago, IL 60612-3798
(312) 738-1336

Medical Physicist

Job Summary

EDUCATION AND TRAINING:
Advanced degree

SALARY RANGE:
Starting—$30,000 to $41,000
Average—$78,000

EMPLOYMENT OUTLOOK:
Good

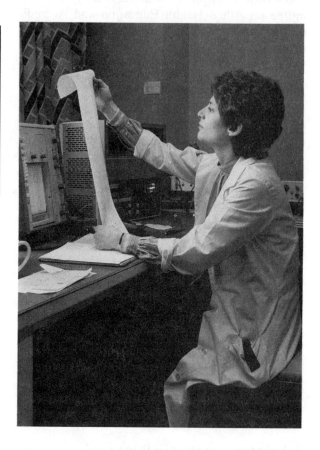

Definition and Nature of the Work

Medical physicists apply the knowledge of physics to all aspects of medicine. In the clinical setting of a hospital, medical physicists provide many important services. They help plan radiation treatment for cancer patients using external radiation beams or internal radioactive sources. They consult with physicians and may work with specific patients. In addition, they are responsible for accurately measuring the radiation administered.

Medical physicists who specialize in nuclear medicine work with physicians in procedures that provide images of the internal organs and determine metabolic rates and blood flow. These images provide physicians with important information that allows them to make a diagnosis.

The equipment used in these diagnostic and treatment procedures is extremely complex. Medical physicists make sure that this equipment functions properly. They also design radiation installations for hospitals and are responsible for safety precautions against the hazards of radiation.

Many medical physicists are involved in the research and design of new medical equipment. They work on new applications for high-energy machines, such as linear accelerators to treat cancer. Diagnostic imaging is constantly being improved with such new techniques as magnetic resonance imaging. Medical physicists are also engaged in research to develop imaging procedures using infrared and ultrasound sources.

More general areas of research for the medical physicist are the use of computers in diagnosis and treatment and the accurate measurement of blood flow and oxygenation in the treatment of heart disease.

Many hospitals that employ medical physicists are medical schools, and the physicists are members of the faculty. Here they help to teach future medical physicists, medical students, and radiographic technologists. In colleges and universities they may teach medical physics, biophysics, and radiobiology to graduate and undergraduate students.

Education and Training Requirements

Graduate training in medical physics is required for all jobs in this field. It takes about 4 years to earn a bachelor's degree and another 1 or 2 years to earn a master's degree. Most medical physicists go on to study for doctoral degrees. Because of the nature of the work, it is important that medical physicists have a good knowledge of physics and basic medical sciences, such as anatomy, physiology, genetics, and biochemistry.

Getting the Job

Your best sources for job openings are your college professors and advisers. The placement office may also be able to help you find a job as a medical physicist. In addition, you can apply directly to hospitals, universities, and government agencies. Other good sources of information are professional associations and publications.

Advancement Possibilities and Employment Outlook

Advancement opportunities are good for medical physicists with a doctoral degree. Medical physicists in hospitals and research centers can advance by taking on more responsibility and heading project teams. Those in teaching positions can advance by moving through the ranks from instructor to full professor.

The employment outlook for medical physicists is good through the year 2005. Although currently fewer than 3,000 medical physicists are employed, this number is expected to grow with the increase in medical technology. New jobs will continue to occur in radiation therapy. Diagnostic radiology and nuclear medicine will also expand.

Working Conditions

Most medical physicists work in hospitals and universities. Their laboratories and classrooms are clean and well lighted. Medical physicists generally work at least 40 hours a week. Overtime is often necessary for medical emergencies and special projects. In order to study and keep up with new developments in the field, medical physicists may work long hours on a regular basis. Medical physicists may conduct research independently or as part of a team. They are often members of a patient's medical team and must be able to communicate their ideas to doctors, students, and sometimes patients both orally and in writing.

Earnings and Benefits

Salaries for medical physicists are similar to those of other physicists. Starting salaries for physicists in private industry average about $30,000 a year for those with a master's degree and $41,000 a year for those with a Ph.D. Experienced physicists who have Ph.D.s and who work in hospitals earn an average salary of $78,000.

Where to Go for More Information

American Association of Physicists in Medicine
One Physics Ellipse
College Park, MD 20740-3846
(301) 209-3350

Medical Record Administrator

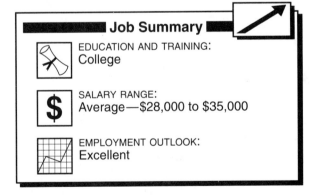

Job Summary

EDUCATION AND TRAINING:
College

SALARY RANGE:
Average—$28,000 to $35,000

EMPLOYMENT OUTLOOK:
Excellent

Definition and Nature of the Work

Medical record administrators, formerly called medical record librarians, prepare and keep records of hospital and clinic patients. These records include medicine given to the patient, surgical operations performed, the patient's diet, and the results of tests. Notes made by physicians and nurses who examine a patient are also part of these records. Medical record administrators are responsible for making sure that these records are complete. They develop systems for keeping the needed information in a usable form. Many systems are computerized. Administrators usually supervise other workers, such as medical record technicians, who take care of the technical and clerical details of medical record keeping.

Medical record administrators often prepare reports on the number of admissions, births, deaths, transfers, and discharges that occur in their hospitals. This information helps hospitals in their planning for community health care. Medical record administrators may help physicians find information they need about a patient or a type of treatment. They sometimes release information to insurance companies or to research institutes. They may testify in court if necessary.

Most medical record administrators work in hospitals. Some work in nursing homes, clinics, public health agencies, medical research centers, or insurance companies. Others work for firms that make machinery or forms for the keeping of medical records. A small number work as consultants for in-

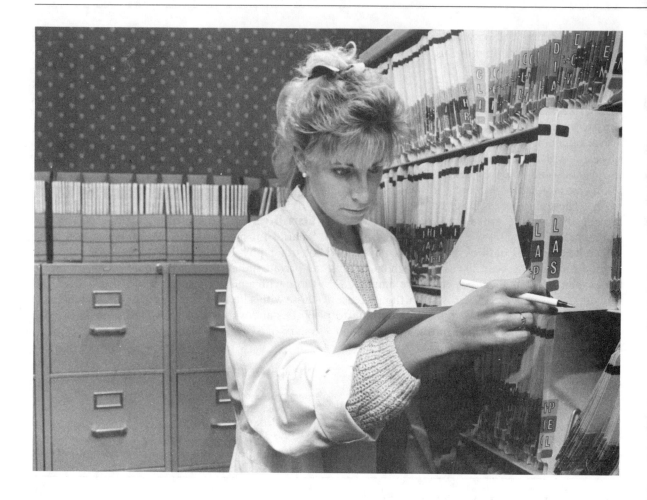

stitutions that do not need a full-time medical record administrator.

Education and Training Requirements

Medical record administrators need 4 years of college. You can get special training leading to a bachelor's degree in medical record administration. Or you can get a degree in another field and then enroll in a 1-year certificate program in medical record administration. When you have completed your training, you are eligible to take an examination given by the American Medical Record Association. If you pass, you become a Registered Record Administrator (RRA).

Getting the Job

The best place to look for your first job is at the placement office of the college where you got your training in medical record administration. The

American Medical Record Association can also provide lists of job openings. Newspaper want ads often include opportunities in the medical record field. Or you can apply directly to hospitals, clinics, research centers, or health agencies.

Advancement Possibilities and Employment Outlook

Advancement in medical record work generally comes with experience. Medical record administrators can become heads of large departments where they supervise many workers. Or they can move into other jobs in hospital administration. They can become consultants for the medical record departments of a number of small hospitals. They can also teach medical record administration courses in colleges and universities.

The employment outlook is excellent through the year 2005, especially for experienced technicians who have completed a formal training program. The demand for medical care is growing. The need for accurate record keeping, especially for insurance purposes and abstracting data, should create opportunities for qualified professionals in this field.

Working Conditions

Medical record departments are usually pleasant places in which to work. Administrators do a good deal of paperwork. They deal with other hospital staff members in addition to their own helpers. They generally work 36 to 40 hours a week.

Medical record administration is a demanding job that requires organizational skills and careful work habits. Administrators must be able to communicate information to others. They are also responsible for seeing that medical information is revealed only to the proper people and organizations.

Earnings and Benefits

Salaries vary depending on the size and type of the place of employment and on the duties and experiences of the worker. Beginning medical record administrators earn a salary that ranges between $20,000 and $27,000 a year. Experienced workers average about $28,000 to $35,000 a year, although some high-level medical record administrators earn more than $47,000 a year. Benefits include paid holidays and vacations, health insurance, and pension plans.

Where to Go for More Information

American Health Information Management
   Association
919 North Michigan Avenue, Suite 1400
Chicago, IL 60611-1683
(312) 787-2672

Nurse Anesthetist

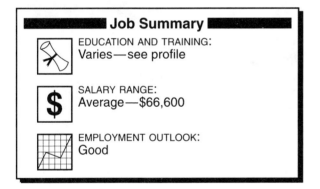

■■■■ **Job Summary** ■■■■

EDUCATION AND TRAINING:
Varies—see profile

SALARY RANGE:
Average—$66,600

EMPLOYMENT OUTLOOK:
Good

Definition and Nature of the Work

Nurse anesthetists are registered nurses (RNs) who have received special training in anesthetics. Anesthetics are drugs that produce anesthesia (a state of painlessness or unconsciousness). Nurse anesthetists work under the supervision of an anesthesiologist (a physician specializing in anesthesia) or another physician. Most work in hospitals. Anesthetists usually work in an operating room during surgery. They sometimes administer anesthetics in the delivery room, in the emergency room, or to dental or psychiatric patients. In small hospitals nurse anesthetists may also administer oxygen in the inhalation therapy department.

Nurse anesthetists generally give anesthetics in the form of a gas or a fluid. They regulate the flow of the anesthetic and watch the patient carefully while it is in effect. They may also give the patient oxygen to prevent shock or other unwanted conditions. Anesthetists keep the physician informed of the patient's condition during an operation. They record the patient's progress. Sometimes nurse anesthetists help to care for the patient during recovery from anesthesia.

Education and Training Requirements

If you want to become a nurse anesthetist, you should take a college preparatory program that includes courses in mathematics, science, and the social sciences. Volunteer or part-time work in a hospital is a valuable experience. After high school you will need to have a bachelor's degree in nursing (BSN) or a bachelor's degree in a related field with either a diploma or associate degree in nursing. You should have at least 1 year of experience working in acute care nursing before enrolling in a special school of anesthesia. Schools of anesthesia are affiliated with hospitals and offer training programs lasting about 2 years. There is also a trend to incorporate this training into a bachelor's or master's degree program. Once you have graduated from an approved school of anesthesia, you are eligible to take the national certifying exam that is given by the Council on Certification of Nurse Anesthetists.

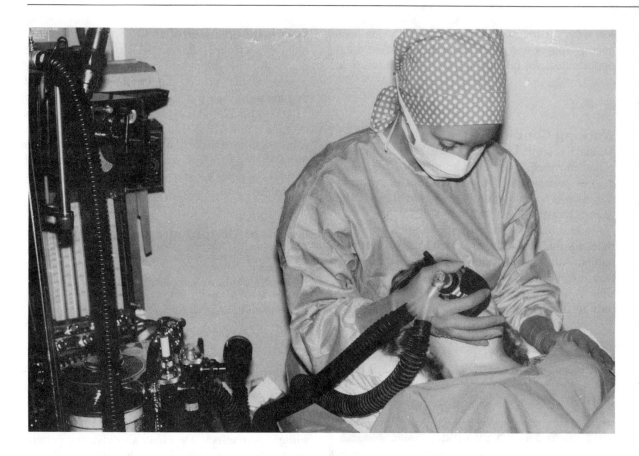

Getting the Job

The American Association of Nurse Anesthetists lists classified ads in its bulletin. Your school placement office can also help you find a job. Sometimes openings for nurse anesthetists are listed in newspaper want ads.

Advancement Possibilities and Employment Outlook

Experienced and skilled nurse anesthetists can expect steady increases in responsibility and income. Some move from smaller hospitals to those offering greater opportunities and rewards. Anesthetists can become supervisors or can specialize in certain difficult types of surgery. Others become teachers.

The employment outlook for nurse anesthetists is good through the year 2005. Currently hospitals in many parts of the country are reporting shortages of registered nurses. Registered nurse recruitment has long been a problem in rural areas, in some big-city hospitals, and in specialty areas, including intensive care, medical-surgical nursing, rehabilitation, geriatrics, and long-term care. Whether the current shortage of nurses will persist through the year 2005 is difficult to predict. Nevertheless, job opportunities look favorable.

Working Conditions

Nurse anesthetists are members of a highly trained medical care team. They must be very careful and responsible in their work. One of their rewards is knowing how important their contribution is. Although the regularly scheduled workweek of many nurse anesthetists is only 35 hours long, they are also on call for additional hours in case of emergency.

Earnings and Benefits

Salaries vary depending on experience and place of employment. Nurse anesthetists usually earn salaries at the top end of the scale for all nurses. Experienced nurse anesthetists generally earn a median salary of $66,600 a year. Benefits include paid vacations and holidays, health insurance, and pension plans.

Where to Go for More Information

American Association of Nurse Anesthetists
222 South Prospect Avenue
Park Ridge, IL 60068
(708) 692-7050

Nurse-Midwife

Job Summary

EDUCATION AND TRAINING:
College plus training

SALARY RANGE:
Starting—$31,000

EMPLOYMENT OUTLOOK:
Good

Definition and Nature of the Work

Nurse-midwives provide routine health care for both pregnant and nonpregnant women. They may also provide counseling and information on childbirth and the care of newborns.

Nurse-midwives perform regular checkups during pregnancy. They evaluate the growth and well-being of the baby and the condition of the mother. While they discuss any problems with a physician, nurse-midwives provide routine treatment to patients. If the pregnancy continues without complication, nurse-midwives provide all prenatal care, assist the mother during labor, and deliver the baby. Following the birth, nurse-midwives make sure that the mother and baby are well and provide follow-up care. If an emergency occurs, nurse-midwives are trained to provide assistance until a doctor arrives.

Nurse-midwives also provide a variety of other services for expectant and new parents. They may lead classes in childbirth instruction, sibling preparation, and care of newborns. They may also counsel parents about the effects a new baby can have on a family.

Nurse-midwives may also provide care for well women and babies and perform routine examinations. They may also offer counseling in health maintenance, fitness, and family nutrition. They can give birth control information to their patients. In many areas, nurse-midwives supervise well-baby and family planning clinics.

Some midwives are known as lay midwives. They generally receive their training from another midwife and are not trained nurses. These midwives are generally found in rural areas and within ethnic communities where such practices are traditional. Many states do not allow lay midwives to practice.

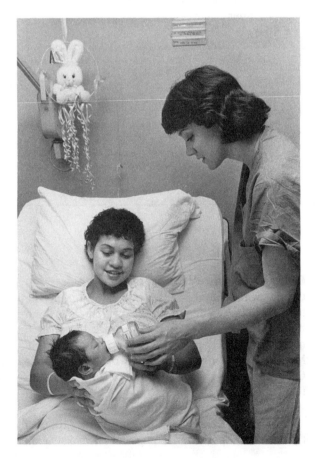

Education and Training Requirements

To become a certified nurse-midwife, you must first become a registered nurse. To do this, high school students should take college preparatory courses. Science and mathematics are important subjects. Other useful courses are English, psychology, sociology, and health. Because entry to nurse-midwife programs is competitive, it is advisable for students to choose a 4-year nursing program that leads to a bachelor's degree. It may soon be necessary for all registered nurses to have 4-year degrees.

Once you are qualified as a registered nurse, a further 8 to 24 months of training are necessary to become a nurse-midwife. Those with bachelor's degrees may apply for master's degree programs in midwifery. These programs last for 12 to 24 months. Those who have graduated from programs approved by the American College of Nurse-Midwives may then take the national certification exam. Once certified, nurse-midwives may have to meet further requirements in the state in which they wish to practice.

Getting the Job

The placement office of your nursing school or college may help you find a position. Want ads can be found in newspapers and nursing journals. Professional organizations, state employment offices, and health-related employment agencies may also have information about job openings. You may apply directly to hospitals, birth centers, public health departments, and health maintenance organizations. The armed services also employ nurse-midwives.

Advancement Possibilities and Employment Outlook

Nurse-midwives are highly trained practitioners and may advance to supervisory and administrative jobs in hospitals, health clinics, public health agencies, family planning clinics, and birth centers. With further education they may teach and do research in universities. Acceptance by the medical community and continued growth in the demand for nurse-midwife services will insure an increase in the number of jobs for nurse-midwives. The employment outlook is good through the year 2005. A large number of jobs will be created within health maintenance organizations, and rural public health departments will continue to need midwives. Currently the number of job openings is greater than the number of qualified nurse-midwives.

Working Conditions

Working conditions vary according to the area and type of facility in which a nurse-midwife works. Some work in modern, well-equipped hospitals and clinics; others work in the pleasant homelike surroundings of a birth center. In rural areas where there are fewer medical facilities, nurse-midwives may have to travel between several small clinics. In poor inner-city and rural areas, nurse-midwives may also travel to visit mothers and babies in their homes. Midwives working in hospitals and clinics usually work a 40-hour week. Those in private practice and working in areas with few medical facilities often work long and irregular hours. Shift work and weekend work are often required.

Earnings and Benefits

Earnings and benefits vary widely. Those working in large hospitals may earn an average starting salary of $31,000 a year. Salaries are lower in smaller hospitals and in rural areas. Nurse-midwives with several years of experience may earn $40,000 or more a year. Earnings for those working in private practice depend on the number of patients seen and on the contract the nurse-midwife has negotiated. Benefits for those working for hospitals or other organizations usually include paid holidays and vacations, health insurance, and retirement plans.

Where to Go for More Information

American Association of Nurse Anesthetists
222 South Prospect Avenue
Park Ridge, IL 60068
(708) 692-7050

American Nurses' Association
600 Maryland Avenue, SW
Washington, DC 20024-2571
(202) 554-4444

National League for Nursing
350 Hudson Street
New York, NY 10014
(212) 989-9393

Occupational Therapist

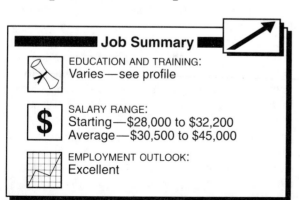

Job Summary

EDUCATION AND TRAINING:
Varies—see profile

SALARY RANGE:
Starting—$28,000 to $32,200
Average—$30,500 to $45,000

EMPLOYMENT OUTLOOK:
Excellent

Definition and Nature of the Work

Occupational therapists plan therapy programs that help patients overcome physical, mental, or emotional disabilities. The programs are designed to help patients become as self-sufficient as possible. Most occupational therapists work in hospitals. Others work in special schools, rehabilitation centers, clinics, and nursing homes. Some are consultants to government and private agencies.

Occupational therapists are part of a health team that includes physicians, physical therapists, and other specialists. This team determines the needs of each patient. For example, a doctor may tell an occupational therapist which muscles a stroke patient should learn to use first. The therapist then decides on an activity to exercise those muscles and hold the patient's interest, as well. For some patients this may be as simple as grasping a ball. Other patients need to practice very basic skills, such as dressing and feeding themselves. Still others can benefit most from learning job skills, such as word processing skills or working with power tools.

Sometimes occupational therapists use recreational therapy to help patients become better able to help themselves. For example, therapists may teach crafts, such as basket weaving, woodworking, or knitting, to get patients to use their muscles and minds in beneficial ways. They often get patients interested in music, drama, or art to help them find ways to express their feelings. Therapists also direct games, sports, and group discussions. These recreational activities are often an important step in encouraging patients to cope with their disabilities. Recreational therapy can help patients to relax, to communicate with other people, and to gain a sense of accomplishment.

Occupational therapists plan programs that set realistic goals for each patient. They work with people of all ages and all backgrounds. They must evaluate each patient's unique set of problems. Therapists often have assistants who help them to carry out these programs.

Education and Training Requirements

To become an occupational therapist, you need a high school education. Then you can follow several paths. You can go to a 4-year college and earn a bachelor's degree in occupational therapy. Or you can take a 14- to 24-month course in occupational therapy, leading to certification, after completing 4 years of college work in another field.

Occupational therapists can become registered after graduation from an approved program. If they pass an exam given by the American Occupational Therapy Association, they become Registered Occupational Therapists (ORTs). Most states require that therapists be licensed.

Getting the Job

Your school placement office can help you to find a job. You can also apply directly to hospitals and clinics. The want ads in newspapers and professional publications are other sources of job leads.

Advancement Possibilities and Employment Outlook

There are several ways for occupational therapists to advance. Therapists working in hospitals or clinics can become senior therapists after several years of experience. Therapists can also become teachers or directors of occupational therapy programs. They can work as consultants too.

The employment outlook is excellent through the year 2005, due to an anticipated demand in the areas of rehabilitation and long-term care. The number of people who need rehabilitative services will rise as advances in medical technology continue to save lives. Also, as the baby-boom generation begins to move into middle age, demand for cardiac rehabilitation programs is expected to increase. Although more people are being trained as occupational therapists, there will be still fewer qualified people than job openings.

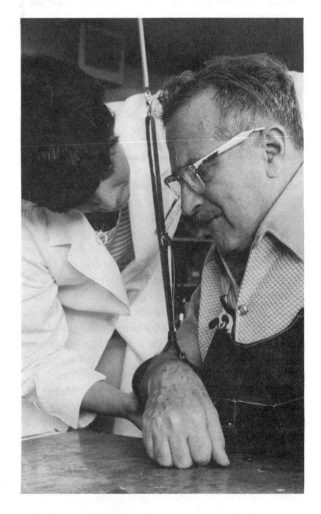

Working Conditions

Most occupational therapists work 40 hours a week. Sometimes evening or weekend work is required. Part-time jobs are also available.

Occupational therapists should be warm and creative people. They work closely with patients and other members of the health care team. They must be able to use their own initiative in planning and carrying out programs.

Earnings and Benefits

Salaries vary depending on education and experience. Starting salaries for occupational therapists range from about $28,000 to $32,200 a year. Ex-

perienced therapists earn, on the average, between $30,500 and $45,000 a year. Administrators earn more than $50,000 a year. Benefits include paid holidays and vacations, health insurance, and pension plans.

Where to Go for More Information

The American Occupational Therapy Association
4720 Montgomery Lane
P.O. Box 31220
Bethesda, MD 20824-1220
(301) 948-9626

American Rehabilitation Counseling Association
5999 Stevenson Avenue
Alexandria, VA 22304-3300
(703) 823-9800

Ophthalmologist

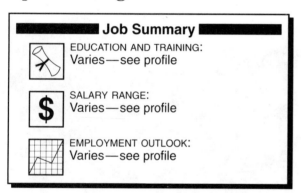

Job Summary

EDUCATION AND TRAINING:
Varies—see profile

SALARY RANGE:
Varies—see profile

EMPLOYMENT OUTLOOK:
Varies—see profile

Definition and Nature of the Work

Ophthalmologists are physicians who specialize in the care of the eye. They treat people with visual problems, such as nearsightedness or crossed eyes. They also treat people with eye injuries or with eye diseases, such as glaucoma or cataracts. Optometrists or family doctors often refer patients with serious eye conditions to ophthalmologists. Because of their medical training, ophthalmologists can recognize disorders elsewhere in the body that can have an effect on the eye. For example, ophthalmologists are sometimes the first to detect brain tumors, diabetes, or multiple sclerosis.

Ophthalmologists use a variety of instruments to examine the eye. For example, they use an ophthalmoscope to see the inner part of the eye. Ophthalmologists can prescribe medicine, contact lenses, and eyeglasses. Sometimes they recommend eye exercises. They perform surgery when necessary. Eye surgery may involve removing a piece of glass

embedded in the eye or transplanting a cornea (the transparent covering of the eye). Because the eye is so small, ophthalmologists usually operate with the help of operating microscopes and magnifying lenses. They must work with great care.

Most ophthalmologists have private practices. However, some work in hospitals, health agencies, or medical colleges. Some teach, do research, or write about their special field.

Education and Training Requirements

Ophthalmologists need extensive training after high school. Most ophthalmologists have 4 years of college and 4 years of medical school. Some medical schools accept students with 3 years of college. After medical school, students begin about 3 years of training as hospital residents in ophthalmology (the study of the structure, function, and diseases of the eye). Usually after 1 or 2 years, residents take the test to be licensed, a requirement in all states. Ophthalmologists must also take an exam for specialty board certification and meet other specialty board requirements.

Getting the Job

Your medical school's placement service can help you find a job or refer you to other doctors who are looking for an associate. This can be helpful, as ophthalmologists need expensive equipment to set up their own offices. Many graduates begin by

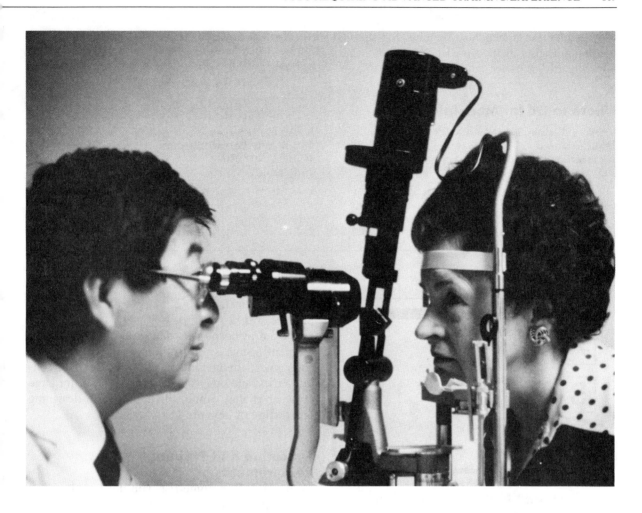

working as an associate with a doctor who has already set up a practice. Others begin work as salaried employees on the staffs of hospitals or in government agencies. You can inquire directly at agencies and hospitals about possible openings. Professional organizations can also give you job information.

Advancement Possibilities and Employment Outlook

Ophthalmologists usually advance by building their practices. Some specialize in one kind of eye care. For example, they may work with children or with elderly people. Or they may concentrate on one disease or disorder, such as detachment of the retina or cataracts. Others teach or do research.

Ophthalmology is one of the specialties in which an oversupply may occur in the future. Predictions vary, although there will be a continuing need for ophthalmologists due to a larger aged population and extended health care benefits.

Working Conditions

Most ophthalmologists are in private practice. They generally spend regularly scheduled hours in their own offices and in the operating room. Because emergencies are unusual, ophthalmologists keep more regular hours than general practitioners. Ophthalmologists must often spend long hours, however, in meetings, study, and research. They must keep up with new developments in their field.

Ophthalmology is an important and respected profession. It requires high intelligence, good depth perception, and excellent coordination.

Earnings and Benefits

Earnings vary with experience, skill, and location. Salaries of medical residents average $28,600 for those in their first year of residency to $36,300 for those in their sixth year. Ophthalmologists with established private practices, however, can earn up to $150,000 a year. Those in private practice must provide their own benefits. Benefits for salaried ophthalmologists include paid holidays and vacations, health insurance, and pension plans.

Where to Go for More Information

American Academy of Ophthalmology
655 Beach Street
San Francisco, CA 94109
(415) 561-8500

The American Medical Association
515 North State Street
Chicago, IL 60610-4377
(312) 464-5000

Society of Eye Surgeons
7801 Norfolk Avenue, Suite 200
Bethesda, MD 20814
(301) 986-1830

Optometrist

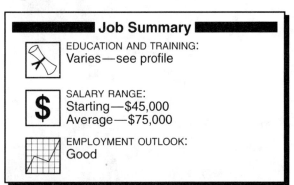

Job Summary

EDUCATION AND TRAINING:
Varies—see profile

SALARY RANGE:
Starting—$45,000
Average—$75,000

EMPLOYMENT OUTLOOK:
Good

Definition and Nature of the Work

Optometrists examine eyes and treat vision problems that do not require drugs or surgery. They preserve and improve sight by prescribing and fitting eyeglasses and contact lenses. They may also give patients eye exercises to correct such problems as crossed eyes. In addition, optometrists often sell eyeglasses or contact lenses that they have prescribed.

Optometrists first talk with patients to find out the history of their eye problems. Then they carefully examine patients' eyes with the help of several instruments. Retinoscopes, for example, help optometrists to see how the patients react to lenses of different strengths. Ophthalmoscopes allow them to see the inside of the eye. After examining patients, optometrists prescribe lenses or other treatment. They help patients with eye problems, such as nearsightedness or farsightedness. If they find eye diseases that need drugs or surgery, they refer patients to ophthalmologists (physicians who specialize in the care of the eye). Sometimes optometrists discover such conditions as diabetes or high blood pressure. They refer patients with these diseases to other medical doctors.

Most optometrists have their own practices. Some practice with a group of optometrists. Others are employed in hospitals, clinics, and health or government agencies. Still others work for insurance companies; for manufacturers of eyeglasses, contact lenses, and other optical equipment; or for large eyewear chains. Some jobs involve the designing and testing of new products.

Education and Training Requirements

To become an optometrist, you must study for at least 6 years after high school. First you need to complete at least 2 or 3 years of college. Your courses should include laboratory sciences and other subjects required by the optometry school that you want to attend. Many students complete 4 years of college before enrolling in an optometry school. In optometry school you will take a 4-year program leading to a Doctor of Optometry (O.D.) degree. Some optometrists may want to specialize in work with the elderly, with children, with the partially sighted, or in vision therapy. These optometrists can go on to study for a master's or doctoral degree, or they may enter a 1-year residency program that is offered for certain optometric specialties.

Optometrists must be licensed before they can work. Each state requires that optometrists graduate from an approved optometry school and pass the state licensing examinations.

Getting the Job

There are a number of ways to enter this field. Some optometrists choose to set up their own practices. Others begin by working with established optometrists. Jobs are also available in clinics, private industry, and in health or government agencies. You can apply directly for a job. You can also get advice from your school placement office or from the American Optometric Association.

Advancement Possibilities and Employment Outlook

Many optometrists become self-employed after some years as a salaried worker or as an associate in a group practice. Other optometrists specialize. They may concentrate on visual problems of children or the aged, on contact lenses, or on aids for the partially sighted. Optometrists who have the additional education and experience can move into jobs in teaching, research, or administration.

The employment outlook for optometrists is good through the year 2005. The maturing of the large baby-boom generation, together with rapid growth in the elderly population in the years ahead, should increase the demand for qualified optometrists. The growth of large eyewear chains will create a need for additional optometrists. However, increased use of optometric assistants and more sophisticated equipment may lessen the demand for new optometrists.

Working Conditions

Optometrists usually work in pleasant surroundings. Those in private practices may supervise assistants. In large offices and in clinics and health and government agencies, optometrists work as members of professional health care teams. Most optometrists work 40 hours a week, often including some evening and Saturday hours. Optometrists in private practice can set their own schedules.

Optometrists have responsible jobs that require close contact with the public. They need manual dexterity and the ability to deal with a wide variety of people. Optometrists in private practice should also have business ability and self-discipline.

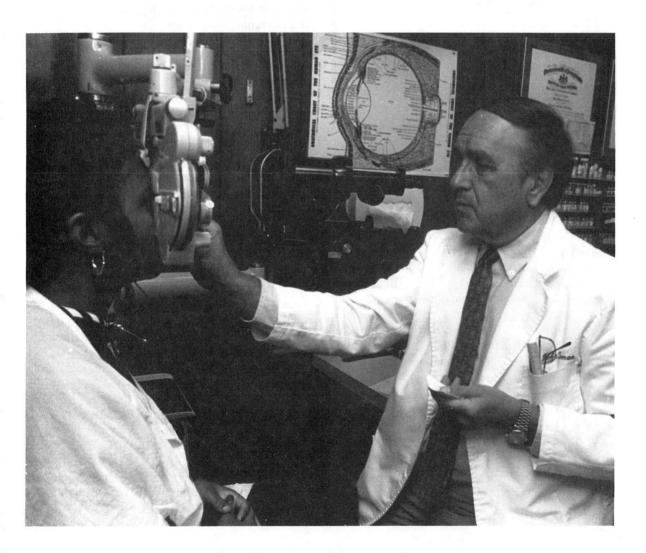

Earnings and Benefits

Earnings depend on experience, location, and area of specialization. Beginning optometrists earn, on the average, about $45,000 a year. Experienced optometrists earn about $75,000 or more a year. Optometrists in private practice must provide their own benefits. Benefits for salaried optometrists usually include paid holidays, sick days, and vacations and health insurance.

Where to Go for More Information

American Optometric Association
243 North Lindbergh Boulevard
St. Louis, MO 63141-7881
(314) 991-4100

National Association of Optometrists and Opticians
18903 South Miles Road
Cleveland, OH 44128
(216) 475-8929

Osteopathic Physician

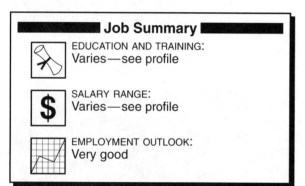

Job Summary

EDUCATION AND TRAINING:
Varies—see profile

SALARY RANGE:
Varies—see profile

EMPLOYMENT OUTLOOK:
Very good

Definition and Nature of the Work

Osteopathic physicians practice a system of health care known as osteopathy. Osteopathy is based on the idea that health is closely related to the structure of the body. Osteopathic physicians study disorders in relation to their effect on the entire body. They stress a special treatment called manipulative therapy. In manipulative therapy osteopathic physicians use their hands to move parts of the patient's body, especially the muscles and bones, into the proper position. This therapy continues until the patient's body systems are all brought back into their correct relationship to one another.

Osteopathic physicians also use the same methods that medical doctors use to diagnose and treat illness and injury. They prescribe drugs, perform surgery, and recommend the proper diet and other kinds of therapy. Over 45 percent of all osteopathic physicians are general practitioners or family doctors. They have office practices and work in hospitals, just as medical doctors do. Almost 15 percent of all osteopathic physicians are specialists. Some of their special fields are surgery, obstetrics and gynecology, pediatrics, psychiatry and neurology, and internal medicine. A small number of osteopathic physicians have salaried positions in osteopathic hospitals and colleges, private industry, and government agencies.

Education and Training Requirements

To become an osteopathic physician, you need extensive training after high school. You should take college courses in science and other subjects required by the osteopathic college that you want to attend. A few students start osteopathic college after only 3 years at a preprofessional college, but most students earn a bachelor's degree first. The 3- to 4-year program in an osteopathic college leads to the degree of Doctor of Osteopathy (D.O.). The training is similar to that given to medical doctors (M.D.s). However, osteopathy puts more emphasis on anatomy and on the relationship between the structure of the body and its functions. Nearly all new graduates of osteopathic colleges spend a year as an intern in an osteopathic hospital. Those who want to specialize must take another 2 to 5 years of training in such areas as surgery or radiology.

In every state osteopathic physicians must be licensed before they can practice. Licensing requirements vary, but in all states osteopathic physicians must graduate from an approved osteopathic college and pass a state board examination.

Getting the Job

Nearly all osteopathic physicians go into private practice. Some open their own practices. Others work for a time as an assistant in the office of an established osteopathic physician. Still others join a group practice with other osteopathic physicians. Some join the staffs of osteopathic hospitals. Professional associations and colleges or hospitals of osteopathy can provide information about opening a practice or finding a salaried position.

Advancement Possibilities and Employment Outlook

Most osteopathic physicians advance by building their practices. Some become specialists. A small number move into positions as teachers, researchers, or administrators. Others write or edit scientific books or journals.

About 5% of the physicians in the United States are osteopathic physicians. The federal government and most states grant osteopathic physicians the same responsibilities and privileges as medical doctors. Some osteopathic physicians serve on the staffs of nonosteopathic hospitals or practice with medical doctors. Most set up their practices in areas where there are osteopathic hospitals or clinics.

The employment outlook for osteopathic physicians is very good through the year 2005. The widespread ability to pay for medical care, a consequence of health insurance and public health programs, is the main reason for projected job growth. The greatest demand for osteopathic physicians should be in rural and suburban areas and in those areas where osteopathic medicine is well known.

Working Conditions

Most osteopathic physicians have their own practices and are able to set their own working conditions. Many work more than 50 or 60 hours a week. Some of this time is spent studying the latest advances in osteopathic medicine. Osteopathic physicians who are family doctors usually work longer and more irregular hours than specialists do.

Osteopathic physicians need good business sense and self-discipline. They should be intelligent and able to deal with a wide variety of people. Good health and stamina are also important if they are to meet the demands of their profession.

Earnings and Benefits

Beginning osteopathic physicians earn about $47,500 a year working for Veterans Administration hospitals. Osteopathic physicians in private practice may earn from $85,000 to $150,000 or more a year.

Osteopathic physicians in private practice must provide their own benefits, such as health insurance and pension funds.

Where to Go for More Information

American Academy of Osteopathy
3500 DePauw Boulevard, Suite 1080
Indianapolis, IN 46286-1136
(317) 879-1881

American Osteopathic Association
142 East Ontario Street
Chicago, IL 60611-2864
(312) 280-5800

American Osteopathic Healthcare Association
5301 Wisconsin Avenue, NW
Washington, DC 20015
(202) 686-1700

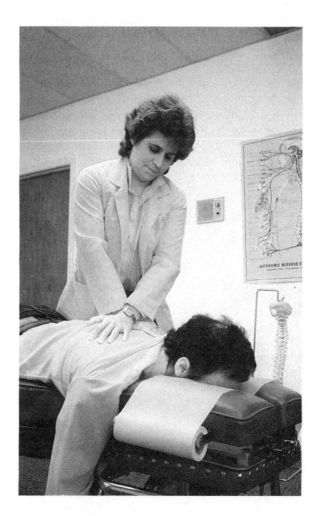

Pharmacist

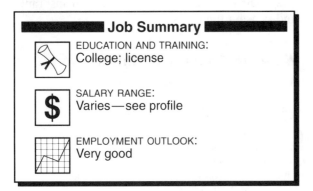

Definition and Nature of the Work

Pharmacists are public health professionals who specialize in the science of drugs. They must know about all kinds of medicines, as well as about the laws that regulate the making and selling of drugs. They dispense drugs that require a doctor's prescription, as well as those that do not. Pharmacists often advise people about the use of the medicines that they supply. They order and store drugs and make sure that they remain safe, pure, and effective. They must also keep careful records of the drugs that they handle.

Most pharmacists work in community pharmacies. These are retail stores that may be owned by the pharmacist or may be part of a chain of drugstores. Community pharmacies may be large or small. They may sell just medical and sickroom needs, or they may carry a wide range of items for the health, grooming, and comfort of their customers. The pharmacist in a community pharmacy may concentrate only on the dispensing of drugs or may manage other areas of the store. Work in a community pharmacy can provide a combined professional and business management career.

Some pharmacists work in hospital or in nursing home pharmacies. These, too, can be either large or small. Hospital pharmacists buy, inspect, store, and distribute drugs. They often keep a drug information library and advise the medical and nursing staffs about new drugs.

Other pharmacists work in the pharmaceutical industry, for firms that make drugs. They may be involved in the research, manufacture, or sale of drugs. Pharmacists are also employed by government agencies and as teachers in colleges and universities. A small number work in specialized areas, such as in the writing or editing of books, articles, or advertisements about drugs.

Education and Training Requirements

To become a pharmacist, you must have at least 5 years of study beyond high school. In most cases you can go to any accredited college that offers the appropriate courses for your first or second year and then transfer to a college of pharmacy. Check the requirements of the college of pharmacy that you want to attend, as requirements vary from college to college. Most colleges of pharmacy award a bachelor's degree at the completion of a 5-year program. Some students go on to get a master's or a doctoral degree in a specialized area of pharmacy. At a few schools, students earn a Doctor of Pharmacy (Pharm. D.) degree after 6 or 7 years of study.

All states require pharmacists to be licensed before they can practice. You need to graduate from an approved college of pharmacy and pass a state licensing board examination. You must also serve an internship or have practical experience under the supervision of a licensed pharmacist.

Getting the Job

Most pharmacists begin their careers as employees in community or hospital pharmacies. The placement service of your college of pharmacy can give you information about these job openings. Or you can apply directly to pharmacies or to firms that make drugs. Professional associations can also provide information to help you get a job or open a pharmacy of your own.

Advancement Possibilities and Employment Outlook

Advancement depends on many factors, including location, type of work, business skill, and ambition of the pharmacist. About 60% of all pharmacists work in community pharmacies. Some go on to open their own pharmacies. Pharmacists who work for chain-owned drugstores can become managers. Pharmacists in hospitals can become directors of pharmacy services. Some pharmacists become administrators in government agencies. Pharmacists working for drug manufacturers can move into executive positions. If they have the necessary education, pharmacists can also advance to high-level positions in teaching or research.

The employment outlook is very good through the year 2005, due to the projected increased pharmaceutical needs of a larger and older population. Scientific advances should make more drug products available for the prevention, diagnosis, and treatment of disease. Expanded use of medicines, along with new developments in administering medication, such as skin patches and implant pumps, will create a need for qualified pharmacists. As consumers become informed about drug advances and as improved health insurance coverage continues to develop, the number of openings in the pharmaceutical field is expected to increase.

Working Conditions

Pharmacists work in clean, pleasant surroundings. Most salaried employees work about 44 hours a week. Self-employed pharmacists usually work longer hours. These usually include some evening and weekend work. Part-time schedules can often be arranged, however.

Pharmacists are often on their feet for long hours. They should be in good health and be able to deal with other professional workers, as well as with the public. They must be responsible people who can do careful and detailed work. Management skills are also an asset.

Earnings and Benefits

Earnings vary depending on experience, skills, and place of employment. Experienced pharmacists can earn salaries of about $37,600 to $51,400 a year. The average salary of pharmacists working in independent drugstores is $45,300; in chain drugstores, $49,800; in hospitals, $50,300; in supermarkets, $51,200; in HMOs, $52,300; and in discount stores, $53,200. Owners of pharmacies, managers of chain drugstores, and high-level administrators often earn much more.

Self-employed pharmacists must provide their own benefits. Benefits for salaried pharmacists generally include paid holidays and vacations, health insurance, and pension plans.

Where to Go for More Information

American Pharmaceutical Association
2215 Constitution Avenue, NW
Washington, DC 20037-2985
(202) 628-4410

National Association of Chain Drug Stores
P.O. Box 1417-D49
Alexandria, VA 22313-1417
(703) 549-3001

National Association of Retail Druggists
205 Daingerfield Road
Alexandria, VA 22314
(703) 683-8200

Pharmacologist

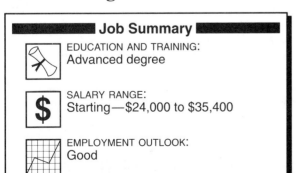

Job Summary

EDUCATION AND TRAINING:
Advanced degree

SALARY RANGE:
Starting—$24,000 to $35,400

EMPLOYMENT OUTLOOK:
Good

Definition and Nature of the Work

Pharmacologists are scientists who develop and test drugs. Their special field is pharmacology, the medical science that studies the effect of drugs on living things. Pharmacologists also do tests to find out whether other substances, such as gases, dusts, or food colorings, are harmful to living things. They study many substances to see whether they have healing powers. They often study the effect of these substances on laboratory animals, such as guinea pigs or monkeys.

There are several areas of specialization in pharmacology. *Clinical pharmacologists* test drugs on human beings. *Toxicologists* study poisonous drugs and other substances, such as chemicals and air pollutants that have harmful effects on living things. *Molecular pharmacologists* concentrate on how the molecules of drugs interact with the molecules of living things. *Neuropharmacologists* study the effect of drugs on the nervous system. *Chemotherapists* test drugs that can kill cancer cells, germs, or viruses without destroying healthy cells. Other areas that pharmacologists specialize in are biochemical pharmacology, cardiovascular pharmacology, behavioral pharmacology, and endocrine pharmacology.

The majority of pharmacologists spend most of their time in special laboratories. They do careful work with scientific instruments. Many also teach and communicate their findings to other scientists. Pharmacologists work in private industry, hospitals, universities, and government agencies.

Education and Training Requirements

To become a pharmacologist, you must first get a bachelor's degree. Your 4-year college program should include courses in science and mathematics, as well as in other areas that will give you a broad

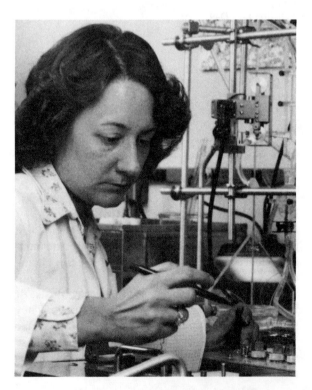

general background. Check the requirements of the college of medicine or pharmacy that you want to attend. You will receive your specialized training in a graduate program that includes theory and laboratory research. You can get a doctoral degree in pharmacology or a related science. Or you can get the degree of Doctor of Medicine (M.D.). Some medical schools have special programs that offer both degrees. You need the Doctor of Medicine degree in order to conduct clinical testing on human beings.

Getting the Job

The placement office at your graduate school can help you to find a job. Professional associations also have job information. Or you can apply directly to the drug company, university, hospital, or government agency for which you want to work.

Advancement Possibilities and Employment Outlook

Most pharmacologists advance by improving their skills. Some continue to take courses throughout their careers. They often become experts in one special area of pharmacology. A pharmacologist can become head of a research team or of a university department.

The employment outlook is good through the year 2005, especially for pharmacologists who have advanced degrees. The projected increase in the middle-aged and elderly populations will increase the demand for trained professionals in all of the life sciences. Also, scientific advances that make more drug products available for the prevention, diagnosis, and treatment of diseases should create many new jobs for pharmacologists.

Working Conditions

Pharmacologists generally work in pleasant surroundings. However, they must spend long hours in the laboratory and in the research library. They must continue to study new findings in their field. As their work is very exacting, they must be both careful and patient. They should also be able to communicate their discoveries to others. Pharmacologists usually find great personal satisfaction in the demanding and important work that they do.

Earnings and Benefits

Salaries vary depending on education, experience, and type of employment. Beginning pharmacologists earn salaries that range from $24,000 to $35,400. Experienced pharmacologists may earn from $38,000 to $55,000 a year. Some workers with many years of experience may earn as much as $66,000 a year. Benefits include paid vacations and holidays, health insurance, and pension plans.

Where to Go for More Information

American Society for Pharmacology and
    Experimental Therapeutics
9650 Rockville Pike
Bethesda, MD 20814-3995
(301) 530-7060

Physical Therapist

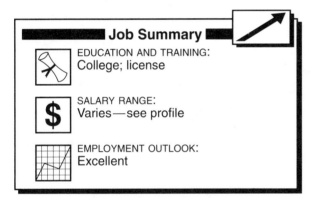

Job Summary

EDUCATION AND TRAINING:
College; license

SALARY RANGE:
Varies—see profile

EMPLOYMENT OUTLOOK:
Excellent

Definition and Nature of the Work

Physical therapists use physical means to help people cope with pain and disability caused by disease or injury. They usually work in hospitals, nursing homes, or rehabilitation centers. Physical therapists are part of a health care team that includes physicians, occupational therapists, and psychologists.

Physical therapists test each patient and design individual programs of treatment. Therapists may use massage to improve muscle condition. They may use cold to reduce swelling or heat to relieve pain. Therapists also teach patients how to do exercises with such equipment as pulleys and weights, stationary bicycles, parallel bars, or inclined surfaces. Physical therapists use a wide variety of other equipment, including whirlpool baths, ultrasonic machines, and ultraviolet and infrared lamps. They also teach patients and their families how to use and care for wheelchairs, braces, canes and crutches, and artificial limbs.

Physical therapists often supervise and instruct aides and assistants who help carry out programs of treatment. Therapists must also keep records and write reports on the progress of each patient.

Education and Training Requirements

You need a college education to become a physical therapist. The shortest route to this career is a 4-year college program leading to a bachelor's degree in physical therapy. If you have a bachelor's degree in another field, you can enroll in an 18-month program that leads to a certificate in physical therapy or in a program that offers a master's degree in physical therapy. To practice as a physical therapist, you must be licensed. Graduation from an approved program and a passing grade on a state board examination will qualify you for a license.

Getting the Job

You can get useful experience while still in high school or college by doing volunteer or part-time work in the physical therapy department of a hospital. Your college placement office can help you find a job. The American Physical Therapy Association may also provide useful job information. You may want to apply directly to hospitals and rehabilitation centers. The want ads in newspapers may be another source for possible job openings.

Advancement Possibilities and Employment Outlook

Experienced therapists can become supervisors of hospital departments. In most cases they need a master's degree to move into administrative, research, or teaching positions.

The job outlook is excellent through the year 2005 due to the rapidly growing need for rehabilitation and long-term care services. Advances in rehabilitation and therapeutic techniques are likely to create additional demand for qualified physical therapists. Although many people are training to become physical therapists, the supply of these workers is expected to fall short of the demand. Opportunities for physical therapists are expected to be best in rehabilitation centers, home health care agencies, and private practice.

Working Conditions

Physical therapists usually work in clean, pleasant, and spacious areas. Some therapists treat patients who are confined to bed or home. Because they deal with patients who may be depressed by their disabilities, physical therapists should be patient and encouraging. They need to be in good health and should be able to work well with their hands.

Most physical therapists work 40 hours a week. Those who prefer flexible hours can usually find part-time or consulting work.

Earnings and Benefits

Salaries vary with education, experience, and place of employment. Beginning physical therapists em-

ployed by the federal government earn, on the average, between $19,200 and $25,200 a year. Experienced physical therapists earn from about $26,600 to $43,600 a year. Some physical therapy supervisors make over $52,000 a year, while those in private practice can earn considerably higher salaries. Benefits for salaried physical therapists include paid holidays and vacations, health insurance, and pension plans. Self-employed therapists must provide their own benefits.

Where to Go for More Information

American Physical Therapy Association
1111 North Fairfax Street
Alexandria, VA 22314-1488
(703) 684-2782

National Association of Rehabilitation Instructors
633 South Washington Street
Alexandria, VA 22314
(703) 836-0850

National Rehabilitation Association
633 South Washington Street
Alexandria, VA 22314
(703) 836-0850

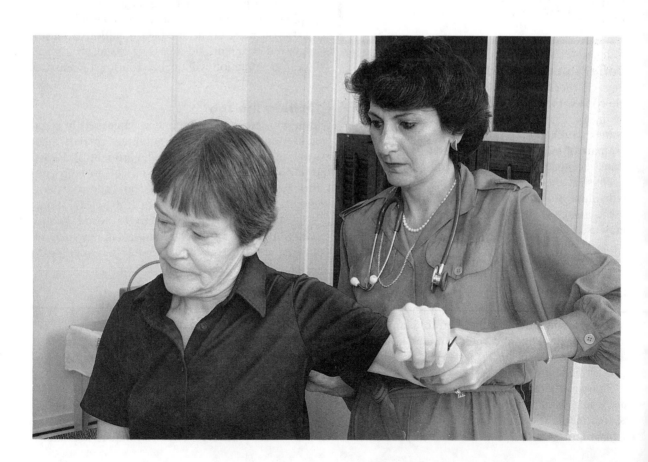

Physician

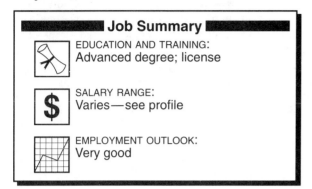

Definition and Nature of the Work

Physicians, or medical doctors, diagnose and treat diseases, injuries, and other disorders. They also try to promote good health and prevent illness. Physicians often supervise other health care workers, such as assistants, nurses, and technicians.

Most American physicians are involved directly in patient care. Only about one-tenth of all physicians in the United States work in areas other than patient care, such as administration or research. The majority of the physicians who provide patient care have their own or group office practices. Others work full time in hospitals.

About one-fifth of the physicians providing patient care are *general practitioners*. They treat a wide variety of the more common health problems. When general practitioners discover illnesses or injuries that need special care, they refer patients to specialists. The other four-fifths of the physicians providing patient care are specialists who work in one particular branch of medicine. There are about 35 major fields of specialization with over 50 different subspecialties. Advances in technology have caused this specialization to increase. New procedures and diagnostic equipment require extensive skills and training. For example, doctors specializing in nuclear medicine have to understand the complex nuclear magnetic resonance imaging machines they use. These machines are used to help other physicians make diagnoses. They produce images that allow the deep internal organs of the body to be examined without surgery.

Other specialists include *surgeons*, who perform operations on patients and who often specialize further in certain kinds of surgery. There are, for example, *orthopedic surgeons*, who operate on diseases and disorders of the joints and bones, and *neurosurgeons*, who use surgery to treat problems of the brain and nervous system. *Plastic surgeons* perform operations that repair or restore damaged parts of the face or body. They use such methods as skin grafts and tissue transplants. There are also surgeons who specialize in colon and rectal surgery or in thoracic surgery, which is surgery of the chest.

Internists are specialists who diagnose and use medicine to treat problems of internal organs, such as the liver, heart, and lungs. *Pediatricians* provide health care for children. *Geriatricians* treat problems and diseases of the elderly. *Obstetricians* care for women during pregnancy and childbirth. *Gynecologists* treat diseases of the female reproductive organs. *Psychiatrists* specialize in emotional problems, and *neurologists* treat disorders of the nervous system. *Family practitioners* concentrate on primary health care for the entire family. Their special training includes surgery, internal medicine, pediatrics, obstetrics and gynecology, psychiatry, and family medicine.

Some other specialists are *anesthesiologists*, who administer anesthetic drugs during surgery or diagnosis, and *dermatologists*, who diagnose and treat diseases of the skin. *Radiologists* use X rays and other forms of radiant energy as tools for diagnosis and treatment. *Ophthalmologists* specialize in the care of the eye. *Orthopedists* deal with problems of the muscles, joints, and bones, and *cardiologists* concentrate on the heart and circulatory system. *Urologists* specialize in the urinary systems of both sexes and in the male reproductive organs. *Otolaryngologists* care for the ears, nose, and throat.

Some physicians are *medical pathologists*, who study changes that disease causes in body chemistry and in organs, tissues, and cells. Others specialize in preventive medicine, which includes public health and occupational medicine. *Physiatrists* work in rehabilitation, a special field in which physical therapy is used to help victims of disabling injuries and diseases, such as arthritis, cerebral palsy, and polio. Other specialists work with allergies and in a wide variety of other special fields.

Education and Training Requirements

Physicians must have extensive training after high school. First they usually go to college for 4 years and earn a bachelor's degree. Some medical schools, however, will accept students after they have completed only 3 years of college. Students who want to be physicians usually major in a science, such as chemistry or biology. Other courses are also important so that the personal and educational development of the student is more well rounded.

Medical schools are increasingly accepting humanities majors with strong science backgrounds. Most medical colleges have 4-year programs that lead to the degree of Doctor of Medicine (M.D.). Some medical colleges have experimented with programs that shorten the total time needed to get the M.D. degree. Further training is then required in a specialty. Such training is known as a residency and lasts from 3 to 7 years.

In every state, physicians need to be licensed before they can practice medicine. Requirements for licensing vary from state to state. Minimal requirements include graduating from an approved medical college and passing a licensing examination. In most states M.D.s must also serve 1 or 2 years of residency in a hospital before they can be licensed.

Physicians who want to work as general practitioners serve a 3-year residency in a field such as general internal medicine. Those who want to become specialists must spend about 3 years as residents in their field. Specialists also need additional practice in their field before they can become certified by the appropriate specialty board. Some physicians who want to go into teaching or research go on to earn a master's or a doctoral degree in a science, such as biochemistry or microbiology.

Getting the Job

Some newly licensed physicians set up their own practices and work alone. Others share offices with other doctors in a group practice or join health maintenance organization (HMO) groups. A small percentage get salaried jobs in hospitals, clinics, government agencies, or private industry. Professional associations and medical colleges can provide information about going into private practice or finding a salaried position.

Advancement Possibilities and Employment Outlook

Most physicians advance by building their practices. They can work at improving their skills in general medicine or in a special field. Some physicians advance by moving into jobs in teaching or research. Others study business administration and become *physician executives*. These doctors then become hospital administrators.

The employment outlook for physicians is very good through the year 2005. Growth and aging of the population will generate a demand for physicians. Those in greatest demand will be in family practice, pediatrics, psychiatry, geriatrics, and internal medicine. The need is especially great in rural and inner-city areas. However, in some geographic areas and in some specialties, there is evidence of an oversupply of M.D.s.

Working Conditions

Physicians generally work in clean, comfortable offices, clinics, or hospitals. Those who have their own practices can control some of their working conditions. Many physicians work long and irregular hours. They must be available to handle emergencies. Some physicians limit their hours or work in specialties that have few emergencies.

Physicians need high intelligence, good health, and self-discipline. They must have good business sense and the ability to organize the work of others. They should be able to deal with many different kinds of people. They should also be careful and responsible workers. Their profession demands that they continue to study new developments in medicine throughout their career.

Earnings and Benefits

Earnings vary widely depending on experience, skill, location, field of specialization, and other factors. Currently M.D.s serving as hospital residents earn between $28,600 and $36,300 a year. After they complete their training, physicians usually increase their income considerably. Currently general practitioners earn about $98,000; internists, $125,000; and radiologists, $223,000.

Self-employed physicians arrange their own benefits. For those who are salaried, benefits generally include paid holidays and vacations, health insurance, and pension plans.

Where to Go for More Information

American College of Physicians
Independence Mall West
Sixth Street at Race
Philadelphia, PA 19106-1572
(215) 351-2400

The American Medical Association
535 North State Street
Chicago, IL 60610-4377
(312) 464-5000

Physician Assistant

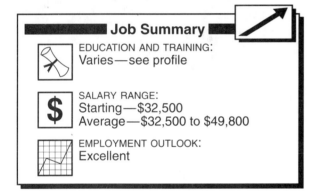

Job Summary

EDUCATION AND TRAINING:
Varies—see profile

SALARY RANGE:
Starting—$32,500
Average—$32,500 to $49,800

EMPLOYMENT OUTLOOK:
Excellent

Definition and Nature of the Work

Physician assistants (PAs) relieve doctors of routine chores and allow doctors to devote more of their time to patient care that requires highly specialized training. Although they are not doctors, physician assistants can do many of the jobs doctors do. Generally they are permitted to perform many tasks that nurses are not trained to handle. Physician assistants work only under the supervision of doctors. They work with doctors and nurses in hospitals, clinics, and private offices. Physician assistants are also called physician extenders and physician associates. Physician assistant is a new profession, which is recognized in most states.

Physician assistants have varied duties. They take patients' medical histories and perform laboratory and blood tests. They perform comprehensive physical exams. They also perform minor surgical pro-

cedures, give first aid, and operate diagnostic and therapeutic equipment. Their duties depend largely on state laws that regulate their activities.

Education and Training Requirements

You need at least a high school education to be admitted to a physician assistant training program. Two years of college is a common requirement. Health care experience may also be a requirement. Many applicants have bachelor's or master's degrees. Programs are taught in medical schools, colleges, community colleges, and teaching hospitals. The programs combine classroom and clinical study and last about 2 years.

Physician assistants' activities are regulated in almost all states. Many states require certification. Most states require registration with the state medical board.

Getting the Job

Your school placement office can help you find a job. You can also apply directly to hospitals, clinics, and doctors' offices in which you would like to work.

Advancement Possibilities and Employment Outlook

Physician assistants advance by accepting more responsibility or by moving into jobs that present a greater challenge. Some become specialists.

The employment outlook for physician assistants is excellent through the year 2005. Anticipated expansion of the health service industry is expected to increase the demand for qualified physician assistants. Also, especially in large health care facilities, such as health maintenance organizations, there will be a greater reliance on physician assistants to provide primary care and assist with medical and surgical procedures.

Working Conditions
The job is very demanding and requires a high degree of commitment. Physician assistants, like doctors, are always on call and generally work 40 to 60 hours a week. Physician assistants have much patient contact. They must be able to work well with patients and other members of the health care team.

Earnings and Benefits
Salaries vary depending on education, experience, and location. The current starting salary for physician assistants averages about $32,500 a year. Experienced physician assistants earn between $32,500 to $49,800 a year. Benefits generally include paid holidays and vacations, health insurance, and pension plans.

Where to Go for More Information
American Academy of Physician Assistants
950 North Washington Street
Alexandria, VA 22314
(703) 836-2272

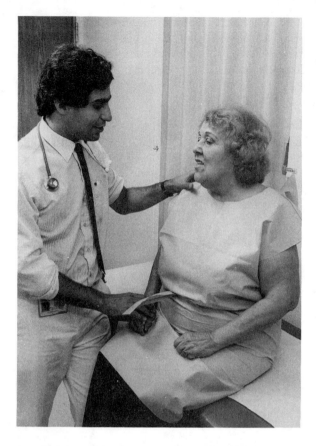

American Association of Medical Assistants
20 North Wacker Drive, Number 1575
Chicago, IL 60606
(312) 899-1500

Association of Physician Assistant Programs
950 North Washington Street
Alexandria, VA 22314-1552
(703) 548-5538

Podiatrist

Job Summary

EDUCATION AND TRAINING:
Advanced degree; license

SALARY RANGE:
Starting—$35,600
Average—$100,300

EMPLOYMENT OUTLOOK:
Very good

Definition and Nature of the Work
Podiatrists are medical practitioners who specialize in the care of the feet. Podiatrists were formerly called chiropodists. They treat people who have sore or badly shaped feet and those who have diseases or injuries of the feet. Podiatrists use special equipment to examine their patients. They may take X rays of the patient's foot. Or they may order laboratory tests to help them diagnose the patient's problem. Podiatrists treat foot problems in several ways. They may manipulate or massage the foot.

They may use other forms of physical therapy, such as whirlpool or paraffin baths. Sometimes they provide the patient with bandages, pads, braces, splints, or other supports. They can prescribe drugs, exercise, or special shoes. Podiatrists can also perform foot surgery, either in their offices or at a hospital. Sometimes foot problems are signs of a general body illness, such as diabetes or heart trouble. When podiatrists find signs of these diseases, they refer the patient to a physician for treatment.

Most podiatrists treat all kinds of foot problems. Some specialize, however. Special fields include foot surgery and orthopedics, which involve treating deformities of foot muscles, joints, or bones. Some podiatrists specialize in podopediatrics, the care of children's feet. Others concentrate on podogeriatrics, the treatment of foot problems of the elderly.

Most podiatrists are in private practice. However, some work in hospitals, podiatric colleges, government agencies, or private clinics.

The employment outlook is very good through the year 2005. The anticipated growth in the elderly population requiring treatment of foot problems should create openings for qualified podiatrists. Also, the popularity of fast-moving sports, such as jogging, tennis, and racquetball, is expected to increase demand in the specialty of podiatric sports medicine.

Working Conditions

Podiatrists generally set their own working conditions. Most work about 40 hours a week, often including some evening and Saturday hours. Schedules are flexible, and some podiatrists work part time. Because emergencies are rare, podiatrists usually keep regular hours.

Podiatrists need good vision and steady nerves. They must work well with their hands. They must

Education and Training Requirements

Admission into a school of podiatry requires at least 3 years of college. Most applicants have a bachelor's degree. In colleges of podiatry, students take a 4-year program leading to the degree of Doctor of Podiatric Medicine (D.P.M.). All states require that podiatrists be licensed. Requirements vary, but in all states podiatrists must at least graduate from an approved college of podiatry and pass a state board exam. A few states also require a 1-year residency.

Getting the Job

Most podiatrists go into private practice. Some newly licensed podiatrists start their own practices. Some buy established practices. Others start by working as assistants in the offices of established podiatrists. Still others take salaried positions until they have the money and experience to open their own practices. Professional associations and colleges of podiatry can provide information about getting started in this field.

Advancement Possibilities and Employment Outlook

Most podiatrists advance by building their practices. Some specialize. A small number of podiatrists move into teaching, research, or administrative positions in hospitals or colleges of podiatry.

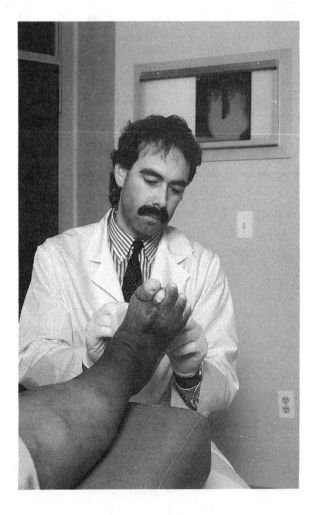

have an aptitude for scientific and technical activities. They should have good business sense and the ability to deal with all kinds of people.

Earnings and Benefits
Earnings vary with experience, skill, and place of work. Currently, beginning podiatrists can earn salaries of about $35,600 a year. Salaries for experienced podiatrists average about $100,300 a year. Salaries for podiatrists with well-established practices may be considerably higher. As most podiatrists are self-employed, they must provide their own health insurance and other benefits.

Where to Go for More Information
American Association of Colleges of Podiatric
    Medicine
1350 Piccard Drive
Rockville, MD 20850-4307
(301) 990-7400

American Podiatric Medical Association
9312 Old Georgetown Road
Bethesda, MD 20814-1621
(301) 571-9200

National Podiatric Medical Association
1706 East 87th Street
Chicago, IL 60617
(312) 374-1616

Prosthetist and Orthotist

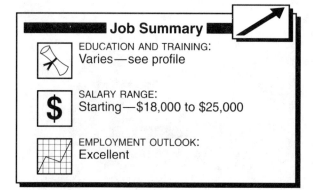

Job Summary

EDUCATION AND TRAINING:
Varies—see profile

SALARY RANGE:
Starting—$18,000 to $25,000

EMPLOYMENT OUTLOOK:
Excellent

Definition and Nature of the Work
Prosthetists and orthotists work with physicians and with physical and occupational therapists to enable patients to use parts of the body that have been damaged or to replace parts that have been lost because of an accident or illness. Prosthetists make and fit artificial limbs. Orthotists make and fit braces to help support parts of the body or to correct malformations.

Working with a doctor's prescription, orthotists and prosthetists examine the patient. They must measure the patient so that the brace or artificial limb will fit exactly. They must design each device to suit the unique needs of its wearer. Orthotists and prosthetists make braces and artificial limbs from various materials, such as wood, steel, aluminum, leather, cloth, rubber, and plastic. They must fit the patient very carefully, often with the help of a doctor and a physical therapist. This team checks to be sure that the device is working as it should. Physical therapists then teach the patient how to use the brace or artificial limb. If the device needs changing, the prosthetist or orthotist makes the necessary adjustments or repairs.

Education and Training Requirements
A bachelor's degree in prosthetics or orthotics is usually required if you want to work as a fully certified practitioner in this field. After a period of supervised clinical practice, college graduates are eligible to take an exam given by the American Board for Certification in Orthotics and Prosthetics. It is also possible to enter this field with an associate degree in any field by completing a certificate program in prosthetics/orthotics, and having a minimum of 4 years of experience in orthotics or prosthetics. One year of this experience in each specialty must be obtained after the certificate program is completed. On passing the proper exams, they become a Certified Orthotist (CO), a Certified Prosthetist (CP), or a Certified Prosthetist-Orthotist (CPO).

Getting the Job
You can apply directly to the places that hire prosthetists and orthotists. These include hospitals, clinics, government agencies, and private compa-

nies. Your school placement office can give you job information. The want ads in newspapers and professional publications may also list job openings.

Advancement Possibilities and Employment Outlook

The possibilities for advancement depend on education, experience, and skill. In large hospitals or clinics prosthetists and orthotists can become department heads. Or they can begin their own practices. Prosthetists and orthotists can also move on to positions in research, sales, or teaching.

The employment outlook is excellent. The field is growing. This is due to the general aging of the population, to disease, and to an increasing number of accidents. More prosthetists and orthotists will be needed to fill the many job openings.

Working Conditions

Most prosthetists and orthotists work in a combination shop-laboratory. Shops can volunteer to be inspected by the American Board for Certification in Orthotics and Prosthetics.

Prosthetists and orthotists must be skilled at using their hands and machinery. They must also be able to deal sympathetically with their patients and to cooperate with doctors and therapists.

Earnings and Benefits

Salaries vary depending on education, experience, and place of employment. Beginning workers who have a bachelor's degree earn from about $18,000 to $25,000 a year. Experienced certified prosthetists and orthotists earn from $36,000 to $59,000 a year. Benefits generally include paid holidays and vacations, health insurance, and pension plans. Self-employed prosthetists and orthotists must provide their own benefits.

Where to Go for More Information

American Academy of Orthotists and Prosthetists
1650 King Street, Suite 500
Alexandria, VA 22314
(703) 836-7118

International Society for Prosthetics and Orthotics
1650 King Street, Suite 500
Alexandria, VA 22314
(708) 836-7114

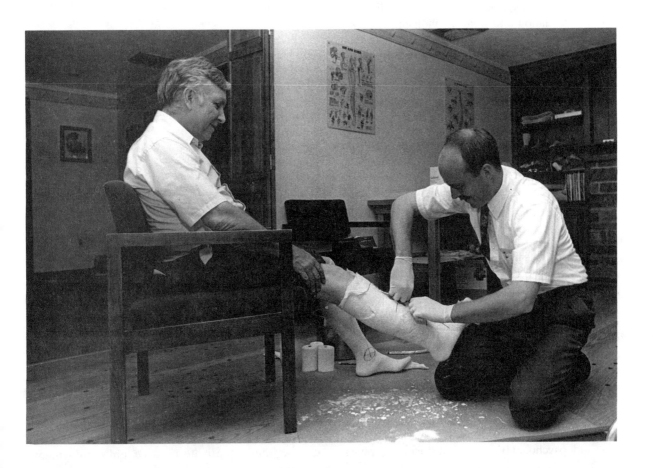

Psychiatrist

Job Summary

EDUCATION AND TRAINING:
Advanced degree; license

SALARY RANGE:
Average—$110,000

EMPLOYMENT OUTLOOK:
Very good

Definition and Nature of the Work

Psychiatrists are physicians who specialize in the prevention, diagnosis, and treatment of mental disorders. They often work with other mental health workers, such as psychologists, occupational therapists, psychiatric nurses, and psychiatric social workers. Psychiatrists deal with many kinds of mental problems. These problems can range from rather mild cases of anxiety to severe disorders that may cause dangerous and bizarre behavior. Psychiatrists work with patients who cannot distinguish reality from fantasy and with those who suffer excessive mood changes. Psychiatrists may also diagnose mental retardation and treat alcoholism.

Psychiatrists talk with patients to learn about their mental problems and examine them to learn about related physical problems. Psychiatrists also use information provided by patients' families or by other mental health workers. They may order laboratory tests or other kinds of diagnostic tests to be done. Psychiatrists are specially trained to recognize the connection between physical and mental disorders. Their training helps them to decide on the proper treatment for each patient.

Psychiatrists use several types of treatment. They can prescribe drugs when needed. They can use shock therapy. They can also use psychotherapy. In psychotherapy psychiatrists use their special training to talk with one or more patients. They help the patients to understand and cope with their problems.

Psychiatrists may work with patients in private offices or in hospitals or clinics. Or they may work in research, studying the causes and treatment of mental illness. Some psychiatrists teach in medical schools or in special psychiatric institutes. Others write or edit psychiatric books or journals. Most psychiatrists combine some of these areas in their work.

Psychiatrists are often confused with psychologists and psychoanalysts. Psychiatrists are physi-

cians who have advanced training in psychiatry. As physicians, they can prescribe medication. Psychologists have either a master's degree or a doctoral degree in psychology. They are not physicians and cannot prescribe drugs or perform surgery. Psychologists are basically scientists who study the reactions of people to their environment. Psychoanalysts are specially trained to practice long-term therapy that investigates the hidden causes of emotional disturbances. Most psychoanalysts are psychiatrists. A few, however, known as lay analysts, are not.

Education and Training Requirements

Psychiatrists need extensive training after high school. They generally spend 4 years in college and another 4 years in medical school. Psychiatrists must also have 3 years of psychiatric training as a resident in a hospital. Usually after 1 or 2 years of residency, psychiatrists must take an examination to be licensed. All states require licensing. Psychiatrists also need additional experience before they are eligible to take an examination for certification as a psychiatrist.

Getting the Job

Psychiatrists who have completed their training can choose between private practice and employment at an institution. Or they can combine the two types of work. Setting up a private practice is not expensive, but it takes time for a beginning psychiatrist to build up a full-time schedule. Many new psychiatrists start by working with an established psychiatrist. Professional associations can provide information about setting up a practice or getting a salaried position.

Advancement Possibilities and Employment Outlook

Psychiatrists usually advance by building their practices. Some become experts in special fields, such as child psychology, educational psychiatry, or legal psychiatry. Others become teachers, researchers, or administrators in colleges, hospitals, or other institutions.

The job outlook is very good through the year 2005. There are many fields open to psychiatrists. For example, health and welfare agencies need the expertise of psychiatrists to treat problems related to aging, family incompatibility, and drug addiction. Currently there is an oversupply of psychiatrists in some areas of the United States. However, some experts predict that there will be a future shortage of psychiatrists, particularly in the area of child psychiatry.

Working Conditions

Psychiatrists in private practice work in pleasant surroundings. They try to create a quiet, peaceful setting so their patients can feel at ease. However, the emotional strain of the work is considerable because of the suffering that psychiatrists see every day. In addition, psychiatrists in private practice must be available to their patients whenever they need help. This makes their working hours somewhat irregular.

Psychiatrists who work in hospitals and clinics often have more regular hours than private practitioners do. This is because they divide the hours that they are on call with the other staff psychiatrists. However, mental hospitals and psychiatric clinics can be very difficult places in which to work. In order to do the work well, psychiatrists must be well balanced and well disciplined. Psychiatrists need high intelligence and the ability to deal with many kinds of patients. They should enjoy the study and research that are needed to prepare for and to continue in this demanding profession.

Earnings and Benefits

Psychiatrists' earnings are similar to those of other physicians. Residents in this field of medicine earn between $28,600 and $36,300 a year. The average salary for an experienced psychiatrist is about $110,000 a year. However, those in private practice may earn as much as $200,000 or more a year. Psychiatrists in private practice must provide their own benefits. Salaried psychiatrists receive paid holidays and vacations, health insurance, and pension plans.

Where to Go for More Information

American College of Psychiatrists
P.O. Box 365
Greenbelt, MD 20768
(301) 345-3534

The American Medical Association
515 North State Street
Chicago, IL 60610-4377
(312) 464-5000

The American Psychiatric Association
1400 K Street, NW
Washington, DC 20005
(202) 682-6000

Psychologist

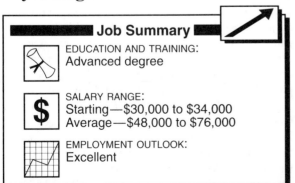

Job Summary

EDUCATION AND TRAINING:
Advanced degree

SALARY RANGE:
Starting—$30,000 to $34,000
Average—$48,000 to $76,000

EMPLOYMENT OUTLOOK:
Excellent

Definition and Nature of the Work

Psychologists are scientists who study behavior. They usually work in jobs that involve teaching, research, or social service. They work in a wide variety of places. Some have private practices. Others work in schools, colleges, clinics, government agencies, or private industry. Psychologists use scientific methods to learn about the behavior of humans and animals. These methods can include tests, laboratory experiments, case histories, or surveys. Psychologists develop theories to help explain how

people react to their environment. They use their knowledge to help change the behavior of people.

There are several areas of specialization within the broad field of psychology. In experimental psychology, for example, psychologists carry out research projects that help them to develop theories about learning, motivation, hearing, or other problems in animal or human behavior. Developmental psychology deals with problems of growth and development and may concentrate on one particular stage of development, such as adolescence or old age. Educational psychology is concerned with learning and teaching and tries to improve the process of education. Other areas of specialization include comparative psychology, social psychology, and psychometrics.

Just as there are many areas of specialization, there are also many kinds of psychologists. The largest group is made up of *clinical psychologists*. They usually help people with emotional problems. They may interview these people, give them tests, and help them to understand and cope with their problems. *School psychologists* work with students in schools. They often give tests to identify gifted, handicapped, and emotionally disturbed students.

They develop programs to educate all types of students within a school system. *Industrial and organizational psychologists* study problems of motivation and morale in offices and factories. They often conduct surveys and give tests to employees, customers, and others. They may advise the company on personnel, management, or marketing problems. Other kinds of psychologists include engineering psychologists, counseling psychologists, and environmental psychologists.

Education and Training Requirements

To be a psychologist, you should first go to a 4-year college and get a bachelor's degree. You can major in psychology or in a related field. Then you will need to get at least a master's degree. A master's degree will qualify you for a limited number of assistant or school counseling jobs. To be employed as a psychologist, you should have a doctoral degree, which usually takes from 3 to 5 years of study after college. To practice clinical or counseling psychology, you generally must have an additional year or more of internship. Unlike psychiatrists, psychologists are not physicians.

All states require that you must be certified or licensed to start a private practice. To become licensed, you usually need a doctoral degree plus 2 years of experience. The American Board of Professional Psychology awards diplomas in clinical, counseling, school, and industrial and organizational psychology. Candidates must have a doctoral degree, 5 years' experience, and professional endorsements.

Getting the Job

Your university placement office can help you to find a job. Want ads in newspapers and professional journals list openings for psychologists. You can also apply directly to the agency for which you want to work. Professional associations can provide information about opening a practice.

Advancement Possibilities and Employment Outlook

Advancement depends on many factors, including education, experience, and other personal qualities. Psychologists with a doctoral degree can move into high-level jobs in research, teaching, counseling, or administration. Those with private practices can build their practices. Some psychologists advance by serving as consultants to government or industry or by writing about their special field.

The employment outlook is excellent through the year 2005. Opportunities will be best for psychologists with doctoral degrees in clinical and counseling psychology, particularly relating to children and the elderly. Currently there is a significant shortage of psychologists trained to deal with the elderly. Many opportunities exist in this area. There will still be keen competition for all teaching jobs.

Working Conditions

Working conditions vary widely. Psychologists in private practice usually have comfortable offices. Their schedules may include some evening and Saturday hours. Most psychologists work 40 hours a week. Hours can be flexible, however, depending on the type of work and the needs of the individual psychologist. School psychologists, for example, often have the same hours as teachers.

Psychologists usually need to spend time studying the latest developments in their field. They need high intelligence and emotional stability. The ability to deal with a wide variety of people is an asset in clinical and counseling psychology. Psychologists involved in research need to be self-disciplined people who are able to do detailed and careful work.

Earnings and Benefits

Salaries vary depending on education, experience, and type of work. Currently clinical psychologists with a doctoral degree earn starting salaries that average about $30,000 to $34,000 a year. Experienced psychologists who work for institutions or corporations earn about $50,000 to $55,000 a year. Psychologists with private practices earn about $48,000 to $76,000 a year. Psychologists in private practice must provide their own benefits, such as health insurance and pension plans. Benefits for salaried psychologists include paid holidays and vacations, health insurance, and pension plans.

Where to Go for More Information

The American Psychological Association
750 First Street, NE
Washington, DC 20002
(202) 336-5500

Recreation Therapist

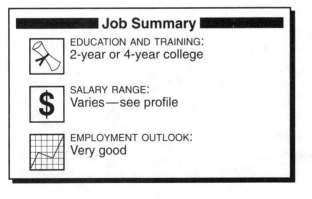

▬▬▬▬ Job Summary ▬▬▬▬

EDUCATION AND TRAINING:
2-year or 4-year college

SALARY RANGE:
Varies—see profile

EMPLOYMENT OUTLOOK:
Very good

Definition and Nature of the Work

Recreation therapists conduct specialized games, sports, crafts, and other leisure activities geared to help people with mental, emotional, and physical disabilities. The recreation programs they provide help the participants overcome or adjust to their difficulties. Therapeutic recreation is offered to individuals of all ages with all types of problems, from children hospitalized for minor surgery to wheelchair-bound elderly people. Recreation therapists are also known as play therapists. In nursing homes recreation therapists are often classified as activities directors.

Mental health facilities, hospitals, correctional institutions, nursing homes, rehabilitation centers and specialized schools, training centers, camps, and residential centers for the disabled all employ recreation therapists. Some therapists develop, as well as conduct, therapeutic recreation programs, and many specialize in a particular type of recreation, such as music, art, dance, drama, or sports.

Education and Training Requirements

Therapist positions require at least a bachelor's degree and sometimes a master's degree, as well. Many colleges and universities offer undergraduate and graduate degree programs in therapeutic recreation or therapeutic education. Some offer programs in music, art, drama, or physical education therapy. Some facilities require certification in some form of therapeutic recreation. Others hire recreation, physical education, or arts majors with experience in therapeutic activities.

Getting the Job

Job notifications are often posted in the special education departments of colleges, and some may be listed in civil service bulletins. Larger facilities often hire aides to work with therapists, and these positions usually do not require a college degree. Working as an aide, possibly while you are pursuing a degree, may give you the added training, experience, and contacts you need to find a job.

Advancement Possibilities and Employment Outlook

Recreation therapists may become program developers, supervisors, or directors of special recreation programs, but this may require further education.

The job outlook for therapists is expected to be very good through the year 2005 as more positions become available in specialized schools and nursing homes. Growth and aging of the population and growth of the number of people with disabilities should increase the demand for qualified recreation therapists. The best opportunities will be available to those therapists with a master's degree.

Working Conditions

Recreation therapists frequently must work evenings and weekends, and those who specialize in sports or outdoor games can anticipate a lot of physical activity. Other conditions will depend largely on the size and type of the facility, the kind of

recreation provided, and the individuals in the program. Therapists may work alone or as part of a professional team. They may be working with one client at a time in a close, one-on-one relationship, or they may work with groups of clients. The work can be demanding and usually requires patience, creativity, and good judgment.

Earnings and Benefits
Salaries vary widely among facilities that employ recreation therapists. The average salary for activities directors working in nursing homes is between $15,000 and $25,000 a year. The average starting salary for all recreation therapists is about $25,600, while those working for the federal government earn an average salary of $33,500. Benefits may include paid vacations, holidays, and sick leave, as well as health insurance and pension plans.

Where to Go for More Information
National Therapeutic Recreation Society
2775 South Quincy Street, Suite 300
Arlington, VA 22206-2204
(703) 578-5548

Registered Nurse

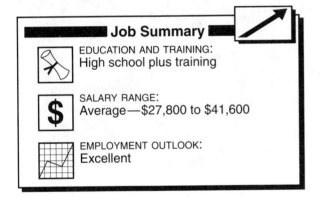

Job Summary

EDUCATION AND TRAINING:
High school plus training

SALARY RANGE:
Average—$27,800 to $41,600

EMPLOYMENT OUTLOOK:
Excellent

Definition and Nature of the Work
Registered nurses (RNs) provide a wide variety of skilled services. They must use considerable judgment in observing and recording the condition of patients. Registered nurses give medication under the direction of a physician. They advise patients and help in their rehabilitation. RNs also work to promote good health and prevent illness.

Registered nurses work in a variety of settings. Most work in hospitals. Others work in nursing homes, rehabilitation centers, and long-term care facilities. Many nurses are general duty nurses. *General duty nurses* focus on the overall care of the patient. They give out medications and keep records of symptoms and progress. General duty nurses also give reports to doctors and supervise practical nurses, nurse's aides, and orderlies.

In hospitals nurses may work in special units, such as critical care, cardiac and burn units, and maternity care. This work often requires special training. Other hospital nurses may be operating room nurses. *Operating room nurses* help out before, during, and after surgery and often stay with patients in the recovery room after operations. Some experienced hospital nurses are head nurses or directors of nursing services. Registered nurses also work as nurse educators or as researchers in hospitals. Other nurses who work in hospitals are *private duty nurses*. They are hired to attend to patients needing special care. Private duty nurses also work in patients' homes and in nursing homes.

In addition, many registered nurses work in private doctors' offices or clinics. These *office nurses* may assist an obstetrician, for example, or a dental surgeon. They may do some office or laboratory work along with their nursing duties.

Registered nurses also work in the community. *Public health nurses* generally work in clinics and help to teach the public about good health practices. They may also care for patients and their families under the supervision of a doctor. *Visiting nurses* carry health care to patients in their homes. *School nurses* and *industrial nurses* promote good health in schools and industries, respectively.

Education and Training Requirements
After you graduate from high school, you can prepare for a career as a registered nurse in one of three ways. You can take a 2-year nursing program in a community college that will lead to an associate degree. Or you can enroll in a diploma program offered by a hospital or independent school of nursing. Diploma programs generally take 3 years to complete. You can also enroll in a college program that leads to a bachelor of science degree. College programs usually take 4 or 5 years to complete. They combine liberal arts courses with scientific and technical training. All programs include practical experience. There is a move toward 2 levels of nursing: technical nursing, which will require an associate degree, and professional nursing, which will

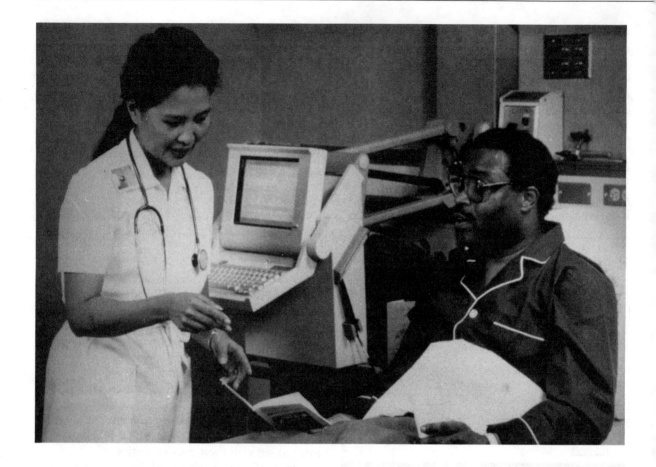

require a bachelor's degree. Only nurses with a bachelor's degree will be eligible for RN licensing. You should check current requirements before deciding on a program.

After you have completed an approved program, you will be eligible to take the national written licensing exam, administered by each state. All states require licensing.

Getting the Job

Nursing school and college placement services can help you find a job. Or you can apply directly to hospitals, clinics, nursing homes, and doctors' offices. For community health jobs, contact public health departments, home health agencies, and visiting nurse associations. The armed services also have openings for nurses. In addition, there are professional nurse registries for private duty nurses.

Advancement Possibilities and Employment Outlook

Advancement in nursing depends on education, experience, and place of employment. Registered nurses can become supervisors of departments or

specialists in a particular field of nursing, such as pediatrics or psychiatry. Nurse practitioners need a master's degree. Those with a bachelor's or a master's degree are more likely to move into the higher-level jobs in these areas. Many positions in research, teaching, or administration require a master's or even a doctoral degree in nursing.

The employment outlook is excellent through the year 2005. Many areas of the United States report significant shortages of registered nurses. Owing to increasing technology, there will also be a demand for RNs to work in physicians' offices. The aging of the population and the trend toward shorter hospital stays will create jobs in nursing facilities and home health care.

Working Conditions

Although particular working conditions vary with the place of employment, nearly all nursing jobs involve close contact with people. Being able to deal with all kinds of people is an important requirement for a nurse. Good health and emotional stability are also valuable assets. Nurses must be careful workers who take their responsibilities seriously. They must follow rigid guidelines to insure the safety of themselves and their patients against infectious diseases.

Registered nurses generally work 40 hours a week. This usually includes some night and weekend shifts, especially for hospital nurses. Many nurses are able to work part time if they choose to do so.

Earnings and Benefits
Salaries for nurses vary depending on education, experience, and area of specialization. The average annual income for all registered nurses is about $27,800 to $41,600. The average salary for head nurses is $47,300 a year. Benefits include paid holidays and vacations, health insurance, and pension plans. In areas where there is an acute shortage of nurses, some employers are offering additional benefits. Those include flex-time, subsidized housing, recruitment bonuses, and free tuition for further

training. Private duty nurses generally charge a daily fee and must provide their own benefits.

Where to Go for More Information
American Assembly for Men in Nursing
P.O. Box 31753
Independence, OH 44131
(216) 524-3504

American Association of Colleges of Nursing
One Dupont Circle, NW, Suite 530
Washington, DC 20036
(202) 463-6930

American Nurses' Association
600 Maryland Avenue, SW
Washington, DC 20024-2571
(202) 554-4444

National League for Nursing
350 Hudson Street
New York, NY 10014
(212) 989-9393

Speech Pathologist and Audiologist

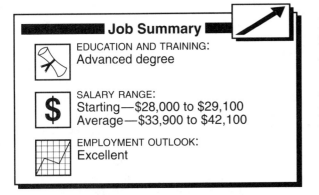

Job Summary

EDUCATION AND TRAINING:
Advanced degree

SALARY RANGE:
Starting—$28,000 to $29,100
Average—$33,900 to $42,100

EMPLOYMENT OUTLOOK:
Excellent

Definition and Nature of the Work
Speech pathologists and audiologists help people who have speech, language, and hearing problems. Speech pathologists are trained in speech and language problems. Audiologists are trained in hearing problems. Many jobs require training in both fields.

Speech pathologists and audiologists give tests to people who have speech and hearing problems. These problems may be caused by injury, illness, or emotional difficulties. Speech pathologists and audiologists may treat brain-damaged and mentally retarded patients and people who have a deformity, such as a cleft palate. Many patients are children who lisp or stutter. Adult patients may be victims of strokes or of cerebral palsy. Speech pathologists

and audiologists often work closely with doctors, psychologists, physical therapists, or classroom teachers. They plan and carry out treatment that takes into account the unique needs of each patient.

The majority of speech pathologists and audiologists work in public schools. Some have private practices. Others work in colleges and universities, clinics, hospitals, special speech and hearing centers, government agencies, and private industry. Some speech pathologists and audiologists work on research projects to design and develop new equipment or methods for treating speech and hearing problems.

Education and Training Requirements
You usually need a master's degree in speech-language pathology or audiology to work in the field. A few jobs are still open, however, to those with only a bachelor's degree and a major in speech or hearing problems. Some states require you to have a teaching certificate to work in public schools. Some states require a license to work in private practice, clinics, or other nonschool settings. Certification and licensing requirements vary from state to state.

Certification by the American Speech-Language-Hearing Association is recommended for those who

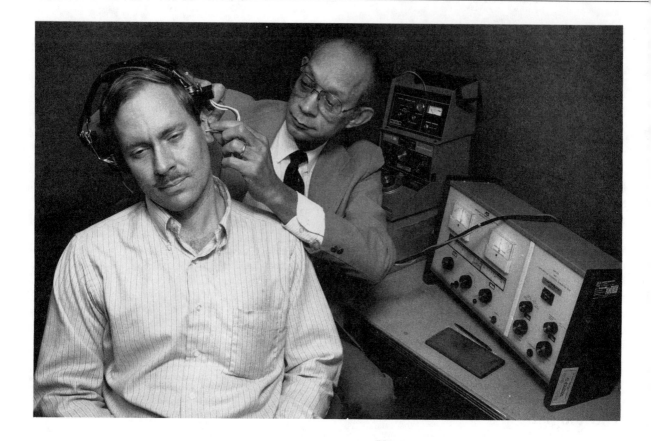

want to advance. You must have a master's degree or its equivalent and a year of work experience. After passing an examination, you will receive a Certificate of Clinical Competence.

Getting the Job
You can apply directly to the school, clinic, or other institution in which you would like to work. Your school placement office or the American Speech-Language-Hearing Association can give you information about job openings. You can also check the want ads in newspapers.

Advancement Possibilities and Employment Outlook
Advancement depends on education and experience. Speech pathologists and audiologists can become supervisors or heads of clinics. They can set up private practices. Those with the necessary training can work as consultants, do research, and write books or articles on speech and hearing problems.

The employment outlook for speech pathologists and audiologists is excellent through the year 2005, particularly for those with advanced degrees. Growth

and aging of the population should increase the number of people with communicative disorders. As recognition and treatment of hearing and speech problems increase, so will the demand for professionals in this field. Competition will be keen for teaching jobs in colleges and universities and in some regions of the United States for positions in hospitals and clinics. In other areas there will be extreme shortages of speech pathologists and audiologists. Job opportunities will depend somewhat on government funding.

Working Conditions
Working conditions are usually pleasant. Speech pathologists and audiologists are part of a health care team. They come into contact with a wide variety of people. They should be patient and able to work well with others.

Many speech pathologists and audiologists work more than 40 hours a week. Their hours are often flexible, and there are part-time jobs available. Speech pathologists and audiologists working in public schools usually have the same schedule that classroom teachers have.

Earnings and Benefits

Salaries vary widely depending on education, experience, and location. Beginning audiologists and speech pathologists in hospitals and medical centers earn average salaries ranging from $28,000 to $29,100 a year. The average salary for experienced speech pathologists and audiologists ranges between $33,900 and $42,100 a year. Benefits usually include paid holidays and vacations, health insurance, and pension plans.

Where to Go for More Information

American Speech-Language-Hearing Association
10801 Rockville Pike
Rockville, MD 20852
(301) 897-5700

National Student Speech Language Hearing
    Association
10801 Rockville Pike
Rockville, MD 20852
(301) 897-5700

Further Reading and Resources

General Career Information—Books

Exploring the Working World

Recommended

The Encyclopedia of Careers and Vocational Guidance, 9th ed., 4 vols., William E. Hopke, et al., eds. New York: Ferguson, 1993. Comprehensive source. Volume 1 is an overview of various fields. Volumes 2, 3, and 4 provide specific information for professional, administrative, technical, engineering, media, and health care careers.

Occupational Outlook Handbook, United States Department of Labor. Washington, DC: United States Government Printing Office, revised biennially. Expands on the *Dictionary of Occupational Titles*. Groups jobs into similar categories. Discusses the nature of the work, the employment outlook, and earnings.

VGM's Careers Encyclopedia, 3rd ed., Craig T. Norback, ed. Lincolnwood, IL: VGM Career Horizons/NTC Publishing Group, 1991. A one-volume guide to 180 careers.

Aid to Career Decisions, D. Arthur. San Diego, CA: Windsong, 1991.
American Almanac of Jobs and Salaries, John W. Wright and Edward J. Dwyer. New York: Avon Books, rev. 1993.
America's Fastest Growing Jobs: A Complete Guide. New York: Gordon Press, 1992.
Career Action Plan, William M. Bloomfield. Bloomington, IL: Meridian Education, 1989.
Career Briefs series. Largo, FL: Careers, Inc. Series of leaflets on many occupations; these are available separately and are revised regularly.
Career Discovery Encyclopedia, C. J. Summerfield, ed., 6 vols. Chicago: Ferguson, 1993.
Career Employment Opportunities Directory, 2nd ed., 4 vols. Santa Monica, CA: Ready Reference Press.
Career Summary series. Largo, FL: Careers, Inc. Series of cards on hundreds of jobs, available separately. Updated regularly.
The Complete Guide to Public Employment, 3rd ed., Ronald Krannich. Manassas, VA: Impact Publications, 1993.
Dictionary of Occupational Titles, 4th ed., United States Department of Labor. Washington, DC: United States Government Printing Office, rev. 1991.

Exploring Careers: The World of Work and You, J. Michael Farr and JoAnn Amore. Indianapolis, IN: JIST Works, 1989.

Great Careers: The Fourth of July Guide to Careers, Internships, and Volunteer Opportunities in the Nonprofit Sector, Devon C. Smith, ed. Garrett Park, MD: Garrett Park Press, 1990.

The Harvard Guide to Careers, 3rd ed., Martha P. Leape and Susan M. Vacca. Cambridge, MA: Harvard University Press, 1991.

Job Search Kit, Thomas R. Wims. Lanham, MD: Roberts Publications, 1992.

Jobs '95, Kathryn Petras. New York: Simon & Schuster, annual.

Jobs Rated Almanac Two, Les Krantz. New York: Pharos Books, rev. 1992.

National Job Bank, 1994, Carter Smith. Boston: Adams, 1993.

Occu-Facts: Facts on Over 565 Careers, Elizabeth Handville, ed. Largo, FL: Careers, Inc., 1989.

Occupational Mini-Brief series. Moravia, NY: Chronicle Guidance Publications. Series of leaflets, available separately.

Occupational Outlook series. Washington, DC: United States Government Printing Office. Briefs, separately published.

Occupational Outlook Quarterly. Washington, DC: Occupational Outlook Service, Bureau of Labor Statistics, current since 1956. Quarterly.

Occupational Projections and Training Data: A Statistical Supplement to the Occupational Outlook Handbook. United States Department of Labor. Washington, DC: United States Government Printing Office, revised biennially.

Professional Careers Sourcebook, 3rd ed. Detroit: Gale, 1993.

Top Professions: The 100 Most Popular, Dynamic, and Profitable Careers in America Today, Nicholas Basta. Princeton, NJ: Peterson's Guides, 1989.

Vocational Careers Sourcebook, Hill, et al. Detroit: Gale, 1992.

Education and Training Opportunities

Recommended

The following four sources are basic directories of information on colleges and universities. They include general information on each school, its address, a listing of the programs offered, the size of the institution, and costs for tuition.

Barron's Top Fifty: An Inside Look at America's Best Colleges, 2nd ed., 2 vols., Tom Fischgrund, ed. Hauppauge, NY: Barron's Educational Series, revised regularly.

The College Blue Book. New York: Macmillan Publishing Co., revised regularly.

Lovejoy's College Guide, Charles T. Straughn and Barbarasue Straughn, ed. New York: Prentice Hall, revised regularly.

Peterson's Guide to Four-Year Colleges, Susan Dilts and Mark Zidzik, eds. Princeton, NJ: Peterson's Guides, revised regularly.

American Universities and Colleges. Hawthorne, NY: De Groyter, revised regularly.

America's Lowest Cost Colleges, 8th ed., Nicholas A. Roes. Barryville, NY: NAR Publications, 1993.

Barron's Guide to Graduate Business Schools, Eugene Miller, ed. Hauppauge, NY: Barron's Educational Series, revised regularly.

Barron's Guide to Law Schools. Hauppauge, NY: Barron's Educational Series, revised regularly.

Barron's Guide to Medical and Dental Schools, Saul Wischitzer, ed. Hauppauge, NY: Barron's Educational Series, 1993.

Bear's Guide to Earning College Degrees Non-Traditionally, 11th ed., John Bear. Benicia, CA: C&B Publishing, 1994.

Chronicle Vocational School Manual, Patricia Hammon, ed. Moravia, NY: Chronicle Guidance Publications, annual.

College Applications and Essays: A How-To Handbook, 2nd ed., Susan D. Van Raalte. New York: Prentice Hall, 1993.

College Comes Sooner Than You Think!, Bonnie Featherstone and Jill Reilly. Dayton, OH: Ohio Psychology Press, 1990.

The College Comparison Guide, Killiaen V. Townsend. Athens, GA: Agee Publishers, 1992.

The College Costs and Financial Aid Handbook, College Board Staff. New York: The College Board, annual.

College Financial Aid Annual, College Research Group of Concord, MA. New York: Prentice Hall, annual.

The College Guide for Parents, Charles Shields. New York: The College Board, rev. 1988.

The College Handbook. New York: The College Board, revised regularly.

College Planning for Gifted Students, 2nd ed., Sandra L. Berger. Reston, VA: Council for Exceptional Children, 1994.

Directory of Internships, Work Experience Programs and On-the-Job Training Opportunities, 2nd ed. Santa Monica, CA: Ready Reference Press.

Four Years: A Knucklehead's Guide to College Life, Russ Clemenza. Midland Park, NJ: Knuthouse, rev. 1990.

Free Money for College: A Guide to More Than 1000 Grants and Scholarships for Undergraduate Study, 3rd ed., Laurie Blum. New York: Facts on File, 1994.

Getting into College: A Guide for Students and Parents, Frank Leana. New York: Farrar, Strauss, & Giroux, 1990.

The Gourman Report: A Rating of Undergraduate Programs in American and International Universities, 7th ed., Jack Gourman. Los Angeles, CA: National Education Standards, 1989.

How to Prepare for the American College Testing Assessment-Act Program, 9th ed., George Ehrenhaft, et al. Hauppauge, NY: Barron's Educational Series, 1991.

Index of Majors and Graduate Degrees. New York: The College Board, annual.

Insider's Guide to the Colleges, Yale Daily News Staff, ed. New York: St. Martin's Press, annual.

National Guide to Educational Credit for Training Programs, American Council on Education. Phoenix, AZ: Oryx Press, rev. 1994.

Peterson's Competitive Colleges, 1994–95, 3rd ed., Susan C. Dilts, ed. Princeton, NJ: Peterson's Guides, 1994.

Peterson's Guide to College Admissions: Getting into the College of Your Choice, 5th ed., R. Fred Zuker. Princeton, NJ: Peterson's Guides, 1991.

Peterson's Guide to Graduate and Professional Programs, Book 1: An Overview, Amy Lefferts, ed. Princeton, NJ: Peterson's Guides, revised regularly.

Peterson's Guide to Two-Year Colleges, Susan Dilts, ed. Princeton, NJ: Peterson's Guides, revised regularly.

Peterson's Paying Less for College, 12th ed. Princeton, NJ: Peterson's Guides, 1994.

Student Access Guide to America's Top 100 Internships, 1995, Mark Oldman. New York: Random House, 1994.

Students, Courses, and Jobs: The Relationship Between Higher Education and the Labor Market, J. L. Brennan. Washington, DC: Taylor and Francis, 1993.

A Student's Guide to College Admissions: Everything Your Guidance Counselor Has No Time to Tell You, Harlow Unger. New York: Facts on File, rev. 1991.

The Ultimate College Shopper's Guide, Heather Evans and Deidre Sullivan. Redding, MA: Addison-Wesley, 1992.

Vocational Education for People with Handicaps, Robert Gaylord-Ross. Mountain View, CA: Mayfield, 1988.

Vocational Education in the Nineteen Nineties II: A Sourcebook for Strategies, Methods, and Materials, Craig Anderson and Lary C. Rampp. Ann Arbor, MI: Prakken Publications, 1993.

Vocational Education: Status in 2-Year Colleges and Early Signs of Change. Upland, PA: Diane Publishing Company, 1994.

Career Goals

Recommended

Personal Career Consultant: A Step-by-Step Guide to Finding a Successful and Satisfying Career, Lehman and Shapiro. New York: Prentice Hall, 1988.

What Color Is Your Parachute?, Richard N. Bolles. Berkeley, CA: Ten Speed Press, revised annually. One of the best sources for career changers and job hunters. Workbook style with exercises to identify skills and interests. Provides comprehensive list of sources including books, agencies, and associations.

Career Anchors: Discovering Your Real Values, Edgar H. Schein. San Diego, CA: Pfeiffer & Co., rev. 1990.

Career Choices: A Guide for Teens and Young Adults, Mindy Bingham and Sandy Stryker. Santa Barbara, CA: Academic Innovations, 1990.

Career Choices and Changes: A Guide for Discovering Who You Are, What You Want, and How to Get It, Mindy Bingham and Sandy Stryker. Santa Monica, CA: Academic Innovations, 1992.

Career Development: Taking Charge of Your Career, 2nd ed., Monica E. Breidenbach. Englewood Cliffs, NJ: Prentice Hall, 1992.

Career Directions, Donna J. Yena. Burr Ridge, IL: Richard D. Irwin, Inc., 1993.

Career Exploration: A Self-Paced Approach, 2nd ed., Charlie Mitchell, et al. Dubuque, IA: Kendall/Hunt, 1992.

The Career Finder: Pathways to Over 1500 Entry-Level Jobs, Lester Schwartz and Irv Brechner. New York: Ballantine Books, 1990.

Career Planning, Martin Mini. Dubuque, IA: Kendall/Hunt, 1994.

Career Planning and Development for College Students and Recent Graduates, John E. Steele and Marilyn S. Morgan. Lincolnwood, IL: NTC Publishing Group, 1991.

Career Planning Q's and A's: A Handbook for Students, Parents, and Professionals, Paul Phifer. Garrett Park, MD: Garrett Park Press, 1990.

Career Planning Today, Randall Powell. Dubuque, IA: Kendall/Hunt, 1994.

Career Workbook: A Tool for Self-Discovery, Marcia A. Perkins-Reed. Portland, OR: High Flight Press, 1989.

Careers Checklist, Arlene S. Hirsch. Lincolnwood, IL: NTC Publishing Group, 1991.

Chronicle Career Index 1994–95, Harriet Scarry, ed. Moravia, NY: Chronicle Guidance Publications, 1994.

College Board Guide to Jobs and Career Planning, 2nd ed., Joyce Slayton Mitchell. New York: College Board, 1994.

College Majors and Careers: A Resource Guide for Effective Life Planning, Phil Phifer. Garrett Park, MD: Garrett Park Press, rev. 1993.

Discover What You're Best At, Barry Gale. New York: Simon & Schuster, rev. 1990.

Guide to Careers Without College, Kathleen S. Abrams. New York: Watts, 1988.

Self-Assessment and Career Development, 3rd ed., James G. Clawson, et al. Englewood Cliffs, NJ: Prentice Hall, 1991.

Getting the Job and Getting Ahead

Recommended

The Complete Job-Search Handbook, Howard Figler. New York: Henry Holt & Co., rev. and expanded 1988. Basic career skills are described and their development and use explained; a positive approach with helpful tips.

The After College Guide to Life, Carole B. Everett and Tracy C. Harkins. Severna Park, MD: Alcove Press, 1993.

Almanac of American Employers, Jack W. Plunkett. Boerne, TX: Corporate Jobs Outlook, rev. 1993.

Fast Track to the Best Job: How to Launch a Successful Career Right Out of College, Bruce J. Bloom. Scarsdale, NY: Blazer Books, 1991.

From School to Work, J. J. Littrell. South Holland, IL: Goodheart-Willcox Co., 1991.

Get the Job You Want: Successful Strategies for Selling Yourself in the Job Market, Signe A. Dayhoff. New Boston, NH: Brick House Publishing, 1990.

Getting Hired in the 'Nineties, 2nd ed., Vicki Spina. Schaumburg, IL: Corporate Image Publications, 1992.

Getting the Job You Want . . . Now!, David H. Roper. New York: Warner Books, 1994.

Job-Finder's Workbook, Chet Muklewicz and Michael Bender. Austin, TX: PRO-ED, 1988.

Job Hotlines U.S.A. 1994–95: The National Telephone Directory of Employer Joblines, Steven A. Wood. Harleysville, PA: Career Communications.

Job Hunter's Yellow Pages, 1994–95: The National Directory of Employment Services, Stephen A. Wood. Harleysville, PA: Career Communications Group.

Jobsearch: The Complete Manual for Job Seekers, 2nd ed., H. Lee Rust. New York: AMACOM, 1990.

Job Search Handbook: The Basics of a Professional Job Search, John Noble. Boston: Adams, Inc., 1988.

Job Search Organizer, Jack O'Brien. Washington, DC: Miranda Associates, 1990.

Job Search That Works, Rick Lamplugh. Los Altos, CA: Crisp Publications, 1991.

Job Seeker's Guide to Private-Public Companies, 4 vols., Charity A. Dorgan. Detroit: Gale, 1993–1995.

Job Seeker's Guide to Success, Atley Host and Cheryl McCann, eds. Minneapolis, MN: Discovery Press, 1990.

Job Seeker's Workbook, Lee A. Boerner. Menomonie, WI: Material Development Center, 1988.

Mentoring at Work: Developmental Relationships in Organizational Life, Kathy E. Kram. Lanham, MD: University Press of America, 1988.

The Student's Guide to Finding a Superior Job, 2nd ed., William A. Cohen. San Diego, CA: Pfeiffer & Co., 1993.

Surviving in the Workplace, Earl Harrell and Cassandra Harrell. Milwaukee: ET Publishing Co., 1993.

Telesearch: Direct Dial the Best Job of Your Life, John Truitt. Ann Arbor, MI: Books Demand UMI.

Work-At-Home Sourcebook, 5th ed., Lynie Arden. Boulder, CO: Live Oak Publications, 1994.

Resumes and Interviews

Recommended

Damn Good Resume Guide, Yana Parker. Berkeley, CA: Ten Speed Press, rev. 1989. Describes how to write a functional resume.

Job Resumes, J. I. Biegeleisen. New York: Berkley Publishing Group, 1991.

The Perfect Resume, Max Eggert. Avenel, NJ: Random House Value, rev. 1994.

Better Resumes for Executives and Professionals, 2nd ed., Robert F. Wilson. Hauppauge, NY: Barron's Educational Series, 1991.

Complete Resume Guide, 4th ed., Marian Faux. New York: Prentice Hall General Reference & Travel, 1991.

Designing Creative Resumes, Gregg Berryman. Los Altos, CA: Crisp Publications, rev. 1991.

Job Interviews, McVey and Associates Staff. Englewood Cliffs, NJ: Cambridge Books, 1988.

Job Interviews That Mean Business, David R. Eyler. New York: Random House, 1992.

Knock 'Em Dead: The Ultimate Job Seeker's Handbook, Martin J. Yate. Boston: Adams, rev. 1994.

Resume Adviser: How to Write and Design a Professional Resume, Thomas M. Sherman and Craig A. Stephen. Scottsdale, AZ: Barrister House, 1992.

Resume Handbook, 2nd ed., BMCC Coop Staff. Dubuque, IA: Kendall/Hunt, 1993.

Resume Handbook, 2nd ed., Arthur Rosenberg and David Hizer. Boston: Adams, Inc., 1990.

The Resume Kit, 2nd ed., Richard H. Beatty. New York: John Wiley & Sons, 1991.

Resume Power: Selling Yourself on Paper, Tom Washington. Bellevue, WA: Mount Vernon Press, 1990.

Resume Writing: A Comprehensive How-to-Do-It Guide, 4th ed. Burdette E. Bostwick. New York: John Wiley & Sons, 1990.

Resume Writing Made Easy, 4th ed., Lola M. Coxford. Gorsuch Scarisbrick, 1991.

Resumes for Better Jobs, 6th. ed., Lawrence D. Brennan. Englewood Cliffs, NJ: Prentice Hall, 1994.

Resumes That Work, 2nd ed., Loretta D. Foxman. New York: John Wiley & Sons, 1992.

Successful Interviewing, Andrew Ambraziejus. Stamford, CT: Longmeadow Press, 1992.

Your Resume: Key to a Better Job, 5th ed., Leonard Corwen. New York: Prentice Hall General Reference & Travel, 1993.

Mid-Career Options

Recommended

Career Change: Everything You Need to Know to Meet New Challenges and Take Control of Your Career. Lincolnwood, IL: NTC Publishing Group, 1995.

Career Burnout: Causes and Cures, Ayala Pines and Elliot Aronson. New York: Free Press, 1988.

Career Redirections for Adults. Portland, OR: Northwest Regional Educational Library.

Careering and Re-Careering for the 1990's: The Complete Guide to Planning Your Future, 2nd ed., Ronald L. Krannich. Manassas, VA: Impact, 1991.

Getting a Job After 50, John S. Morgan. Princeton, NJ: Petrocelli Books, 1990.

Guide for the Employee Who Is Losing His or Her Job, Dorri Jacobs. New York: Programs on Change, 1992.

Guide for the Employee Who Is to Be Relocated, Dorri Jacobs. New York: Programs on Change, 1992.

Guide for the Employee Who Is Up for a Promotion, 3rd ed., Dorri Jacobs. New York: Programs on Change, 1992.

Equality of Opportunity

Recommended

Coping with Sexual Harassment, Beryl Black, ed. New York: The Rosen Publishing Group, rev. 1992. Helpful in giving direct ways to respond to and prevent sexual harassment at work.

Routes into the Mainstream: Career Choices of Women and Minorities, Sue E. Berryman. Columbus, OH: Center On Education and Training For Employment, 1988.

The Black Resource Guide, 10th ed. Washington, DC: Black Resource Guide, 1992.

Coping with Discrimination, Gabrielle Edwards. New York: The Rosen Publishing Group, rev. 1992.

Directory of Career Resources for Minorities. Santa Monica, CA: Ready Reference Press.

Equal Opportunity. Hauppauge, NY: Equal Opportunity Publications, published 3 times a year.

Every Woman's Guide to Career Success, Denise Dudley. Mission, KS: Skill Path Publications, rev. 1991.

Exploring Non-Traditional Jobs for Women, Rose Neufield. New York: The Rosen Publishing Group, rev. 1989.

Financial Aid for Minorities. Garrett Park, MD: Garrett Park Press, 1994.

Financial Aid for the Disabled and Their Families, 1994–1996, 6th ed., Gail A. Schlachter and R. David Weber. San Carlos, CA: Reference Services Press, 1994.

Resume Guide for Women of the Nineties, Kim Marino. Berkeley, CA: Ten Speed Press, 1992.

Women and Work, Susan Bullock. Atlantic Highlands, NJ: Humanities Press, 1994.

Lists and Indexes of Career and Vocational Information

Career Index, Gretchen S. Baldauf. Westport, CT: Greenwood Press, 1990.

The Career Source Encyclopedia, Career Associates Staff. Danbury, CT: Grolier, 1993.

Chronicle Career Index. Moravia, NY: Chronicle Guidance Publications, annual publication.

Dictionary of Holland Occupational Codes (DHOC), 2nd ed., Gary D. Gottfredson and John L. Holland. Lutz, FL: Psychological Assessment Resources, 1989.

Dictionary of Occupational Titles, United States Department of Labor. Washington, DC: United States Government Printing Office, rev. 1991.

Monthly Catalog of United States Government Publications. Washington, DC: United States Government Printing Office, monthly publication.

Vertical File Index. New York: Wilson, monthly publication.

Where the Jobs Are: A Comprehensive Directory of 1200 Journals Listing Career Opportunities, S. Norman Feingold and Glenda Ann Hansard-Winkler. Garrett Park, MD: Garrett Park Press, 1989.

Where to Start Career Planning: Essential Resource Guide for Career Planning and Job Hunting, 8th ed., Pamela L. Feodoroff and Carolyn Lloyd Lindquist. Princeton, NJ: Peterson's Guides (distr.), 1991.

General Career Information—Audiovisual Materials

Exploring the Working World

Career Assessment. Video; student worksheets; guide. Charleston, WV: Cambridge Job Search.

Career Choice: A Lifelong Process. Video; guide. Mount Kisco, NY: Guidance Associates.

Career Cluster Decisions. Video; guide. Charleston, WV: Cambridge Job Search.

Career Exploration: A Job Seeker's Guide to the OOH, DOT, and GOE. Video. Charleston, WV: Cambridge Job Search.

Career Goals: The Window to Success. Video; student workbook. Mansfield, OH: Opportunities for Learning, Inc.

Career Plan. Video; guide. Charleston, WV: Cambridge Job Search.

Career Planning: Putting Your Skills to Work. 2 videos; guide. Mansfield, OH: Opportunities for Learning, Inc.

Career Planning Steps. Video. Charleston, WV: Cambridge Job Search.

Career Self-Assessment: Where Do You Fit? Video; guide. Mount Kisco, NY: Guidance Associates.

Career Values: What Really Matters to You? Video; guide. Mount Kisco, NY: Guidance Associates.

Investigating the World of Work. Video; manual. Charleston, WV: Cambridge Job Search.

Jobs for the 21st Century. Video; guide. Mount Kisco, NY: Guidance Associates.

Kaleidoscope of Careers. 5 videos; manual. Mansfield, OH: Opportunities for Learning, Inc.

Learning for Earning. Video; guide. Charleston, WV: Cambridge Job Search.

Me and Jobs. Video; student workbooks; manual. Mansfield, OH: Opportunities for Learning, Inc.

New Tomorrows. Video. Mansfield, OH: Opportunities for Learning, Inc.

Occupational Preparation. Video; manual. Charleston, WV: Cambridge Job Search.

Preparing for the Jobs of the 1990s: What You Should Know. Video; guide. Mount Kisco, NY: Guidance Associates.

School-to-Work Transition. Video; guide. Charleston, WV: Cambridge Job Search.

Self-Awareness and Your Career Options. Video; manual. Charleston, WV: Cambridge Job Search.

Setting Career Goals the Video Way. Video. Charleston, WV: Cambridge Job Search.

The Ten Fastest Growing Careers: Jobs for the Future. Video; guide. Mount Kisco, NY: Guidance Associates.

Voyage: An Introduction to Career/Life Planning. Video. Mansfield, OH: Opportunities for Learning, Inc.

Where Do You Want to Work? Video. Mansfield, OH: Opportunities for Learning, Inc.

Why Work? Working for a Living. Video. New York: Educational Design, Inc.

Your Future: Planning Through Career Exploration. Video. Bloomington, IL: Meridian Education Corporation.

Your Interests: Related to Work Activities. Video. Bloomington, IL: Meridian Education Corporation.

Your Temperaments: Related to Work Situations. Video. Bloomington, IL: Meridian Education Corporation.

Getting the Job and Getting Ahead

Communicating on the Job. Video. Bowling Green, KY: Southern School Media.

The Complete Video Guide to Job Hunting. Video. Charleston, WV: Cambridge Job Search.

Dialing for Jobs. Video. Mansfield, OH: Opportunities for Learning, Inc.

Finding a Company That's Right for You. Video. Mansfield, OH: Opportunities for Learning, Inc.

Getting a Good Start. Video; guide. Bloomington, IL: Meridian Education Corporation.

Getting Along on the Job: Interpersonal Work Skills. Video. Mansfield, OH: Opportunities for Learning, Inc.

Given the Opportunity: A Guide to Interaction in the Workplace. Video. Bloomington, IL: Meridian Education Corporation.

If At First . . . How To Get a Job and Keep It. Video. Mount Kisco, NY: Vocational Media Associates.

If You Really Want to Get Ahead . . . Video. Mansfield, OH: Opportunities for Learning, Inc.

The Interview. Video. Olathe, KS: RMI Media Productions.

Interview Techniques and Resume Tips for the Job Applicant. Video. Mansfield, OH: Opportunities for Learning, Inc.

Job Survival Kit. Video. Charleston, WV: Cambridge Job Search.

Job Survival Skills: Working With Others. Video. Mount Kisco, NY: Vocational Media Associates.

Keeping Your Job. Video. Olathe, KS: RMI Media Productions.

Learning Seed's Job Search Strategies. Video. Lake Zurich, IL: The Learning Seed.

Locating Potential Employers. Video. Olathe, KS: RMI Media Productions.

Making It On Your First Job. Video. Olathe, KS: RMI Media Productions.

Moving Up or Out. Video. Lake Zurich, IL: The Learning Seed.

Power Interviewing. Video. Charleston, WV: Cambridge Job Search.

Resumes That Get Interviews. Video. Mount Kisco, NY: Vocational Media Associates.

Sell Yourself: Successful Job Interviewing. Video. Lake Zurich, IL: The Learning Seed.

Shhh! I'm Finding a Job: The Library and Your Self-Directed Job Search. Video; guide. Charleston, WV: Cambridge Job Search.

Tough Times: Finding the Jobs. Video. Charleston, WV: Cambridge Job Search.

Unemployment: A Plan of Action. Video. Mansfield, OH: Opportunities for Learning, Inc.

The Video Resume Writer. Video. Charleston, WV: Cambridge Job Search.

What Employers Expect. Video. Bowling Green, KY: Southern School Media.

Your Resume and Other Job Search Skills. Video; guide. Mansfield, OH: Opportunities for Learning, Inc.

General Career Information—Computer Software

The Cambridge Career Counseling System. 2 disks for IBM. Charleston, WV: Cambridge Job Search.

Career Area Interest Checklist. Disk for Apple or IBM. Bloomington, IL: Meridian Education Corporation.

Career Compass. Disk for IBM. Bloomington, IL: Meridian Education Corporation.

Career Compusearch. Disk for Apple or IBM. Bloomington, IL: Meridian Education Corporation.

Career Counselor. Disk for Apple. Mansfield, OH: Opportunities for Learning, Inc.

Career Development Plan. 2 disks for IBM. Charleston, WV: Cambridge Job Search.

Career Directions. Disk for IBM. Charleston, WV: Cambridge Job Search.

Career Finder. Disk for Apple or IBM. Bloomington, IL: Meridian Education Corporation.

Career Match. Disk for Apple or IBM. Charleston, WV: Cambridge Job Search.

Career Scan V. Disk for Apple or IBM. Mansfield, OH: Opportunities for Learning, Inc.

Career System 2000. 7 disks for Apple. Mansfield, OH: Opportunities for Learning, Inc.

Careers of the Future. 3 disks for Apple or IBM. Mansfield, OH: Opportunities for Learning, Inc.

Computerized Career Assessment and Planning. 8 disks for Apple. Mansfield, OH: Opportunities for Learning, Inc.

Computerized Career Information System. 5 disks for Apple or IBM. Mansfield, OH: Opportunities for Learning, Inc.

Computerized Dictionary of Occupational Titles. 16 disks for IBM. Largo, FL: Careers, Inc.

Emerging Occupations. Disk for Apple or IBM. Mansfield, OH: Opportunities for Learning, Inc.

Encyclopedia of Careers and Vocational Guidance. CD-ROM. Largo, FL: Careers, Inc.

How to Win Your Job Search. Disk for IBM. Charleston, WV: Cambridge Job Search.

Interview Skills of the Future. CD-ROM for Apple. Charleston, WV: Cambridge Job Search.

Job Hunter's Survival Kit. 2 disks for Apple or IBM. Mansfield, OH: Opportunities for Learning, Inc.

Job-O. Disk for Apple or IBM. Mansfield, OH: Opportunities for Learning, Inc.

Job Search Skills for the 21st Century. CD-ROM for Apple. Charleston, WV: Cambridge Job Search.

Jobs in Today's World. Disk for Apple or IBM. Mansfield, OH: Opportunities for Learning, Inc.

Life and Career Planning: The Future Is Yours. Disk for Apple or IBM. Mansfield, OH: Opportunities for Learning, Inc.

MSPI: Exploring Career Goals and College Courses. Disk for Apple or IBM. Charleston, WV: Cambridge Job Search.

Multimedia Career Center. 2 CD-ROMs. Bloomington, IL: Meridian Education Corporation.

The Multimedia Career Path. CD-ROM for Apple. Charleston, WV: Cambridge Job Search.

The Multimedia Guide to Occupational Exploration. 2 CD-ROMs. Bloomington, IL: Meridian Education Corporation.

Occu-Facts 2000. Disk for Apple or IBM. Largo, FL: Careers, Inc.

Occupational Outlook Handbook on CD-ROM. CD-ROM for IBM. Largo, FL: Careers, Inc.

The Perfect Resume. 2 disks for IBM. Mansfield, OH: Opportunities for Learning, Inc.

Resume Express: The Multimedia Guide. CD-ROM for Apple. Charleston, WV: Cambridge Job Search.

The Right Job Application. Disk for IBM. Charleston, WV: Cambridge Job Search.

Successful Interviewing. Disk for Apple or IBM. Mansfield, OH: Opportunities for Learning, Inc.

Career and Vocational Information on Health

General

Books

Recommended

AHA Guide to the Health Care Field. Washington, DC: American Hospital Association, updated annually. Directory of hospitals throughout the United States. Lists hospital administrators, numbers of beds, occupancy percentages, and services available.

Careers in Health Care. Lincolnwood, IL: NTC Publishing Group, 1995. Provides job descriptions, educational qualifications, and salary information for more than 80 jobs.

Chronicle Health Occupations Guidebook, Paul Downes, ed. Moravia, NY: Chronicle Guidance Publications, rev. 1994.

Brief Introduction to Health Occupations, Shirley Badasch. Englewood Cliffs, NJ: Prentice Hall, 1994.

Careers in Health and Fitness, Jackie Heron. New York: The Rosen Publishing Group, rev. 1990.

Careers in Health Care, Rachel Epstein. New York: Chelsea House, 1989.

Diversified Health Occupations, 3rd ed., Louise Simmers. Albany, NY: Delmar Publishers, 1993.

Health Careers Today, Resource Kit. St. Louis, MO: Mosby-Year Book, 1991.

Health Occupations: Excerpts from the Occupational Outlook Handbook, Englewood Cliffs, NJ: Prentice Hall, 1993.

Health Occupations: Explorations and Career Planning, Birchenall and Streight. St. Louis, MO: Mosby-Year Book, 1989.

Job Opportunities in Health Care, 1994. Princeton, NJ: Peterson's Guides.

New Careers in Hospitals, Lois S. Sigel. New York: The Rosen Publishing Group, 1990.

Opportunities in Hospital Administration Careers, Donald Snook. Lincolnwood, IL: NTC Publishing Group, 1989.

Audiovisual Materials

Career Success Series: Medicine. Video. Mansfield, OH: Opportunities for Learning, Inc.

Careers in Health. Video. Bloomington, IL: Meridian Education Corporation.

Careers in Health Services: Occupations for You. Video; guide. Mount Kisco, NY: Guidance Associates.

Health-Related Cluster. Video. Mount Kisco, NY: Vocational Media Associates.

Health Services Careers. Video. Olathe, KS: RMI Media Productions.

Medicine. Video. New York: Educational Design, Inc.

School to Work: Health Occupations. Video. Bloomington, IL: Meridian Education Corporation.

Technical Careers in Health. Video. Bloomington, IL: Meridian Education Corporation.

Dentists, Dental Assistants, and Dental Technicians

Books

Recommended

Careers in Dentistry: Is It for You, Adele S. Doherty. Brentwood, TN: DSH Publishing Company, 1992.

Career Directions for Dental Hygienists, Regina D. Thomas. Holmdel, NJ: Career Directions Press, 1992.

Certified Dental Technician (CDT), Jack Rudman. Syosset, NY: National Learning Corporation, 1993.

Opportunities in Dental Care Careers, Bonnie Kendall. Lincolnwood, IL: NTC Publishing Group, 1991.

Audiovisual Materials

Career Profiles: Health Related Fields—Dental Assistant. Video; guide. Mansfied, OH: Opportunities for Learning, Inc.

Career Profiles: Health Related Fields—Dental Laboratory Technician. Video; guide. Mansfield, OH: Opportunities for Learning, Inc.

Career Success Videos: Dental Hygienics. Video. Mansfield, OH: Opportunities for Learning, Inc.

Video Career Library: Allied Health Fields. Video. Bowling Green, KY: Southern School Media. Includes profiles of dental assistant, dental hygienist, and dental laboratory technician.

Video Career Library: Medicine & Related Fields. Video. Bowling Green, KY: Southern School Media. Includes profile of dentist.

Medical Assistants, Technicians, and Technologists

Books

Recommended

Opportunities in Paramedical Careers, Alex Kacen. Lincolnwood, IL: NTC Publishing Group, 1994. Employment outlook, earnings, educational requirements, and educational opportunities are all considered.

The Administrative Medical Assistant, 3rd ed., Mary E. Kinn. Philadelphia: W. B. Saunders Co., 1993.

Opportunities in Medical Imaging Careers, Clifford J. Sherry. New York: VCH Publishers, 1993.

Audiovisual Materials

Career Encounters: Radiology. Video. Charleston, WV: Cambridge Job Search.

Day in a Career Series: Medical Health Aide. Video. Charleston, WV: Cambridge Job Search.

Day in a Career Series: X-Ray Technologist. Video. Charleston, WV: Cambridge Job Search.

Medical Assisting Profession. Video. Mansfield, OH: Opportunities for Learning, Inc.

Medical Assisting Video Series. 12 videos. Albany, NY: Delmar Publishers.

Tech Prep and Health Occupations. Video. Bloomington, IL: Meridian Education Corporation. Includes profiles of surgical technologist, medical assistant, medical records technician, and radiologic technologist.

Technical Careers in Health. Video. Bloomington, IL: Meridian Education Corporation.

Vocational Visions: Health-Related Cluster. Video. Mount Kisco, NY: Guidance Associates. Includes profiles of surgical technician and medical assistant.

Nursing and Dietetics

Books

Recommended

Your Career in Nursing, Lila Anastas. New York: National League for Nursing, 2nd ed., 1988. A career guide for nursing students and recent graduates.

Accreditation-Approval Manual for Dietetic Education Programs, 2nd ed., The American Dietetic Association Staff. Chicago: American Dietetic Association, 1991.

Developing Your Career in Nursing, Desmond Cormack, ed. New York: Chapman & Hall, 1990.

Directions in Community Health Nursing, J. Sullivan. Cambridge, MA: Blackwell Science Publications, 1989.

Exploring Careers in Nursing, Jackie Heron. New York: The Rosen Publishing Group, rev. 1990.

Guide to Surviving Nursing School, Regan. Springhouse, PA: Springhouse Publishing Company, 1991.

Mosby's Tour Guide to Nursing School: A Student's Road Survival Kit, 3rd ed., Melodie Chenevert. St. Louis, MO: Mosby-Year Book, 1994.

Nursing School Entrance Examinations, 12th ed., Marion F. Gooding. New York: Arco Test Publishing, 1993.

Opportunities in Nursing Careers, Keville Frederickson. Lincolnwood, IL: NTC Publishing Group, 1989.

Audiovisual Materials

Career Encounters: Nursing. Video. Mansfield, OH: Opportunities for Learning, Inc.

Career Profiles: Health Related Fields—Nursing: RN and LPN. Video; guide. Mansfield, OH: Opportunities for Learning, Inc.

Career Success Series: Nursing and Paramedics.Video. Mansfield, OH: Opportunities for Learning, Inc.

Nursing: A Career for All Reasons. Video. Mansfield, OH: Opportunities for Learning, Inc.

Nursing Assistant Procedures Video Series. 12 videos. Albany, NY: Delmar Publishers.

Work-A-Day America: Nursing Aides. Video. Mansfield, OH: Opportunities for Learning, Inc.

Pharmacy

Books

Opportunities in Pharmacy Careers, Fred B. Gable. Lincolnwood, IL: NTC Publishing Group, 1990.

Pharmacy College Admission Test (PCAT), Jack Rudman. Syosset, NY: National Learning Corporation, 1991.

Pharmacy College Admission Test Student Guide, David M. Tarlow. St. Louis, MO: Datar Publishing, 1993.

Pharmacy Education and Careers: The APhA Resource Book, Vicki L. Meade, ed. Washington, DC: American Pharmaceutical Association, 1988.

Audiovisual Materials

Career Success Series: Physicians and Health Practitioners. Video. Mansfield, OH: Opportunities for Learning, Inc.

The Video Career Library: Physicians and Health Practitioners. Video. Olathe, KS: RMI Media Productions. Includes profile of pharmacist.

Physicians and Specialized Practitioners

Books

Recommended

Exploring Careers in Medicine, Carolyn Simpson and Penelope Hall. New York: The Rosen Publishing Group, 1993. Working conditions, career advancement, job duties, and areas of specialization are all considered.

Barron's Guide to Medical and Dental Schools, 6th ed., Saul Wischnitzer. Hauppauge, NY: Barron's Educational Series, 1993.

Careers in Medicine: Traditional and Alternative Opportunities, T. Donald Rucker and Martin D. Keller. Garrett Park, MD: Garrett Park Press, 1990.

Opportunities in Physician Careers, Jan Sugar-Webb. Lincolnwood, IL: NTC Publishing Group, 1992.

Opportunities in Psychology Careers, Donald Super and Charles M. Super. Lincolnwood, IL: NTC Publishing Group, 1994.

Optometry, Frank M. Kitchell. Lincolnwood, IL: NTC Publishing Group, 1991.

Working in Partnership: Clinicians and Careers in the Management of Longstanding Mental Illness, Liz Kuipers and Paul Bebbington. Newton, MA: Butterworth-Heinemann, 1991.

Audiovisual Materials

Career Encounters: Physician. Video. Charleston, WV: Cambridge Job Search.

Career Encounters: Podiatric Medicine. Video. Charleston, WV: Cambridge Job Search.

Career Encounters: Psychology. Video. Charleston, WV: Cambridge Job Search.

Career Encounters: Radiology. Video. Charleston, WV: Cambridge Job Search.

Exploring Careers in Psychology. Video. Mount Kisco, NY: Guidance Associates.

Physicians & Health Practitioners. Video. Largo, FL: Careers, Inc.

Video Career Library: Medicine & Related Fields. Video. Bowling Green, KY: Southern School Media.

Therapists

Books

Careers in Occupational Therapy, Margaret F. Brown. New York: The Rosen Group, 1989.

Opportunities in Occupational Therapy Careers, Marie-Louise Franciscus, Marguerite Abbot, and Zona R. Weeks. Lincolnwood, IL: NTC Publishing Group, 1994.

Audiovisual Materials

Career Profiles: Health Related Fields—Occupational Therapy Assistant. Video; guide. Mansfield, OH: Opportunities for Learning, Inc.

Video Career Library: Careers in Allied Health I. Video. Bloomington, IL: Meridian Education Corporation. Includes profiles of physical therapist and occupational therapist.

Vocational Visions Career Series: Physical Therapist. Video. Charleston, WV: Cambridge Job Search.

Related Health Careers

Books

Recommended

Being a Health Unit Coordinator, 3rd ed., Kay Cox. Englewood Cliffs, NJ: Prentice Hall, 1990. Describes on-the-job experiences.

Allied Health Education Directory, 19th ed. Chicago, IL: American Medical Association, 1993.

Allied Health Professions Admission Test (A.H.P.A.T.): The Betz Guide, Aftab Hassan. Rockville, MD: Betz Publishing Company, 1994.

Health Careers Today, Gerdin. St. Louis, MO: Mosby-Year Book, 1990.

Health Careers: Undergraduate Careers in the Health Professions, Michael Beard and Yasmen Simonian. Dubuque, IA: Kendall-Hunt, 1994.

Healthcare Career Directory—Medical-Technical, Bradley J. Morgan and Joseph M. Palmisano, eds. Detroit, MI: Gale Research, 1994.

Paramedical Careers, 6 vols. Santa Monica, CA. Ready Reference Press, 1988.

Audiovisual Materials

Health Information Services. Video. Mansfield, OH: Opportunities for Learning, Inc.

Video Career Library: Allied Health Fields. Video. Bowling Green, KY: Southern School Media.

Directory of Institutions Offering Career Training

The information in this directory was generated from the IPEDS (Integrated Postsecondary Education Data System) database of the U.S. Department of Education. It includes only regionally or nationally accredited institutions offering postsecondary occupational training in health. Because college catalogs and directories of colleges and universities are readily available elsewhere, this directory does not include institutions that offer only bachelor's and advanced degrees.

Dental Assistant Technology

ALABAMA

Community College of the Air Force
Maxwell Air Force Base
Montgomery 36112

ARIZONA

Apollo College
3870 North Oracle Rd.
Tucson 85705

Apollo College-Phoenix, Inc.
8503 North 27th Ave.
Phoenix 85051

Apollo College-Tri City, Inc.
630 West Southern Ave.
Mesa 85210

The Bryman School
4343 North 16th St.
Phoenix 85016

Institute of Medical and Dental
  Technology
20 East Main St.
Mesa 85201

The Laural School
2538 North Eighth St.
Phoenix 85006

CALIFORNIA

Allan Hancock College
800 South College Dr.
Santa Maria 93454

Citrus College
1000 West Foothill Blvd.
Glendora 91741-1899

Concorde Career Institute
4150 Lankershim Blvd.
North Hollywood 91602

Concorde Career Institute
123 Camino De La Reina
San Diego 92108

Concorde Career Institute
1290 North First St.
San Jose 95112

Concorde Career Institute
6850 Van Nuys Blvd.
Van Nuys 91405

Concorde Career Institute Campus
600 North Sierra Way
San Bernardino 92410

Diablo Valley College
321 Golf Club Rd.
Pleasant Hill 94523

Donald Vocational School
1833 West Eighth St.
Los Angeles 90057

Galen College of Medical and Dental
  Assistants
1325 North Wishon Ave.
Fresno 93728

Galen College of Medical and Dental
  Assistants
1604 Ford Ave.
Modesto 95350

Galen College of Medical and Dental
  Assistants
3746 West Mineral King
Visalia 93277

Huntington College of Dental Technology
7466 Edinger Ave.
Huntington Beach 92647

Institute of Business and Medical
  Technology
75-110 Saint Charles Place
Palm Desert 92260

National Education Center-Bryman
  Campus
1120 North Brookhurst St.
Anaheim 92801

National Education Center-Bryman
  Campus
5350 Atlantic Ave.
Long Beach 90805

National Education Center-Bryman
  Campus
1017 Wilshire Blvd.
Los Angeles 90017

National Education Center-Bryman
  Campus
3505 North Hart Ave.
Rosemead 91770

National Education Center-Bryman
  Campus
731 Market St.
San Francisco 94103

National Education Center-Bryman
  Campus
2015 Naglee Ave.
San Jose 95128

National Education Center-Bryman
  Campus
20835 Sherman Way
Winnetka 91306

Nova Institute of Health Technology
2400 South Western Ave.
Los Angeles 90018

Nova Institute of Health Technology
520 North Euclid Ave.
Ontario 91762

Nova Institute of Health Technology
11416 Whittier Blvd.
Whittier 90601

Orange Coast College
2701 Fairview Rd.
Costa Mesa 92626

San Joaquin Valley College
201 New Stine Rd.
Bakersfield 93309

San Joaquin Valley College
3333 North Bond
Fresno 93726

San Joaquin Valley College
8400 West Mineral King Ave.
Visalia 93291

Santa Rosa Junior College
1501 Mendocino Ave.
Santa Rosa 95401-4395

Southern California College of
  Medical-Dental Care
1717 South Brookhurst
Anaheim 92804

Western Career College
170 Bay Fair Mall
San Leandro 94578

COLORADO

Concorde Career Institute
770 Grant St.
Denver 80203

Front Range Community College
3645 West 112th Ave.
Westminster 80030

Heritage College of Health Careers
12 Lakeside Ln.
Denver 80212

CONNECTICUT

Huntington Institute, Inc.
193 Broadway
Norwich 06360

FLORIDA

Concorde Career Institute
7960 Arlington Expwy.
Jacksonville 32211

Concorde Career Institute
4202 West Spruce St.
Tampa 33607

Florida Community College at
  Jacksonville
501 West State St.
Jacksonville 32202

Palm Beach Community College
4200 Congress Ave.
Lake Worth 33461

Southern College
5600 Lake Underhill Rd.
Orlando 32807

GEORGIA

Albany Technical Institute
1021 Lowe Rd.
Albany 31708

Atlanta College of Medical Dental
  Careers
1240 West Peachtree St. NE
Atlanta 30309-2906

Medix Schools
2480 Windy Hill Rd.
Marietta 30067

IDAHO

American Institute of Health Technology,
  Inc.
6600 Emerald
Boise 83704

ILLINOIS

Kaskaskia College
27210 College Rd.
Centralia 62801

Parkland College
2400 West Bradley Ave.
Champaign 61821

VIP Schools, Inc.
600n McClurg Ct.
Chicago 60611-3044

INDIANA

Indiana University-Purdue University at
  Indianapolis
355 North Lansing
Indianapolis 46202

Professional Career Institute
2611 Waterfront Pkwy., East Dr.
Indianapolis 46214-2028

KANSAS

Bryan Institute
1004 South Oliver
Wichita 67218

LOUISIANA

Delta Schools, Inc.
4549 Johnston St.
Lafayette 70503

Delta Schools, Inc.
413 West Admiral Doyle
New Iberia 70560

Domestic Health Care Institute
4826 Jamestown Ave.
Baton Rouge 70808

Eastern College of Health Vocations
3540 I-10 Service Rd. S
Metairie 70001

Spencer College
2902 Florida St.
Baton Rouge 70802

MARYLAND

Medix Schools
1017 York Rd.
Towson 21204-9840

MASSACHUSETTS

National Education Center-Bryman
Campus
323 Boylston St.
Brookline 02146

Northeastern University
360 Huntington Ave.
Boston 02115

MICHIGAN

Delta College
University Center 48710

Ferris State University
901 South State St.
Big Rapids 49307

Grand Rapids Community College
143 Bostwick Ave. NE
Grand Rapids 49505

Grand Rapids Educational Center
1750 Woodworth NE
Grand Rapids 49505

Grand Rapids Educational Center
5349 West Main
Kalamazoo 49009

Ross Medical Education Center
1036 Gilbert St.
Flint 48532

Ross Medical Education Center
1188 North West Ave.
Jackson 49202

Ross Medical Education Center
913 West Holmes
Lansing 48910

Ross Medical Education Center
4054 Bay Rd.
Saginaw 48603

Ross Medical Education Center
26417 Hoover Rd.
Warren 48089

MINNESOTA

Concorde Career Institute, Inc.
12 North 12th St.
Minneapolis 55403

Lakeland Medical and Dental Academy
1402 West Lake St.
Minneapolis 55408

Northeast Metro Technical College
3300 Century Ave. N
White Bear Lake 55110

Range Technical College-Hibbing
Campus
2900 East Beltline
Hibbing 55746

MISSISSIPPI

Hinds Community College-Raymond
Campus
Raymond 39154

MISSOURI

Al-Med Academy
10963 Saint Charles Rock Rd.
Saint Louis 63074

Concorde Career Institute
3239 Broadway
Kansas City 64111

Missouri School for Doctors' Assistants
10121 Manchester Rd.
Saint Louis 63122

Saint Louis Community College-Forest
Park
5600 Oakland Ave.
Saint Louis 63110

NEVADA

American Academy for Career Education
3120 East Desert Inn Rd.
Las Vegas 89121

Professional Careers
3305 Spring Mountain Rd.
Las Vegas 89120

NEW HAMPSHIRE

New Hampshire Technical Institute
11 Institute Dr.
Concord 03301

NEW JERSEY

Berdan Institute
265 Rte. 46
Totowa 07512

Camden County College
P.O. Box 200
Blackwood 08012

Empire Technical School of New Jersey
576 Central Ave.
East Orange 07018

NEW YORK

Continental Dental Assistant School
633 Jefferson Rd.
Rochester 14623

Mandl School
254 West 54th St.
New York 10019

New York School for Medical and
Dental Assistants
116-16 Queens Blvd.
Forest Hills 11375

Techno-Dent Training Center
101 West 31st St.
New York 10001

NORTH CAROLINA

Alamance Community College
P.O. Box 8000
Graham 27253

Guilford Technical Community College
P.O. Box 309
Jamestown 27282

OHIO

Akron Medical-Dental Institute
733 West Market St.
Akron 44303

Aristotle Institute of Medical-Dental
Technology
5900 Westerville Rd.
Westerville 43081

Cleveland Institute of Dental-Medical
Assistants
1836 Euclid Ave.
Cleveland 44115

Cleveland Institute of Dental-Medical
Assistants
5564 Mayfield Rd.
Lyndhurst 44124

Cleveland Institute of Dental-Medical
Assistants
5733 Hopkins Rd.
Mentor 44060

Eastland Career Center
4465 South Hamilton Rd.
Groveport 43125

Institute of Medical-Dental Technology
375 Glensprings Dr.
Cincinnati 45246

OKLAHOMA

Bryan Institute
2843 East 51st St.
Tulsa 74105-1709

Kiamichi AVTS SD #7-Talihina Campus
Rte. 2 & Hwy. 63A, P.O. Box 1800
Talihina 74571

Metro Tech Vocational Technical Center
1900 Springlake Dr.
Oklahoma City 73111

OREGON

Apollo College-Portland, Inc.
2600 Southeast 98th Ave.
Portland 97266

College of America
921 Southwest Washington
Portland 97205

Lane Community College
4000 East 30th Ave.
Eugene 97405

Portland Community College
P.O. Box 19000
Portland 97280-0990

PENNSYLVANIA

Academy of Medical Arts and Business
279 Boas St.
Harrisburg 17102

Career Training Academy
703 Fifth Ave.
New Kensington 15068

Community College of Philadelphia
1700 Spring Garden St.
Philadelphia 19130

Delaware Valley Academy of Medical
and Dental Assistants
6539 Roosevelt Blvd.
Philadelphia 19149

Median School of Allied Health Careers
125 Seventh St.
Pittsburgh 15222-3400

RHODE ISLAND

Community College of Rhode Island
400 East Ave.
Warwick 02886-1805

TENNESSEE

Chattanooga State Technical Community
College
4501 Amnicola Hwy.
Chattanooga 37406

Memphis Area Vocational-Technical
School
550 Alabama Ave.
Memphis 38105-3799

Shelbyville State Area Vocational
Technical School
1405 Madison St.
Shelbyville 37160

TEXAS

Allied Health Careers
5424 Hwy. 290 W
Austin 78735

ATI Health Education Center
8150 Brookriver Dr.
Dallas 75247

ATI Health Education Center
1200 Summit Ave.
Fort Worth 76102

Bryan Institute
1719 Pioneer Pkwy. W
Arlington 76013

Career Centers of Texas El Paso, Inc.
8375 Burnham Dr.
El Paso 79907

San Antonio College of Medical and
Dental Assistants-Central
4205 San Pedro Ave.
San Antonio 78212

San Antonio College of Medical and
Dental Assistants-South
3900 North 23rd
McAllen 78501

Texas State Technical College-Waco
Campus
3801 Campus Dr.
Waco 76705

UTAH

American Institute of Medical-Dental
    Technology
1675 North 200 West
Provo 84604

Bryman School
1144 West 3300 South
Salt Lake City 84119-3330

Provo College
1450 West 820 North
Provo 84601

VIRGINIA

Career Development Center
605 Thimble Shoals
Newport News 23606

National Business College
1813 East Main St.
Salem 24153

Riverside Regional Medical
    Center-School of Professional Nursing
500 J Clyde Morris Blvd.
Newport News 23601

WASHINGTON

Bates Technical College
1101 South Yakima Ave.
Tacoma 98405

Bellingham Technical College
3028 Lindbergh Ave.
Bellingham 98225

Eton Technical Institute
209 East Casino Rd.
Everett 98204

Eton Technical Institute
31919 Sixth Ave. S
Federal Way 98063

Eton Technical Institute
3649 Frontage Rd.
Port Orchard 98366

Lake Washington Technical College
11605 132nd Ave. NE
Kirkland 98034

Seattle Vocational Institute
315 22nd Ave. S
Seattle 98144

Spokane Community College
North 1810 Greene Ave.
Spokane 99207

Trend College
North 214 Wall St.
Spokane 99201

WISCONSIN

Fox Valley Technical College
1825 North Bluemound Dr.
Appleton 54913-2277

Western Wisconsin Technical College
304 North Sixth St., P.O. Box 908
La Crosse 54602-0908

Dental Laboratory Technology

CALIFORNIA

California Vocational College
538 41st Ave.
San Francisco 94121

Dental Technology Institute
1937 West Chapman Ave.
Orange 92668

Huntington College of Dental Technology
7466 Edinger Ave.
Huntington Beach 92647

Nova Institute of Health Technology
11416 Whittier Blvd.
Whittier 90601

Simi Valley Adult School
3192 Los Angeles Ave.
Simi Valley 93065

ILLINOIS

Midwest Institute of Technology
3712 West Montrose Ave.
Chicago 60618

MICHIGAN

High-Tech Learning, Inc.
7531 East Eight Mile Rd.
Warren 48091

NEW YORK

Penaranda Institute of Dental School
40-17 82nd St.
Jackson Heights 11373

Techno-Dent Training Center
101 West 31st St.
New York 10001

TENNESSEE

Memphis Area Vocational-Technical
    School
550 Alabama Ave.
Memphis 38105-3799

TEXAS

ATI Health Education Center
8150 Brookriver Dr.
Dallas 75247

ATI Health Education Center
1200 Summit Ave.
Fort Worth 76102

Texas Dental Technology School
2414 Broadway Blvd.
Houston 77012-3612

Dental Hygiene Technology

ARIZONA

Phoenix College
1202 West Thomas Rd.
Phoenix 85013

CALIFORNIA

Cabrillo College
6500 Soquel Dr.
Aptos 95003

Foothill College
12345 El Monte Rd.
Los Altos Hills 94022

Pasadena City College
1570 East Colorado Blvd.
Pasadena 91106

Riverside Community College
4800 Magnolia Ave.
Riverside 92506-1299

West Los Angeles College
4800 Freshman Dr.
Culver 90230

CONNECTICUT

Tunxis Community College
Rtes. 6 and 177
Farmington 06032

University of Bridgeport
380 University Ave.
Bridgeport 06601

DELAWARE

Delaware Technical and Community
    College-Stanton-Wilmington
400 Stanton-Christiana Rd.
Newark 19702

FLORIDA

Miami-Dade Community College
300 Northeast Second Ave.
Miami 33132

Palm Beach Community College
4200 Congress Ave.
Lake Worth 33461

Pensacola Junior College
1000 College Blvd.
Pensacola 32504

Saint Petersburg Junior College
P.O. Box 13489
Saint Petersburg 33733

Santa Fe Community College
3000 Northwest 83rd St.
Gainesville 32601

GEORGIA

Darton College
2400 Gillionville Rd.
Albany 31707

Dekalb College
3251 Panthersville Rd.
Decatur 30034

Medical College of Georgia
1120 15th St.
Augusta 30912

ILLINOIS

Illinois Central College
One College Dr.
East Peoria 61635

Parkland College
2400 West Bradley Ave.
Champaign 61821

Prairie State College
202 Halsted St.
Chicago Heights 60411

Southern Illinois University-Carbondale
Carbondale 62901

William Rainey Harper College
1200 West Algonquin Rd.
Palatine 60067-7398

INDIANA

Indiana University-Northwest
3400 Broadway
Gary 46408

Indiana University-Purdue University at
    Indianapolis
355 North Lansing
Indianapolis 46202

KANSAS

Johnson County Community College
12345 College Blvd.
Overland Park 66210-1299

Wichita State University
1845 Fairmount
Wichita 67260

KENTUCKY

Lexington Community College
Cooper Dr.
Lexington 40506

LOUISIANA

Louisiana State University Medical
    Center
433 Bolivar St.
New Orleans 70112

MAINE

Westbrook College
716 Stevens Ave.
Portland 04103

MARYLAND

Allegany Community College
Willowbrook Rd.
Cumberland 21502

Baltimore City Community College
2901 Liberty Heights Ave.
Baltimore 21215

MASSACHUSETTS

Bristol Community College
777 Elsbree St.
Fall River 02720

Forsyth School for Dental Hygienists
140 the Fenway
Boston 02115

Middlesex Community College
Springs Rd.
Bedford 01730

MICHIGAN

Ferris State University
901 South State St.
Big Rapids 49307

Grand Rapids Community College
143 Bostwick Ave. NE
Grand Rapids 49505

Mott Community College
1401 East Court St.
Flint 48503

Oakland Community College
2480 Opdyke Rd.
Bloomfield Hills 48304-2266

University of Detroit-Mercy
P.O. Box 19900
Detroit 48219-0900

MINNESOTA

Normandale Community College
9700 France Ave. S
Bloomington 55431

MISSOURI

Saint Louis Community College-Forest
Park
5600 Oakland Ave.
Saint Louis 63110

NEW HAMPSHIRE

New Hampshire Technical Institute
11 Institute Dr.
Concord 03301

NEW JERSEY

Bergen Community College
400 Paramus Rd.
Paramus 07652

Camden County College
P.O. Box 200
Blackwood 08012

Middlesex County College
155 Mill Rd., P.O. Box 3050
Edison 08818-3050

Union County College
1033 Springfield Ave.
Cranford 07016

NEW MEXICO

University of New Mexico-Main Campus
Albuquerque 87131

NEW YORK

Broome Community College
P.O. Box 1017
Binghamton 13902

CUNY New York City Technical College
300 Jay St.
Brooklyn 11201

Erie Community College-North Campus
Main St. and Youngs Rd.
Williamsville 14221

Hudson Valley Community College
80 Vandenburgh Ave.
Troy 12180

Monroe Community College
1000 East Henrietta Rd.
Rochester 14623

Onondaga Community College
Rte. 173
Syracuse 13215

SUNY College of Technology at
Farmingdale
Melville Rd.
Farmingdale 11735

NORTH CAROLINA

Central Piedmont Community College
P.O. Box 35009
Charlotte 28235

Guilford Technical Community College
P.O. Box 309
Jamestown 27282

NORTH DAKOTA

North Dakota State College of Science
800 North Sixth St.
Wahpeton 58076

OHIO

Cuyahoga Community College District
700 Carnegie Ave.
Cleveland 44115-2878

Shawnee State University
940 Second St.
Portsmouth 45662

University of Cincinnati-Raymond
Walters College
9555 Plainfield Rd.
Blue Ash 45236

Youngstown State University
410 Wick Ave.
Youngstown 44555

OREGON

Lane Community College
4000 East 30th Ave.
Eugene 97405

PENNSYLVANIA

Community College of Philadelphia
1700 Spring Garden St.
Philadelphia 19130

Harcum Junior College
Morris and Montgomery Ave.
Bryn Mawr 19010

ICS-International Correspondence
Schools
Oak St. and Pawnee Ave.
Scranton 18515

Luzerne County Community College
1333 South Prospect St.
Nanticoke 18634

Northampton County Area Community
College
3835 Green Pond Rd.
Bethlehem 18017

Pennsylvania College of Technology
One College Ave.
Williamsport 17701

RHODE ISLAND

Community College of Rhode Island
400 East Ave.
Warwick 02886-1805

SOUTH CAROLINA

Greenville Technical College
Station B, P.O. Box 5616
Greenville 29606-5616

Midlands Technical College
P.O. Box 2408
Columbia 29202

Trident Technical College
P.O. Box 118067
Charleston 29423-8067

SOUTH DAKOTA

University of South Dakota
414 East Clark St.
Vermillion 57069-2390

TENNESSEE

East Tennessee State University
P.O. Box 70716
Johnson City 37614

Tennessee State University
3500 John Merritt Blvd.
Nashville 37209-1561

TEXAS

Tyler Junior College
P.O. Box 9020
Tyler 75711

University of Texas Health Science
Center
P.O. Box 20036
Houston 77225

University of Texas Health Science
Center-San Antonio
7703 Floyd Curl Dr.
San Antonio 78284

UTAH

American Institute of Medical-Dental
Technology
1675 North 200 West
Provo 84604

Weber State University
3750 Harrison Blvd.
Ogden 84408

VIRGINIA

Wytheville Community College
1000 East Main St.
Wytheville 24382

WASHINGTON

Clark College
1800 East McLoughlin Blvd.
Vancouver 98663

Shoreline Community College
16101 Greenwood Ave. N
Seattle 98133

WEST VIRGINIA

West Liberty State College
West Liberty 26074

WISCONSIN

North Central Technical College
1000 Campus Dr.
Wausau 54401-1899

Northeast Wisconsin Technical College
2740 West Mason St., P.O. Box 19042
Green Bay 54307-9042

Wisconsin Area Vocational Training and
Adult Education System District
Number Four
3550 Anderson St.
Madison 53704

EEG and EKG Technology

CALIFORNIA

Institute of Computer Technology
3200 Wilshire Blvd.
Los Angeles 90010

Orange Coast College
2701 Fairview Rd.
Costa Mesa 92626

Southern California College of
Medical-Dental Care
1717 South Brookhurst
Anaheim 92804

FLORIDA

Pasco-Hernando Community College
36727 Blanton Rd.
Dade City 33525-7599

Technical Career Institute
720 Northwest 27th Ave.
Miami 33125

ILLINOIS

Medical Careers Institute
116 South Michigan Ave.
Chicago 60603

Saint John's Hospital School of EEG
800 East Carpenter
Springfield 62769

MICHIGAN

Carnegie Institute
550 Stephenson Hwy.
Troy 48083

MISSOURI

Saint Louis College of Health Careers
4484 West Pine
Saint Louis 63108

NEW JERSEY

Hudson County Area Vocational
    Technical School-Bayonne Center
West 30th St.
Bayonne 07002

Hudson County Area Vocational
    Technical School-North Hudson Center
8511 Tonnelle Ave.
North Bergen 07047

NEW YORK

Niagara County Community College
3111 Saunders Settlement Rd.
Sanborn 14132

PENNSYLVANIA

American Center Technical Arts
1930 Chestnut St.
Philadelphia 19103

TEXAS

Career Centers of Texas El Paso, Inc.
8375 Burnham Dr.
El Paso 79907

Laboratory Animal Care Technology

COLORADO

Institute for Nuclear Medical Education
5171 Eldorado Springs Dr.
Boulder 80303

CONNECTICUT

Huntington Institute, Inc.
193 Broadway
Norwich 06360

FLORIDA

Beacon Career Institute, Inc.
2900 Northwest 183rd St.
Miami 33056

Lee County Vocational-Technical Center
3800 Michigan Ave.
Fort Myers 33916

Miriam Vocational School, Inc.
7311 West Flagler St.
Miami 33144

Sarasota County Technical Institute
4748 Beneva Rd.
Sarasota 34233-1798

MINNESOTA

Saint Cloud Technical College
1540 Northway Dr.
Saint Cloud 56303

Saint Paul Technical College
235 Marshall Ave.
Saint Paul 55102

NEW JERSEY

Star Technical Institute-Ocean Township
2105 Hwy. 35
Ocean Township 07712

OHIO

Professional Skills Institute
1232 Flaire Dr.
Toledo 43615

PENNSYLVANIA

Allied Medical Careers, Inc.
2901 Pittston Ave.
Scranton 18505

Allied Medical Careers, Inc.
104 Woodward Hill Rd.
Edwardsville 18704

RHODE ISLAND

Community College of Rhode Island
400 East Ave.
Warwick 02886-1805

TENNESSEE

Nashville State Area Vocational
    Technical School
100 White Bridge Rd.
Nashville 37209

WEST VIRGINIA

Seneca Phlebotomy Institute
1756 H Mileground Plaza
Morgantown 26505

WISCONSIN

Saint Joseph's Hospital School of
    Medical Technology
611 Saint Joseph's Ave.
Marshfield 54449

Licensed Practical Nursing

ALABAMA

Bessemer State Technical College
P.O. Box 308
Bessemer 35021

Bevill State Community College
P.O. Drawer K
Sumiton 35148

Central Alabama Community College
P.O. Box 699
Alexander 35010

Douglas MacArthur Technical College
P.O. Box 649
Opp 36467

G C Wallace State Community College
P.O. Drawer 1049
Selma 36702-1049

Gadsden State Community College
P.O. Box 227
Gadsden 35902-0227

George C Wallace State Community
    College-Dothan
Rte. 6, P.O. Box 62
Dothan 36303-9234

George C Wallace State Community
    College-Hanceville
801 Main St. NW, P.O. Box 2000
Hanceville 35077-2000

Harry M Ayers State Technical College
1801 Coleman Rd., P.O. Box 1647
Anniston 36202

J F Drake State Technical College
3421 Meridian St. N
Huntsville 35811

Jefferson Davis Community
    College-Brewton Campus
Alco Dr.
Brewton 36426

John C Calhoun State Community
    College
P.O. Box 2216
Decatur 35609-2216

Northwest Alabama Community College
Rte. 3, P.O. Box 77
Phil Campbell 35581

Opelika State Technical College
P.O. Box 2268
Opelika 36803-2268

Reid State Technical College
P.O. Box 588
Evergreen 36401

Shelton State Community College
202 Skyland Blvd.
Tuscaloosa 35405

Shoals Community College
P.O. Box 2545
Muscle Shoals 35662

Southern Union State Junior College
Roberts St.
Wadley 36276

Trenholm State Technical College
1225 Air Base Blvd.
Montgomery 36108

ARIZONA

Central Arizona College
8470 North Overfield Rd.
Coolidge 85228-9778

Gateway Community College
108 North 40th St.
Phoenix 85034

Mesa Community College
1833 West Southern Ave.
Mesa 85202

Mohave Community College
1971 Jagerson Ave.
Kingman 86401

Pima Community College
2202 West Anklam Rd.
Tucson 85709-0001

ARKANSAS

Arkansas Valley Technical Institute
Hwy. 23 N, P.O. Box 506
Ozark 72949

Baptist Schools of Nursing and Allied
    Health
11900 College Glenn Rd.
Little Rock 72210-2820

Black River Technical College
Hwy. 304, P.O. Box 468
Pocahontas 72455

Cossatot Technical College
P.O. Box 960
De Queen 71832

Cotton Boll Technical Institute
P.O. Box 36
Burdette 72321

Crowley's Ridge Technical School
P.O. Box 925
Forrest City 72335

Foothills Technical Institute
1800 East Moore St., P.O. Box 909
Searcy 72143

Northwest Technical Institute
P.O. Box A
Springdale 72765

Pines Technical College
1900 Hazel
Pine Bluff 71603

Pulaski Technical College
3000 West Scenic Dr.
North Little Rock 72118

Quapaw Technical Institute
201 Vo-Tech Dr.
Hot Springs 71913

Red River Technical College
P.O. Box 140
Hope 71801

Rice Belt Vocational Technical School
P.O. Box 427
Dewitt 72042

Westark Community College
P.O. Box 3649
Fort Smith 72913

CALIFORNIA

Butte College
3536 Butte Campus Dr.
Oroville 95965

Casa Loma College-Sylmar
14445 Olive View Dr.
Sylmar 91342

Casa Loma College-Los Angeles
3761 Stocker
Los Angeles 90008

Cerro Coso Community College
3000 College Heights Blvd.
Ridgecrest 93555-7777

Citrus College
1000 West Foothill Blvd.
Glendora 91741-1899

Concorde Career Institute
4150 Lankershim Blvd.
North Hollywood 91602

Concorde Career Institute Campus
600 North Sierra Way
San Bernardino 92410

Crafton Hills College
11711 Sand Canyon Rd.
Yucaipa 92399-1799

El Camino College
16007 Crenshaw Blvd.
Torrance 90506

Glendale Community College
1500 North Verdugo Rd.
Glendale 91208-2894

Hacienda La Puente Unified School
District-Valley Vocational Center
15959 East Gale Ave.
La Puente 91749

Lassen College
Hwy. 139, P.O. Box 3000
Susanville 96130

Los Angeles Training Technical College
400 West Washington Blvd.
Los Angeles 90015-4181

Maric College of Medical Careers
7202 Princess View Dr.
San Diego 92120

Maric College of Medical Careers
1300 Rancheros Dr.
San Marcos 92069

Maric College of Medical Careers-Vista
Campus
1593C East Vista Way
Vista 92084

Merced College
3600 M St.
Merced 95348-2898

Mission College
3000 Mission College Blvd.
Santa Clara 95054-1897

Mount San Jacinto College
1499 North State St.
San Jacinto 92383-2399

Napa Valley College
2277 Napa Vallejo Hwy.
Napa 94558

Pacific Coast College
1261 Third Ave.
Chula Vista 91911-3237

Pacific Coast College
16001 Ventura Blvd.
Encino 91436

Pacific Coast College
118 West Fifth St.
Santa Ana 92701

Porterville College
100 East College Ave.
Porterville 93257

Sacramento City College
3835 Freeport Blvd.
Sacramento 95822

San Diego City College
1313 12th Ave.
San Diego 92101

Santa Barbara City College
721 Cliff Dr.
Santa Barbara 93109-2394

Sierra College
5000 Rocklin Rd.
Rocklin 95677

Yuba College
2088 North Beale Rd.
Marysville 95901

COLORADO

Boulder Valley Area Vocational
Technical Center
6600 East Arapahoe
Boulder 80303

Community College of Denver
P.O. Box 173363
Denver 80217

Front Range Community College
3645 West 112th Ave.
Westminster 80030

Northeastern Junior College
100 College Dr.
Sterling 80751

Otero Junior College
1802 Colorado Ave.
La Junta 81050

Pikes Peak Community College
5675 South Academy Blvd.
Colorado Springs 80906-5498

Pueblo College of Business &
Technology
330 Lake Ave.
Pueblo 81004

Pueblo Community College
900 West Orman Ave.
Pueblo 81004

Red Rocks Community College
13300 West Sixth Ave.
Golden 80401

San Juan Basin Area Vocational School
P.O. Box 970
Cortez 81321

San Luis Valley Area Vocational School
1011 Main St.
Alamosa 81101

T H Pickens Technical Center
500 Buckley Rd.
Aurora 80011

Trinidad State Junior College
600 Prospect St.
Trinidad 81082

DELAWARE

Delaware Technical and Community
College-Southern Campus
P.O. Box 610
Georgetown 19947

Delaware Technical and Community
College-Terry Campus
1832 North Dupont Pkwy.
Dover 19901

DISTRICT OF COLUMBIA

Harrison Center for Career Education
624 Ninth St. NW
Washington 20001

FLORIDA

Atlantic Vocational Technical Center
4700 Coconut Creek Pkwy.
Coconut Creek 33063

Brevard Community College
1519 Clearlake Rd.
Cocoa 32922

Central Florida Community College
P.O. Box 1388
Ocala 34478

Charlotte Vocational-Technical Center
18300 Toledo Blade Blvd.
Port Charlotte 33948-3399

Daytona Beach Community College
1200 Volusia Ave.
Daytona Beach 32114

Florida Community College at
Jacksonville
501 West State St.
Jacksonville 32202

Indian River Community College
3209 Virginia Ave.
Fort Pierce 34981

James Lorenzo Walker Vocational
Technical Center
3702 Estey Ave.
Naples 33942

Lake City Community College
Rte. 3, P.O. Box 7
Lake City 32055

Lake County Area Vocational-Technical
Center
2001 Kurt St.
Eustis 32726

Lee County Vocational-Technical Center
3800 Michigan Ave.
Fort Myers 33916

Lewis M Lively Area
Vocational-Technical Center
500 North Appleyard Dr.
Tallahassee 32304

Lindsey Hopkins Technical Education
Center
750 Northwest 20th St.
Miami 33127

Manatee Vocational-Technical Center
5603 34th St. W
Bradenton 34210

Miami Lakes Technical Education Center
5780 Northwest 158th St.
Miami Lakes 33169

North Florida Junior College
Turner Davis Dr.
Madison 32340

North Technical Education Center
7071 Garden Rd.
Riviera Beach 33404

Pasco-Hernando Community College
36727 Blanton Rd.
Dade City 33525-7599

Pensacola Junior College
1000 College Blvd.
Pensacola 32504

Pinellas Technical Education
Center-Clearwater Campus
6100 154th Ave. N
Clearwater 34620

Pinellas Technical Education
Centers-Saint Pete Campus
901 34th St. S
Saint Petersburg 33711

Robert Morgan Vocational Technical
Center
18180 Southwest 122nd Ave.
Miami 33177

Saint Augustine Technical Center
2980 Collins Ave.
Saint Augustine 32095

Santa Fe Community College
3000 Northwest 83rd St.
Gainesville 32601

Sarasota County Technical Institute
4748 Beneva Rd.
Sarasota 34233-1798

Seminole Community College
100 Weldon Blvd.
Sanford 32773-6199

Sheridan Vocational Center
5400 West Sheridan St.
Hollywood 33021

South Florida Community College
600 West College Dr.
Avon Park 33825

South Technical Education Center
1300 Southwest 30th Ave.
Boynton Beach 33426-9099

Washington-Holmes Area
Vocational-Technical Center
209 Hoyt St.
Chipley 32428

William T McFatter Vocational
Technical Center
6500 Nova Dr.
Davie 33317

Withlacoochee Technical Institute
1201 West Main St.
Inverness 32650

GEORGIA

Albany Technical Institute
1021 Lowe Rd.
Albany 31708

Athens Area Technical Institute
U.S. Hwy. 29 N
Athens 30610-0399

Atlanta Area Technical School
1560 Stewart Ave. SW
Atlanta 30310

Augusta Technical Institute
3116 Deans Bridge Rd.
Augusta 30906

Bainbridge College
Hwy. 84 E
Bainbridge 31717

Ben Hill-Irwin Technical Institute
P.O. Box 1069
Fitzgerald 31750

Brunswick College
Altama at Fourth St.
Brunswick 31523

Carroll Technical Institute
997 South Hwy. 16
Carrollton 30117

Chattahoochee Technical Institute
980 South Cobb Dr.
Marietta 30060-3398

Columbus Technical Institute
928 45th St.
Columbus 31904-6572

Coosa Valley Technical Institute
112 Hemlock St.
Rome 30161

Dalton School of Health
Occupations-Practical Nursing
1221 Elkwood Dr.
Dalton 30720

Dekalb Technical Institute
495 North Indian Creek Dr.
Clarkston 30021

Flint River Technical Institute
1533 Hwy. 19 S
Thomaston 30286

Griffin Technical Institute
501 Varsity Rd.
Griffin 30223

Heart of Georgia Technical Institute
Rte. 5, P.O. Box 136
Dublin 31021

Macon Technical Institute
3300 Macon Tech Dr.
Macon 31206

Middle Georgia Technical Institute
1311 Corder Rd.
Warner Robins 31088

Moultrie Area Technical Institute
P.O. Box 520
Moultrie 31776

North Georgia Technical Institute
Georgia Hwy. 197, P.O. Box 65
Clarkesville 30523

Pickens Technical Institute
100 Pickens Tech Dr.
Jasper 30143

Savannah Technical Institute
5717 White Bluff Rd.
Savannah 31499

South College
709 Mall Blvd.
Savannah 31406

South Georgia Technical Institute
728 Souther Field Rd.
Americus 31709

Swainsboro Technical Institute
201 Kite Rd.
Swainsboro 30401

Thomas Technical Institute
P.O. Box 1578
Thomasville 31799

Valdosta Technical Institute
4089 Valtech Rd.
Valdosta 31602-9796

HAWAII

Kapiolani Community College
4303 Diamond Head Rd.
Honolulu 96816

IDAHO

Boise State University
1910 University Dr.
Boise 83725

College of Southern Idaho
P.O. Box 1238
Twin Falls 83301

Idaho State University
741 South Seventh Ave.
Pocatello 83209

ILLINOIS

Black Hawk College-Quad-Cities
6600 34th Ave.
Moline 61265

Capital Area School of Practical Nursing
2201 Toronto Rd., RR 11
Springfield 62707-8645

Carl Sandburg College
2232 South Lake Storey Rd.
Galesburg 61401

Chicago Public Schools Practical Nursing
  Program
2040 West Adams St.
Chicago 60612

City College of Chicago-Chicago
  City-Wide College
226 West Jackson Blvd.
Chicago 60606-6997

Danville Area Community College
2000 East Main St.
Danville 61832

Decatur School of Practical Nursing
300 East Eldorado St.
Decatur 62523

Elgin Community College
1700 Spartan Dr.
Elgin 60123

F W Olin Vocational School of Practical
  Nursing
4200 Humbert Rd.
Alton 62002

Highland Community College
2998 West Pearl City Rd.
Freeport 61032-9341

Illinois Eastern Community
  Colleges-Olney Central College
RR 3
Olney 62450

Illinois Valley Community College
2578 East 350th Rd.
Oglesby 61348

Jacksonville School of Practical Nursing
49 North Central Park Plaza
Jacksonville 62650

John A Logan College
Carterville 62918

John Wood Community College
150 South 48th St.
Quincy 62301-9147

Joliet Township Hospital School of
  Practical Nursing
201 East Jefferson St.
Joliet 60432

Kankakee Community College
P.O. Box 888
Kankakee 60901

Kaskaskia College
27210 College Rd.
Centralia 62801

Lake Land College
5001 Lake Land Blvd.
Mattoon 61938

Rend Lake College
Rte. 1
Ina 62846

Shawnee Community College
Shawnee College Rd.
Ullin 62992

South Suburban College
15800 South State St.
South Holland 60473

Southeastern Illinois College
3575 College Rd.
Harrisburg 62946

Spoon River College
RR 1
Canton 61520

Triton College
2000 Fifth Ave.
River Grove 60171

William Rainey Harper College
1200 West Algonquin Rd.
Palatine 60067-7398

INDIANA

Anderson Area Vocational-Technical
  School
325 West 38th St.
Anderson 46013

Indiana Vocational Technical
  College-Central Indiana
One West 26th St.
Indianapolis 46206-1763

Indiana Vocational Technical
  College-Columbus
4475 Central Ave.
Columbus 47203

Indiana Vocational Technical
  College-East Central
4301 South Cowan Rd., P.O. Box 3100
Muncie 47302

Indiana Vocational Technical
  College-Lafayette
3208 Ross Rd., P.O. Box 6299
Lafayette 47903

Indiana Vocational Technical
  College-North Central
1534 West Sample St.
South Bend 46619

Indiana Vocational Technical
  College-Northeast
3800 North Anthony Blvd.
Fort Wayne 46805

Indiana Vocational Technical
  College-Northwest
1440 East 35th Ave.
Gary 46409

Indiana Vocational Technical
  College-South Central
8204 Hwy. 311
Sellersburg 47172

Indiana Vocational Technical
  College-Southeast
590 Ivy Tech Dr., P.O. Box 209
Madison 47250

Indiana Vocational Technical
  College-Southwest
3501 First Ave.
Evansville 47710

Indiana Vocational Technical
  College-Wabash Valley
7999 U.S. Hwy. 41
Terre Haute 47802-4898

Indiana Vocational Technical
  College-Whitewater
2325 Chester Blvd., P.O. Box 1145
Richmond 47374

J Everett Light Career Center
1901 East 86th St.
Indianapolis 46240

Vincennes University
1002 North First St.
Vincennes 47591

IOWA

Des Moines Community College
2006 Ankeny Blvd.
Ankeny 50021

Eastern Iowa Community College District
306 West River Dr.
Davenport 52801-1221

Hawkeye Institute of Technology
1501 East Orange Rd.
Waterloo 50704

Indian Hills Community College
525 Grandview
Ottumwa 52501

Iowa Central Community College
330 Ave. M
Fort Dodge 50501

Iowa Lakes Community College
19 South Seventh St.
Estherville 51334

Iowa Valley Community College
P.O. Box 536
Marshalltown 50158

Iowa Western Community College
2700 College Rd., P.O. Box 4C
Council Bluffs 51502

North Iowa Area Community College
500 College Dr.
Mason City 50401

Northeast Iowa Community College
Hwy. 150 S, P.O. Box 400
Calmar 52132-0400

Saint Luke's School of Nursing
2720 Stone Park Blvd.
Sioux City 51104-0263

Southeastern Community College
1015 South Gear Ave., P.O. Drawer F
West Burlington 52655-0605

Southwestern Community College
1501 Townline
Creston 50801

Western Iowa Technical Community
  College
4647 Stone Ave., P.O. Box 265
Sioux City 51102-0265

KANSAS

Barton County Community College
Rte. 3, P.O. Box 136Z
Great Bend 67530

Colby Community College
1255 South Range
Colby 67701

Dodge City Community College
2501 North 14th Ave.
Dodge City 67801

Flint Hills Technical School
3301 West 18th St.
Emporia 66801

Johnson County Area
  Vocational-Technical School
311 East Park
Olathe 66061

Kansas City Area Vocational Technical
  School
2220 North 59th St.
Kansas City 66104

KAW Area Vocational-Technical School
5724 Huntoon
Topeka 66604

Manhattan Area Technical Center
3136 Dickens Ave.
Manhattan 66502

Neosho County Community College
1000 South Allen
Chanute 66720

North Central Kansas Area Vocational
   Technical School
Hwy. 24, P.O. Box 507
Beloit 67420

Northeast Kansas Area Vocational
   Technical School
1501 West Riley St., P.O. Box 277
Atchison 66002

Seward County Community College
P.O. Box 1137
Liberal 67905-1137

Wichita Area Vocational Technical
   School
428 South Broadway
Wichita 67202-3910

KENTUCKY

Ashland State Vocational Technical
   School
4818 Roberts Dr.
Ashland 41102

Humana Health Institute-Louisville
612 South Fourth St.
Louisville 40202

Kentucky Department for Adult &
   Technical Education-Central Kentucky
   SVTS
104 Vo Tech Rd.
Lexington 40510

Kentucky Technical-Hazard State
   Vocational Technical School
101 Vo-Tech Dr.
Hazard 41701

Kentucky Technical-Jefferson State
   Vocational Technical School
727 West Chestnut
Louisville 40203

Kentucky Technical-Somerset Campus
230 Airport Rd.
Somerset 42501

Kentucky Technical-West Kentucky
   State Vocational Technical School
P.O. Box 7408
Paducah 42002-7408

Letcher County Vocational Center
610 Circle Dr.
Whitesburg 41858

Mayo State Vocational Technical School
Third St.
Paintsville 41240

Spencerian College
4627 Dixie Hwy.
Louisville 40216

LOUISIANA

Alexandria Regional Technical Institute
4311 South MacArthur Dr.
Alexandria 71302-3137

Bastrop Vocational-Technical Institute
Kammell St., P.O. Box 1120
Bastrop 71221-1120

Cameron College
2740 Canal St.
New Orleans 70119

Delta-Ouachita Regional-Technical
   Institute
609 Vocational Pkwy.
West Monroe 71291

Florida Parishes Technical Institute
P.O. Box 130
Greensburg 70441

Gulf Area Technical Institute
1115 Clover St.
Abbeville 70510

Huey P Long Technical Institute
303 South Jones St.
Winnfield 71483

Jefferson Davis Technical Institute
P.O. Box 1327
Jennings 70546

Jefferson Technical Institute
5200 Blair Dr.
Metairie 70001

Lafayette Regional Technical Institute
1101 Bertrand Dr., P.O. Box 4909
Lafayette 70502-4909

Lamar Salter Vocational-Technical
   School
Rte. 2, P.O. Box 25
Leesville 71446

New Orleans Regional Technical Institute
980 Navarre Ave.
New Orleans 70124

Northwest Louisiana Technical Institute
P.O. Box 835
Minden 71058-0835

Our Lady of the Lake College of Nursing
   & Allied Health
5345 Brittany Dr.
Baton Rouge 70808

Ruston Technical Institute
1010 James St.
Ruston 71273-1070

Shreveport-Bossier Regional Technical
   Institute
2010 North Market St., P.O. Box 78527
Shreveport 71137-8527

Sidney N Collier Technical Institute
3727 Louisa St.
New Orleans 70126

Slidell Technical Institute
1000 Canulette Rd., P.O. Box 827
Slidell 70459

Southwest School of Health Careers
2424 Williams Blvd., Plaza 24 Center
Kenner 70062

Sowela Regional Technical Institute
3820 Legion St., P.O. Box 16950
Lake Charles 70601

Sullivan Technical Institute
1710 Sullivan Dr.
Bogalusa 70427

T H Harris Technical Institute
337 East South St., P.O. Box 713
Opelousas 70570

West Jefferson Technical Institute
475 Manhattan Blvd.
Harvey 70058

Young Memorial Technical Institute
P.O. Box 2148
Morgan City 70381

MAINE

Central Maine Medical Center School of
   Nursing
300 Main St.
Lewiston 04240

Eastern Maine Technical College
354 Hogan Rd.
Bangor 04401

Northern Maine Technical College
33 Edgemont Dr.
Presque Isle 04769

Southern Maine Technical College
Fort Rd.
South Portland 04106

MARYLAND

Harford Community College
401 Thomas Run Rd.
Bel Air 21015

Johnston School of Practical Nursing
201 East University Pkwy.
Baltimore 21218-2895

Wor-Wic Community College
1409 Wesley Dr.
Salisbury 21801-7131

MASSACHUSETTS

Assabet Valley Regional Vocational
   Technical School
215 Fitchburg St.
Marlborough 01752

Becker College-Worcester
61 Sever St.
Worcester 01615-0071

Berkshire Community College
1350 West St.
Pittsfield 01201-5786

Blue Hills Regional Technical School
800 Randolph St.
Canton 02021

Bristol Community College
777 Elsbree St.
Fall River 02720

Diman Regional Technical Institute
Stonehaven Rd.
Fall River 02723

Essex Agricultural-Technical Institute
562 Maple St., P.O. Box 562
Hathorne 01937

Fisher College
118 Beacon St.
Boston 02116

Lemuel Shattuck Hospital School of
   Practical Nursing
180 Morton St.
Jamaica Plain 02130

Massachusetts Bay Community College
50 Oakland St.
Wellesley Hills 02181

Massachusetts Soldiers Home School of
   Practical Nursing
91 Crest Ave.
Chelsea 02150

Northern Essex Community College
Elliott Way
Haverhill 01830-2399

Quincy College
34 Coddington St.
Quincy 02169

Southeastern Technical Institute
250 Foundry St.
South Easton 02375

Tewksbury State Hospital School of
   Practical Nursing
East St.
Tewksbury 01876

Upper Cape Cod Regional Vocational
   Technical School
220 Sandwich Rd.
Bourne 02532

William J Dean Technical High School
1045 Main St.
Holyoke 01040

Worcester Technical Institute
251 Belmont St.
Worcester 01605

Youville Hospital School of Practical
   Nursing
1575 Cambridge St.
Cambridge 02238

MICHIGAN

Alpena Community College
666 Johnson St.
Alpena 49707

Bay De Noc Community College
2001 North Lincoln Rd.
Escanaba 49289

Delta College
University Center 48710

Gogebic Community College
East 4946 Jackson Rd.
Ironwood 49938

Grand Rapids Community College
143 Bostwick Ave. NE
Grand Rapids 49505

Jackson Community College
2111 Emmons Rd.
Jackson 49201

Kalamazoo Valley Community College
6767 West O Ave.
Kalamazoo 49009

Kirtland Community College
10775 North Saint Helen Rd.
Roscommon 48653

Mid Michigan Community College
1375 South Clare Ave.
Harrison 48625

Montcalm Community College
2800 College Dr.
Sidney 48885

Mott Community College
1401 East Court St.
Flint 48503

Muskegon Community College
221 South Quarterline Rd.
Muskegon 49442

Northern Michigan University
1401 Presque Isle
Marquette 49855

Oakland Community College
2480 Opdyke Rd.
Bloomfield Hills 48304-2266

Saint Clair County Community College
323 Erie, P.O. Box 5015
Port Huron 48061-5015

Schoolcraft College
18600 Haggerty Rd.
Livonia 48152

West Shore Community College
3000 North Stiles
Scottville 49454

MINNESOTA

Albert Lea-Mankato Technical College
1920 Lee Blvd.
North Mankato 56003

Alexandria Technical College
1601 Jefferson St.
Alexandria 56308

Brainerd-Staples Technical
College-Brainerd Campus
300 Quince St.
Brainerd 56401

Dakota County Technical College
1300 East 145th St.
Rosemount 55068

Duluth Technical College
2101 Trinity Rd.
Duluth 55811

Fergus Falls Community College
1414 College Way
Fergus Falls 56537

Hennepin Technical College
1820 North Xenium Ln.
Plymouth 55441

Hutchinson-Willmar Technical
College-Willmar Campus
P.O. Box 1097
Willmar 56201

Minneapolis Technical College
1415 Hennepin Ave.
Minneapolis 55403

Minnesota Riverland Technical
College-Austin Campus
1900 Eighth Ave. NW
Austin 55912

Minnesota Riverland Technical
College-Faribault Campus
1225 Southwest Third St.
Faribault 55021

Minnesota Riverland Technical
College-Rochester Campus
1926 College View Rd. SE
Rochester 55904

Northwest Technical College-Detroit
Lakes
900 Hwy. 34 E
Detroit Lakes 56501

Northwest Technical College-East Grand
Forks
Hwy. 220 N
East Grand Forks 56721

Northwest Technical College-Thief River
Falls
1301 Hwy. 1 E
Thief River Falls 56701

Rainy River Community College
Hwy. 11 and 71
International Falls 56649

Red Wing-Winona Technical
College-Red Wing Campus
Hwy. 58 at Pioneer Rd.
Red Wing 55066

Red Wing-Winona Technical
College-Winona Campus
1250 Homer Rd., P.O. Box 409
Winona 55987

Saint Cloud Technical College
1540 Northway Dr.
Saint Cloud 56303

Saint Paul Technical College
235 Marshall Ave.
Saint Paul 55102

Worthington Community College
1450 College Way
Worthington 56187

MISSISSIPPI

East Mississippi Community College
P.O. Box 158
Scooba 39358

Hinds Community College-Raymond
Campus
Raymond 39154

Holmes Community College
Hill St.
Goodman 39079

Jones County Junior College
Front St.
Ellisville 39437

Meridian Community College
910 Hwy. 19 N
Meridian 39307

Mississippi Delta Community College
P.O. Box 668
Moorhead 38761

Mississippi Gulf Coast Community
College
Central Office, P.O. Box 67
Perkinston 39573

Northeast Mississippi Community
College
Cunningham Blvd.
Booneville 38829

Northwest Mississippi Community
College
Hwy. 51 N
Senatobia 38668

Pearl River Community College
Station A
Poplarville 39470

Southwest Mississippi Community
College
College Dr.
Summit 39666

MISSOURI

Columbia Area Vocational Technical
School
4203 South Providence Rd.
Columbia 65203

Gibson Technical Center
P.O. Box 169
Reeds Spring 65737

Hannibal Area Vocational Technical
School
4550 McMasters Ave.
Hannibal 63401

Jefferson College
1000 Viking Dr.
Hillsboro 63050

Lester E Cox Medical Center of
Radiologic Technology
3801 South National Ave.
Springfield 65807

Lutheran Medical Center School of
Nursing
3547 South Jefferson Ave.
Saint Louis 63118

Mexico Public School Practical Nursing
620 East Monroe
Mexico 65265

Mineral Area College
P.O. Box 1000
Flat River 63601

Nichols Career Center
609 Union
Jefferson City 65101

North Central Missouri College
1301 Main St.
Trenton 64683

Northwest Missouri Area Vocational
Technical School
1515 South Munn
Maryville 64468

Poplar Bluff School District Practical
Nurse Program
P.O. Box 47
Poplar Bluff 63901

Rolla Area Vocational-Technical School
1304 East Tenth St.
Rolla 65401

Saint Charles County Community College
4601 Mid Rivers Mall Dr.
Saint Peter's 63376

Saint Louis Board of Education-Practical
Nursing Program
3815 McCausland Ave.
Saint Louis 63109

Saint Louis College of Health Careers
4484 West Pine
Saint Louis 63108

Sanford-Brown Business College
12006 Manchester Rd.
Des Peres 63131

Sikeston Area Vocational Technical
School
1002 Virginia
Sikeston 63801

State Fair Community College
3201 West 16th
Sedalia 65301-2199

Waynesville Area Vocational School
810 Roosevelt
Waynesville 65583

MONTANA

Billings Vocational Technical Center
3803 Central Ave.
Billings 59102

Great Falls Vocational Technical Center
2100 16th Ave. S
Great Falls 59405

Helena Vocational-Technical Center
1115 North Roberts St.
Helena 59601

Missoula Vocational Technical Center
909 South Ave. W
Missoula 59801

NEBRASKA

Central Community College-Grand Island
P.O. Box 4903
Grand Island 68802

Metropolitan Community College Area
P.O. Box 3777
Omaha 68103

Mid Plains Community College
416 North Jeffers
North Platte 69101

Northeast Community College
801 East Benjamin, P.O. Box 469
Norfolk 68702-0469

Southeast Community College-Lincoln
Campus
8800 O St.
Lincoln 68520

Western Nebraska Community College
1601 East 27th St. NE
Scottsbluff 69361-1899

NEVADA

Community College of Southern Nevada
3200 East Cheyenne Ave.
Las Vegas 89030

NEW HAMPSHIRE

New Hampshire Technical College at
Claremont
One College Dr.
Claremont 03743

Saint Joseph's Hospital School of
Practical Nursing & Health
Occupations
Five Woodward Ave.
Nashua 03060

NEW JERSEY

Bergen Pines Colorado Hospital School
of Practical Nursing
East Ridgewood Ave.
Paramus 07652

Charles E Gregory School of Nursing
530 New Brunswick Ave.
Perth Amboy 08861

Hudson County Area Vocational
Technical School-Bayonne Center
West 30th St.
Bayonne 07002

Mountainside Hospital School of Nursing
Bay and Highland Aves.
Montclair 07042

Salem Community College
460 Hollywood Ave.
Carneys Point 08069

Union County College
1033 Springfield Ave.
Cranford 07016

NEW MEXICO

Clovis Community College
417 Schepps Blvd.
Clovis 88101

Northern New Mexico Community
College
1002 North Onate St.
Espanola 87532

NEW YORK

Hospital for Special Surgery Practical
Nursing
535 East 70th St.
New York 10021

Iona College
715 North Ave.
New Rochelle 10801

Isabella G Hart School of Practical
Nursing
1425 Portland Ave.
Rochester 14621

Marion S Whelan School of Nursing of
Geneva General Hospital
196-198 North St.
Geneva 14456

Niagara County Community College
3111 Saunders Settlement Rd.
Sanborn 14132

North Country Community College
20 Winona Ave., P.O. Box 89
Saranac Lake 12983

Oswego County Boces
Colorado Rte. 64
Mexico 13114

Saint Francis School of Practical Nursing
2221 West State St.
Olean 14760-1984

St. Vincent's Medical Center of
Richmond-School of Nursing
Two Gridley Ave.
Staten Island 10303

SUNY Westchester Commmunity College
75 Grasslands Rd.
Valhalla 10595

NORTH CAROLINA

Asheville Buncombe Technical
Community College
340 Victoria Rd.
Asheville 28801

Caldwell Community College and
Technical Institute
P.O. Box 600
Lenoir 28645

Carteret Community College
3505 Arendell St.
Morehead City 28557

Central Carolina Community College
1105 Kelly Dr.
Sanford 27330

Durham Technical Community College
1637 Lawson St.
Durham 27703

Forsyth Technical Community College
2100 Silas Creek Pkwy.
Winston-Salem 27103

Montgomery Community College
P.O. Box 787
Troy 27371

Richmond Community College
P.O. Box 1189
Hamlet 28345

Rockingham Community College
P.O. Box 38
Wentworth 27375-0038

Rowan-Cabarrus Community College
P.O. Box 1595
Salisbury 28145-1595

Surry Community College
South Main St.
Dobson 27017-0304

NORTH DAKOTA

Dickinson State University
Third St. and Eighth Ave. W
Dickinson 58601

North Dakota State College of Science
800 North Sixth St.
Wahpeton 58076

OHIO

Akron Adult Vocational Services
147 Park St.
Akron 44308

Akron School of Practical Nursing
619 Sumner St.
Akron 44311

Apollo School of Practical Nursing
3325 Shawnee Rd.
Lima 45806-1454

Ashtabula County Joint Vocational
School
1565 Rte. 167
Jefferson 44047

Belmont Technical College
120 Fox Shannon Place
Saint Clairsville 43950

Bowling Green Area School of Practical
Nursing
140 South Grove St.
Bowling Green 43402

Butler County JVS District-D Russel Lee
Career Center
3603 Hamilton Middletown Rd.
Hamilton 45011

Canton City School Practical Nurse
Program
1253 Third St. SE
Canton 44707-4798

Central School of Practical Nursing
3300 Chester Ave.
Cleveland 44114

Choffin Career Center
200 East Wood St.
Youngstown 44503

Clark State Community College
570 East Leffel Ln.
Springfield 45505

Ehove School of Practical
Nursing-Ehove Career Center
316 West Mason Rd.
Milan 44848

Gallia Jackson Vinton JUSD
P.O. Box 157
Rio Grande 45674

Hannah E Mullins School of Practical
Nursing
2094 East State St.
Salem 44460

Health Occupations Program-Columbus
Public School
100 Arcadia Ave.
Columbus 43202

Hocking Technical College
3301 Hocking Pkwy.
Nelsonville 45764

Jefferson Technical College
4000 Sunset Blvd.
Steubenville 43952-3598

Lawrence County Joint Vocational School
Rte. 2 Getaway
Chesapeake 45619

Lorain County Community College
1005 North Abbe Rd.
Elyria 44035

Marymount School of Practical Nursing
12300 McCracken Rd.
Garfield Heights 44125

North Central Technical College
2441 Kenwood Circle, P.O. Box 698
Mansfield 44901

Northwest Technical College
22-600 South Rte. 34 & Rte. 1, P.O. Box
246A
Archbold 43502-9990

Ohio Hi Point Joint Vocational School
District
2280 SR 540
Bellefontaine 43311

Parma School of Practical Nursing
6726 Ridge Rd.
Parma 44129

Pickaway Ross Joint Vocational School
District
895 Crouse Chapel Rd.
Chillicothe 45601-9010

Portage Lakes Career Center
4401 Shriver Rd., P.O. Box 248
Greensburg 44232-0248

Scioto County Joint Vocational School
District
Rte. 2 Houston Hollow Rd.
Lucasville 45648

Toledo School of Practical Nursing
1602 Washington St., Whitney Building
Toledo 43624

Upper Valley Joint Vocational School
8811 Career Dr.
Piqua 45356

W Howard Nicol School of Practical
Nursing
4401 Shriver Rd., P.O. Box 248
Greensburg 44232-0248

Walsh College
2020 Easton St. NW
North Canton 44720-3396

Washington State Community College
710 Colegate Dr.
Marietta 45750

Wayne Adult School of Practical Nursing
518 West Prospect St.
Smithville 44677-0378

OKLAHOMA

Caddo-Kiowa Area Vocational Technical
School
P.O. Box 190
Fort Cobb 73038

Francis Tuttle Area Vocational-Technical
Center
12777 North Rockwell Ave.
Oklahoma City 73142-2789

Gordon Cooper Area Vocational
Technical School
4801 North Harrison
Shawnee 74801

Great Plains Area Vocational-Technical
School
4500 West Lee Blvd.
Lawton 73505

Kiamichi AVTS SD #7-Hugo Campus
107 South 15th, P.O. Box 699
Hugo 74743

Kiamichi AVTS SD #7-McCurtain
Campus
Hwy. 70 N, Rte. 3, P.O. Box 177
Idabel 74745

Kiamichi AVTS SD #7-Poteau Campus
1509 South McKenna, P.O. Box 825
Poteau 74953

Metro Tech Vocational Technical Center
1900 Springlake Dr.
Oklahoma City 73111

Pioneer Area Vocational-Technical
School
2101 North Ash
Ponca City 74601

Pontotoc Skill Development Center
601 West 33rd
Ada 74820

Red River Area Vocational-Technical
School
3300 West Bois Darc
Duncan 73533

Southwest Area Vocational-Technical
Center
1121 North Spurgeon
Altus 73521

OREGON

Blue Mountain Community College
P.O. Box 100
Pendleton 97801

Central Oregon Community College
2600 Northwest College Way
Bend 97701

Chemeketa Community College
P.O. Box 14007
Salem 97309-7070

Clackamas Community College
19600 Molalla Ave.
Oregon City 97045

Lane Community College
4000 East 30th Ave.
Eugene 97405

PENNSYLVANIA

Altoona Area Vocational Technical
School
1500 Fourth Ave.
Altoona 16602

Fayette County Area Vocational
Technical School of Practical Nursing
RD 2, P.O. Box 122A
Uniontown 15401

Frankford Hospital School of Nursing
4918 Penn St.
Philadelphia 19124

Franklin Colorado Area Vocational
Technical School-Practical Nursing
Program
2463 Loop Rd.
Chambersburg 17201

Gannon University
109 West Sixth St.
Erie 16541

Harrisburg Area Community
College-Harrisburg Campus
One Hacc Dr.
Harrisburg 17110

Lawrence County Vocational-Technical
School Practical Nursing
750 Phelps Way
New Castle 16101-5099

Lehigh County Community College
4525 Education Park Dr.
Schnecksville 18078-2598

Mercer County Area Vocational
Technical School
P.O. Box 152
Mercer 16137-0152

Northampton County Area Community
College
3835 Green Pond Rd.
Bethlehem 18017

Pennsylvania College of Technology
One College Ave.
Williamsport 17701

Practical Nursing Program of
Lackawanna Vocational Technology
School
3201 Rockwell Ave.
Scranton 18508

Roxborough Memorial Hospital
5800 Ridge Ave.
Philadelphia 19128

Saint Francis Medical Center School of
Nursing
400 45th St.
Pittsburgh 15201

Saint Luke's Hospital School of Nursing
801 Ostrum
Bethlehem 18015

Schuykill County Area Vocational
Technical School
Pottsville Minersville Hwy.
Mar Lin 17951-0110

Western Area Vocational Technical
School of Practical Nursing
RD 1, P.O. Box 178-A
Canonsburg 15317

Wilkes-Barre Area Vocational-Technical
School of Practical Nursing
North End Station Jumper Rd., P.O. Box
1699
Wilkes-Barre 18705-0699

RHODE ISLAND

Community College of Rhode Island
400 East Ave.
Warwick 02886-1805

SOUTH CAROLINA

Greenville Technical College
Station B, P.O. Box 5616
Greenville 29606-5616

Midlands Technical College
P.O. Box 2408
Columbia 29202

Orangeburg-Calhoun Technical College
3250 Saint Matthew's Rd.
Orangeburg 29115

Piedmont Technical College
P.O. Drawer 1467
Greenwood 29648

Spartanburg Technical College
Hwy. I-85, P.O. Drawer 4386
Spartanburg 29305

Trident Technical College
P.O. Box 118067
Charleston 29423-8067

SOUTH DAKOTA

Lake Area Vocational Technical Institute
230 11th St. NE
Watertown 57201

Western Dakota Vocational Technical
Institute
1600 Sedivy
Rapid City 57701

TENNESSEE

Athens State Area Vocational-Technical
School
1635 Vo Tech Dr., P.O. Box 848
Athens 37371-0848

Chattanooga State Technical Community
College
4501 Amnicola Hwy.
Chattanooga 37406

Covington State Area Vocational
Technical School
P.O. Box 249
Covington 38019

Crossville State Area Vocational
Technical School
P.O. Box 2959
Crossville 38557

Dickson State Area Vocational-Technical
School
740 Hwy. 46
Dickson 37055

Elizabethton State Area Vocational
Technical School
1500 Arney St., P.O. Box 789
Elizabethton 37643

Harriman State Area
Vocational-Technical School
P.O. Box 1109
Harriman 37748

Jacksboro State Area
Vocational-Technical School
Rte. 1
Jacksboro 37757

Jackson State Area Vocational Technical
School
McKellar Airport
Jackson 38301

Knoxville State Area
Vocational-Technical School
1100 Liberty St.
Knoxville 37919

Livingston State Area
Vocational-Technical School
P.O. Box 219
Livingston 38570

McMinnville State Area Vocational
Technical School
Vo Tech Dr.
McMinnville 37110

Memphis Area Vocational-Technical
School
550 Alabama Ave.
Memphis 38105-3799

Morristown State Area
Vocational-Technical School
821 West Louise Ave.
Morristown 37813

Nashville State Area Vocational
Technical School
100 White Bridge Rd.
Nashville 37209

Paris State Area Vocational-Technical
School
312 South Wilson St.
Paris 38242

Shelbyville State Area Vocational
Technical School
1405 Madison St.
Shelbyville 37160

Whiteville State Area
Vocational-Technical School
P.O. Box 489
Whiteville 38075

TEXAS

Amarillo College
P.O. Box 447
Amarillo 79178

Austin Community College
5930 Middle Fiskville Rd.
Austin 78752

Baptist Memorial Hospital
System-Institute of Health Education
111 Dallas St.
San Antonio 78205

Bee County College
3800 Charco Rd.
Beeville 78102

Blinn College
902 College Ave.
Brenham 77833

Central Texas College
P.O. Box 1800
Killeen 76540-9990

Chenier
6300 Richmond
Houston 77057

Cisco Junior College
Rte. 3, P.O. Box 3
Cisco 76437

Clarendon College
P.O. Box 968
Clarendon 79226

Cooke County College
1525 West California
Gainesville 76240

Del Mar College
101 Baldwin
Corpus Christi 78404-3897

Delta Career Institute
1310 Pennsylvania Ave.
Beaumont 77701

El Centro College
Main and Lamar
Dallas 75202

Galveston College
4015 Ave. Q
Galveston 77550

Hill College
P.O. Box 619
Hillsboro 76645

Houston Community College System
22 Waugh Dr., P.O. Box 7849
Houston 77270-7849

Howard County Junior College District
1001 Birdwell Ln.
Big Spring 79720

Huntsville Memorial Hospital School
Vocational Nursing
3000 I-4 S
Huntsville 77340

Kilgore College
1100 Broadway
Kilgore 75662-3299

Lamar University-Orange
410 Front St.
Orange 77630

Lamar University-Port Arthur
1500 Proctor St.
Port Arthur 77640

Laredo Junior College
West End Washington St.
Laredo 78040

Lee College
511 South Whiting St.
Baytown 77520-4703

McLennan Community College
1400 College Dr.
Waco 76708

Memorial City Medical Center School of
Vocational Nursing
920 Frostwood
Houston 77024-2434

Navarro College
3200 West Seventh
Corsicana 75110

North Harris Montgomery Community
College District
250 North Sam Houston Pkwy. E
Houston 77060

Northeast Texas Community College
P.O. Box 1307
Mount Pleasant 75456

Odessa College
201 West University
Odessa 79764

Panola College
West Panola St.
Carthage 75633

Paris Junior College
2400 Clarksville St.
Paris 75460

PCI Health Training Center
8101 John Carpenter Fwy.
Dallas 75247

Ranger Junior College
College Circle
Ranger 76470

Saint Philip's College
2111 Nevada St.
San Antonio 78203

San Jacinto College-North Campus
5800 Uvalde
Houston 77049

San Jacinto College-South Campus
13735 Beamer Rd.
Houston 77089

Schreiner College
2100 Memorial Blvd.
Kerrville 78028

South Plains College
1401 College Ave.
Levelland 79336

Tarleton State University
Tarleton Station
Stephenville 76402

Temple Junior College
2600 South First St.
Temple 76504-7435

Texarkana College
2500 North Robison Rd.
Texarkana 75501

Texas Southmost College
80 Fort Brown
Brownsville 78520

Texas State Technical
College-Sweetwater Campus
300 College Dr.
Sweetwater 79556

Trinity Valley Community College
500 South Prairieville
Athens 75751

Vernon Regional Junior College
4400 College Dr.
Vernon 76384-4092

Victoria College
2200 East Red River
Victoria 77901

Weatherford College
308 East Park Ave.
Weatherford 76086

Western Texas College
6200 South College Ave.
Snyder 79549

Wharton County Junior College
911 Boling Hwy.
Wharton 77488

UTAH

College of Eastern Utah
400 East 400 North
Price 84501

Davis Applied Technology Center
550 East 300 South
Kaysville 84037

Salt Lake Community College
P.O. Box 30808
Salt Lake City 84130

Uintah Basin Applied Technology Center
1100 East Lagoon St.
Roosevelt 84066

Utah Valley Community College
800 West 1200 South
Orem 84058

Weber State University
3750 Harrison Blvd.
Ogden 84408

VERMONT

Fanny Allen School of Practical Nursing
29 Ethan Allen Ave.
Colchester 05446-3339

Putnam Memorial School of Practical
Nursing
150 Hospital Dr.
Bennington 05201

Thompson School for Practical Nurses
30 Maple St.
Brattleboro 05301

VIRGINIA

Career Development Center
605 Thimble Shoals
Newport News 23606

CDI-Career Education Center
5361 Virginia Beach Blvd.
Virginia Beach 23462

Petersburg Public Schools Practical
Nursing Program
Blandford School, 816 East Bank St.
Petersburg 23803

Richmond Public School of Practical
Nursing
2020 Westwood Ave.
Richmond 23230

Roanoke Memorial Hospital School of
Practical Nursing
P.O. Box 13367
Roanoke 24033

Tidewater Technical
616 Denbigh Blvd.
Newport News 23602

WASHINGTON

Bates Technical College
1101 South Yakima Ave.
Tacoma 98405

Bellingham Technical College
3028 Lindbergh Ave.
Bellingham 98225

Centralia College
600 West Locust St.
Centralia 98531

Clark College
1800 East McLoughlin Blvd.
Vancouver 98663

Columbia Basin College
2600 North 20th Ave.
Pasco 99301

Everett Community College
801 Wetmore Ave.
Everett 98201

Grays Harbor College
1620 Edward P Smith Dr.
Aberdeen 98520

Green River Community College
12401 Southeast 320th St.
Auburn 98002

Lower Columbia College
P.O. Box 3010
Longview 98632

North Seattle Community College
9600 College Way N
Seattle 98103

Olympic College
1600 Chester Ave.
Bremerton 98310-1699

Skagit Valley College
2405 College Way
Mount Vernon 98273

South Puget Sound Community College
2011 Mottman Rd. SW
Olympia 98512

Spokane Community College
North 1810 Greene Ave.
Spokane 99207

Walla Walla Community College
500 Tausick Way
Walla Walla 99362

Wenatchee Valley College
1300 Fifth St.
Wenatchee 98801

Yakima Valley Community College
P.O. Box 1647
Yakima 98907

WEST VIRGINIA

B M Spurr School of Practical Nursing
800 Wheeling Ave.
Glen Dale 26038

Fred W Eberle School of Practical
Nursing
Rte. 5, P.O. Box 2
Buckhannon 26201

James Rumsey Vocational Technical
Center
Rte. 6, P.O. Box 268
Martinsburg 25401

Logan-Mingo School of Practical Nursing
Three Mile Curve, P.O. Box 1747
Logan 25601

Mercer County Vocational-Technical
Center
1397 Stafford Dr.
Princeton 24740

Raleigh County Vocational-Technical
Center
410-1/2 Stanaford Rd.
Beckley 25801

Roane-Jackson Technical Center
4800 Spencer Rd.
Leroy 25252-9700

Wood County Vocational School of
Practical Nursing
1515 Blizzard Dr.
Parkersburg 26101-6424

WISCONSIN

Chippewa Valley Technical College
620 West Clairemont Ave.
Eau Claire 54701

Fox Valley Technical College
1825 North Bluemound Dr.
Appleton 54913-2277

Milwaukee Area Technical College
700 West State St.
Milwaukee 53233

Wisconsin Area Vocational Training and
Adult Education System-Moraine Park
235 North National Ave., P.O. Box 1940
Fond Du Lac 54936-1940

Wisconsin Area Vocational Training and
Adult Education System District
Number Four
3550 Anderson St.
Madison 53704

WYOMING

Central Wyoming College
2660 Peck Ave.
Riverton 82501

Sheridan College
P.O. Box 1500
Sheridan 82801

Western Wyoming Community College
P.O. Box 428
Rock Springs 82902

Medical Assistant Technology

ALABAMA

Capps College
3100 Cottage Hill Rd.
Mobile 36606

Coastal Training Institute
5950 Monticello Dr.
Montgomery 36117

Community College of the Air Force
Maxwell Air Force Base
Montgomery 36112

Gadsden Business College
750 Forrest Ave.
Gadsden 35901

Gadsden Business College-Anniston
P.O. Box 1575
Anniston 36202-1575

George C Wallace State Community
College-Dothan
Rte. 6, P.O. Box 62
Dothan 36303-9234

National Career College
1351 McFarland Blvd. E
Tuscaloosa 35405

New World College of Business
P.O. Box 2287
Anniston 36201

ARIZONA

Apollo College
3870 North Oracle Rd.
Tucson 85705

Apollo College-Phoenix, Inc.
8503 North 27th Ave.
Phoenix 85051

Apollo College-Tri City, Inc.
630 West Southern Ave.
Mesa 85210

Apollo College-Westridge, Inc.
7502 West Thomas Rd.
Phoenix 85033

The Bryman School
4343 North 16th St.
Phoenix 85016

Gateway Community College
108 North 40th St.
Phoenix 85034

Institute of Medical and Dental
Technology
20 East Main St.
Mesa 85201

The Laural School
2538 North Eighth St.
Phoenix 85006

Long Medical Institute
4126 North Black Canyon Hwy.
Phoenix 85017

Occupational Training Center
4136 North 75th Ave.
Phoenix 85033

Pima Medical Institute
2300 East Broadway Rd.
Tempe 85282

Pima Medical Institute
3350 East Grant Rd.
Tucson 85716

Tucson College
7302-10 East 22nd St.
Tucson 85710

ARKANSAS

Eastern College of Health Vocations
6423 Forbing Rd.
Little Rock 72209

CALIFORNIA

Advanced Computer Training School
2160 North Winery
Fresno 93703

American College of Optechs
4021 Rosewood Ave.
Los Angeles 90004

American School of X-Ray
13723 Harvard Place
Gardena 90249

Andon College
1314 H St.
Modesto 95354

Andon College
1201 North El Dorado St.
Stockton 95202

Assert, Inc.
16270 Raymer St.
Van Nuys 91406

Cabot College
41 East 12th St.
National City 91950

California Paramedic and Technical
College
4550 La Sierra Ave.
Riverside 92505

Canterbury Career Schools
1090 East Washington St.
Colton 92324

Canterbury Career Schools, Inc.
114 North Sunrise Ave.
Roseville 95661

Career West Academy
2505B Zanella Way
Chico 95928

Career West Academy
2505B Zanella Way
Chico 95928

Chabot College
25555 Hesperian Blvd.
Hayward 94545

Citrus College
1000 West Foothill Blvd.
Glendora 91741-1899

City College of San Francisco
50 Phelan Ave.
San Francisco 94112

Concorde Career Institute
4150 Lankershim Blvd.
North Hollywood 91602

Concorde Career Institute
123 Camino De La Reina
San Diego 92108

Concorde Career Institute
1290 North First St.
San Jose 95112

Concorde Career Institute
6850 Van Nuys Blvd.
Van Nuys 91405

Concorde Career Institute Campus
600 North Sierra Way
San Bernardino 92410

Dickinson-Warren Business College
1001 South 57th St.
Richmond 94804

Donald Vocational School
1833 West Eighth St.
Los Angeles 90057

Educorp Career College
230 East Third St.
Long Beach 90802

Foothill College
12345 El Monte Rd.
Los Altos Hills 94022

Galen College of Medical and Dental
Assistants
1325 North Wishon Ave.
Fresno 93728

Galen College of Medical and Dental
Assistants
1604 Ford Ave.
Modesto 95350

Galen College of Medical and Dental
Assistants
3746 West Mineral King
Visalia 93277

Hacienda La Puente Unified School
District-Valley Vocational Center
15959 East Gale Ave.
La Puente 91749

Institute for Business and Technology
2550 Scott Blvd.
Santa Clara 95050

Institute of Business and Medical
Technology
75-110 Saint Charles Place
Palm Desert 92260

Institute of Business Technology
5607 Capistrano
Woodland Hills 90303

Institute of Computer Technology
3200 Wilshire Blvd.
Los Angeles 90010

Maric College of Medical Careers
7202 Princess View Dr.
San Diego 92120

Maric College of Medical Careers
1300 Rancheros Dr.
San Marcos 92069

Maric College of Medical Careers-Vista
Campus
1593C East Vista Way
Vista 92084

McKinnon Institute of Professional
Massage and Bodywork
3798 Grand Ave.
Oakland 94610-1594

Modern Technology School of X-Ray
1232 East Katella Ave.
Anaheim 92805

Modern Technology School of X-Ray
6180 Laurel Canyon Blvd.
North Hollywood 91606

MTI Business College, Inc.
6006 North El Dorado St.
Stockton 95207-4349

National Career Education
6060 Sunrise Vista Dr.
Citrus Heights 95610

National Education Center-Bryman
Campus
1120 North Brookhurst St.
Anaheim 92801

National Education Center-Bryman
Campus
5350 Atlantic Ave.
Long Beach 90805

National Education Center-Bryman
Campus
1017 Wilshire Blvd.
Los Angeles 90017

National Education Center-Bryman
Campus
1600 Broadway
Oakland 94612

National Education Center-Bryman
Campus
3505 North Hart Ave.
Rosemead 91770

National Education Center-Bryman
Campus
731 Market St.
San Francisco 94103

National Education Center-Bryman
Campus
2015 Naglee Ave.
San Jose 95128

National Education Center-Bryman
Campus
4212 West Artesia Blvd.
Torrance 90504

National Education Center-Bryman
Campus
20835 Sherman Way
Winnetka 91306

National Education Center-Sawyer
Campus
8475 Jackson Rd.
Sacramento 95826

National Education Center-Skadron
College of Business
825 East Hospitality Ln.
San Bernardino 92408

Newbridge College
700 El Camino Real
Tustin 92680

Nova Institute of Health Technology
2400 South Western Ave.
Los Angeles 90018

Nova Institute of Health Technology
520 North Euclid Ave.
Ontario 91762

Nova Institute of Health Technology
11416 Whittier Blvd.
Whittier 90601

Phillips College-Inland Empire Campus
4300 Central Ave.
Riverside 92506

Platt College-San Diego
6250 El Cajon Blvd.
San Diego 92115

San Joaquin Valley College
201 New Stine Rd.
Bakersfield 93309

San Joaquin Valley College
3333 North Bond
Fresno 93726

San Joaquin Valley College
8400 West Mineral King Ave.
Visalia 93291

Santa Barbara Business College
211 South Real Rd.
Bakerfield 93309

Santa Barbara Business College
4333 Hansen Ave.
Fremont 94536

Santa Barbara Business College-Santa
Maria Branch
303 East Plaza Dr.
Santa Maria 93454

Sawyer College at Ventura
2101 East Gonzales Rd.
Oxnard 93030

Shasta College
P.O. Box 496006
Redding 96049

Simi Valley Adult School
3192 Los Angeles Ave.
Simi Valley 93065

Southern California College of
Medical-Dental Care
1717 South Brookhurst
Anaheim 92804

Technical Health Careers School
11603 South Western Ave.
Los Angeles 90047

Technical School of Orthopedics
1101 South Winchester Blvd.
San Jose 95128

Travel and Trade Career Institute
3635 Atlantic Ave.
Long Beach 90807

United Education Institute
3727 West Sixth St.
Los Angeles 90020

Watterson College
1165 East Colorado Blvd.
Pasadena 91106

Watterson College Pacific
815 North Oxnard Blvd.
Oxnard 93030

Watterson College-Business
1422 South Azusa Ave.
West Covina 91791

Western Career College
8909 Folsom Blvd.
Sacramento 95826

Western Career College
170 Bay Fair Mall
San Leandro 94578

COLORADO

Blair Junior College
828 Wooten Rd.
Colorado Springs 80915

Concorde Career Institute
770 Grant St.
Denver 80203

Denver Technical College at Colorado
Springs
225 South Union Blvd.
Colorado Springs 80910

Heritage College of Health Careers
12 Lakeside Ln.
Denver 80212

Medical Careers Training Center
4020 South College
Fort Collins 80525

PPI Health Careers School
2345 North Academy Blvd.
Colorado Springs 80909

CONNECTICUT

Branford Hall Career Institute
Nine Business Park Dr.
Branford 06405

Huntington Institute, Inc.
193 Broadway
Norwich 06360

Stone Academy
1315 Dixwell Ave.
Hamden 06514

DELAWARE

Star Technical Institute
631 West Newport Pike, Graystone Plaza
Wilmington 19804

DISTRICT OF COLUMBIA

Harrison Center for Career Education
624 Ninth St. NW
Washington 20001

National Education Center-Capitol Hill
    Campus
810 First St. NE
Washington 20002

FLORIDA

Career Training Institute
101 West Main St.
Leesburg 34748

Career Training Institute
2120 West Colonial
Orlando 32804

Concorde Career Institute
7960 Arlington Expwy.
Jacksonville 32211

Concorde Career Institute
4000 North State Rd. 7
Lauderdale Lake 33319

Concorde Career Institute
285 Northwest 199th St.
Miami 33169

Concorde Career Institute
4202 West Spruce St.
Tampa 33607

Florida School of Business
405 East Polk St.
Tampa 33602

Garces Commercial College
1301 Southwest First
Miami 33135

Keiser College of Technology
1500 Northwest 49th St.
Fort Lauderdale 33309

Martin Technical College
1901 Northwest Seventh St.
Miami 33125

Miami Lakes Technical Education Center
5780 Northwest 158th St.
Miami Lakes 33169

Miami Technical College
14701 Northwest Seventh Ave.
North Miami 33168

Miriam Vocational School, Inc.
7311 West Flagler St.
Miami 33144

National Education Center-Bauder
    College Campus
7955 Northwest 12th St.
Miami 33126-1823

National School of Technology, Inc.
4355 West 16th Ave.
Hialeah 33012

National School of Technology, Inc.
16150 Northeast 17th Ave.
North Miami Beach 33162

Orlando College
5500-5800 Diplomat Circle
Orlando 32810

Phillips Junior College
2401 North Harbor City Blvd.
Melbourne 32935

Politechnical Institute of Florida
1405 Southwest 107th Ave.
Miami 33174

Ross Technical Institute
1490 South Military Trail
West Palm Beach 33415

Santa Fe Community College
3000 Northwest 83rd St.
Gainesville 32601

Tampa College
3319 West Hillsborough Ave.
Tampa 33614

Technical Career Institute
720 Northwest 27th Ave.
Miami 33125

Webster College, Inc.
5623 U.S. Hwy. 19 S
New Port Richey 34652

William T McFatter Vocational
    Technical Center
6500 Nova Dr.
Davie 33317

GEORGIA

Atlanta Area Technical School
1560 Stewart Ave. SW
Atlanta 30310

Atlanta College of Medical Dental
    Careers
1240 West Peachtree St. NE
Atlanta 30309-2906

Augusta Technical Institute
3116 Deans Bridge Rd.
Augusta 30906

Branell Institute
1000 Circle 75 Pkwy.
Atlanta 30339

Draughons College-Atlanta
1430 Peachtree St.
Atlanta 30309

Gwinnett Technical Institute
1250 Atkinson Rd., P.O. Box 1505
Lawrenceville 30246-1505

Meadows College of Business
832 South Slappey Blvd.
Albany 31701

Medix Schools
2480 Windy Hill Rd.
Marietta 30067

National Education Center-Bryman
    Campus
40 Marietta St. NW
Atlanta 30303

Valdosta Technical Institute
4089 Valtech Rd.
Valdosta 31602-9796

HAWAII

Medical Assistant School of Hawaii, Inc.
1149 Bethel
Honolulu 96813

IDAHO

American Institute of Health Technology,
    Inc.
6600 Emerald
Boise 83704

College of Southern Idaho
P.O. Box 1238
Twin Falls 83301

Ricks College
Rexburg 83460-4107

ILLINOIS

National Education Center-Bryman
    Campus
17 North State St.
Chicago 60602

National Education Center-Bryman
    Campus
4101 West 95th St.
Oak Lawn 60453-1000

INDIANA

Davenport College-Merrillville
8200 Georgia St.
Merrillville 46410

Indiana Vocational Technical
    College-North Central
1534 West Sample St.
South Bend 46619

Indiana Vocational Technical
    College-Northeast
3800 North Anthony Blvd.
Fort Wayne 46805

Indiana Vocational Technical
    College-South Central
8204 Hwy. 311
Sellersburg 47172

Indiana Vocational Technical
    College-Southwest
3501 First Ave.
Evansville 47710

International Business College
3811 Illinois Rd.
Fort Wayne 46804

Michiana College
1030 East Jefferson Blvd.
South Bend 46617

Professional Career Institute
2611 Waterfront Pkwy., East Dr.
Indianapolis 46214-2028

IOWA

Des Moines Community College
2006 Ankeny Blvd.
Ankeny 50021

Kirkwood Community College
P.O. Box 2068
Cedar Rapids 52406

Palmer College of Chiropractic
1000 Brady St.
Davenport 52803

Spencer School of Business
217 West Fifth St., P.O. Box 5065
Spencer 51301

KANSAS

Bryan Institute
1004 South Oliver
Wichita 67218

Johnson County Area
    Vocational-Technical School
311 East Park
Olathe 66061

Liberal Area Vocational Technical School
P.O. Box 1599
Liberal 67905-1599

Topeka Technical College
1620 Northwest Gage
Topeka 66618

KENTUCKY

Careercom Junior College of Business
1102 South Virginia St.
Hopkinsville 42240

Kentucky College of Business
628 East Main St.
Lexington 40508

Owensboro Junior College of Business
1515 East 18th St., P.O. Box 1350
Owensboro 42303

Spencerian College
4627 Dixie Hwy.
Louisville 40216

LOUISIANA

Ayers Institute, Inc.
2924 Knight St.
Shreveport 71105

Cameron College
2740 Canal St.
New Orleans 70119

Coastal College
2001 Canal St.
New Orleans 70112

Coastal College-Hammond
119 Yokum Rd.
Hammond 70403

Coastal College-Houma
2318 West Park Ave.
Houma 70364

Coastal College-Slidell
320 Howze Beach Rd.
Slidell 70461

Commercial College
2640 Youree Dr.
Shreveport 71104

Commercial College of Baton Rouge
5677 Florida Blvd.
Baton Rouge 70806

Delta Career College
1900 Cameron St.
Lafayette 70506-1608

Delta Schools, Inc.
4549 Johnston St.
Lafayette 70503

Delta Schools, Inc.
413 West Admiral Doyle
New Iberia 70560

Domestic Health Care Institute
4826 Jamestown Ave.
Baton Rouge 70808

Eastern College of Health Vocations
3540 I-10 Service Rd. S
Metairie 70001

National Education Center-Bryman
    Campus
2322 Canal St.
New Orleans 70119

Southern Technical College
303 Rue Louis XIV
Lafayette 70508

Southwest School of Health Careers
2424 Williams Blvd., Plaza 24 Center
Kenner 70062

Spencer College
2902 Florida St.
Baton Rouge 70802

MAINE

Andover College
901 Washington Ave.
Portland 04103

Beal College
629 Main St.
Bangor 04401

Mid-State College
88 East Hardscrabble Rd.
Auburn 04210

MARYLAND

Essex Community College
7201 Rossville Blvd.
Baltimore 21237

Medix Schools
1017 York Rd.
Towson 21204-9840

National Education Center-Temple
School Campus
3601 O'Donnell St.
Baltimore 21224

MASSACHUSETTS

Aquinas College at Newton
15 Walnut Park
Newton 02158

Associated Technical Institute
345 West Cummings Park
Woburn 01801

Bunker Hill Community College
New Rutherford Ave.
Boston 02129

Fisher College
118 Beacon St.
Boston 02116

National Education Center-Bryman
Campus
323 Boylston St.
Brookline 02146

The Salter School
458 Bridge St.
Springfield 01103

The Salter School
155 Ararat St.
Worcester 01606

MICHIGAN

American Career Academy
15160 West Eight Mile Rd.
Oak Park 48237

Carnegie Institute
550 Stephenson Hwy.
Troy 48083

Delta College
University Center 48710

Detroit Business Institute
115 State St.
Detroit 48226

Detroit Business Institute-Downriver
19100 Fort St.
Riverview 48192

Grand Rapids Educational Center
1750 Woodworth NE
Grand Rapids 49505

Grand Rapids Educational Center
5349 West Main
Kalamazoo 49009

Lansing Community College
419 North Capitol Ave.
Lansing 48901-7210

Macomb Community College
14500 Twelve Mile Rd.
Warren 48093-3896

National Education Center-Bryman
Campus
4244 Oakman Blvd.
Detroit 48204

National Education Center-National
Institute of Technology
18000 Newburgh Rd.
Livonia 48152

National Education Center-National
Institute of Technology
2620 Remico St. SW
Wyoming 49509

Payne-Pulliam School of Trade and
Commerce, Inc.
2345 Cass Ave.
Detroit 48201

Pontiac Business Institute-Oxford
775 West Drahner Rd.
Oxford 48371

Professional Careers Institute
23300 Greenfield Ave.
Oak Park 48237

Ross Business Institute
37065 South Gratiot
Clinton Township 48036

Ross Business Institute
1285 North Telegraph
Monroe 48161

Ross Business Institute
22293 Eureka
Taylor 48180

Ross Medical Education Center
1036 Gilbert St.
Flint 48532

Ross Medical Education Center
2035 28th St. SE
Grand Rapids 49508

Ross Medical Education Center
1188 North West Ave.
Jackson 49202

Ross Medical Education Center
913 West Holmes
Lansing 48910

Ross Medical Education Center
950 Norton Ave., Park Row Mall
Roosevelt Park 49441

Ross Medical Education Center
4054 Bay Rd.
Saginaw 48603

Ross Medical Education Center
26417 Hoover Rd.
Warren 48089

Ross Medical Education Center
253 Summit Dr.
Waterford 48328

Ross Technical Institute
4703 Washtenaw
Ann Arbor 48108-1411

Ross Technical Institute
5757 Whitmore Lake Rd.
Brighton 48116

Ross Technical Institute
1553 Woodward
Detroit 48226

Ross Technical Institute
20820 Greenfield Rd.
Oak Park 48237

Schoolcraft College
18600 Haggerty Rd.
Livonia 48152

Technical Career Institute
35205 Gratoit
Clinton 48043

MINNESOTA

Concorde Career Institute, Inc.
12 North 12th St.
Minneapolis 55403

Duluth Business University, Inc.
412 West Superior St.
Duluth 55802

Globe College of Business
175 Fifth St. E, P.O. Box 60
Saint Paul 55101-2901

Lakeland Medical and Dental Academy
1402 West Lake St.
Minneapolis 55408

Medical Institute of Minnesota
5503 Green Valley Dr.
Bloomington 55437

Northwest Technical College-East Grand
Forks
Hwy. 220 N
East Grand Forks 56721

Rochester Community College
851 30th Ave. SE
Rochester 55904-4999

MISSISSIPPI

Moore Career College
1500 North 31st Ave.
Hattiesburg 39401

Moore Career College
2460 Terry Rd.
Jackson 39204

Moore Career College
1500 Hwy. 19 N
Meridian 39303

Northeast Mississippi Community
College
Cunningham Blvd.
Booneville 38829

MISSOURI

Al-Med Academy
10963 Saint Charles Rock Rd.
Saint Louis 63074

Bryan Institute
12184 Natural Bridge Rd.
Bridgeton 63044

Concorde Career Institute
3239 Broadway
Kansas City 64111

Eastern Jackson County College of
Allied Health
808 South 15th St.
Blue Springs, 64015

Metro Business College
1407 Southwest Blvd.
Jefferson City 65109

Metro Business College
2305 North Bishop Hwy. 63 N
Rolla 65401

Metro Business College of Cape
Girardeau
1732 North Kingshighway
Cape Girardeau 63701

Midwest Institute for Medical Assistants
112 West Jefferson
Kirkwood 63122

Missouri School for Doctors' Assistants
10121 Manchester Rd.
Saint Louis 63122

Phillips Junior College
1010 West Sunshine
Springfield 65807

Saint Louis College of Health Careers
4484 West Pine
Saint Louis 63108

Tad Technical Institute
7910 Troost Ave.
Kansas City 64131

NEBRASKA

Institute of Computer Science
808 South 74th Place, 7400 Court
Building
Omaha 68114

Omaha College of Health Careers
10845 Harney St.
Omaha 68154

Southeast Community College-Lincoln
Campus
8800 O St.
Lincoln 68520

NEVADA

American Academy for Career Education
3120 East Desert Inn Rd.
Las Vegas 89121

Canterbury Career Schools
2215C Renaissance Dr.
Las Vegas 89119

NEW HAMPSHIRE

New Hampshire Technical College at
Claremont
One College Dr.
Claremont 03743

NEW JERSEY

American Business Academy
66 Moore St.
Hackensack 07601

Barclay Career School
28 South Harrison St.
East Orange 07017

Berdan Institute
265 Rte. 46
Totowa 07512

Business Training Institute
Four Forest Ave.
Paramus 07652

Dover Business College
15 East Blackwell St.
Dover 07801

Dover Business College
East 81 & Rte. 4 W
Paramus 07652

Drake College of Business
Nine Caldwell Place
Elizabeth 07201

Ho-Ho-Kus School
27 South Franklin Tpke.
Ramsey 07446

Omega Institute
Rte. 130 S, Cinnaminson Mall
Cinnaminson 08077

Star Technical Institute
2224 U.S. Hwy. 130, Park Plaza
Edgewater Park 08010

Star Technical Institute
1255 Rte. 70
Lakewood 08701

Star Technical Institute
1386 South Delsea Dr.
Vineland 08360

Star Technical Institute-Deptford
251 Delsea Dr.
Deptford 08104

Star Technical Institute-Ocean Township
2105 Hwy. 35
Ocean Township 07712

NEW MEXICO

Franklin Medical College-Branch Campus
2400 Louisiana Blvd. NE
Albuquerque 87110

Pima Medical Institute
2201 San Pedro NE
Albuquerque 87110

NEW YORK

Bayley Seton Hospital School Physicians
   Assistant
75 Vanderbilt Ave.
Staten Island 10304

Blake Business School-New York City
20 Cooper Square
New York 10003

Bryant and Stratton Business
   Institute-Buffalo
1028 Main St.
Buffalo 14202

Hudson Valley Community College
80 Vandenburgh Ave.
Troy 12180

Mandl School
254 West 54th St.
New York 10019

New York School for Medical and
   Dental Assistants
116-16 Queens Blvd.
Forest Hills 11375

Suburban Technical School
2650 Sunrise Hwy.
East Islip 11730

Suburban Technical School
175 Fulton Ave.
Hempstead 11550

NORTH CAROLINA

Central Piedmont Community College
P.O. Box 35009
Charlotte 28235

Miller-Motte Business College
606 South College Rd.
Wilmington 28403

NORTH DAKOTA

Interstate Business College
520 East Main Ave.
Bismarck 58501

Interstate Business College
2720 32nd Ave. SW
Fargo 58103

OHIO

Akron Medical-Dental Institute
733 West Market St.
Akron 44303

American School of Technology
2100 Morse Rd.
Columbus 43229

Aristotle Institute of Medical-Dental
   Technology
5900 Westerville Rd.
Westerville 43081

Belmont Technical College
120 Fox Shannon Place
Saint Clairsville 43950

Boheckers Business College
326 East Main St.
Ravenna 44266

Cleveland Institute of Dental-Medical
   Assistants
1836 Euclid Ave.
Cleveland 44115

Cleveland Institute of Dental-Medical
   Assistants
5564 Mayfield Rd.
Lyndhurst 44124

Cleveland Institute of Dental-Medical
   Assistants
5733 Hopkins Rd.
Mentor 44060

Columbus Para Professional Institute
1077 Lexington Ave.
Columbus 43201

Cuyahoga Community College District
700 Carnegie Ave.
Cleveland 44115-2878

ESI Career Center
25301 Euclid Ave.
Euclid 44117

ESI Career Center
1985 North Ridge Rd. E
Lorain 44055

Fairfield Career Center
4000 Columbus Lancaster Rd.
Carroll 43112

Institute of Medical-Dental Technology
4452 Eastgate Blvd.
Cincinnati 45245

Institute of Medical-Dental Technology
375 Glensprings Dr.
Cincinnati 45246

Knox County Career Center
306 Martinsburg Rd.
Mount Vernon 43050

Mahoning County Joint Vocational
   School District
7300 North Palmyra Rd.
Canfield 44406

MTI Business College
1901 East 13th St.
Cleveland 44114

National Education Center
14445 Broadway Ave.
Cleveland 44125

National Education Center-National
   Institute of Technology
1225 Orlen Ave.
Cuyahoga Falls 44221

Professional Skills Institute
1232 Flaire Dr.
Toledo 43615

RETS Technical Center
116 Westpark Rd.
Centerville 45459

Sawyer College of Business
3150 Mayfield Rd.
Cleveland Heights 44118

Southwestern College of Business
225 West First St.
Dayton 45402

Stautzenberger College
5355 Southwyck Blvd.
Toledo 43614

Technology Education Center
288 South Hamilton Rd.
Columbus 43213

Tri-County Vocational School
15675 SR 691
Nelsonville 45764

Trumbull County Joint Vocational
   School District
528 Educational Hwy.
Warren 44483

University of Toledo
2801 West Bancroft
Toledo 43606

Warren County Career Center
3525 N SR 48
Lebanon 45036-1099

OKLAHOMA

Bryan Institute
2843 East 51st St.
Tulsa 74105-1709

Central Oklahoma Area Vocational
   Technical School
1720 South Main
Sapulpa 74030

De Marge College
3608 Northwest 58th
Oklahoma City 73112

Francis Tuttle Area Vocational-Technical
   Center
12777 North Rockwell Ave.
Oklahoma City 73142-2789

Platt College
6125 West Reno
Okc 73127

Southern Oklahoma Area
   Vocational-Technical Center
2610 Sam Noble Pkwy.
Ardmore 73401

Wright Business School
2219 Southwest 74th St.
Oklahoma City 73159

OREGON

Apollo College-Portland, Inc.
2600 Southeast 98th Ave.
Portland 97266

College of America
921 Southwest Washington
Portland 97205

Pioneer Pacific College
25195 Southwest Parkway Ave.
Wilsonville 97070

Western Business College
505 Southwest Sixth Ave.
Portland 97204

PENNSYLVANIA

Academy of Medical Arts and Business
279 Boas St.
Harrisburg 17102

Allied Medical Careers, Inc.
2901 Pittston Ave.
Scranton 18505

Allied Medical Careers, Inc.
104 Woodward Hill Rd.
Edwardsville 18704

Altoona Area Vocational Technical
   School
1500 Fourth Ave.
Altoona 16602

Antonelli Medical and Professional
   Institute
1700 Industrial Hwy.
Pottstown 19464

Berks Technical Institute
832 North Park Rd., Four Park Plaza
Wyomissing 19610

Career Training Academy
244 Center Rd.
Monroeville 15146

Career Training Academy
703 Fifth Ave.
New Kensington 15068

The Craft Institute
Nine South 12th St.
Philadelphia 19107

Delaware Valley Academy of Medical
   and Dental Assistants
6539 Roosevelt Blvd.
Philadelphia 19149

Duffs Business Institute
110 Ninth St.
Pittsburgh 15222

ICM School of Business
10-14 Wood St.
Pittsburgh 15222

J H Thompson Academies
2910 State St.
Erie 16508

Median School of Allied Health Careers
125 Seventh St.
Pittsburgh 15222-3400

National Education Center-Thompson
   Institute Campus
5650 Derry St.
Harrisburg 17111

National Education Center-Thompson
   Institute Campus
3440 Market St.
Philadelphia 19104

North Hills School of Health Occupations
1500 Northway Mall
Pittsburgh 15237

Sawyer School
717 Liberty Ave.
Pittsburgh 15222

Star Technical Institute-Kingston
212 Wyoming Ave.
Kingston 18704

Star Technical Institute-Whitehall
1541 Alta Dr.
Whitehall 18052

SOUTH CAROLINA

Central Carolina Technical College
506 North Guignard Dr.
Sumter 29150

Trident Technical College
P.O. Box 118067
Charleston 29423-8067

TENNESSEE

Davidson Technical College
212 Pavilion Blvd.
Nashville 37217-1002

Draughons College
3200 Elvis Presley Blvd.
Memphis 38116

Fugazzi College
5042 Linbar Dr.
Nashville 37217

Medical Career College
537 Main St.
Nashville 37206

TEXAS

The Academy of Health Care Professions
1919 Northloop W
Houston 77008

ATI Health Education Center
8150 Brookriver Dr.
Dallas 75247

ATI Health Education Center
1200 Summit Ave.
Fort Worth 76102

Avalon Vocational Technical Institute
1407 Texas St.
Fort Worth 76102

Avalon Vocational Technical Institute
4241 Tanglewood
Odessa 79762

Bradford School of Business
4669 Southwest Fwy.
Houston 77027

Bryan Institute
1719 Pioneer Pkwy. W
Arlington 76013

Career Centers of Texas El Paso, Inc.
8375 Burnham Dr.
El Paso 79907

International Career School
7647 Belfort
Houston 77061

National Education Center-Bryman
Campus
9724 Beechnut
Houston 77036

National Education Center-Bryman
Campus
16416 North Chase Dr.
Houston 77060

National Education Center-NIT Campus
3622 Fredericksburg Rd.
San Antonio 78201

PCI Health Training Center
8101 John Carpenter Fwy.
Dallas 75247

San Antonio College of Medical and
Dental Assistants-Central
4205 San Pedro Ave.
San Antonio 78212

San Antonio College of Medical and
Dental Assistants-South
3900 North 23rd
McAllen 78501

San Antonio College of Medical and
Dental Assistants
5280 Medical Dr.
San Antonio 78229

Southern Career Institute, Inc.
2301 South Congress
Austin 78704

Southern Careers Institute-South Texas
3233 North 38th
McAllen 78501

Southwest School of Business and
Technical Careers
602 West South Cross
San Antonio 78221

Southwest School of Medical Assistants
201 West Sheridan
San Antonio 78204

Western Technical Institute
4710 Alabama St., P.O. Box M
El Paso 79951

UTAH

American Institute of Medical-Dental
Technology
1675 North 200 West
Provo 84604

Bryman School
1144 West 3300 South
Salt Lake City 84119-3330

Stevens-Henager College of Business
2168 Washington Blvd.
Ogden 84401

Stevens-Henager College of Business
25 East 1700 South
Provo 84606-6157

VIRGINIA

Career Development Center
605 Thimble Shoals
Newport News 23606

Commonwealth College
300 Boush St.
Norfolk 23510

Commonwealth College
4160 Virginia Beach Blvd.
Virginia Beach 23452

Dominion Business School
4142-1 Melrose Ave.
Roanoke 24017

National Education Center-Kee Business
College Campus
861 Glenrock Rd.
Norfolk 23502

National Education Center-Kee Business
College Campus
6301 Midlothian Tpke.
Richmond 23225

Tidewater Technical
1760 East Little Creek Rd.
Norfolk 23518

Tidewater Technical
2697 Dean Dr.
Virginia Beach 23452

WASHINGTON

Eton Technical Institute
209 East Casino Rd.
Everett 98204

Eton Technical Institute
31919 Sixth Ave. S
Federal Way 98063

Eton Technical Institute
3649 Frontage Rd.
Port Orchard 98366

Pima Medical Institute
1627 Eastlake Ave. E
Seattle 98102

Seattle Vocational Institute
315 22nd Ave. S
Seattle 98144

Spokane Community College
North 1810 Greene Ave.
Spokane 99207

Trend College
North 214 Wall St.
Spokane 99201

WEST VIRGINIA

Boone County Career & Technical Center
P.O. Box 50B
Danville 25053

Huntington Junior College
900 Fifth Ave.
Huntington 25701

Opportunities Industrialization
Center-North Central West Virginia
120 Jackson St.
Fairmont 26554

West Virginia Career College
148 Willey St.
Morgantown 26505

WISCONSIN

Blackhawk Technical College
P.O. Box 5009
Janesville 53547

Mid-State Technical College-Main
Campus
500 32nd St. N
Wisconsin Rapids 54494

Milwaukee Area Technical College
700 West State St.
Milwaukee 53233

Northeast Wisconsin Technical College
2740 West Mason St., P.O. Box 19042
Green Bay 54307-9042

Waukesha County Technical College
800 Main St.
Pewaukee 53072

Western Wisconsin Technical College
304 North Sixth St., P.O. Box 908
La Crosse 54602-0908

Wisconsin Area Vocational Training and
Adult Education System District
Number Four
3550 Anderson St.
Madison 53704

Wisconsin Indianhead Technical College
505 Pine Ridge Dr., P.O. Box 10B
Shell Lake 54871

Medical and Biological Laboratory Technology

ALABAMA

Capps College
3100 Cottage Hill Rd.
Mobile 36606

Community College of the Air Force
Maxwell Air Force Base
Montgomery 36112

Jefferson State Community College
2601 Carson Rd.
Birmingham 35215-3098

University of Alabama at Birmingham
UAB MJH 107 2010
Birmingham 35294-2010

ARIZONA

Apollo College
3870 North Oracle Rd.
Tucson 85705

Apollo College-Phoenix, Inc.
8503 North 27th Ave.
Phoenix 85051

Institute of Medical and Dental
Technology
20 East Main St.
Mesa 85201

Long Medical Institute
4126 North Black Canyon Hwy.
Phoenix 85017

Occupational Training Center
4136 North 75th Ave.
Phoenix 85033

Phoenix College
1202 West Thomas Rd.
Phoenix 85013

Pima Medical Institute
2300 East Broadway Rd.
Tempe 85282

Tucson College
7302-10 East 22nd St.
Tucson 85710

ARKANSAS

Arkansas Valley Technical Institute
Hwy. 23 N, P.O. Box 506
Ozark 72949

Carti School of Radiation Therapy
Technology
P.O. Box 5210
Little Rock 72215

CALIFORNIA

American School of X-Ray
13723 Harvard Place
Gardena 90249

Associated Technical College
1670 Wilshire Blvd.
Los Angeles 90017

Butte College
3536 Butte Campus Dr.
Oroville 95965

Cabot College
41 East 12th St.
National City 91950

El Camino College
16007 Crenshaw Blvd.
Torrance 90506

Glendale Career College
1021 Grandview Ave.
Glendale 91201

Grossmont College
8800 Grossmont College Dr.
El Cajon 92020

Hacienda La Puente Unified School
District-Valley Vocational Center
15959 East Gale Ave.
La Puente 91749

Ila Institute
202 West Lincoln Ave.
Orange 92665-1058

Institute for Business and Technology
2550 Scott Blvd.
Santa Clara 95050

Loma Linda University
Loma Linda 92350

Maric College of Medical Careers
1300 Rancheros Dr.
San Marcos 92069

McKinnon Institute of Professional
Massage and Bodywork
3798 Grand Ave.
Oakland 94610-1594

Modern Technology School of X-Ray
1232 East Katella Ave.
Anaheim 92805

Modern Technology School of X-Ray
6180 Laurel Canyon Blvd.
North Hollywood 91606

National Career Education
6060 Sunrise Vista Dr.
Citrus Heights 95610

Newbridge College
700 El Camino Real
Tustin 92680

Nova Institute of Health Technology
2400 South Western Ave.
Los Angeles 90018

Nova Institute of Health Technology
11416 Whittier Blvd.
Whittier 90601

Orange Coast College
2701 Fairview Rd.
Costa Mesa 92626

Simi Valley Adult School
3192 Los Angeles Ave.
Simi Valley 93065

Technical School of Orthopedics
1101 South Winchester Blvd.
San Jose 95128

COLORADO

Institute for Nuclear Medical Education
5171 Eldorado Springs Dr.
Boulder 80303

North Colorado Medical Center School
of Medical Technology
1801 16th St.
Greeley 80631

PPI Health Careers School
2345 North Academy Blvd.
Colorado Springs 80909

Regis University
3333 Regis Blvd.
Denver 80221-1099

CONNECTICUT

Department of Education Hartford
Hospital School of Allied Health
312 ConklinSeymour St.
Hartford 06115

Housatonic Community College
510 Barnum Ave.
Bridgeport 06608

Huntington Institute, Inc.
193 Broadway
Norwich 06360

South Central Community College
60 Sargent Dr.
New Haven 06511

DELAWARE

Delaware Technical and Community
College-Southern Campus
P.O. Box 610
Georgetown 19947

Delaware Technical and Community
College Stanton-Wilmington
400 Stanton-Christiana Rd.
Newark 19702

DISTRICT OF COLUMBIA

Harrison Center for Career Education
624 Ninth St. NW
Washington 20001

FLORIDA

Beacon Career Institute, Inc.
2900 Northwest 183rd St.
Miami 33056

Brevard Community College
1519 Clearlake Rd.
Cocoa 32922

Florida Community College at
Jacksonville
501 West State St.
Jacksonville 32202

H W Brewster Technical Center
2222 North Tampa St.
Tampa 33602-2196

Keiser College of Technology
1500 Northwest 49th St.
Fort Lauderdale 33309

Lake City Community College
Rte. 3, P.O. Box 7
Lake City 32055

Lee County Vocational-Technical Center
3800 Michigan Ave.
Fort Myers 33916

Miami-Dade Community College
300 Northeast Second Ave.
Miami 33132

Miriam Vocational School, Inc.
7311 West Flagler St.
Miami 33144

National School of Technology, Inc.
4355 West 16th Ave.
Hialeah 33012

National School of Technology, Inc.
16150 Northeast 17th Ave.
North Miami Beach 33162

Pasco-Hernando Community College
36727 Blanton Rd.
Dade City 33525-7599

Santa Fe Community College
3000 Northwest 83rd St.
Gainesville 32601

Sarasota County Technical Institute
4748 Beneva Rd.
Sarasota 34233-1798

Sheridan Vocational Center
5400 West Sheridan St.
Hollywood 33021

Ultrasound Diagnostic School
10199 Southside Blvd., Grand Parc
Jacksonville 32250

Ultrasound Diagnostic School
9950 Princess Palm Ave.
Tampa 33619

William T McFatter Vocational
Technical Center
6500 Nova Dr.
Davie 33317

GEORGIA

Atlanta College of Medical Dental
Careers
1240 West Peachtree St. NE
Atlanta 30309-2906

Branell Institute
1000 Circle 75 Pkwy.
Atlanta 30339

Columbus College
4225 University Ave.
Columbus 31907-5645

Dekalb Technical Institute
495 North Indian Creek Dr.
Clarkston 30021

Fulton Dekalb Hospital Authority-Grady
Memorial Hospital
80 Butler St., P.O. Box 26044
Atlanta 30335-3801

ILLINOIS

Medical Careers Institute
116 South Michigan Ave.
Chicago 60603

Methodist Medical Center of
Illinois-Medical Technology
221 Northeast Glen Oak Ave.
Peoria 61636-0001

Oakton Community College
1600 East Golf Rd.
Des Plaines 60016

Swedish American Hospital School of
Surgical Technology
1400 Charles St.
Rockford 61104-1257

Triton College
2000 Fifth Ave.
River Grove 60171

INDIANA

Vincennes University
1002 North First St.
Vincennes 47591

IOWA

Des Moines Community College
2006 Ankeny Blvd.
Ankeny 50021

Iowa Methodist Medical Center-Clinical
Laboratory Science Program
1200 Pleasant St.
Des Moines 50309-1406

Palmer College of Chiropractic
1000 Brady St.
Davenport 52803

Saint Luke's Regional Medical
Center-School of Medical Technology
2720 Stone Park Blvd.
Sioux City 51104

KANSAS

Seward County Community College
P.O. Box 1137
Liberal 67905-1137

Wichita Area Vocational Technical
School
428 South Broadway
Wichita 67202-3910

KENTUCKY

Spencerian College
4627 Dixie Hwy.
Louisville 40216

University of Louisville
South Third St.
Louisville 40292-0001

LOUISIANA

Delgado Community College
615 City Park Ave.
New Orleans 70119

Eastern College of Health Vocations
3540 I-10 Service Rd. S
Metairie 70001

New Orleans Regional Technical Institute
980 Navarre Ave.
New Orleans 70124

Our Lady of the Lake Medical
Center-School of Medical Technology
5000 Hennessy Blvd.
Baton Rouge 70808

MARYLAND

Hagerstown Business College
18618 Crestwood Dr.
Hagerstown 21742

Ultrasound Diagnostic School
1320 Fenwick Ln.
Silver Spring 20910

MASSACHUSETTS

Middlesex Community College
Springs Rd.
Bedford 01730

Northeastern University
360 Huntington Ave.
Boston 02115

Springfield Technical Community
College
Armory Square
Springfield 01105

Ultrasound Diagnostic School
33 Boston Post Rd. W
Marlborough 01752

MICHIGAN

Carnegie Institute
550 Stephenson Hwy.
Troy 48083

Krainz Woods Academy of Medical
 Laboratory Technology
4327 East Seven Mile Rd.
Detroit 48234

Marygrove College
8425 West McNichols Rd.
Detroit 48221

Northern Michigan University
1401 Presque Isle
Marquette 49855

Oakland Community College
2480 Opdyke Rd.
Bloomfield Hills 48304-2266

Schoolcraft College
18600 Haggerty Rd.
Livonia 48152

MINNESOTA

Duluth Technical College
2101 Trinity Rd.
Duluth 55811

Fergus Falls Community College
1414 College Way
Fergus Falls 56537

Lakeland Medical and Dental Academy
1402 West Lake St.
Minneapolis 55408

Mayo School of Health-Related Sciences
200 First St. SW
Rochester 55905

Medical Institute of Minnesota
5503 Green Valley Dr.
Bloomington 55437

North Hennepin Community College
7411 85th Ave. N
Brooklyn Park 55445

Northwest Technical College-East Grand
 Forks
Hwy. 220 N
East Grand Forks 56721

Range Technical College-Hibbing
 Campus
2900 East Beltline
Hibbing 55746

Saint Cloud Technical College
1540 Northway Dr.
Saint Cloud 56303

Saint Paul Technical College
235 Marshall Ave.
Saint Paul 55102

MISSISSIPPI

Mississippi Gulf Coast Community
 College
Central Office, P.O. Box 67
Perkinston 39573

MISSOURI

Al-Med Academy
10963 Saint Charles Rock Rd.
Saint Louis 63074

Saint John's Regional Health Center
 School of Medical Technology
1235 East Cherokee
Springfield 65804-2263

Saint Louis Community College-Forest
 Park
5600 Oakland Ave.
Saint Louis 63110

Trinity Lutheran Hospital School of
 Histological Technology
3030 Baltimore
Kansas City 64108

NEW JERSEY

Bergen Community College
400 Paramus Rd.
Paramus 07652

Drake College of Business
Nine Caldwell Place
Elizabeth 07201

Hudson County Area Vocational
 Technical School-Bayonne Center
West 30th St.
Bayonne 07002

Omega Institute
Rte. 130 S, Cinnaminson Mall
Cinnaminson 08077

Saint Joseph's Hospital School of
 Medical Technology
703 Main St.
Paterson 07503

Star Technical Institute
1255 Rte. 70
Lakewood 08701

Star Technical Institute-Ocean Township
2105 Hwy. 35
Ocean Township 07712

Ultrasound Diagnostic School
675 Rte. 1 & Atgill Ln., Plaza One
Iselin 08830

University of Medicine and Dentistry of
 New Jersey
30 Bergen St.
Newark 07107

NEW MEXICO

Albuquerque Technical-Vocational
 Institute
525 Buena Vista SE
Albuquerque 87106

New Mexico Junior College
5317 Lovington Hwy.
Hobbs 88240

Pima Medical Institute
2201 San Pedro NE
Albuquerque 87110

NEW YORK

Dutchess Community College
Pendell Rd.
Poughkeepsie 12601

Hudson Valley Community College
80 Vandenburgh Ave.
Troy 12180

Institute of Allied Medical Professions
106 Central Park S
New York 10019

Mandl School
254 West 54th St.
New York 10019

Monroe Community College
1000 East Henrietta Rd.
Rochester 14623

New York School for Medical and
 Dental Assistants
116-16 Queens Blvd.
Forest Hills 11375

NYU Medical Center Allied Health
 Education
342 East 26th St.
New York 10010

Saint Vincent's Hospital Medical
 Technology Program
153 West 11th St.
New York 10011

SUNY College of Technology at
 Farmingdale
Melville Rd.
Farmingdale 11735

SUNY Westchester Commmunity College
75 Grasslands Rd.
Valhalla 10595

Syrit Computer School Systems
1760 53rd St.
Brooklyn 11204

Ultrasound Diagnostic School
One Old Country Rd.
Carle Place 11514

Ultrasound Diagnostic School
2269 Saw Mill River Pkwy.
Elmsford 10523

Ultrasound Diagnostic School
121 West 27th St.
New York 10001

NORTH CAROLINA

Alamance Community College
P.O. Box 8000
Graham 27253

Caldwell Community College and
 Technical Institute
P.O. Box 600
Lenoir 28645

Halifax Community College
P.O. Drawer 809
Weldon 27890

Northern Hospital of Surry Colorado
 School of Medical Laboratory
 Technology
830 Rockford St., P.O. Box 1101
Mount Airy 27030

Pitt Community College
Hwy. 11 S, P.O. Drawer 7007
Greenville 27835-7007

Southwestern Community College
275 Webster Rd.
Sylva 28779

Wake Technical Community College
9101 Fayetteville Rd.
Raleigh 27603-5696

NORTH DAKOTA

Trinity School of Medical Technology
Three Burdick Expwy.
Minot 58701

OHIO

Akron Medical-Dental Institute
733 West Market St.
Akron 44303

Cincinnati Technical College
3520 Central Pkwy.
Cincinnati 45223

Cleveland Institute of Dental-Medical
 Assistants
1836 Euclid Ave.
Cleveland 44115

Cleveland Institute of Dental-Medical
 Assistants
5564 Mayfield Rd.
Lyndhurst 44124

Cleveland Institute of Dental-Medical
 Assistants
5733 Hopkins Rd.
Mentor 44060

Columbus State Community College
550 East Spring St., P.O. Box 1609
Columbus 43216

Cuyahoga Community College District
700 Carnegie Ave.
Cleveland 44115-2878

Kettering College of Medical Arts
3737 Southern Blvd.
Kettering 45429-1299

Marion Technical College
1467 Mount Vernon Ave.
Marion 43302-5694

Owens Technical College
30335 Oregon Rd., P.O. Box 10000
Toledo 43699-1947

Professional Skills Institute
1232 Flaire Dr.
Toledo 43615

Riverside School of Medical Technology
1600 North Superior St.
Toledo 43604

Tri-Rivers Career Center
2222 Marion Mount Gilead Rd.
Marion 43302

Trumbull County Joint Vocational
 School District
528 Educational Hwy.
Warren 44483

OKLAHOMA

Tulsa Junior College
6111 East Skelly Dr.
Tulsa 74135

OREGON

Concorde Career Institute
1827 Northeast 44th Ave.
Portland 97213

PENNSYLVANIA

Abington Memorial Hospital Medical
 Technology Program
1200 Old York Rd.
Abington 19001

Allied Medical Careers, Inc.
2901 Pittston Ave.
Scranton 18505

Allied Medical Careers, Inc.
104 Woodward Hill Rd.
Edwardsville 18704

Chambersburg Hospital Medical
 Laboratory Technical School
112 North Seventh St., P.O. Box 187
Chambersburg 17201

Community College of Allegheny County
800 Allegheny Ave.
Pittsburgh 15233-1895

Community College of Philadelphia
1700 Spring Garden St.
Philadelphia 19130

Conemaugh Valley Memorial Hospital
1086 Franklin St.
Johnstown 15905-4398

Divine Providence Hospital School of
Medical Technology
1100 Grampian Blvd.
Williamsport 17754

Edinboro University of Pennsylvania
Edinboro 16444

Gwynedd-Mercy College
Sumneytown Pike
Gwynedd Valley 19437

Johnson Technical Institute
3427 North Main Ave.
Scranton 18508

Mount Aloysius College
One College Dr.
Cresson 16630-1999

North Hills School of Health Occupations
1500 Northway Mall
Pittsburgh 15237

Pennsylvania State University-New
Kensington Campus
3550 Seventh Street Rd.
New Kensington 15068

Ultra Sound Diagnosis School
12901 Townsend Ave.
Philadelphia 19154

Ultrasound Diagnostic School
5830 Ellsworth Ave.
Pittsburgh 15232

Western School of Health & Business
Careers
411 Seventh Ave.
Pittsburgh 15219

Wilkes-Barre General Hospital-School of
Medical Technology
North River and Auburn
Wilkes-Barre 18764

RHODE ISLAND

Community College of Rhode Island
400 East Ave.
Warwick 02886-1805

SOUTH CAROLINA

Central Carolina Technical College
506 North Guignard Dr.
Sumter 29150

Midlands Technical College
P.O. Box 2408
Columbia 29202

Orangeburg-Calhoun Technical College
3250 Saint Matthew's Rd.
Orangeburg 29115

Trident Technical College
P.O. Box 118067
Charleston 29423-8067

SOUTH DAKOTA

Presentation College
1500 North Main
Aberdeen 57401

Southeast Vocational Technical Institute
2301 Career Place
Sioux Falls 57107

TENNESSEE

Nashville State Area Vocational
Technical School
100 White Bridge Rd.
Nashville 37209

Roane State Community College
Patton Ln.
Harriman 37748

Shelby State Community College
P.O. Box 40568
Memphis 38174-0568

TEXAS

The Academy of Health Care Professions
1919 Northloop W
Houston 77008

Austin Community College
5930 Middle Fiskville Rd.
Austin 78752

Del Mar College
101 Baldwin
Corpus Christi 78404-3897

El Centro College
Main and Lamar
Dallas 75202

El Paso Community College
P.O. Box 20500
El Paso 79998

Houston Community College System
22 Waugh Dr., P.O. Box 7849
Houston 77270-7849

Microcomputer Technology Institute
7277 Regency Square Blvd.
Houston 77036

Saint Philip's College
2111 Nevada St.
San Antonio 78203

San Antonio College of Medical and
Dental Assistants
5280 Medical Dr.
San Antonio 78229

Texas State Technical College-Waco
Campus
3801 Campus Dr.
Waco 76705

Ultrasound Diagnostic School
102 Decker Ct.
Irving 75062

Wadley Regional Medical Center School
of Medical Technology
1000 Pine St.
Texarkana 75501

WASHINGTON

Pima Medical Institute
1627 Eastlake Ave. E
Seattle 98102

Shoreline Community College
16101 Greenwood Ave. N
Seattle 98133

Spokane Community College
North 1810 Greene Ave.
Spokane 99207

WEST VIRGINIA

Boone County Career & Technical Center
P.O. Box 50B
Danville 25053

Seneca Phlebotomy Institute
1756 H Mileground Plaza
Morgantown 26505

West Virginia University Hospital School
of Radiation Technology
Medical Center Dr., P.O. Box 8062
Morgantown 26506-8062

WISCONSIN

Chippewa Valley Technical College
620 West Clairemont Ave.
Eau Claire 54701

Marshfield Clinic-Saint Joseph Hospital
School of Cytotechnology
1000 North Oak Ave.
Marshfield 54449

Milwaukee Area Technical College
700 West State St.
Milwaukee 53233

Saint Joseph's Hospital School of
Medical Technology
611 Saint Joseph's Ave.
Marshfield 54449

Saint Luke's Medical Center-School of
Diagnostic Medical Sonography
2900 West Oklahoma Ave.
Milwaukee 53215

Western Wisconsin Technical College
304 North Sixth St., P.O. Box 908
La Crosse 54602-0908

Wisconsin Area Vocational Training and
Adult Education System District
Number Four
3550 Anderson St.
Madison 53704

Medical Emergency Technology

ALABAMA

Bessemer State Technical College
P.O. Box 308
Bessemer 35021

George C Wallace State Community
College-Hanceville
801 Main St. NW, P.O. Box 2000
Hanceville 35077-2000

University of Alabama at Birmingham
UAB MJH 107 2010
Birmingham 35294-2010

University of Alabama in Huntsville
Huntsville 35899

University of South Alabama
245 Administration Building
Mobile 36688

ARIZONA

Phoenix College
1202 West Thomas Rd.
Phoenix 85013

Pima Community College
2202 West Anklam Rd.
Tucson 85709-0001

CALIFORNIA

Canterbury Career Schools
1090 East Washington St.
Colton 92324

Crafton Hills College
11711 Sand Canyon Rd.
Yucaipa 92399-1799

Daniel Freeman Hospital Paramedic
School
333 North Prairie Ave.
Inglewood 90301-4514

Imperial Valley College
P.O. Box 158
Imperial 92251-0158

Medical Help Training School
2072 Clayton Rd.
Concord 94519

Pacoima Skills Center-Lausd
13323 Louvre St.
Pacoima 91331

Simi Valley Adult School
3192 Los Angeles Ave.
Simi Valley 93065

Skyline College
3300 College Dr.
San Bruno 94066

COLORADO

Aims Community College
P.O. Box 69
Greeley 80632

Colorado Mountain College
P.O. Box 10001
Glenwood Springs 81602

Morgan Community College
17800 County Rd. 20
Fort Morgan 80701

San Juan Basin Area Vocational School
P.O. Box 970
Cortez 81321

San Luis Valley Area Vocational School
1011 Main St.
Alamosa 81101

FLORIDA

Brevard Community College
1519 Clearlake Rd.
Cocoa 32922

Broward Community College
225 East Las Olas Blvd.
Fort Lauderdale 33301

Central Florida Community College
P.O. Box 1388
Ocala 34478

Daytona Beach Community College
1200 Volusia Ave.
Daytona Beach 32114

Hillsborough Community College
P.O. Box 31127
Tampa 33631-3127

Indian River Community College
3209 Virginia Ave.
Fort Pierce 34981

Lake City Community College
Rte. 3, P.O. Box 7
Lake City 32055

Lake County Area Vocational-Technical
Center
2001 Kurt St.
Eustis 32726

Manatee Vocational-Technical Center
5603 34th St. W
Bradenton 34210

Palm Beach Community College
4200 Congress Ave.
Lake Worth 33461

Pasco-Hernando Community College
36727 Blanton Rd.
Dade City 33525-7599

Pensacola Junior College
1000 College Blvd.
Pensacola 32504

Saint Petersburg Junior College
P.O. Box 13489
Saint Petersburg 33733

Santa Fe Community College
3000 Northwest 83rd St.
Gainesville 32601

Seminole Community College
100 Weldon Blvd.
Sanford 32773-6199

South Florida Community College
600 West College Dr.
Avon Park 33825

Tallahassee Community College
444 Appleyard Dr.
Tallahassee 32304-2895

Valencia Community College
P.O. Box 3028
Orlando 32802

GEORGIA

Dekalb Technical Institute
495 North Indian Creek Dr.
Clarkston 30021

Gwinnett Technical Institute
1250 Atkinson Rd., P.O. Box 1505
Lawrenceville 30246-1505

ILLINOIS

City College of Chicago-Chicago
City-Wide College
226 West Jackson Blvd.
Chicago 60606-6997

Columbus Hospital-Emergency Medical
Technology Program
2520 North Lakeview
Chicago 60614

Southeastern Illinois College
3575 College Rd.
Harrisburg 62946

INDIANA

Sawyer College-Hammond
6040 Hohman Ave.
Hammond 46320

IOWA

North Iowa Area Community College
500 College Dr.
Mason City 50401

KANSAS

Allen County Community College
1801 North Cottonwood
Iola 66749

Cloud County Community College
2221 Campus Dr., P.O. Box 1002
Concordia 66901-1002

Colby Community College
1255 South Range
Colby 67701

Johnson County Community College
12345 College Blvd.
Overland Park 66210-1299

Salina Area Vocational Technical School
2562 Scanlan Ave.
Salina 67401

LOUISIANA

Hammond Area Technical Institute
P.O. Box 489
Hammond 70404

Huey P Long Technical Institute
303 South Jones St.
Winnfield 71483

MARYLAND

Baltimore City Community College
2901 Liberty Heights Ave.
Baltimore 21215

MICHIGAN

Davenport College
415 East Fulton
Grand Rapids 49503

Lansing Community College
419 North Capitol Ave.
Lansing 48901-7210

MINNESOTA

Northeast Metro Technical College
3300 Century Ave. N
White Bear Lake 55110

MISSISSIPPI

University of Mississippi Medical Center
2500 North State St.
Jackson 39216

MISSOURI

Cape Girardeau Area
Vocational-Technical School
301 North Clark Ave.
Cape Girardeau 63701

Rolla Area Vocational-Technical School
1304 East Tenth St.
Rolla 65401

MONTANA

Great Falls Vocational Technical Center
2100 16th Ave. S
Great Falls 59405

NEW HAMPSHIRE

New Hampshire Technical Institute
11 Institute Dr.
Concord 03301

NEW YORK

Hudson Valley Community College
80 Vandenburgh Ave.
Troy 12180

NORTH DAKOTA

Med Center One EMS Education
P.O. Box 5525
Bismarck 58505

OHIO

Akron Adult Vocational Services
147 Park St.
Akron 44308

Butler County JVS District-D Russel Lee
Career Center
3603 Hamilton Middletown Rd.
Hamilton 45011

Columbus State Community College
550 East Spring St., P.O. Box 1609
Columbus 43216

Lima Technical College
4240 Campus Dr.
Lima 45804

Tri-Rivers Career Center
2222 Marion Mount Gilead Rd.
Marion 43302

OKLAHOMA

Oklahoma City Community College
7777 South May Ave.
Oklahoma City 73159

TENNESSEE

Shelby State Community College
P.O. Box 40568
Memphis 38174-0568

Walters State Community College
500 South Davy Crockett Pkwy.
Morristown 37813-6899

TEXAS

Texas State Technical
College-Sweetwater Campus
300 College Dr.
Sweetwater 79556

UTAH

Bridgerland Applied Technology Center
1301 North 600 West
Logan 84321

WISCONSIN

Blackhawk Technical College
P.O. Box 5009
Janesville 53547

Fox Valley Technical College
1825 North Bluemound Dr.
Appleton 54913-2277

Gateway Technical College
3520 30th Ave.
Kenosha 53144-1690

Lakeshore Vocational Training and Adult
Education System District
1290 North Ave.
Cleveland 53015

Mid-State Technical College-Main
Campus
500 32nd St. N
Wisconsin Rapids 54494

North Central Technical College
1000 Campus Dr.
Wausau 54401-1899

Northeast Wisconsin Technical College
2740 West Mason St., P.O. Box 19042
Green Bay 54307-9042

Waukesha County Technical College
800 Main St.
Pewaukee 53072

Wisconsin Area Vocational Training and
Adult Education System-Moraine Park
235 North National Ave., P.O. Box 1940
Fond Du Lac 54936-1940

Wisconsin Area Vocational Training and
Adult Education System District
Number Four
3550 Anderson St.
Madison 53704

Medical Illustrating

ARIZONA

Pima Medical Institute
2815 South Alma School Rd.
Mesa 85210

CALIFORNIA

West Hills College
300 Cherry Ln.
Coalinga 93210

MICHIGAN

Ferndale Medical Careers, Inc.
22720 Woodward
Ferndale 48220

Muskegon Business College
141 Hartfort St.
Muskegon 49442

OHIO

Ohio State University-Main Campus
1800 Cannon Dr.
Columbus 43210

Medical Record Technology

ALABAMA

Capps College
3100 Cottage Hill Rd.
Mobile 36606

Community College of the Air Force
Maxwell Air Force Base
Montgomery 36112

Walker College
1411 Indiana Ave.
Jasper 35501

ARIZONA

Arizona Institute of Business and
Technology
925 South Gilbert Rd.
Mesa 85204

Arizona Institute of Business and
Technology
6049 North 43rd Ave.
Phoenix 85019

The Bryman School
4343 North 16th St.
Phoenix 85016

Gateway Community College
108 North 40th St.
Phoenix 85034

Tucson College
7302-10 East 22nd St.
Tucson 85710

ARKANSAS

Foothills Technical Institute
1800 East Moore St., P.O. Box 909
Searcy 72143

CALIFORNIA

Advanced Computer Training School
2160 North Winery
Fresno 93703

Allan Hancock College
800 South College Dr.
Santa Maria 93454

Business Training Center
17870 Hwy. 18
Apple Valley 92307

California Career College
123 East Gish Rd.
San Jose 95112

California College for Health Science
222 West 24th St.
National City 91950

California Paramedic and Technical
College
4550 La Sierra Ave.
Riverside 92505

Canterbury Career Schools, Inc.
114 North Sunrise Ave.
Roseville 95661

Career Development Center
255 East Bonita Ave.
Pomona 91767

Concorde Career Institute
600 North Sierra Way
San Bernardino 92410

Concorde Career Institute
123 Camino De La Reina
San Diego 92108

Concorde Career Institute
1290 North First St.
San Jose 95112

Concorde Career Institute
6850 Van Nuys Blvd.
Van Nuys 91405

Empire College School of Business
3033 Cleveland Ave.
Santa Rosa 95403

ESO Women's Programs Center
1445 Oakland Rd.
San Jose 95112

Hacienda La Puente Unified School
District-Valley Vocational Center
15959 East Gale Ave.
La Puente 91749

Institute for Business and Technology
2550 Scott Blvd.
Santa Clara 95050

Larson Training Centers, Inc.
2041 West Orangewood Ave.
Orange 92668

Maric College of Medical Careers
7202 Princess View Dr.
San Diego 92120

Maric College of Medical Careers
1300 Rancheros Dr.
San Marcos 92069

Maric College of Medical Careers-Vista
Campus
1593C East Vista Way
Vista 92084

Mount Saint Mary's College
12001 Chalon Rd.
Los Angeles 90049

MTI Business College, Inc.
6006 North El Dorado St.
Stockton 95207-4349

National Career Education
6060 Sunrise Vista Dr.
Citrus Heights 95610

National Education Center-Bryman
Campus
5350 Atlantic Ave.
Long Beach 90805

National Education Center-Bryman
Campus
1017 Wilshire Blvd.
Los Angeles 90017

National Education Center-Bryman
Campus
3505 North Hart Ave.
Rosemead 91770

National Education Center-Bryman
Campus
4212 West Artesia Blvd.
Torrance 90504

National Education Center-Sawyer
Campus
8475 Jackson Rd.
Sacramento 95826

Newbridge College
700 El Camino Real
Tustin 92680

Nova Institute of Health Technology
11416 Whittier Blvd.
Whittier 90601

San Joaquin Valley College
8400 West Mineral King Ave.
Visalia 93291

Santa Barbara Business College
211 South Real Rd.
Bakerfield 93309

Summit Career College
1330 East Cooley Dr.
Colton 92324

COLORADO

Arapahoe Community College
2500 West College Dr.
Littleton 80160-9002

Concorde Career Institute
770 Grant St.
Denver 80203

Denver Academy of Court Reporting
220 Ruskin Dr.
Colorado Springs 80910

Heritage College of Health Careers
12 Lakeside Ln.
Denver 80212

Medical Careers Training Center
4020 South College
Fort Collins 80525

DELAWARE

Star Technical Institute
631 West Newport Pike, Graystone Plaza
Wilmington 19804

FLORIDA

Atlantic Vocational Technical Center
4700 Coconut Creek Pkwy.
Coconut Creek 33063

Beacon Career Institute, Inc.
2900 Northwest 183rd St.
Miami 33056

Concorde Career Institute
7960 Arlington Expwy.
Jacksonville 32211

Concorde Career Institute
4202 West Spruce St.
Tampa 33607

Daytona Beach Community College
1200 Volusia Ave.
Daytona Beach 32114

H W Brewster Technical Center
2222 North Tampa St.
Tampa 33602-2196

Miami-Dade Community College
300 Northeast Second Ave.
Miami 33132

Pasco-Hernando Community College
36727 Blanton Rd.
Dade City 33525-7599

Pensacola Junior College
1000 College Blvd.
Pensacola 32504

Sarasota County Technical Institute
4748 Beneva Rd.
Sarasota 34233-1798

Sheridan Vocational Center
5400 West Sheridan St.
Hollywood 33021

Webster College, Inc.
5623 U.S. Hwy. 19 S
New Port Richey 34652

Withlacoochee Technical Institute
1201 West Main St.
Inverness 32650

GEORGIA

Branell Institute
1000 Circle 75 Pkwy.
Atlanta 30339

Interactive Learning Systems
5600 Roswell Rd., Prado Mall
Atlanta 30342

Medix Schools
2480 Windy Hill Rd.
Marietta 30067

HAWAII

Cannon's International Business College
of Honolulu
1500 Kapiolani Blvd.
Honolulu 96816

Medical Assistant School of Hawaii, Inc.
1149 Bethel
Honolulu 96813

IDAHO

American Institute of Health Technology,
Inc.
6600 Emerald
Boise 83704

ILLINOIS

American Health Information
Management Association
919 North Michigan Ave.
Chicago 60611

Belleville Area College
2500 Carlyle Rd.
Belleville 62221

Lewis and Clark Community College
5800 Godfrey Rd.
Godfrey 62035

Medical Careers Institute
116 South Michigan Ave.
Chicago 60603

INDIANA

Indiana University-Northwest
3400 Broadway
Gary 46408

Professional Career Institute
2611 Waterfront Pkwy., East Dr.
Indianapolis 46214-2028

Saint Margaret Hospital Medical
Technology Program
5454 Hohman Ave.
Hammond 46320

IOWA

Indian Hills Community College
525 Grandview
Ottumwa 52501

KANSAS

Dodge City Community College
2501 North 14th Ave.
Dodge City 67801

KENTUCKY

Eastern Kentucky University
Lancaster Ave.
Richmond 40475

Interactive Learning Systems
6612 Dixie Hwy.
Florence 41042

LOUISIANA

American School of Business
702 Professional Dr. N
Shreveport 71105

Ayers Institute, Inc.
2924 Knight St.
Shreveport 71105

Commercial College
2640 Youree Dr.
Shreveport 71104

MARYLAND

Essex Community College
7201 Rossville Blvd.
Baltimore 21237

Medix Schools
1017 York Rd.
Towson 21204-9840

Woodbridge Business Institute
309 East Main St.
Salisbury 21801

MASSACHUSETTS

Associated Technical Institute
345 West Cummings Park
Woburn 01801

National Education Center-Bryman
Campus
323 Boylston St.
Brookline 02146

MICHIGAN

American Career Academy
15160 West Eight Mile Rd.
Oak Park 48237

Baker College of Flint
G1050 West Bristol Rd.
Flint 48507

Baker College of Muskegon
141 Hartford St.
Muskegon 49442

Carnegie Institute
550 Stephenson Hwy.
Troy 48083

Davenport College-Kalamazoo Branch
4123 West Main St.
Kalamazoo 49006-2791

Dorsey Business Schools
31542 Gratiot
Roseville 48066

Dorsey Business Schools
24901 Northwestern Hwy.
Southfield 48075

Dorsey Business Schools
15755 Northline Rd.
Southgate 48195

Dorsey Business Schools
34841 Veterans Plaza
Wayne 48184

Ferris State University
901 South State St.
Big Rapids 49307

Grand Rapids Educational Center
1750 Woodworth NE
Grand Rapids 49505

Grand Rapids Educational Center
5349 West Main
Kalamazoo 49009

Henry Ford Community College
5101 Evergreen Rd.
Dearborn 48128

High-Tech Learning, Inc.
7531 East Eight Mile Rd.
Warren 48091

High-Tech Learning, Inc.-Southfield
20755 Greenfield
Southfield 48075

National Education Center-Bryman
Campus
4244 Oakman Blvd.
Detroit 48204

Pontiac Business Institute-Oxford
775 West Drahner Rd.
Oxford 48371

SER Business and Technical Institute
9301 Michigan Ave.
Detroit 47210-2095

MINNESOTA

Concorde Career Institute, Inc.
12 North 12th St.
Minneapolis 55403

Hennepin Technical College
1820 North Xenium Ln.
Plymouth 55441

Minnesota Riverland Technical
College-Rochester Campus
1926 College View Rd. SE
Rochester 55904

Northwest Technical College-East Grand
Forks
Hwy. 220 N
East Grand Forks 56721

Saint Paul Technical College
235 Marshall Ave.
Saint Paul 55102

MISSISSIPPI

Amherst Career Center
201 West Park Ave.
Greenwood 38930

MISSOURI

Concorde Career Institute
3239 Broadway
Kansas City 64111

Miss Vanderschmidt's Secretarial School
4625 Lindell Blvd.
Saint Louis 63108

Missouri School for Doctors' Assistants
10121 Manchester Rd.
Saint Louis 63122

Penn Valley Community College
3201 Southwest Trafficway
Kansas City 64111

Saint Louis College of Health Careers
4484 West Pine
Saint Louis 63108

Sikeston Area Vocational Technical
School
1002 Virginia
Sikeston 63801

NEBRASKA

College of Saint Mary
1901 South 72nd St.
Omaha 68124

NEVADA

Professional Careers
3305 Spring Mountain Rd.
Las Vegas 89120

NEW HAMPSHIRE

New England School of Business
Services
136 Harvey Rd.
Londonderry 03053

NEW JERSEY

Berdan Institute
265 Rte. 46
Totowa 07512

Business Training Institute
Four Forest Ave.
Paramus 07652

Star Technical Institute
1255 Rte. 70
Lakewood 08701

NEW MEXICO

Albuquerque Technical-Vocational
Institute
525 Buena Vista SE
Albuquerque 87106

NEW YORK

CUNY Borough of Manhattan
Community College
199 Chambers St.
New York 10007

Monroe Community College
1000 East Henrietta Rd.
Rochester 14623

NORTH CAROLINA

Central Piedmont Community College
P.O. Box 35009
Charlotte 28235

Kings College
322 Lamar Ave.
Charlotte 28204

Pitt Community College
Hwy. 11 S, P.O. Drawer 7007
Greenville 27835-7007

OHIO

Chase School of Medical Transcription
Ten West Streetsboro St.
Hudson 44236

Cincinnati Technical College
3520 Central Pkwy.
Cincinnati 45223

Cleveland Institute of Dental-Medical
Assistants
1836 Euclid Ave.
Cleveland 44115

Cleveland Institute of Dental-Medical
Assistants
5564 Mayfield Rd.
Lyndhurst 44124

Cleveland Institute of Dental-Medical
Assistants
5733 Hopkins Rd.
Mentor 44060

National Education Center
14445 Broadway Ave.
Cleveland 44125

Pioneer Joint Vocational School District
27 Ryan Rd., P.O. Box 309
Shelby 44875

OKLAHOMA

De Marge College
3608 Northwest 58th
Oklahoma City 73112

Francis Tuttle Area Vocational-Technical
Center
12777 North Rockwell Ave.
Oklahoma City 73142-2789

Pontotoc Skill Development Center
601 West 33rd
Ada 74820

Wright Business School
2219 Southwest 74th St.
Oklahoma City 73159

OREGON

Chemeketa Community College
P.O. Box 14007
Salem 97309-7070

Concorde Career Institute
1827 Northeast 44th Ave.
Portland 97213

Portland Community College
P.O. Box 19000
Portland 97280-0990

PENNSYLVANIA

Allied Medical Careers, Inc.
2901 Pittston Ave.
Scranton 18505

Allied Medical Careers, Inc.
104 Woodward Hill Rd.
Edwardsville 18704

Antonelli Medical and Professional
Institute
1700 Industrial Hwy.
Pottstown 19464

Bidwell Training Center, Inc.
1815 Metropolitan St.
Pittsburgh 15233

Community College of Allegheny County
800 Allegheny Ave.
Pittsburgh 15233-1895

Computer Learning Network
2900 Fairway Dr.
Altoona 16602

Delaware County Community College
901 South Media Line Rd.
Media 19063

Median School of Allied Health Careers
125 Seventh St.
Pittsburgh 15222-3400

National Education Center-Allentown
Business School Campus
1501 Lehigh St.
Allentown 18103

National Education Center-Thompson
Institute Campus
3440 Market St.
Philadelphia 19104

Star Technical Institute-Whitehall
1541 Alta Dr.
Whitehall 18052

RHODE ISLAND

New England Institute of Technology
2500 Post Rd.
Warwick 02886

SOUTH DAKOTA

National College
321 Kansas City St.
Rapid City 57701

TENNESSEE

Davidson Technical College
212 Pavilion Blvd.
Nashville 37217-1002

Fugazzi College
5042 Linbar Dr.
Nashville 37217

Medical Career College
537 Main St.
Nashville 37206

Nashville State Area Vocational
Technical School
100 White Bridge Rd.
Nashville 37209

Roane State Community College
Patton Ln.
Harriman 37748

TEXAS

The Academy of Health Care Professions
1919 Northloop W
Houston 77008

American Commercial College
3177 Executive Dr.
San Angelo 76904

Brazos Business College
1702 South Texas Ave.
Bryan 77802

Career Centers of Texas El Paso, Inc.
8375 Burnham Dr.
El Paso 79907

Metro Business Academy
3225B Commerce, P.O. Box 7609
Amarillo 79114-7609

PCI Health Training Center
8101 John Carpenter Fwy.
Dallas 75247

Saint Philip's College
2111 Nevada St.
San Antonio 78203

San Antonio College of Medical and
Dental Assistants
5280 Medical Dr.
San Antonio 78229

Texas School of Business, Inc.
711 Airtex Dr.
Houston 77073

Texas School of Business-Southwest, Inc.
10250 Bissonnet
Houston 77036

Texas State Technical College-Harlingen
Campus
2424 Boxwood
Harlingen 78550-3697

UTAH

Bridgerland Applied Technology Center
1301 North 600 West
Logan 84321

Provo College
1450 West 820 N
Provo 84601

VIRGINIA

Career Development Center
605 Thimble Shoals
Newport News 23606

CDI-Career Education Center
5361 Virginia Beach Blvd.
Virginia Beach 23462

WASHINGTON

Clark College
1800 East McLoughlin Blvd.
Vancouver 98663

Eton Technical Institute
209 East Casino Rd.
Everett 98204

Eton Technical Institute
31919 Sixth Ave. S
Federal Way 98063

Eton Technical Institute
3649 Frontage Rd.
Port Orchard 98366

Lower Columbia College
P.O. Box 3010
Longview 98632

Spokane Community College
North 1810 Greene Ave.
Spokane 99207

Tacoma Community College
5900 South 12th St.
Tacoma 98465

WEST VIRGINIA

Marshall University
400 Hal Greer Blvd.
Huntington 25755

West Virginia Business College
215 West Main St.
Clarksburg 26301

West Virginia Business College
1052 Main St.
Wheeling 26003

WISCONSIN

Chippewa Valley Technical College
620 West Clairemont Ave.
Eau Claire 54701

Gateway Technical College
3520 30th Ave.
Kenosha 53144-1690

Mid-State Technical College-Main
Campus
500 32nd St. N
Wisconsin Rapids 54494

Milwaukee Area Technical College
700 West State St.
Milwaukee 53233

Northeast Wisconsin Technical College
2740 West Mason St., P.O. Box 19042
Green Bay 54307-9042

Waukesha County Technical College
800 Main St.
Pewaukee 53072

Western Wisconsin Technical College
304 North Sixth St., P.O. Box 908
La Crosse 54602-0908

Nurse's Aide

ALABAMA

Bevill State Community College
P.O. Drawer K
Sumiton 35148

Reid State Technical College
P.O. Box 588
Evergreen 36401

Trenholm State Technical College
1225 Air Base Blvd.
Montgomery 36108

ARIZONA

Eastern Arizona College
Church St.
Thatcher 85552-0769

Gateway Community College
108 North 40th St.
Phoenix 85034

Pima Community College
2202 West Anklam Rd.
Tucson 85709-0001

Pima Medical Institute
3350 East Grant Rd.
Tucson 85716

Tucson College
7302-10 East 22nd St.
Tucson 85710

ARKANSAS

Arkansas Valley Technical Institute
Hwy. 23 N, P.O. Box 506
Ozark 72949

Black River Technical College
Hwy. 304, P.O. Box 468
Pocahontas 72455

Crowley's Ridge Technical School
P.O. Box 925
Forrest City 72335

Eastern College of Health Vocations
6423 Forbing Rd.
Little Rock 72209

Gateway Technical College
P.O. Box 3350
Batesville 72503

Great Rivers Vocational-Technical School
P.O. Box 747
McGehee 71654

CALIFORNIA

Allan Hancock College
800 South College Dr.
Santa Maria 93454

Allied Nursing Center, Inc.
3806 Beverly Blvd.
Los Angeles 90004

American School of X-Ray
13723 Harvard Place
Gardena 90249

Butte College
3536 Butte Campus Dr.
Oroville 95965

Educorp Career College
230 East Third St.
Long Beach 90802

Hacienda La Puente Unified School
District-Valley Vocational Center
15959 East Gale Ave.
La Puente 91749

Mission College
3000 Mission College Blvd.
Santa Clara 95054-1897

Nova Institute of Health Technology
520 North Euclid Ave.
Ontario 91762

Santa Rosa Junior College
1501 Mendocino Ave.
Santa Rosa 95401-4395

Simi Valley Adult School
3192 Los Angeles Ave.
Simi Valley 93065

COLORADO

Colorado Mountain College
P.O. Box 10001
Glenwood Springs 81602

PPI Health Careers School
2345 North Academy Blvd.
Colorado Springs 80909

San Luis Valley Area Vocational School
1011 Main St.
Alamosa 81101

CONNECTICUT

Connecticut Business Institute
809 Main St.
East Hartford 06108

Connecticut Business Institute
984 Chapel St.
New Haven 06511

Connecticut Business Institute
605 Broad St.
Stratford 06497

FLORIDA

Atlantic Vocational Technical Center
4700 Coconut Creek Pkwy.
Coconut Creek 33063

Beacon Career Institute, Inc.
2900 Northwest 183rd St.
Miami 33056

Branell Institute
1700 Halstead Blvd.
Tallahassee 32308

Brevard Community College
1519 Clearlake Rd.
Cocoa 32922

Career City College
1317 Northeast Fourth Ave.
Fort Lauderdale 33304

Charlotte Vocational-Technical Center
18300 Toledo Blade Blvd.
Port Charlotte 33948-3399

Crown Business Institute
1223 Southwest Fourth St.
Miami 33135

Daytona Beach Community College
1200 Volusia Ave.
Daytona Beach 32114

Florida Community College at
Jacksonville
501 West State St.
Jacksonville 32202

Florida School of Business
2990 Northwest 81st Terrace
Miami 33147

Florida School of Business
405 East Polk St.
Tampa 33602

Garces Commercial College
1301 Southwest First
Miami 33135

H W Brewster Technical Center
2222 North Tampa St.
Tampa 33602-2196

James Lorenzo Walker Vocational
Technical Center
3702 Estey Ave.
Naples 33942

Lee County Vocational-Technical Center
3800 Michigan Ave.
Fort Myers 33916

Lindsey Hopkins Technical Education
Center
750 Northwest 20th St.
Miami 33127

Manatee Vocational-Technical Center
5603 34th St. W
Bradenton 34210

Miriam Vocational School, Inc.
7311 West Flagler St.
Miami 33144

Pensacola Junior College
1000 College Blvd.
Pensacola 32504

Pinellas Technical Education
Centers-Saint Pete Campus
901 34th St. S
Saint Petersburg 33711

Radford M Locklin Vocational Technical
Center
5330 Berryhill Rd.
Milton 32570

Robert Morgan Vocational Technical
Center
18180 Southwest 122nd Ave.
Miami 33177

Santa Fe Community College
3000 Northwest 83rd St.
Gainesville 32601

Sarasota County Technical Institute
4748 Beneva Rd.
Sarasota 34233-1798

Seminole Community College
100 Weldon Blvd.
Sanford 32773-6199

South Florida Community College
600 West College Dr.
Avon Park 33825

Suwannee-Hamilton Area Vocational and
Adult Center
415 Southwest Pinewood Dr.
Live Oak 32060

U.S. Schools
100 North Plaza
Miami 33147

Washington-Holmes Area
Vocational-Technical Center
209 Hoyt St.
Chipley 32428

Withlacoochee Technical Institute
1201 West Main St.
Inverness 32650

GEORGIA

Branell Institute
5255 Snapfinger Park Dr.
Decatur 30035

Draughons College-Atlanta
1430 Peachtree St.
Atlanta 30309

Kerr Business College
2623 Washington Rd., P.O. Box 1986
Augusta 30903

Kerr Business College
P.O. Box 976
La Grange 30241

Meadows Junior College
1170 Brown Ave.
Columbus 31906

Pointe Career Institute
44 Broad St. NW
Atlanta 30303

ILLINOIS

Belleville Area College
2500 Carlyle Rd.
Belleville 62221

Career Academy
Five South Wabash Ave.
Chicago 60605

City College of Chicago-Chicago
City-Wide College
226 West Jackson Blvd.
Chicago 60606-6997

John Wood Community College
150 South 48th St.
Quincy 62301-9147

Kishwaukee College
21193 Malta Rd.
Malta 60150

Lake Land College
5001 Lake Land Blvd.
Mattoon 61938

Lewis and Clark Community College
5800 Godfrey Rd.
Godfrey 62035

McHenry County College
8900 U.S. Hwy. 14
Crystal Lake 60012

Pointe Career Institute
11 East Adams St.
Chicago 60603

Rock Valley College
3301 North Mulford Rd.
Rockford 61114

Sauk Valley Community College
173 Rte. 2
Dixon 61021

Shawnee Community College
Shawnee College Rd.
Ullin 62992

Waubonsee Community College
Rte. 47 at Harter Rd.
Sugar Grove 60554-0901

IOWA

North Iowa Area Community College
500 College Dr.
Mason City 50401

KANSAS

Cloud County Community College
2221 Campus Dr., P.O. Box 1002
Concordia 66901-1002

Colby Community College
1255 South Range
Colby 67701

Johnson County Area
Vocational-Technical School
311 East Park
Olathe 66061

KAW Area Vocational-Technical School
5724 Huntoon
Topeka 66604

Liberal Area Vocational Technical School
P.O. Box 1599
Liberal 67905-1599

Salina Area Vocational Technical School
2562 Scanlan Ave.
Salina 67401

KENTUCKY

Ashland State Vocational Technical
School
4818 Roberts Dr.
Ashland 41102

LOUISIANA

Ascension College
320 East Ascension St.
Gonzales 70737

Ascension Vocational-Technical School
P.O. Box 38
Sorrento 70778

Avoyelles Technical Institute
Hwy. 107, P.O. Box 307
Cottonport 71327

Baton Rouge Regional Technical Institute
3250 North Acadian Hwy. E
Baton Rouge 70805

Cameron College
2740 Canal St.
New Orleans 70119

Charles B Coreil Technical Institute
Industrial Park Ward I, P.O. Box 296
Ville Platte 70586

Claiborne Technical Institute
3001 Minden Rd.
Homer 71040

Coastal College
2001 Canal St.
New Orleans 70112

Coastal College-Bossier City
5520 Industrial Dr.
Bossier City 71112

Coastal College-Hammond
119 Yokum Rd.
Hammond 70403

Coastal College-Houma
2318 West Park Ave.
Houma 70364

Coastal College-Slidell
320 Howze Beach Rd.
Slidell 70461

Concordia Technical Institute
East E Wallace Blvd., P.O. Box 152
Ferriday 71334

Delta Career College
3900 Lee St., P.O. Box 1528
Alexandria 71302-3837

Delta Career College
1900 Cameron St.
Lafayette 70506-1608

Delta Career College
4358 Hwy. 84 W
Vidalia 71373

Delta Career College-Medical Support
Division
1702 Hudson Ln.
Monroe 71201

Delta Schools, Inc.
4549 Johnston St.
Lafayette 70503

Delta Schools, Inc.
413 West Admiral Doyle
New Iberia 70560

Domestic Health Care Institute
4826 Jamestown Ave.
Baton Rouge 70808

Eastern College of Health Vocations
3540 I-10 Service Rd. S
Metairie 70001

Elaine P Nunez Community College
3700 La Fontaine St.
Chalmette 70043

Evangeline Vocational Technical School
P.O. Box 68
Saint Martinville 70582

Huey P Long Technical Institute
303 South Jones St.
Winnfield 71483

Louisiana Institute of Technology
3412 Williams Blvd.
Kenner 70065

Mansfield Technical Institute
P.O. Box 1236
Mansfield 71052

New Orleans Regional Technical Institute
980 Navarre Ave.
New Orleans 70124

Sabine Valley Vocational-Technical
School
Hwy. 171 S
Many 71449

Southwest School of Health Careers
2424 Williams Blvd., Plaza 24 Center
Kenner 70062

T H Harris Technical Institute
337 East South St., P.O. Box 713
Opelousas 70570

Thibodaux Area Technical Institute
1425 Tiger Dr., P.O. Box 1831
Thibodaux 70302-1831

MARYLAND

Automation Academy
17 South Charles St.
Baltimore 21201

Pointe Career Institute
201 East Baltimore St.
Baltimore 21202

MASSACHUSETTS

Assabet Valley Regional Vocational
  Technical School
215 Fitchburg St.
Marlborough 01752

MICHIGAN

Detroit Business Institute
115 State St.
Detroit 48226

Ross Medical Education Center
15670 East Eight Mile Rd.
Detroit 48205

Ross Medical Education Center
1036 Gilbert St.
Flint 48532

Ross Medical Education Center
913 West Holmes
Lansing 48910

Ross Medical Education Center
950 Norton Ave., Park Row Mall
Roosevelt Park 49441

Ross Medical Education Center
4054 Bay Rd.
Saginaw 48603

Ross Technical Institute
1553 Woodward
Detroit 48226

Ross Technical Institute
20820 Greenfield Rd.
Oak Park 48237

MINNESOTA

Duluth Technical College
2101 Trinity Rd.
Duluth 55811

Itasca Community College
1851 Hwy. 169 E
Grand Rapids 55744

Northeast Metro Technical College
3300 Century Ave. N
White Bear Lake 55110

MISSISSIPPI

Northwest Mississippi Community
  College
Hwy. 51 N
Senatobia 38668

MISSOURI

Cape Girardeau Area
  Vocational-Technical School
301 North Clark Ave.
Cape Girardeau 63701

Saint Louis College of Health Careers
4484 West Pine
Saint Louis 63108

Sikeston Area Vocational Technical
  School
1002 Virginia
Sikeston 63801

MONTANA

Dawson Community College
300 College Dr.
Glendive 59330

Great Falls Vocational Technical Center
2100 16th Ave. S
Great Falls 59405

NEBRASKA

Opportunity Industrialization Center
  Omaha
2725 North 24th St.
Omaha 68110

NEW MEXICO

Albuquerque Technical-Vocational
  Institute
525 Buena Vista SE
Albuquerque 87106

Crownpoint Institute of Technology
P.O. Box 849
Crownpoint 87313

Franklin Medical College-Branch Campus
2400 Louisiana Blvd. NE
Albuquerque 87110

Pima Medical Institute
2201 San Pedro NE
Albuquerque 87110

NEW YORK

A Business Career Institute, Inc.
91-31 Queens Blvd.
Elmhurst 11373

Cashier Training Institute
500 Eighth Ave.
New York 10018

CM First Step Training Center
1360 Fulton St.
Brooklyn 11216

Municipal Training Center
26 Court St.
Brooklyn 11242

New York Training Institute for Nlp
145 Ave. of the Americas
New York 10012

Silhouette
3187 Steinway St.
Long Island City 11103

Suburban Technical School
2650 Sunrise Hwy.
East Islip 11730

Suburban Technical School
175 Fulton Ave.
Hempstead 11550

Superior Career Institute, Inc.
116 West 14th St.
New York 10011

Travel Institute
15 Park Row
New York 10038

NORTH CAROLINA

Brunswick Community College
P.O. Box 30
Supply 28462

Coastal Carolina Community College
444 Western Blvd.
Jacksonville 28546-6877

Craven Community College
800 College Ct.
New Bern 28562

Piedmont Community College
P.O. Box 1197
Roxboro 27573

Roanoke-Chowan Community College
Rte. 2, P.O. Box 46A
Ahoskie 27910

Robeson Community College
P.O. Box 1420
Lumberton 28359

NORTH DAKOTA

Meyer Vocational Technical School
2045 Northwest Third, P.O. Box 2126
Minot 58702

OHIO

Gallia Jackson Vinton JUSD
P.O. Box 157
Rio Grande 45674

Madison Local Schools-Madison Adult
  Education
600 Esley Ln.
Mansfield 44905

Pointe Career Institute
1140 Euclid Ave.
Cleveland 44115

Tri-Rivers Career Center
2222 Marion Mount Gilead Rd.
Marion 43302

OKLAHOMA

Mid-Del College
3420 South Sunnylane
Del City 73115

Southwest Area Vocational-Technical
  Center
1121 North Spurgeon
Altus 73521

Tulsa Colorado Area Vocational
  Technical School District 18
3802 North Peoria
Tulsa 74106

OREGON

Southwestern Oregon Community
  College
1988 Newmark Ave.
Coos Bay 97420

PENNSYLVANIA

Advanced Career Training
Southwest Corner 69th & Market
Upper Darby 19082

Allied Medical Careers, Inc.
2901 Pittston Ave.
Scranton 18505

Allied Medical Careers, Inc.
104 Woodward Hill Rd.
Edwardsville 18704

American Institute of Design
1616 Orthodox St.
Philadelphia 19124

Antonelli Medical and Professional
  Institute
1700 Industrial Hwy.
Pottstown 19464

Delaware County Institute of Training
615 Ave. of the States
Chester 19013

McKeesport Hospital School of Nursing
  Assistants
1500 Fifth Ave.
McKeesport 15132

Pennsylvania State University-Allentown
  Campus
6090 Mohr Ln.
Fogelsville 18051-9733

Pointe Career Institute
40 North Second St.
Philadelphia 19106

Presbyterian Home Nurse Assistant
  School
P.O. Box 551
Philipsburg 16866

SOUTH CAROLINA

Chris Logan Career College
1125 15-401 Bypass
Bennettsville 29512

Chris Logan Career College
P.O. Box 261
Myrtle Beach 29578-0261

Chris Logan Career College
256 South Pike Rd.
Sumter 29150

Trident Technical College
P.O. Box 118067
Charleston 29423-8067

TENNESSEE

Davidson Technical College
212 Pavilion Blvd.
Nashville 37217-1002

Draughons College
3200 Elvis Presley Blvd.
Memphis 38116

Elizabethton State Area Vocational
  Technical School
1500 Arney St., P.O. Box 789
Elizabethton 37643

Hohenwald State Area
  Vocational-Technical School
813 West Main
Hohenwald 38462-2201

Knoxville State Area
  Vocational-Technical School
1100 Liberty St.
Knoxville 37919

Medical Career College
537 Main St.
Nashville 37206

Memphis Area Vocational-Technical
  School
550 Alabama Ave.
Memphis 38105-3799

Paris State Area Vocational-Technical
  School
312 South Wilson St.
Paris 38242

Rice College
1515 Magnolia Ave. NE
Knoxville 37917

Rice College
2485 Union Extended
Memphis 38112

TEXAS

Branell Institute
7505 Fannin
Houston 77054

Brazos Business College
1702 South Texas Ave.
Bryan 77802

Chenier
2816 Loop 306
San Angelo 76904

Delta Career Institute
1310 Pennsylvania Ave.
Beaumont 77701

Draughons College of Nursing Assistants
2725 West Seventh St.
Fort Worth 76107

Houston Medical Career Training, Inc.
2420 Garland Dr.
Houston 77087

Southern Careers Institute-South Texas
3233 North 38th
McAllen 78501

Southwest School of Business and
Technical Careers
100 Main St.
Eagle Pass 78852

Southwest School of Business and
Technical Careers
602 West South Cross
San Antonio 78221

Texas State Technical College-Harlingen
Campus
2424 Boxwood
Harlingen 78550-3697

Transworld Academy, Inc.
6220 West Park
Houston 77057

UTAH

Bridgerland Applied Technology Center
1301 North 600 West
Logan 84321

Salt Lake Community College-Skills
Center
South City Campus, 1575 South State St.
Salt Lake City 84115

VIRGINIA

Blue Ridge Nursing Home School
Commerce St., P.O. Box 459
Stuart 24171

Career Development Center
605 Thimble Shoals
Newport News 23606

Career Training Center
2600 Memorial Ave.
Lynchburg 24501

Career Training Center
4000 West Broad St.
Richmond 23230

Southside Training Skill Center
Nottoway County
P.O. Box 258
Crewe 23930

Tidewater Technical
616 Denbigh Blvd.
Newport News 23602

Tidewater Technical
1760 East Little Creek Rd.
Norfolk 23518

Tidewater Technical
2697 Dean Dr.
Virginia Beach 23452

WASHINGTON

Bates Technical College
1101 South Yakima Ave.
Tacoma 98405

Lower Columbia College
P.O. Box 3010
Longview 98632

Yakima Valley Community College
P.O. Box 1647
Yakima 98907

WEST VIRGINIA

Opportunities Industrialization
Center-North Central West Virginia
120 Jackson St.
Fairmont 26554

WISCONSIN

Blackhawk Technical College
P.O. Box 5009
Janesville 53547

Fox Valley Technical College
1825 North Bluemound Dr.
Appleton 54913-2277

Gateway Technical College
3520 30th Ave.
Kenosha 53144-1690

Lakeshore Vocational Training and Adult
Education System District
1290 North Ave.
Cleveland 53015

Mid-State Technical College-Main
Campus
500 32nd St. N
Wisconsin Rapids 54494

Milwaukee Area Technical College
700 West State St.
Milwaukee 53233

Nicolet Vocational Training and Adult
Education System District
P.O. Box 518
Rhinelander 54501

North Central Technical College
1000 Campus Dr.
Wausau 54401-1899

Northeast Wisconsin Technical College
2740 West Mason St., P.O. Box 19042
Green Bay 54307-9042

Southwest Wisconsin Technical College
Hwy. 18 E
Fennimore 53809

Waukesha County Technical College
800 Main St.
Pewaukee 53072

Western Wisconsin Technical College
304 North Sixth St., P.O. Box 908
La Crosse 54602-0908

Wisconsin Area Vocational Training and
Adult Education System-Moraine Park
235 North National Ave., P.O. Box 1940
Fond Du Lac 54936-1940

Wisconsin Area Vocational Training and
Adult Education System District
Number Four
3550 Anderson St.
Madison 53704

Wisconsin Indianhead Technical College
505 Pine Ridge Dr., P.O. Box 10B
Shell Lake 54871

Occupational Therapy Technology

CALIFORNIA

Imperial Valley College
P.O. Box 158
Imperial 92251-0158

COLORADO

Aims Community College
P.O. Box 69
Greeley 80632

CONNECTICUT

Manchester Community College
60 Bidwell St., P.O. Box 1045
Manchester 06040-1046

FLORIDA

Charlotte Vocational-Technical Center
18300 Toledo Blade Blvd.
Port Charlotte 33948-3399

ILLINOIS

College of Du Page
Lambert Rd. and 22nd St.
Glen Ellyn 60137

IOWA

Kirkwood Community College
P.O. Box 2068
Cedar Rapids 52406

KANSAS

Allen County Community College
1801 North Cottonwood
Iola 66749

Cloud County Community College
2221 Campus Dr., P.O. Box 1002
Concordia 66901-1002

Colby Community College
1255 South Range
Colby 67701

Kansas City Area Vocational Technical
School
2220 North 59th St.
Kansas City 66104

KAW Area Vocational-Technical School
5724 Huntoon
Topeka 66604

Neosho County Community College
1000 South Allen
Chanute 66720

North Central Kansas Area Vocational
Technical School
Hwy. 24, P.O. Box 507
Beloit 67420

Salina Area Vocational Technical School
2562 Scanlan Ave.
Salina 67401

Wichita Area Vocational Technical
School
428 South Broadway
Wichita 67202-3910

LOUISIANA

Northeast Louisiana University
700 University Ave.
Monroe 71209

MASSACHUSETTS

Quinsigamond Community College
670 West Boylston St.
Worcester 01606

MICHIGAN

Grand Rapids Community College
143 Bostwick Ave. NE
Grand Rapids 49505

Schoolcraft College
18600 Haggerty Rd.
Livonia 48152

Wayne County Community College
801 West Fort St.
Detroit 48226

MINNESOTA

Duluth Technical College
2101 Trinity Rd.
Duluth 55811

Hibbing Community College
1515 East 25th St.
Hibbing 55746

Northeast Metro Technical College
3300 Century Ave. N
White Bear Lake 55110

MISSOURI

Jefferson College
1000 Viking Dr.
Hillsboro 63050

Saint Louis Community College-Forest
Park
5600 Oakland Ave.
Saint Louis 63110

NEW YORK

CUNY La Guardia Community College
31-10 Thomson Ave.
Long Island City 11101

Erie Community College-North Campus
Main St. and Youngs Rd.
Williamsville 14221

Herkimer County Community College
Reservoir Rd.
Herkimer 13350-1598

Rockland Community College
145 College Rd.
Suffern 10901

NORTH DAKOTA

North Dakota State College of Science
800 North Sixth St.
Wahpeton 58076

OKLAHOMA

Metro Tech Vocational Technical Center
1900 Springlake Dr.
Oklahoma City 73111

Oklahoma City Community College
7777 South May Ave.
Oklahoma City 73159

PENNSYLVANIA

Community College of Allegheny County
800 Allegheny Ave.
Pittsburgh 15233-1895

Harcum Junior College
Morris and Montgomery Ave.
Bryn Mawr 19010

Median School of Allied Health Careers
125 Seventh St.
Pittsburgh 15222-3400

Mount Aloysius College
One College Dr.
Cresson 16630-1999

TENNESSEE

Shelby State Community College
P.O. Box 40568
Memphis 38174-0568

TEXAS

Houston Community College System
22 Waugh Dr., P.O. Box 7849
Houston 77270-7849

WASHINGTON

Green River Community College
12401 Southeast 320th St.
Auburn 98002

Spokane Falls Community College
West 3410 Fort George Wright Dr.
Spokane 99204

WISCONSIN

Fox Valley Technical College
1825 North Bluemound Dr.
Appleton 54913-2277

Milwaukee Area Technical College
700 West State St.
Milwaukee 53233

Wisconsin Area Vocational Training and
Adult Education System District
Number Four
3550 Anderson St.
Madison 53704

Optical Technology

ARIZONA

The Bryman School
4343 North 16th St.
Phoenix 85016

CALIFORNIA

American College of Optechs
4021 Rosewood Ave.
Los Angeles 90004

Concorde Career Institute
6850 Van Nuys Blvd.
Van Nuys 91405

National Career Education
6060 Sunrise Vista Dr.
Citrus Heights 95610

National Education Center-Bryman
Campus
1120 North Brookhurst St.
Anaheim 92801

National Education Center-Bryman
Campus
731 Market St.
San Francisco 94103

National Education Center-Bryman
Campus
2015 Naglee Ave.
San Jose 95128

National Education Center-Sawyer
Campus
5500 South Eastern
Commerce 90043

FLORIDA

Miami-Dade Community College
300 Northeast Second Ave.
Miami 33132

ILLINOIS

National Education Center-Bryman
Campus
17 North State St.
Chicago 60602

MASSACHUSETTS

Worcester Technical Institute
251 Belmont St.
Worcester 01605

MICHIGAN

Detroit Institute of Ophthalmology
15415 East Jefferson Ave.
Grosse Pointe Park 48230

Ferris State University
901 South State St.
Big Rapids 49307

NEW YORK

Allied Health Program in Orthoptics &
Opthalmic Technology
310 East 14th St.
New York 10003

CUNY New York City Technical College
300 Jay St.
Brooklyn 11201

Erie Community College-North Campus
Main St. and Youngs Rd.
Williamsville 14221

Interboro Institute
450 West 56th St.
New York 10019

TEXAS

National Education Center-Bryman
Campus
16416 North Chase Dr.
Houston 77060

San Antonio College of Medical and
Dental Assistants
5280 Medical Dr.
San Antonio 78229

UTAH

American Institute of Medical-Dental
Technology
1675 North 200 West
Provo 84604

WISCONSIN

Lakeshore Vocational Training and Adult
Education System District
1290 North Ave.
Cleveland 53015

Pharmaceutical Technology

ALABAMA

Community College of the Air Force
Maxwell Air Force Base
Montgomery 36112

ARIZONA

Apollo College
3870 North Oracle Rd.
Tucson 85705

Long Medical Institute
4126 North Black Canyon Hwy.
Phoenix 85017

Pima Community College
2202 West Anklam Rd.
Tucson 85709-0001

CALIFORNIA

American College of Optechs
4021 Rosewood Ave.
Los Angeles 90004

Cabot College
41 East 12th St.
National City 91950

California Paramedic and Technical
College
4550 La Sierra Ave.
Riverside 92505

California Paramedic and Technical
College
3745 Long Beach Blvd.
Long Beach 90807

Concorde Career Institute Campus
600 North Sierra Way
San Bernardino 92410

Donald Vocational School
1833 West Eighth St.
Los Angeles 90057

Healthstaff Training Institute, Inc.
1505 East 17th St.
Santa Ana 92701

Western Career College
170 Bay Fair Mall
San Leandro 94578

COLORADO

Concorde Career Institute
770 Grant St.
Denver 80203

FLORIDA

Beacon Career Institute, Inc.
2900 Northwest 183rd St.
Miami 33056

Technical Career Institute
720 Northwest 27th Ave.
Miami 33125

GEORGIA

Atlanta College of Medical Dental
Careers
1240 West Peachtree St. NE
Atlanta 30309-2906

IDAHO

American Institute of Health Technology,
Inc.
6600 Emerald
Boise 83704

MICHIGAN

Academy of Health Careers
27301 Dequindre
Madison Hgts 48071

Ferris State University
901 South State St.
Big Rapids 49307

MINNESOTA

Northeast Metro Technical College
3300 Century Ave. N
White Bear Lake 55110

MISSOURI

Al-Med Academy
10963 Saint Charles Rock Rd.
Saint Louis 63074

Saint Louis College of Health Careers
4484 West Pine
Saint Louis 63108

OREGON

Apollo College-Portland, Inc.
2600 Southeast 98th Ave.
Portland 97266

College of America
921 Southwest Washington
Portland 97205

PENNSYLVANIA

Allied Medical Careers, Inc.
2901 Pittston Ave.
Scranton 18505

Allied Medical Careers, Inc.
104 Woodward Hill Rd.
Edwardsville 18704

Bidwell Training Center, Inc.
1815 Metropolitan St.
Pittsburgh 15233

North Hills School of Health Occupations
1500 Northway Mall
Pittsburgh 15237

TEXAS

Amarillo College
P.O. Box 447
Amarillo 79178

WASHINGTON

North Seattle Community College
9600 College Way N
Seattle 98103

WISCONSIN

Milwaukee Area Technical College
700 West State St.
Milwaukee 53233

Physical Therapy Technology

ALABAMA

Community College of the Air Force
Maxwell Air Force Base
Montgomery 36112

George C Wallace State Community
College-Hanceville
801 Main St. NW, P.O. Box 2000
Hanceville 35077-2000

University of Alabama at Birmingham
UAB MJH 107 2010
Birmingham 35294-2010

ARIZONA

Long Medical Institute
4126 North Black Canyon Hwy.
Phoenix 85017

Pima Medical Institute
2300 East Broadway Rd.
Tempe 85282

ARKANSAS

University of Central Arkansas
201 Donaghey Ave.
Conway 72035-0001

CALIFORNIA

Cerritos College
11110 Alondra Blvd.
Norwalk 90650

De Anza College
21250 Stevens Creek Blvd.
Cupertino 95014

Imperial Valley College
P.O. Box 158
Imperial 92251-0158

Loma Linda University
Loma Linda 92350

Sawyer College at Ventura
2101 East Gonzales Rd.
Oxnard 93030

Watterson College Pacific
815 North Oxnard Blvd.
Oxnard 93030

COLORADO

Aims Community College
P.O. Box 69
Greeley 80632

CONNECTICUT

Manchester Community College
60 Bidwell St., P.O. Box 1045
Manchester 06040-1046

FLORIDA

Broward Community College
225 East Las Olas Blvd.
Fort Lauderdale 33301

Charlotte Vocational-Technical Center
18300 Toledo Blade Blvd.
Port Charlotte 33948-3399

Miami-Dade Community College
300 Northeast Second Ave.
Miami 33132

Saint Petersburg Junior College
P.O. Box 13489
Saint Petersburg 33733

GEORGIA

Gwinnett Technical Institute
1250 Atkinson Rd., P.O. Box 1505
Lawrenceville 30246-1505

IDAHO

American Institute of Health Technology,
Inc.
6600 Emerald
Boise 83704

ILLINOIS

Belleville Area College
2500 Carlyle Rd.
Belleville 62221

Morton College
3801 South Central Ave.
Cicero 60650

KANSAS

Allen County Community College
1801 North Cottonwood
Iola 66749

Cloud County Community College
2221 Campus Dr., P.O. Box 1002
Concordia 66901-1002

Colby Community College
1255 South Range
Colby 67701

Kansas City Area Vocational Technical
School
2220 North 59th St.
Kansas City 66104

KAW Area Vocational-Technical School
5724 Huntoon
Topeka 66604

Neosho County Community College
1000 South Allen
Chanute 66720

North Central Kansas Area Vocational
Technical School
Hwy. 24, P.O. Box 507
Beloit 67420

Salina Area Vocational Technical School
2562 Scanlan Ave.
Salina 67401

Wichita Area Vocational Technical
School
428 South Broadway
Wichita 67202-3910

MARYLAND

Baltimore City Community College
2901 Liberty Heights Ave.
Baltimore 21215

MASSACHUSETTS

Becker College-Worcester
61 Sever St.
Worcester 01615-0071

Newbury College, Inc.
129 Fisher Ave.
Brookline 02146

MICHIGAN

Delta College
University Center 48710

Macomb Community College
14500 Twelve Mile Rd.
Warren 48093-3896

MINNESOTA

Anoka-Ramsey Community College
11200 Mississippi Blvd.
Coon Rapids 55433

College of Saint Catherine-Saint Mary's
Campus
2500 South Sixth St.
Minneapolis 55454

MISSOURI

Jefferson College
1000 Viking Dr.
Hillsboro 63050

NEW JERSEY

University of Medicine and Dentistry of
New Jersey
30 Bergen St.
Newark 07107

NEW YORK

CUNY Kingsborough Community
College
2001 Oriental Blvd.
Brooklyn 11235

CUNY La Guardia Community College
31-10 Thomson Ave.
Long Island City 11101

Genesee Community College
One College Rd.
Batavia 14020

Nassau Community College
One Education Dr.
Garden City 11530

Suffolk County Community
College-Ammerman Campus
533 College Rd.
Selden 11784

NORTH CAROLINA

Central Piedmont Community College
P.O. Box 35009
Charlotte 28235

OHIO

Cuyahoga Community College District
700 Carnegie Ave.
Cleveland 44115-2878

Kent State University-East Liverpool
Regional Campus
400 East Fourth St.
East Liverpool 43920

Stark Technical College
6200 Frank Ave. NW
Canton 44720

OKLAHOMA

Metro Tech Vocational Technical Center
1900 Springlake Dr.
Oklahoma City 73111

OREGON

Mount Hood Community College
26000 Southeast Stark St.
Gresham 97030

PENNSYLVANIA

Community College of Allegheny County
800 Allegheny Ave.
Pittsburgh 15233-1895

Harcum Junior College
Morris and Montgomery Ave.
Bryn Mawr 19010

Lehigh County Community College
4525 Education Park Dr.
Schnecksville 18078-2598

Pennsylvania State University-Hazleton
  Campus
Highacres
Hazleton 18201

SOUTH CAROLINA

Trident Technical College
P.O. Box 118067
Charleston 29423-8067

TENNESSEE

Volunteer State Community College
1360 Nashville Pike
Gallatin 37066

TEXAS

Amarillo College
P.O. Box 447
Amarillo 79178

Houston Community College System
22 Waugh Dr., P.O. Box 7849
Houston 77270-7849

Tarrant County Junior College District
1500 Houston St.
Fort Worth 76102

Transworld Academy, Inc.
6220 West Park
Houston 77057

VIRGINIA

Northern Virginia Community College
4001 Wakefield Chapel Rd.
Annandale 22003

WASHINGTON

Green River Community College
12401 Southeast 320th St.
Auburn 98002

WISCONSIN

Milwaukee Area Technical College
700 West State St.
Milwaukee 53233

Northeast Wisconsin Technical College
2740 West Mason St., P.O. Box 19042
Green Bay 54307-9042

Psychiatric and Mental Health Technology

ALABAMA

Chauncey Sparks State Technical College
P.O. Drawer 580
Eufaula 36027

Gadsden State Community College
P.O. Box 227
Gadsden 35902-0227

George C Wallace State Community
  College-Hanceville
801 Main St. NW, P.O. Box 2000
Hanceville 35077-2000

Patrick Henry State Junior College
P.O. Box 2000
Monroeville 36460

ALASKA

University of Alaska-Anchorage
3211 Providence Dr.
Anchorage 99508

University of Alaska-Fairbanks
Signers Hall
Fairbanks 99775

ARIZONA

Apollo College
3870 North Oracle Rd.
Tucson 85705

Apollo College-Tri City, Inc.
630 West Southern Ave.
Mesa 85210

Apollo College-Westridge, Inc.
7502 West Thomas Rd.
Phoenix 85033

Glendale Community College
6000 West Olive Ave.
Glendale 85302

Maricopa Skill Center
1245 East Buckeye
Phoenix 85034-4101

Phoenix College
1202 West Thomas Rd.
Phoenix 85013

Pima Community College
2202 West Anklam Rd.
Tucson 85709-0001

Rio Salado Community College
640 North First Ave.
Phoenix 85003

CALIFORNIA

Allan Hancock College
800 South College Dr.
Santa Maria 93454

Allied Nursing Center, Inc.
3806 Beverly Blvd.
Los Angeles 90004

American River College
4700 College Oak Dr.
Sacramento 95841

American School of X-Ray
13723 Harvard Place
Gardena 90249

Behavior Science Research and
  Education Center
260 Maple Ct.
Ventura 93003

Butte College
3536 Butte Campus Dr.
Oroville 95965

California Nannie College
910 Howe Ave.
Sacramento 95825

California Paramedic and Technical
  College
4550 La Sierra Ave.
Riverside 92505

California Paramedic and Technical
  College
3745 Long Beach Blvd.
Long Beach 90807

Citrus College
1000 West Foothill Blvd.
Glendora 91741-1899

Cypress College
9200 Valley View
Cypress 90630

De Anza College
21250 Stevens Creek Blvd.
Cupertino 95014

Foothill College
12345 El Monte Rd.
Los Altos Hills 94022

Fresno City College
1101 East University Ave.
Fresno 93741

Glendale Community College
1500 North Verdugo Rd.
Glendale 91208-2894

Griffin and Wong Institute for Education
  and Training
3258 Fourth Ave.
San Diego 92103

Hacienda La Puente Unified School
  District-Valley Vocational Center
15959 East Gale Ave.
La Puente 91749

Hypnosis Motivation Institute
18607 Ventura Blvd.
Tarzana 91356

Hypnotism Training Institute of Los
  Angeles
700 South Central
Glendale 91204

Imperial Valley College
P.O. Box 158
Imperial 92251-0158

L & P School of Professional
  Hypnotherapy
12941 Gilbert
Garden Grove 92641

Marin Regional Occupational Program
P.O. Box 4925
San Rafael 94913

Merced College
3600 M St.
Merced 95348-2898

Mission College
3000 Mission College Blvd.
Santa Clara 95054-1897

Mount San Antonio College
1100 North Grand
Walnut 91789

Mueller College of Holistic Studies
4607 Park Blvd.
San Diego 92116

Napa Valley College
2277 Napa Vallejo Hwy.
Napa 94558

Pacific College of Oriental Medicine
7445 Mission Valley Rd.
San Diego 92108

Pacific Oaks College
Five Westmoreland Place
Pasadena 91103

Porterville College
100 East College Ave.
Porterville 93257

Santa Rosa Junior College
1501 Mendocino Ave.
Santa Rosa 95401-4395

Simi Valley Adult School
3192 Los Angeles Ave.
Simi Valley 93065

Ventura College
4667 Telegraph Rd.
Ventura 93003

Yuba College
2088 North Beale Rd.
Marysville 95901

COLORADO

Aims Community College
P.O. Box 69
Greeley 80632

Community College of Denver
P.O. Box 173363
Denver 80217

Medical Careers Training Center
4020 South College
Fort Collins 80525

Modern Institute of Reflexology
7043 West Colfax Ave.
Lakewood 80215

Morgan Community College
17800 County Rd. 20
Fort Morgan 80701

Red Rocks Community College
13300 West Sixth Ave.
Golden 80401

CONNECTICUT

Asnuntuck Community College
170 Elm St.
Enfield 06082

Housatonic Community College
510 Barnum Ave.
Bridgeport 06608

Manchester Community College
60 Bidwell St., P.O. Box 1045
Manchester 06040-1046

Mattatuck Community College
750 Chase Pkwy.
Waterbury 06708

Middlesex Community College
100 Training Hill Rd.
Middletown 06457

Mitchell College
437 Pequot Ave.
New London 06320

Mohegan Community College
Mahan Dr., P.O. Box 629
Norwich 06360

Northwestern Connecticut Community
  College
Park Place E
Winsted 06098

Norwalk Community Technical College
188 Richards Ave.
Norwalk 06854

South Central Community College
60 Sargent Dr.
New Haven 06511

Tunxis Community College
Rtes. 6 and 177
Farmington 06032

DELAWARE

Delaware Technical and Community
College-Southern Campus
P.O. Box 610
Georgetown 19947

Delaware Technical and Community
College-Terry Campus
1832 North Dupont Pkwy.
Dover 19901

Delaware Technical and Community
College Stanton-Wilmington
400 Stanton-Christiana Rd.
Newark 19702

DISTRICT OF COLUMBIA

Howard University
2400 Sixth St. NW
Washington 20059

Pointe Career Institute
529 14th St. NW
Washington 20004

FLORIDA

Career Training Institute
101 West Main St.
Leesburg 34748

Charlotte Vocational-Technical Center
18300 Toledo Blade Blvd.
Port Charlotte 33948-3399

Daytona Beach Community College
1200 Volusia Ave.
Daytona Beach 32114

Florida Community College at
Jacksonville
501 West State St.
Jacksonville 32202

Lee County Vocational-Technical Center
3800 Michigan Ave.
Fort Myers 33916

Sarasota County Technical Institute
4748 Beneva Rd.
Sarasota 34233-1798

Seminole Community College
100 Weldon Blvd.
Sanford 32773-6199

Sheridan Vocational Center
5400 West Sheridan St.
Hollywood 33021

GEORGIA

Dekalb College
3251 Panthersville Rd.
Decatur 30034

Saint Joseph Hospital School of
Histologic Technique
5665 Peachtree Dunwoody Rd. NE
Atlanta 30342

ILLINOIS

City College of Chicago-Harold
Washington
30 East Lake St.
Chicago 60601

College of Du Page
Lambert Rd. and 22nd St.
Glen Ellyn 60137

Elgin Community College
1700 Spartan Dr.
Elgin 60123

Montay College
3750 Peterson Ave.
Chicago 60659-3115

Moraine Valley Community College
10900 South 88th Ave.
Palos Hills 60465-0937

Prairie State College
202 Halsted St.
Chicago Heights 60411

Swedish American Hospital School of
Radiation Technology Therapy
1400 Charles St.
Rockford 61104-2298

Triton College
2000 Fifth Ave.
River Grove 60171

Waubonsee Community College
Rte. 47 at Harter Rd.
Sugar Grove 60554-0901

William Rainey Harper College
1200 West Algonquin Rd.
Palatine 60067-7398

INDIANA

Indiana University-Purdue University at
Fort Wayne
2101 Coliseum Blvd. E
Fort Wayne 46805

IOWA

Iowa Lakes Community College
19 South Seventh St.
Estherville 51334

KANSAS

Allen County Community College
1801 North Cottonwood
Iola 66749

Cloud County Community College
2221 Campus Dr., P.O. Box 1002
Concordia 66901-1002

Colby Community College
1255 South Range
Colby 67701

Cowley County Community College
125 South Second St.
Arkansas City 67005

Johnson County Area
Vocational-Technical School
311 East Park
Olathe 66061

Kansas City Area Vocational Technical
School
2220 North 59th St.
Kansas City 66104

KAW Area Vocational-Technical School
5724 Huntoon
Topeka 66604

Neosho County Community College
1000 South Allen
Chanute 66720

North Central Kansas Area Vocational
Technical School
Hwy. 24, P.O. Box 507
Beloit 67420

Salina Area Vocational Technical School
2562 Scanlan Ave.
Salina 67401

Washburn University of Topeka
1700 College Ave.
Topeka 66621

Wichita Area Vocational Technical
School
428 South Broadway
Wichita 67202-3910

KENTUCKY

Northern Kentucky University
University Dr.
Highland Heights 41099

LOUISIANA

Phillips Junior College
822 South Clearview Pkwy.
New Orleans 70123

Southern University-New Orleans
6400 Press Dr.
New Orleans 70126

MAINE

University of Maine at Augusta
University Heights
Augusta 04330-9410

MARYLAND

Allegany Community College
Willowbrook Rd.
Cumberland 21502

Anne Arundel Community College
101 College Pkwy.
Arnold 21012

Baltimore City Community College
2901 Liberty Heights Ave.
Baltimore 21215

Dundalk Community College
7200 Sollers Point Rd.
Dundalk 21222

Essex Community College
7201 Rossville Blvd.
Baltimore 21237

MASSACHUSETTS

Bristol Community College
777 Elsbree St.
Fall River 02720

Bunker Hill Community College
New Rutherford Ave.
Boston 02129

Lawrence Memorial Hospital School of
Nursing
170 Governors Ave.
Medford 02155

Middlesex Community College
Springs Rd.
Bedford 01730

Mount Wachusett Community College
444 Green St.
Gardner 01440

North Shore Community College
One Ferncroft Rd.
Danvers 01923

Northern Essex Community College
Elliott Way
Haverhill 01830-2399

Quinsigamond Community College
670 West Boylston St.
Worcester 01606

Springfield Technical Community
College
Armory Square
Springfield 01105

Stonehill College
Washington St.
North Easton 02357

MICHIGAN

Delta College
University Center 48710

Lansing Community College
419 North Capitol Ave.
Lansing 48901-7210

Macomb Community College
14500 Twelve Mile Rd.
Warren 48093-3896

Mott Community College
1401 East Court St.
Flint 48503

Oakland Community College
2480 Opdyke Rd.
Bloomfield Hills 48304-2266

Wayne County Community College
801 West Fort St.
Detroit 48226

MINNESOTA

College of Saint Catherine-Saint Mary's
Campus
2500 South Sixth St.
Minneapolis 55454

Minneapolis Community College
1501 Hennepin Ave.
Minneapolis 55403

Saint Cloud Technical College
1540 Northway Dr.
Saint Cloud 56303

University of Minnesota-Crookston
105 Selvig Hall
Crookston 56716

MISSISSIPPI

Phillips Junior College
942 Beach Dr.
Gulfport 39507

MISSOURI

Jefferson College
1000 Viking Dr.
Hillsboro 63050

NEBRASKA

Central Community College-Grand Island
P.O. Box 4903
Grand Island 68802

Institute of Computer Science
808 South 74th Place, 7400 Court
Building
Omaha 68114

Omaha College of Health Careers
10845 Harney St.
Omaha 68154

Opportunity Industrialization Center
Omaha
2725 North 24th St.
Omaha 68110

Southeast Community College-Lincoln
Campus
8800 O St.
Lincoln 68520

NEW HAMPSHIRE

Keene State College
229 Main
Keene 03431

New Hampshire Technical Institute
11 Institute Dr.
Concord 03301

NEW JERSEY

Camden County College
P.O. Box 200
Blackwood 08012

Star Technical Institute-Deptford
251 Delsea Dr.
Deptford 08104

NEW MEXICO

Hypnosis Career Institute
10701 Lomas NE
Albuquerque 87112

Northern New Mexico Community
College
1002 North Onate St.
Espanola 87532

NEW YORK

CUNY Kingsborough Community
College
2001 Oriental Blvd.
Brooklyn 11235

Erie Community College-City Campus
121 Ellicott St.
Buffalo 14203

Mercy College-Main Campus
555 Broadway
Dobbs Ferry 10522

New York Training Institute for Nlp
145 Ave. of the Americas
New York 10012

Rochester Institute of Technology
One Lamb Memorial Dr.
Rochester 14623-0887

Saint Joseph's College-Main Campus
245 Clinton Ave.
Brooklyn 11205-3688

Saint Joseph's College-Suffolk Campus
155 Roe Blvd.
Patchogue 11772

Sullivan County Community College
Le Roy Rd., P.O. Box 4002
Loch Sheldrake 12759-4002

NORTH CAROLINA

Duke University
103 Allen Building
Durham 27706

Southeastern Community College
P.O. Box 151
Whiteville 28472

Wake Technical Community College
9101 Fayetteville Rd.
Raleigh 27603-5696

Wayne Community College
P.O. Box 8002
Goldsboro 27533-8002

Western Piedmont Community College
1001 Burkemont Ave.
Morganton 28655-9978

OHIO

Belmont Technical College
120 Fox Shannon Place
Saint Clairsville 43950

Columbus State Community College
550 East Spring St., P.O. Box 1609
Columbus 43216

English Nanny and Governess School
30 South Franklin St.
Chagrin Falls 44022

Kettering College of Medical Arts
3737 Southern Blvd.
Kettering 45429-1299

Muskingum Area Technical College
1555 Newark Rd.
Zanesville 43701

North Central Technical College
2441 Kenwood Circle, P.O. Box 698
Mansfield 44901

Sinclair Community College
444 West Third St.
Dayton 45402

University of Toledo
2801 West Bancroft
Toledo 43606

OKLAHOMA

Central Oklahoma Area Vocational
Technical School
Three Court Circle
Drumright 74030

Kiamichi AVTS SD #7-McCurtain
Campus
Hwy. 70 N & Rte. 3, P.O. Box 177
Idabel 74745

Metro Tech Vocational Technical Center
1900 Springlake Dr.
Oklahoma City 73111

OREGON

Chemeketa Community College
P.O. Box 14007
Salem 97309-7070

Mount Hood Community College
26000 Southeast Stark St.
Gresham 97030

PENNSYLVANIA

Bucks County Community College
Swamp Rd.
Newtown 18940

Community College of Allegheny County
800 Allegheny Ave.
Pittsburgh 15233-1895

Community College of Philadelphia
1700 Spring Garden St.
Philadelphia 19130

Edinboro University of Pennsylvania
Edinboro 16444

Harcum Junior College
Morris and Montgomery Ave.
Bryn Mawr 19010

Manor Junior College
700 Fox Chase Rd.
Jenkintown 19046

Mercer County Area Vocational
Technical School
P.O. Box 152
Mercer 16137-0152

Pennsylvania College of Technology
One College Ave.
Williamsport 17701

Pennsylvania State University-Main
Campus
201 Old Main
University Park 16802

Reading Area Community College
P.O. Box 1706
Reading 19603

Sawyer School
717 Liberty Ave.
Pittsburgh 15222

Seton Hill College
Greensburg 15601

Ursuline Center, Inc.
201 South Winebiddle St.
Pittsburg 15224

RHODE ISLAND

Community College of Rhode Island
400 East Ave.
Warwick 02886-1805

SOUTH CAROLINA

York Technical College
452 South Anderson Rd.
Rock Hill 29730

SOUTH DAKOTA

Lake Area Vocational Technical Institute
230 11th St. NE
Watertown 57201

TENNESSEE

Shelby State Community College
P.O. Box 40568
Memphis 38174-0568

TEXAS

ATI Health Education Center
8150 Brookriver Dr.
Dallas 75247

ATI Health Education Center
1200 Summit Ave.
Fort Worth 76102

Career Academy, Inc.
32 Oak Lawn Village
Texarkana 75501

Career Centers of Texas El Paso, Inc.
8375 Burnham Dr.
El Paso 79907

Cisco Junior College
Rte. 3, P.O. Box 3
Cisco 76437

Eastfield College
3737 Motley Dr.
Mesquite 75150

El Paso Community College
P.O. Box 20500
El Paso 79998

Houston Community College System
22 Waugh Dr., P.O. Box 7849
Houston 77270-7849

Howard County Junior College District
1001 Birdwell Ln.
Big Spring 79720

McLennan Community College
1400 College Dr.
Waco 76708

PCI Health Training Center
8101 John Carpenter Fwy.
Dallas 75247

San Antonio College of Medical and
Dental Assistants
5280 Medical Dr.
San Antonio 78229

Tarrant County Junior College District
1500 Houston St.
Fort Worth 76102

UTAH

Bridgerland Applied Technology Center
1301 North 600 West
Logan 84321

VERMONT

Community College of Vermont
P.O. Box 120
Waterbury 05676

VIRGINIA

Blue Ridge Community College
P.O. Box 80
Weyers Cave 24486

Central Virginia Community College
3506 Wards Rd.
Lynchburg 24502

Danville Community College
1008 South Main St.
Danville 24541

Eastern Shore Community College
29300 Lankford Hwy.
Melfa 23410

Germanna Community College
P.O. Box 339
Locust Grove 22508

J Sargeant Reynolds Community College
P.O. Box 85622
Richmond 23285-5622

John Tyler Community College
13101 Jefferson Davis Hwy.
Chester 23831-5399

Lord Fairfax Community College
173 Skirmisher Ln., P.O. Box 47
Middletown 22645

Mountain Empire Community College
P.O. Drawer 700
Big Stone Gap 24219

New River Community College
P.O. Drawer 1127
Dublin 24084

Northern Virginia Community College
4001 Wakefield Chapel Rd.
Annandale 22003

Patrick Henry Community College
P.O. Box 5311
Martinsville 24115-5311

Paul D Camp Community College
100 North College Dr., P.O. Box 737
Franklin 23851

Rappahannock Community College
Glenns Campus, P.O. Box 287
Glenns 23149

Southside Virginia Community College
Rte. 1, P.O. Box 60
Alberta 23821

Southwest Virginia Community College
P.O. Box SVCC
Richlands 24641

Thomas Nelson Community College
P.O. Box 9407
Hampton 23670

Tidewater Community College
Rte. 135
Portsmouth 23703

Virginia Highlands Community College
P.O. Box 828
Abingdon 24210

Virginia Western Community College
3095 Colonial Ave.
Roanoke 24015

WASHINGTON

Edmonds Community College
20000 68th Ave. W
Lynnwood 98036

Lake Washington Technical College
11605 132nd Ave. NE
Kirkland 98034

Pierce College
9401 Farwest Dr. SW
Tacoma 98498

Spokane Falls Community College
West 3410 Fort George Wright Dr.
Spokane 99204

Tacoma Community College
5900 South 12th St.
Tacoma 98465

Yakima Valley Community College
P.O. Box 1647
Yakima 98907

WEST VIRGINIA

Opportunities Industrialization
  Center-North Central West Virginia
120 Jackson St.
Fairmont 26554

WISCONSIN

C Ross Educational Center
4041 North Richards
Milwaukee 53212

Chippewa Valley Technical College
620 West Clairemont Ave.
Eau Claire 54701

Lac Courte Oreilles Ojibwa Community
  College
Rte. 2, P.O. Box 2357
Hayward 54843

Waukesha County Technical College
800 Main St.
Pewaukee 53072

Western Wisconsin Technical College
304 North Sixth St., P.O. Box 908
La Crosse 54602-0908

Wisconsin Indianhead Technical College
505 Pine Ridge Dr., P.O. Box 10B
Shell Lake 54871

Radiologic Technology

ALABAMA

Community College of the Air Force
Maxwell Air Force Base
Montgomery 36112

Gadsden State Community College
P.O. Box 227
Gadsden 35902-0227

George C Wallace State Community
  College-Hanceville
801 Main St. NW, P.O. Box 2000
Hanceville 35077-2000

Jefferson State Community College
2601 Carson Rd.
Birmingham 35215-3098

University of Alabama at Birmingham
UAB MJH 107 2010
Birmingham 35294-2010

University of South Alabama
245 Administration Building
Mobile 36688

ARIZONA

The Bryman School
4343 North 16th St.
Phoenix 85016

Gateway Community College
108 North 40th St.
Phoenix 85034

ARKANSAS

Arkansas Valley Technical Institute
Hwy. 23 N, P.O. Box 506
Ozark 72949

Carti School of Radiation Therapy
  Technology
P.O. Box 5210
Little Rock 72215

Sparks Regional Medical Center School
  of Radiography
1311 South Eye St.
Fort Smith 72917-7006

CALIFORNIA

American School of X-Ray
13723 Harvard Place
Gardena 90249

Butte College
3536 Butte Campus Dr.
Oroville 95965

Cabrillo College
6500 Soquel Dr.
Aptos 95003

Cancer Foundation Schools of
  Technology
300 West Pueblo St.
Santa Barbara 93105

Chaffey Community College
5885 Haven Ave.
Rancho Cucamonga 91737-3002

Charles R Drew University of Medicine
  and Science
1621 East 120th St.
Los Angeles 90059

Cypress College
9200 Valley View
Cypress 90630

Educorp Career College
230 East Third St.
Long Beach 90802

Foothill College
12345 El Monte Rd.
Los Altos Hills 94022

Fresno City College
1101 East University Ave.
Fresno 93741

Loma Linda University
Loma Linda 92350

Long Beach City College
4901 East Carson St.
Long Beach 90808

Merced College
3600 M St.
Merced 95348-2898

Modern Technology School of X-Ray
6180 Laurel Canyon Blvd.
North Hollywood 91606

Mount San Antonio College
1100 North Grand
Walnut 91789

Nova Institute of Health Technology
2400 South Western Ave.
Los Angeles 90018

Nova Institute of Health Technology
11416 Whittier Blvd.
Whittier 90601

Orange Coast College
2701 Fairview Rd.
Costa Mesa 92626

San Diego Mesa College
7250 Mesa College Dr.
San Diego 92111-4998

San Joaquin General Hospital School of
  Radiation Technology
P.O. Box 1020
Stockton 95201

Santa Barbara City College
721 Cliff Dr.
Santa Barbara 93109-2394

Santa Rosa Junior College
1501 Mendocino Ave.
Santa Rosa 95401-4395

Yuba College
2088 North Beale Rd.
Marysville 95901

COLORADO

Community College of Denver
P.O. Box 173363
Denver 80217

CONNECTICUT

Saint Vincent's Medical Center of
  Nuclear Medicine
2800 Main St.
Bridgeport 06606

South Central Community College
60 Sargent Dr.
New Haven 06511

DELAWARE

Delaware Technical and Community
  College Stanton-Wilmington
400 Stanton-Christiana Rd.
Newark 19702

DISTRICT OF COLUMBIA

George Washington University
2121 Eye St. NW
Washington 20052

FLORIDA

Hillsborough Community College
P.O. Box 31127
Tampa 33631-3127

National School of Technology, Inc.
4355 West 16th Ave.
Hialeah 33012

Pensacola Junior College
1000 College Blvd.
Pensacola 32504

Saint Petersburg Junior College
P.O. Box 13489
Saint Petersburg 33733

Santa Fe Community College
3000 Northwest 83rd St.
Gainesville 32601

GEORGIA

De Kalb Medical Center School of
  Radiation Technology
2701 North Decatur Rd.
Decatur 30033

Fulton Dekalb Hospital Authority Grady
  Memorial Hospital
80 Butler St., P.O. Box 26044
Atlanta 30335-3801

Medical Center, Inc.-School of
  Radiologic Technology
710 Center St., P.O. Drawer 85
Columbus 31994-2299

Medical College of Georgia
1120 15th St.
Augusta 30912

HAWAII

Kapiolani Community College
4303 Diamond Head Rd.
Honolulu 96816

ILLINOIS

Belleville Area College
2500 Carlyle Rd.
Belleville 62221

College of Du Page
Lambert Rd. and 22nd St.
Glen Ellyn 60137

Cook County Hospital School of X-Ray
Technology
1825 West Harrison St.
Chicago 60612

Kaskaskia College
27210 College Rd.
Centralia 62801

Methodist Medical Center of
Illinois-Medical Technology
221 Northeast Glen Oak Ave.
Peoria 61636-0001

Moraine Valley Community College
10900 South 88th Ave.
Palos Hills 60465-0937

Rockford Memorial Hospital School of
X-Ray Technology
2400 North Rockton Ave.
Rockford 61103

Southern Illinois University-Carbondale
Carbondale 62901

Swedish American Hospital School of
Surgical Technology
1400 Charles St.
Rockford 61104-1257

Triton College
2000 Fifth Ave.
River Grove 60171

INDIANA

Ball State University
2000 University Ave.
Muncie 47306

Indiana University-Purdue University at
Indianapolis
355 North Lansing
Indianapolis 46202

Saint Joseph Medical Center School of
Radiology
700 Broadway
Fort Wayne 46802

IOWA

University of Iowa
Iowa City 52242

KANSAS

Fort Hays State University
600 Park St.
Hays 67601-4099

Labette Community College
200 South 14th
Parsons 67357

Washburn University of Topeka
1700 College Ave.
Topeka 66621

KENTUCKY

Kentucky Technical-Bowling Green
State Vocational Technical School
1845 Loop Dr., P.O. Box 6000
Bowling Green 42101

Lexington Community College
Cooper Dr.
Lexington 40506

Morehead State University
University Blvd.
Morehead 40351

LOUISIANA

Delgado Community College
615 City Park Ave.
New Orleans 70119

MAINE

Southern Maine Technical College
Fort Rd.
South Portland 04106

MARYLAND

Essex Community College
7201 Rossville Blvd.
Baltimore 21237

Prince Georges Community College
301 Largo Rd.
Largo 23701-1243

MASSACHUSETTS

Bunker Hill Community College
New Rutherford Ave.
Boston 02129

Holyoke Community College
303 Homestead Ave.
Holyoke 01040

Massasoit Community College
One Massasoit Blvd.
Brockton 02402

Northeastern University
360 Huntington Ave.
Boston 02115

Springfield Technical Community
College
Armory Square
Springfield 01105

MICHIGAN

Carnegie Institute
550 Stephenson Hwy.
Troy 48083

Ferris State University
901 South State St.
Big Rapids 49307

Grand Rapids Community College
143 Bostwick Ave. NE
Grand Rapids 49505

Lansing Community College
419 North Capitol Ave.
Lansing 48901-7210

William Beaumont Hospital
3601 West 13 Mile Rd.
Royal Oak 48073-6769

MINNESOTA

Mayo School of Health-Related Sciences
200 First St. SW
Rochester 55905

Northwest Technical College-East Grand
Forks
Hwy. 220 N
East Grand Forks 56721

Rochester Community College
851 30th Ave. SE
Rochester 55904-4999

MISSISSIPPI

University of Mississippi Medical Center
2500 North State St.
Jackson 39216

MISSOURI

Research Medical Center School of
Nuclear Medical Technology
2316 East Meyer Blvd.
Kansas City 64132

Saint Louis Community College-Forest
Park
5600 Oakland Ave.
Saint Louis 63110

Saint Luke's College
4426 Wornall Rd.
Kansas City 64111

NEW HAMPSHIRE

New Hampshire Technical Institute
11 Institute Dr.
Concord 03301

NEW JERSEY

Bergen Community College
400 Paramus Rd.
Paramus 07652

Hudson Area School of Radiologic
Technology
29 East 29th St.
Bayonne 07002

Middlesex County College
155 Mill Rd., P.O. Box 3050
Edison 08818-3050

Overlook Hospital School of Nuclear
Medical Technology
99 Beauvoir Ave., P.O. Box 220
Summit 07902-0220

University of Medicine and Dentistry of
New Jersey
30 Bergen St.
Newark 07107

NEW YORK

Bellevue Hospital Center School of
Radiation Technology
First Ave. and 27th St.
New York 10016

Broome Community College
P.O. Box 1017
Binghamton 13902

Catholic Medical Center-Program of
Radiography
89-15 Woodhaven Blvd.
Woodhaven 11421

CUNY New York City Technical College
300 Jay St.
Brooklyn 11201

Hudson Valley Community College
80 Vandenburgh Ave.
Troy 12180

Institute of Allied Medical Professions
23d 106 Central Park S
New York 10019

Monroe Community College
1000 East Henrietta Rd.
Rochester 14623

Nassau Community College
One Education Dr.
Garden City 11530

Saint Luke's Memorial Hospital Center
Champlin Rd., P.O. Box 479
Utica 13503-0479

SUNY Health Science Center at Syracuse
750 East Adams St.
Syracuse 13210

SUNY Westchester Commmunity College
75 Grasslands Rd.
Valhalla 10595

Trocaire College
110 Red Jacket Pkwy.
Buffalo 14220

NORTH CAROLINA

Edgecombe Community College
2009 West Wilson St.
Tarboro 27886

Forsyth Technical Community College
2100 Silas Creek Pkwy.
Winston-Salem 27103

Pitt Community College
Hwy. 11 S, P.O. Drawer 7007
Greenville 27835-7007

Southwestern Community College
275 Webster Rd.
Sylva 28779

OHIO

Cuyahoga Community College District
700 Carnegie Ave.
Cleveland 44115-2878

Kent State University-Salem Regional
Campus
2491 South Rte. 45 S
Salem 44460

Kettering College of Medical Arts
3737 Southern Blvd.
Kettering 45429-1299

Lima Technical College
4240 Campus Dr.
Lima 45804

Lorain County Community College
1005 North Abbe Rd.
Elyria 44035

Owens Technical College
30335 Oregon Rd., P.O. Box 10000
Toledo 43699-1947

Sinclair Community College
444 West Third St.
Dayton 45402

Tri-Rivers Career Center
2222 Marion Mount Gilead Rd.
Marion 43302

University of Cincinnati-Raymond
Walters College
9555 Plainfield Rd.
Blue Ash 45236

OREGON

Concorde Career Institute
1827 Northeast 44th Ave.
Portland 97213

Oregon Health Science University
3181 Southwest Sam Jackson Rd.
Portland 97201

Portland Community College
P.O. Box 19000
Portland 97280-0990

PENNSYLVANIA

Community College of Allegheny County
800 Allegheny Ave.
Pittsburgh 15233-1895

Crozer-Chester Medical Center-Allied
Health Program
One Medical Center Blvd.
Upland 19013

Gannon University
109 West Sixth St.
Erie 16541

Harrisburg Area Community
College-Harrisburg Campus
One Hacc Dr.
Harrisburg 17110

North Hills School of Health Occupations
1500 Northway Mall
Pittsburgh 15237

Northampton County Area Community
College
3835 Green Pond Rd.
Bethlehem 18017

Ohio Valley Hospital School of
Radiologic Technology
Heckel Rd.
McKees Rocks 15136

Wilkes-Barre General Hospital-School of
Medical Technology
North River and Auburn
Wilkes-Barre 18764

RHODE ISLAND

Community College of Rhode Island
400 East Ave.
Warwick 02886-1805

Rhode Island Hospital School of Nuclear
Medicine
593 Eddy St.
Providence 02903

Rhode Island Hospital School of
Radiation Therapy
593 Eddy St.
Providence 02903

SOUTH CAROLINA

Greenville Technical College
Station B, P.O. Box 5616
Greenville 29606-5616

Horry-Georgetown Technical College
P.O. Box 1966
Conway 29526

Trident Technical College
P.O. Box 118067
Charleston 29423-8067

TENNESSEE

Chattanooga State Technical Community
College
4501 Amnicola Hwy.
Chattanooga 37406

East Tennessee State University
P.O. Box 70716
Johnson City 37614

Roane State Community College
Patton Ln.
Harriman 37748

Shelby State Community College
P.O. Box 40568
Memphis 38174-0568

TEXAS

Amarillo College
P.O. Box 447
Amarillo 79178

Austin Community College
5930 Middle Fiskville Rd.
Austin 78752

El Centro College
Main and Lamar
Dallas 75202

El Paso Community College
P.O. Box 20500
El Paso 79998

Galveston College
4015 Ave. Q
Galveston 77550

Houston Community College System
22 Waugh Dr., P.O. Box 7849
Houston 77270-7849

Lamar University-Beaumont
4400 Mlk, P.O. Box 10001
Beaumont 77710

McLennan Community College
1400 College Dr.
Waco 76708

Midwestern State University
3410 Taft Blvd.
Wichita Falls 76308-2099

Moncrief Radiation Center School of
Radiation Therapy
1450 Eighth Ave.
Fort Worth 76104

Saint Philip's College
2111 Nevada St.
San Antonio 78203

San Jacinto College-Central Campus
8060 Spencer Hwy.
Pasadena 77505

Ultrasound Diagnostic School
102 Decker Ct.
Irving 75062

UTAH

Utah Valley Hospital School of Radiogic
Technology
1034 North Fifth West St.
Provo 84603

VIRGINIA

Tidewater Community College
Rte. 135
Portsmouth 23703

WASHINGTON

Bellevue Community College
3000 Landerholm Circle SE
Bellevue 98007-6484

Tacoma Community College
5900 South 12th St.
Tacoma 98465

Yakima Valley Community College
P.O. Box 1647
Yakima 98907

WEST VIRGINIA

West Virginia University Hospital School
of Radiation Technology
Medical Center Dr., P.O. Box 8062
Morgantown 26506-8062

WISCONSIN

Mercy Medical Center School of
Radiologic Technology
631 Hazel St.
Oshkosh 54902

Milwaukee Area Technical College
700 West State St.
Milwaukee 53233

Saint Joseph's Hospital School of
Medical Technology
611 Saint Joseph's Ave.
Marshfield 54449

Saint Luke's Medical Center-School of
Diagnostic Medical Sonography
2900 West Oklahoma Ave.
Milwaukee 53215

Registered Nursing

ALABAMA

Bishop State Community College
351 North Broad St.
Mobile 36690

Coosa Valley Medical Center School of
Nursing
315 West Hickory St.
Sylacauga 35150

G C Wallace State Community College
P.O. Drawer 1049
Selma 36702-1049

Gadsden State Community College
P.O. Box 227
Gadsden 35902-0227

George C Wallace State Community
College-Dothan
Rte. 6, P.O. Box 62
Dothan 36303-9234

George C Wallace State Community
College-Hanceville
801 Main St. NW, P.O. Box 2000
Hanceville 35077-2000

Jefferson Davis Community
College-Brewton Campus
Alco Dr.
Brewton 36426

Jefferson State Community College
2601 Carson Rd.
Birmingham 35215-3098

John C Calhoun State Community
College
P.O. Box 2216
Decatur 35609-2216

Livingston University
Station One
Livingston 35470

Mobile College
P.O. Box 13220
Mobile 36663-0220

Northeast Alabama State Community
College
Hwy. 35 W
Rainsville 35986

Northwest Alabama Community College
Rte. 3, P.O. Box 77
Phil Campbell 35581

Samford University
800 Lakeshore Dr.
Birmingham 35229

Shelton State Community College
202 Skyland Blvd.
Tuscaloosa 35405

Southern Union State Junior College
Roberts St.
Wadley 36276

Troy State University-Main Campus
University Ave.
Troy 36082

Walker College
1411 Indiana Ave.
Jasper 35501

ALASKA

University of Alaska-Anchorage
3211 Providence Dr.
Anchorage 99508

ARIZONA

Arizona Western College
P.O. Box 929
Yuma 85366

Central Arizona College
8470 North Overfield Rd.
Coolidge 85228-9778

Cochise College
4190 West Hwy. 80
Douglas 85607-9724

Gateway Community College
108 North 40th St.
Phoenix 85034

Glendale Community College
6000 West Olive Ave.
Glendale 85302

Mesa Community College
1833 West Southern Ave.
Mesa 85202

Mohave Community College
1971 Jagerson Ave.
Kingman 86401

Phoenix College
1202 West Thomas Rd.
Phoenix 85013

Pima Community College
2202 West Anklam Rd.
Tucson 85709-0001

Scottsdale Community College
9000 East Chaparral Rd.
Scottsdale 85253

Yavapai College
1100 East Sheldon St.
Prescott 86301

ARKANSAS

Arkansas State University-Main Campus
P.O. Box 790
State University 72467

Arkansas Valley Technical Institute
Hwy. 23 N, P.O. Box 506
Ozark 72949

Baptist Schools of Nursing and Allied
Health
11900 College Glenn Rd.
Little Rock 72210-2820

East Arkansas Community College
Newcastle Rd.
Forrest City 72335

Garland County Community College
100 College Dr.
Hot Springs 71913

Jefferson School of Nursing
1515 West 42nd Ave.
Pine Bluff 71603

Mississippi County Community College
P.O. Box 1109
Blytheville 72316-1109

North Arkansas Community College
Pioneer Ridge
Harrison 72601

Phillips County Community College
P.O. Box 785
Helena 72342

Southern Arkansas University-Main
Campus
SAU Box 1288
Magnolia 71753

University of Arkansas-Fayetteville
Administration
Fayetteville 72701

University of Arkansas-Little Rock
2801 South University Ave.
Little Rock 72204

University of Arkansas-Monticello
P.O. Box 3598
Monticello 71655

Westark Community College
P.O. Box 3649
Fort Smith 72913

CALIFORNIA

Allan Hancock College
800 South College Dr.
Santa Maria 93454

American River College
4700 College Oak Dr.
Sacramento 95841

Antelope Valley College
3041 West Ave. K
Lancaster 93534

Bakersfield College
1801 Panorama Dr.
Bakersfield 93305-1299

Cabrillo College
6500 Soquel Dr.
Aptos 95003

Cerritos College
11110 Alondra Blvd.
Norwalk 90650

Chabot College
25555 Hesperian Blvd.
Hayward 94545

Chaffey Community College
5885 Haven Ave.
Rancho Cucamonga 91737-3002

City College of San Francisco
50 Phelan Ave.
San Francisco 94112

College of Marin
Kentfield 94904

College of San Mateo
1700 West Hillsdale Blvd.
San Mateo 94402

College of the Canyons
26455 North Rockwell Canyon Rd.
Santa Clarita 91355

College of the Desert
43-500 Monterey St.
Palm Desert 92260

College of the Redwoods
7351 Tompkins Hill Rd.
Eureka 95501-9302

College of the Sequoias
915 South Mooney Blvd.
Visalia 93277

Compton Community College
1111 East Artesia Blvd.
Compton 90221

Contra Costa College
2600 Mission Bell Dr.
San Pablo 94806

Crafton Hills College
11711 Sand Canyon Rd.
Yucaipa 92399-1799

Cuesta College
P.O. Box 8106
San Luis Obispo 93403-8106

De Anza College
21250 Stevens Creek Blvd.
Cupertino 95014

El Camino College
16007 Crenshaw Blvd.
Torrance 90506

Fresno City College
1101 East University Ave.
Fresno 93741

Gavilan College
5055 Santa Teresa Blvd.
Gilroy 95020

Glendale Community College
1500 North Verdugo Rd.
Glendale 91208-2894

Golden West College
15744 Golden West
Huntington Beach 92647

Grossmont College
8800 Grossmont College Dr.
El Cajon 92020

Hartnell College
156 Homestead Ave.
Salinas 93901

Imperial Valley College
P.O. Box 158
Imperial 92251-0158

Loma Linda University
Loma Linda 92350

Long Beach City College
4901 East Carson St.
Long Beach 90808

Los Angeles County Medical Center
School of Nursing
Muir Hall
Los Angeles 90033-1084

Los Angeles Harbor College
1111 Figueroa Place
Wilmington 90744

Los Angeles Pierce College
6201 Winnetka Ave.
Woodland Hills 91371

Los Angeles Training Technical College
400 West Washington Blvd.
Los Angeles 90015-4181

Los Angeles Valley College
5800 Fulton Ave.
Van Nuys 91401

Los Medanos College
2700 East Leland Rd.
Pittsburg 94565

Maric College of Medical Careers
7202 Princess View Dr.
San Diego 92120

Maric College of Medical Careers
1300 Rancheros Dr.
San Marcos 92069

Merced College
3600 M St.
Merced 95348-2898

Merritt College
12500 Campus Dr.
Oakland 94619

Mira Costa College
One Barnard Dr.
Oceanside 92056-3899

Modesto Junior College
435 College Ave.
Modesto 95350-9977

Monterey Peninsula College
980 Fremont Blvd.
Monterey 93940-4799

Moorpark College
7075 Campus Rd.
Moorpark 93021

Mount Saint Mary's College
12001 Chalon Rd.
Los Angeles 90049

Mount San Antonio College
1100 North Grand
Walnut 91789

Napa Valley College
2277 Napa Vallejo Hwy.
Napa 94558

Ohlone College
43600 Mission Blvd.
Fremont 94539

Pacific Union College
Institutional Research
Angwin 94508-9707

Palomar College
1140 West Mission
San Marcos 92069-1487

Pasadena City College
1570 East Colorada Blvd.
Pasadena 91106

Rancho Santiago College
17th at Bristol
Santa Ana 92706

Rio Hondo College
3600 Workman Mill Rd.
Whittier 90601-1699

Riverside Community College
4800 Magnolia Ave.
Riverside 92506-1299

Sacramento City College
3835 Freeport Blvd.
Sacramento 95822

San Diego City College
1313 12th Ave.
San Diego 92101

San Joaquin Delta College
5151 Pacific Ave.
Stockton 95207

Santa Barbara City College
721 Cliff Dr.
Santa Barbara 93109-2394

Santa Monica College
1900 Pico Blvd.
Santa Monica 90405-1628

Santa Rosa Junior College
1501 Mendocino Ave.
Santa Rosa 95401-4395

Shasta College
P.O. Box 496006
Redding 96049

Sierra College
5000 Rocklin Rd.
Rocklin 95677

Solano County Community College
District
4000 Suisun Valley Rd.
Suisun 94585

Southwestern College
900 Otay Lakes Rd.
Chula Vista 92010

Ventura College
4667 Telegraph Rd.
Ventura 93003

Victor Valley College
18422 Bear Valley Rd.
Victorville 92392-9699

Yuba College
2088 North Beale Rd.
Marysville 95901

COLORADO

Arapahoe Community College
2500 West College Dr.
Littleton 80160-9002

Community College of Denver
P.O. Box 173363
Denver 80217

Front Range Community College
3645 West 112th Ave.
Westminster 80030

Mesa State College
P.O. Box 2647
Grand Junction 81502

Otero Junior College
1802 Colorado Ave.
La Junta 81050

Pikes Peak Community College
5675 South Academy Blvd.
Colorado Springs 80906-5498

Pueblo College of Business &
Technology
330 Lake Ave.
Pueblo 81004

Pueblo Community College
900 West Orman Ave.
Pueblo 81004

Red Rocks Community College
13300 West Sixth Ave.
Golden 80401

Trinidad State Junior College
600 Prospect St.
Trinidad 81082

CONNECTICUT

Bridgeport Hospital School of Nursing
200 Mill Hill Ave.
Bridgeport 06610

Greater Hartford Community College
61 Woodland St.
Hartford 06105-2354

Mattatuck Community College
750 Chase Pkwy.
Waterbury 06708

Mohegan Community College
Mahan Dr., P.O. Box 629
Norwich 06360

Norwalk Community Technical College
188 Richards Ave.
Norwalk 06854

Quinnipiac College
Mount Carmel Ave.
Hamden 06518

Saint Francis Hospital School of Nursing
260 Ashley St.
Hartford 06105

Saint Mary's Hospital School of Nursing
41 John St.
Waterbury 06708

St. Vincent's College of Nursing
2800 Main St.
Bridgeport 06606

Wilcox College of Nursing
28 Crescent St.
Middletown 06457

DELAWARE

Delaware Technical and Community
College-Southern Campus
P.O. Box 610
Georgetown 19947

Delaware Technical and Community
College Stanton-Wilmington
400 Stanton-Christiana Rd.
Newark 19702

FLORIDA

Brevard Community College
1519 Clearlake Rd.
Cocoa 32922

Broward Community College
225 East Las Olas Blvd.
Fort Lauderdale 33301

Central Florida Community College
P.O. Box 1388
Ocala 34478

Daytona Beach Community College
1200 Volusia Ave.
Daytona Beach 32114

Edison Community College
8099 College Pkwy. SW
Fort Myers 33906-6210

Florida Community College at
Jacksonville
501 West State St.
Jacksonville 32202

Florida Keys Community College
5901 West College Rd.
Key West 33040

Gulf Coast Community College
5230 West Hwy. 98
Panama City 32401

Hillsborough Community College
P.O. Box 31127
Tampa 33631-3127

Indian River Community College
3209 Virginia Ave.
Fort Pierce 34981

Lake City Community College
Rte. 3, P.O. Box 7
Lake City 32055

Lake County Area Vocational-Technical
Center
2001 Kurt St.
Eustis 32726

Lake-Sumter Community College
9501 U.S. Hwy. 441
Leesburg 34788-8751

Manatee Community College
5840 26th St. W
Bradenton 34207

Miami-Dade Community College
300 Northeast Second Ave.
Miami 33132

North Florida Junior College
Turner Davis Dr.
Madison 32340

North Technical Education Center
7071 Garden Rd.
Riviera Beach 33404

Palm Beach Community College
4200 Congress Ave.
Lake Worth 33461

Pasco-Hernando Community College
36727 Blanton Rd.
Dade City 33525-7599

Pensacola Junior College
1000 College Blvd.
Pensacola 32504

Pinellas Technical Education
Centers-Saint Pete Campus
901 34th St. S
Saint Petersburg 33711

Polk Community College
999 Ave. H NE
Winter Haven 33881

Saint Petersburg Junior College
P.O. Box 13489
Saint Petersburg 33733

Santa Fe Community College
3000 Northwest 83rd St.
Gainesville 32601

Seminole Community College
100 Weldon Blvd.
Sanford 32773-6199

Tallahassee Community College
444 Appleyard Dr.
Tallahassee 32304-2895

Valencia Community College
P.O. Box 3028
Orlando 32802

GEORGIA

Abraham Baldwin Agricultural College
ABAC 9, 2802 Moore Hwy.
Tifton 31794-2601

Armstrong State College
11935 Abercorn St.
Savannah 31419

Augusta College
2500 Walton Way
Augusta 30910

Brunswick College
Altama at Fourth St.
Brunswick 31523

Clayton State College
5900 Lee St., P.O. Box 285
Morrow 30260

Columbus College
4225 University Ave.
Columbus 31907-5645

Dalton College
213 North College Dr.
Dalton 30720

Darton College
2400 Gillionville Rd.
Albany 31707

Dekalb College
3251 Panthersville Rd.
Decatur 30034

Floyd College
P.O. Box 1864
Rome 30162-1864

Georgia Southwestern College
800 Wheatley St.
Americus 31709-4693

Gordon College
419 College Dr.
Barnesville 30204

Kennesaw State College
P.O. Box 444
Marietta 30061

La Grange College
601 Broad St.
La Grange 30240

Macon College
100 College Station Dr.
Macon 31297

Middle Georgia College
1100 Second St. SE
Cochran 31014-1599

North Georgia College
College Ave.
Dahlonega 30597

South Georgia College
100 West College Park Dr.
Douglas 31533

West Georgia College
Carrollton 30118-0001

HAWAII

Hawaii Community College
200 West Kawili St.
Hilo 96720-4091

Kapiolani Community College
4303 Diamond Head Rd.
Honolulu 96816

Maui Community College
310 Kaahumanu Ave.
Kahului 96732

University of Hawaii at Manoa
2444 Dole St.
Honolulu 96822

IDAHO

Boise State University
1910 University Dr.
Boise 83725

College of Southern Idaho
P.O. Box 1238
Twin Falls 83301

Lewis-Clark State College
Eighth Ave. and Sixth St.
Lewiston 83501

North Idaho College
1000 West Garden Ave.
Coeur D'Alene 83814

Ricks College
Rexburg 83460-4107

ILLINOIS

Belleville Area College
2500 Carlyle Rd.
Belleville 62221

Black Hawk College-Quad-Cities
6600 34th Ave.
Moline 61265

Carl Sandburg College
2232 South Lake Storey Rd.
Galesburg 61401

City College of Chicago-Olive-Harvey
College
10001 South Woodlawn Ave.
Chicago 60628

City College of Chicago-Kennedy-King
College
6800 South Wentworth Ave.
Chicago 60621

City College of Chicago-Richard J Daley
College
7500 South Pulaski Rd.
Chicago 60652

City College of Chicago-Truman College
1145 Wilson Ave.
Chicago 60640

City College of Chicago-Malcolm X
College
1900 West Van Buren
Chicago 60612

College of Du Page
Lambert Rd. and 22nd St.
Glen Ellyn 60137

College of Lake County
19351 West Washington St.
Grays Lake 60030-1198

Elgin Community College
1700 Spartan Dr.
Elgin 60123

Highland Community College
2998 West Pearl City Rd.
Freeport 61032-9341

Illinois Central College
One College Dr.
East Peoria 61635

Illinois Eastern Community
Colleges-Olney Central College
RR 3
Olney 62450

Illinois Valley Community College
2578 East 350th Rd.
Oglesby 61348

John A Logan College
Carterville 62918

Joliet Junior College
1216 Houbolt Ave.
Joliet 60436

Kankakee Community College
P.O. Box 888
Kankakee 60901

Kaskaskia College
27210 College Rd.
Centralia 62801

Kishwaukee College
21193 Malta Rd.
Malta 60150

Lake Land College
5001 Lake Land Blvd.
Mattoon 61938

Lewis and Clark Community College
5800 Godfrey Rd.
Godfrey 62035

Lincoln Land Community College
Shepherd Rd.
Springfield 62194-9256

Methodist Medical Center of Illinois
School of Nursing
221 Northeast Glen Oak Ave.
Peoria 61636

Moraine Valley Community College
10900 South 88th Ave.
Palos Hills 60465-0937

Morton College
3801 South Central Ave.
Cicero 60650

Oakton Community College
1600 East Golf Rd.
Des Plaines 60016

Parkland College
2400 West Bradley Ave.
Champaign 61821

Prairie State College
202 Halsted St.
Chicago Heights 60411

Ravenswood Hospital Medical Center
2318 West Irving Park Rd.
Chicago 60618-3824

Rend Lake College
Rte. 1
Ina 62846

Rock Valley College
3301 North Mulford Rd.
Rockford 61114

Saint Francis Hospital School of Nursing
319 Ridge Ave.
Evanston 60202

Shawnee Community College
Shawnee College Rd.
Ullin 62992

South Suburban College
15800 South State St.
South Holland 60473

Southeastern Illinois College
3575 College Rd.
Harrisburg 62946

Trinity School of Nursing
501 Tenth Ave.
Moline 61265

Triton College
2000 Fifth Ave.
River Grove 60171

Waubonsee Community College
Rte. 47 at Harter Rd.
Sugar Grove 60554-0901

William Rainey Harper College
1200 West Algonquin Rd.
Palatine 60067-7398

INDIANA

Ball State University
2000 University Ave.
Muncie 47306

Bethel College
1001 West McKinley Ave.
Mishawaka 46545

Indiana State University
210 North Seventh St.
Terre Haute 47809

Indiana University-East
2325 Chester Blvd.
Richmond 47374

Indiana University-Kokomo
2300 South Washington
Kokomo 46902

Indiana University-Northwest
3400 Broadway
Gary 46408

Indiana University-Purdue University at
Fort Wayne
2101 Coliseum Blvd. E
Fort Wayne 46805

Indiana University-Purdue University at
Indianapolis
355 North Lansing
Indianapolis 46202

Indiana University-South Bend
1700 Mishawaka Ave.
South Bend 46615

Indiana Vocational Technical
College-North Central
1534 West Sample St.
South Bend 46619

Indiana Vocational Technical
College-Southeast
590 Ivy Tech Dr., P.O. Box 209
Madison 47250

Indiana Vocational Technical
College-Southwest
3501 First Ave.
Evansville 47710

Indiana Vocational Technical
College-Whitewater
2325 Chester Blvd., P.O. Box 1145
Richmond 47374

Lutheran College of Health Professions
3024 Fairfield Ave.
Fort Wayne 46807

Marian College
3200 Cold Spring Rd.
Indianapolis 46222-1997

Purdue University-Calumet Campus
2233 171st St.
Hammond 46323

Purdue University-North Central Campus
U.S. Hwy. 421 & Indiana Toll Rd.
Westville 46391

Saint Elizabeth Hospital School of
Nursing
1508 Tippecanoe St.
Lafayette 47904-2198

University of Indianapolis
1400 East Hanna Ave.
Indianapolis 46227

University of Southern Indiana
8600 University Blvd.
Evansville 47712

Vincennes University
1002 North First St.
Vincennes 47591

IOWA

Allen Memorial Hospital-Allied Health
Programs
1825 Logan Ave.
Waterloo 50703

Des Moines Community College
2006 Ankeny Blvd.
Ankeny 50021

Eastern Iowa Community College District
306 West River Dr.
Davenport 52801-1221

Hawkeye Institute of Technology
1501 East Orange Rd.
Waterloo 50704

Indian Hills Community College
525 Grandview
Ottumwa 52501

Iowa Central Community College
330 Ave. M
Fort Dodge 50501

Iowa Lakes Community College
19 South Seventh St.
Estherville 51334

Iowa Methodist School of Nursing
1117 Pleasant St.
Des Moines 50309

Iowa Valley Community College
P.O. Box 536
Marshalltown 50158

Iowa Western Community College
2700 College Rd., P.O. Box 4C
Council Bluffs 51502

Jennie Edmundson Memorial Hospital
School of Nursing
933 East Pierce St., P.O. Box 2C
Council Bluffs 51502

Kirkwood Community College
P.O. Box 2068
Cedar Rapids 52406

Mercy Hospital Medical Center School
of Nursing
6th and University
Des Moines 50314

North Iowa Area Community College
500 College Dr.
Mason City 50401

Northeast Iowa Community College
Hwy. 150 S, P.O. Box 400
Calmar 52132-0400

Saint Luke's School of Nursing
2720 Stone Park Blvd.
Sioux City 51104-0263

Southeastern Community College
1015 South Gear Ave., P.O. Drawer F
West Burlington 52655-0605

Southwestern Community College
1501 Townline
Creston 50801

Western Iowa Technical Community
College
4647 Stone Ave., P.O. Box 265
Sioux City 51102-0265

KANSAS

Baker University
8th and Grove
Baldwin City 66006

Barton County Community College
Rte. 3, P.O. Box 136Z
Great Bend 67530

Butler County Community College
901 South Haverhill Rd.
El Dorado 67042

Cloud County Community College
2221 Campus Dr., P.O. Box 1002
Concordia 66901-1002

Colby Community College
1255 South Range
Colby 67701

Dodge City Community College
2501 North 14th Ave.
Dodge City 67801

Fort Scott Community College
2108 South Horton
Fort Scott 66701

Garden City Community College
801 Campus Dr.
Garden City 67846

Hesston College
P.O. Box 3000
Hesston 67062

Hutchinson Community College
1300 North Plum St.
Hutchinson 67501

Johnson County Area
Vocational-Technical School
311 East Park
Olathe 66061

Johnson County Community College
12345 College Blvd.
Overland Park 66210-1299

Kansas City Area Vocational Technical
School
2220 North 59th St.
Kansas City 66104

Kansas City Kansas Community College
7250 State Ave.
Kansas City 66112

Kansas Newman College
3100 McCormick Ave.
Wichita 67213-2097

Kansas Wesleyan University
100 East Claflin
Salina 67401-6196

Labette Community College
200 South 14th
Parsons 67357

Neosho County Community College
1000 South Allen
Chanute 66720

Seward County Community College
P.O. Box 1137
Liberal 67905-1137

KENTUCKY

Ashland Community College
1400 College Dr.
Ashland 41101

Eastern Kentucky University
Lancaster Ave.
Richmond 40475

Elizabethtown Community College
College Street Rd.
Elizabethtown 42701

Hazard Community College
Hazard 41701

Henderson Community College
2660 South Green St.
Henderson 42420

Hopkinsville Community College
North Dr.
Hopkinsville 42240

Jefferson Community College
109 East Broadway
Louisville 40202

Kentucky State University
East Main St.
Frankfort 40601

Kentucky Wesleyan College
3000 Frederica St., P.O. Box 1039
Owensboro 42302-1039

Lees College
601 Jefferson
Jackson 41339

Lexington Community College
Cooper Dr.
Lexington 40506

Madisonville Community College
University Dr.
Madisonville 42431

Maysville Community College
Maysville 41056

Midway College
512 Stephens St.
Midway 40347-1120

Morehead State University
University Blvd.
Morehead 40351

Northern Kentucky University
University Dr.
Highland Heights 41099

Paducah Community College
P.O. Box 7380
Paducah 42002-7380

Prestonsburg Community College
Bert Combs Dr.
Prestonsburg 41653

Somerset Community College
808 Monticello Rd.
Somerset 42501

Southeast Community College
300 College Rd.
Cumberland 40823

Western Kentucky University
1526 Russellville Rd.
Bowling Green 42101-3576

LOUISIANA

Baton Rouge General Medical Center
School of Nursing
3616 North Blvd.
Baton Rouge 70806

Delta Junior College-Baton Rouge
7290 Exchange Place
Baton Rouge 70806

Huey P Long Technical Institute
303 South Jones St.
Winnfield 71483

Louisiana State University-Alexandria
8100 Hwy. 71 S
Alexandria 71302-9633

Louisiana State University-Eunice
P.O. Box 1129
Eunice 70535

Louisiana State University Medical
Center
433 Bolivar St.
New Orleans 70112

Louisiana Technical University
Tech Station, P.O. Box 3168
Ruston 71272

Nicholls State University
University Station
Thibodaux 70310

Northwestern State University of
Louisiana
College Ave.
Natchitoches 71497

Our Lady of the Lake College of Nursing
& Allied Health
5345 Brittany Dr.
Baton Rouge 70808

MAINE

Central Maine Medical Center School of
Nursing
300 Main St.
Lewiston 04240

Kennebec Valley Technical College
92 Western Ave.
Fairfield 04937-1367

Northern Maine Technical College
33 Edgemont Dr.
Presque Isle 04769

Southern Maine Technical College
Fort Rd.
South Portland 04106

University of Maine at Augusta
University Heights
Augusta 04330-9410

MARYLAND

Allegany Community College
Willowbrook Rd.
Cumberland 21502

Anne Arundel Community College
101 College Pkwy.
Arnold 21012

Baltimore City Community College
2901 Liberty Heights Ave.
Baltimore 21215

Catonsville Community College
800 South Rolling Rd.
Catonsville 21228

Cecil Community College
1000 North East Rd.
North East 21901-1999

Charles County Community College
Mitchell Rd., P.O. Box 910
La Plata 20646

Essex Community College
7201 Rossville Blvd.
Baltimore 21237

Frederick Community College
7932 Opossumtown Pike
Frederick 21702

Hagerstown Junior College
11400 Robinwood Dr.
Hagerstown 21742-6590

Harbor Hospital Center School of Nursing
3001 South Hanover St.
Baltimore 21225

Harford Community College
401 Thomas Run Rd.
Bel Air 21015

Howard Community College
Little Patuxent Pkwy.
Columbia 21044

Montgomery College of Takoma Park
Takoma Ave. and Fenton St.
Takoma Park 20912

Prince Georges Community College
301 Largo Rd.
Largo 23701-1243

Wor-Wic Community College
1409 Wesley Dr.
Salisbury 21801-7131

MASSACHUSETTS

Atlantic Union College
South Lancaster 01561

Bay State Medical Center School of
Nursing
759 Chestnut St.
Springfield 01199

Berkshire Community College
1350 West St.
Pittsfield 01201-5786

Bristol Community College
777 Elsbree St.
Fall River 02720

Bunker Hill Community College
New Rutherford Ave.
Boston 02129

Cape Cod Community College
Rte. 132
West Barnstable 02668

Catherine Laboure College
2120 Dorchester Ave.
Boston 02124

Fisher College
118 Beacon St.
Boston 02116

Framingham Union School of
Nursing-Merrowest Medical Center
85 Lincoln St.
Framingham 01701

Greenfield Community College
One College Dr.
Greenfield 01301-9739

Holyoke Community College
303 Homestead Ave.
Holyoke 01040

Massachusetts Bay Community College
50 Oakland St.
Wellesley Hills 02181

Massachusetts Soldiers Home School of
Practical Nursing
91 Crest Ave.
Chelsea 02150

Massasoit Community College
One Massasoit Blvd.
Brockton 02402

Middlesex Community College
Springs Rd.
Bedford 01730

Mount Wachusett Community College
444 Green St.
Gardner 01440

North Shore Community College
One Ferncroft Rd.
Danvers 01923

Northern Essex Community College
Elliott Way
Haverhill 01830-2399

Quincy College
34 Coddington St.
Quincy 02169

Quinsigamond Community College
670 West Boylston St.
Worcester 01606

Saint Elizabeth's Hospital School of
Nursing
159 Washington St.
Brighton 02135

Somerville Hospital School of Nursing
125 Lowell St.
Somerville 02143

Springfield Technical Community
College
Armory Square
Springfield 01105

MICHIGAN

Alpena Community College
666 Johnson St.
Alpena 49707

Bay De Noc Community College
2001 North Lincoln Rd.
Escanaba 49289

Bronson Methodist Hospital
252 East Lovell St.
Kalamazoo 49007

Delta College
University Center 48710

Ferris State University
901 South State St.
Big Rapids 49307

Grand Rapids Community College
143 Bostwick Ave. NE
Grand Rapids 49505

Great Lakes Junior College of Business
310 South Washington Ave.
Saginaw 48607

Henry Ford Community College
5101 Evergreen Rd.
Dearborn 48128

Henry Ford Hospital School of Nursing
2921 West Grand Blvd.
Detroit 48202

Hurley Medical Center School of Nursing
701 West Eighth Ave.
Flint 48502

Jackson Community College
2111 Emmons Rd.
Jackson 49201

Kalamazoo Valley Community College
6767 West O Ave.
Kalamazoo 49009

Kellogg Community College
450 North Ave.
Battle Creek 49017

Kirtland Community College
10775 North Saint Helen Rd.
Roscommon 48653

Lake Michigan College
2755 East Napier
Benton Harbor 49022

Lansing Community College
419 North Capitol Ave.
Lansing 48901-7210

Macomb Community College
14500 Twelve Mile Rd.
Warren 48093-3896

Mid Michigan Community College
1375 South Clare Ave.
Harrison 48625

Monroe County Community College
1555 South Raisinville Rd.
Monroe 48161

Montcalm Community College
2800 College Dr.
Sidney 48885

Mott Community College
1401 East Court St.
Flint 48503

Muskegon Community College
221 South Quarterline Rd.
Muskegon 49442

North Central Michigan College
1515 Howard St.
Petoskey 49770

Northwestern Michigan College
1701 East Front St.
Traverse City 49684

Oakland Community College
2480 Opdyke Rd.
Bloomfield Hills 48304-2266

Saint Clair County Community College
323 Erie, P.O. Box 5015
Port Huron 48061-5015

Schoolcraft College
18600 Haggerty Rd.
Livonia 48152

Southwestern Michigan College
58900 Cherry Grove Rd.
Dowagiac 49047-9793

Suomi College
601 Quincy St.
Hancock 49930

University of Detroit-Mercy
P.O. Box 19900
Detroit 48219-0900

Washtenaw Community College
P.O. Drawer 1
Ann Arbor 48016

Wayne County Community College
801 West Fort St.
Detroit 48226

West Shore Community College
3000 North Stiles
Scottville 49454

MINNESOTA

Anoka-Ramsey Community College
11200 Mississippi Blvd.
Coon Rapids 55433

Austin Community College
1600 Eighth Ave. NW
Austin 55912

Brainerd Community College
501 West College Dr.
Brainerd 56401

College of Saint Catherine-Saint Mary's
Campus
2500 South Sixth St.
Minneapolis 55454

Hibbing Community College
1515 East 25th St.
Hibbing 55746

Inver Hills Community College
5445 College Trail
Inver Grove Heights 55076

Lakewood Community College
3401 Century Ave. N
White Bear Lake 55110

Minneapolis Community College
1501 Hennepin Ave.
Minneapolis 55403

Normandale Community College
9700 France Ave. S
Bloomington 55431

North Hennepin Community College
7411 85th Ave. N
Brooklyn Park 55445

Northland Community College
Hwy. 1 E
Thief River Falls 56701

Rochester Community College
851 30th Ave. SE
Rochester 55904-4999

Willmar Community College
P.O. Box 797
Willmar 56201-0797

MISSISSIPPI

Alcorn State University
P.O. Box 359
Lorman 39096

Hinds Community College-Raymond
Campus
Raymond 39154

Holmes Community College
Hill St.
Goodman 39079

Itawamba Community College
602 West Hill St.
Fulton 38843

Jones County Junior College
Front St.
Ellisville 39437

Meridian Community College
910 Hwy. 19 N
Meridian 39307

Mississippi Delta Community College
P.O. Box 668
Moorhead 38761

Mississippi Gulf Coast Community
College
Central Office, P.O. Box 67
Perkinston 39573

Mississippi University for Women
P.O. Box W1600
Columbus 39701

Northeast Mississippi Community
College
Cunningham Blvd.
Booneville 38829

Northwest Mississippi Community
College
Hwy. 51 N
Senatobia 38668

Pearl River Community College
Station A
Poplarville 39470

Southwest Mississippi Community
College
College Dr.
Summit 39666

MISSOURI

Barnes College
416 South Kings Hwy.
Saint Louis 63110

Central Methodist College
411 Central Methodist Square
Fayette 65248

East Central College
P.O. Box 529
Union 63084

Hannibal-Lagrange College
2800 Palmyra Rd.
Hannibal 63401

Jefferson College
1000 Viking Dr.
Hillsboro 63050

Lincoln University
820 Chestnut
Jefferson City 65102-0029

Lutheran Medical Center School of
Nursing
3547 South Jefferson Ave.
Saint Louis 63118

Mineral Area College
P.O. Box 1000
Flat River 63601

Missouri Baptist Medical Center School
of Nursing
3015 North Ballas Rd.
Saint Louis 63131

Missouri Southern State College
3950 East Newman Rd.
Joplin 64801-1595

Moberly Area Community College
College and Rollins St.
Moberly 65270

North Central Missouri College
1301 Main St.
Trenton 64683

Park College
87 River Park Dr.
Parkville 64152-3795

Penn Valley Community College
3201 Southwest Trafficway
Kansas City 64111

Saint Charles County Community College
4601 Mid Rivers Mall Dr.
Saint Peter's 63376

Saint John's School of Nursing
4431 South Fremont
Springfield 65804-2263

Saint Louis Community College-Forest
Park
5600 Oakland Ave.
Saint Louis 63110

Saint Luke's College
4426 Wornall Rd.
Kansas City 64111

Sanford-Brown Business College
12006 Manchester Rd.
Des Peres 63131

Southeast Missouri State University
One University Plaza
Cape Girardeau 63701

Southwest Missouri State
University-West Plains
128 Garfield
West Plains 65775

State Fair Community College
3201 West 16th
Sedalia 65301-2199

Three Rivers Community College
Three Rivers Blvd.
Poplar Bluff 63901

Waynesville Area Vocational School
810 Roosevelt
Waynesville 65583

MONTANA

Miles Community College
2715 Dickinson
Miles City 59301

Northern Montana College
P.O. Box 7751
Havre 59501

Salish Kootenai Community College
P.O. Box 117
Pablo 59855

NEBRASKA

Bryan Memorial Hospital School of
Nursing
5000 Sumner St.
Lincoln 68506-1398

Central Community College-Grand Island
P.O. Box 4903
Grand Island 68802

College of Saint Mary
1901 South 72nd St.
Omaha 68124

Metropolitan Community College Area
P.O. Box 3777
Omaha 68103

Northeast Community College
801 East Benjamin, P.O. Box 469
Norfolk 68702-0469

Southeast Community College-Lincoln
Campus
8800 O St.
Lincoln 68520

NEVADA

Community College of Southern Nevada
3200 East Cheyenne Ave.
Las Vegas 89030

Truckee Meadows Community College
7000 Dandini Blvd.
Reno 89512

Western Nevada Community College
2201 West Nye Ln.
Carson City 89703

NEW HAMPSHIRE

New Hampshire Technical College at
Berlin
2020 Riverside Dr.
Berlin 03570

New Hampshire Technical College at
Claremont
One College Dr.
Claremont 03743

New Hampshire Technical College at
Manchester
1066 Front St.
Manchester 03102

New Hampshire Technical College at
Stratham
277 Portsmouth Ave.
Stratham 03885

New Hampshire Technical Institute
11 Institute Dr.
Concord 03301

Rivier College
429 Main St.
Nashua 03060

NEW JERSEY

Ann May School of Nursing-Jersey
Shore Medical Center
1945 Rte. 33
Neptune 07754

Atlantic Community College
5100 Black Horse Pike
Mays Landing 08330-2699

Bergen Community College
400 Paramus Rd.
Paramus 07652

Brookdale Community College
Newman Springs Rd.
Lincroft 07738-1599

Burlington County College
Rte. 530
Pemberton 08068

Camden County College
P.O. Box 200
Blackwood 08012

Charles E Gregory School of Nursing
530 New Brunswick Ave.
Perth Amboy 08861

County College of Morris
214 Center Grove Rd.
Randolph 07869

Cumberland County College
College Dr., P.O. Box 517
Vineland 08360

Englewood Hospital Medical Center
School of Nursing
55 West Demarest Ave.
Englewood 07631

Essex County College
303 University Ave.
Newark 07102

Felician College
260 South Main St.
Lodi 07644

Gloucester County College
Tanyard Rd. & RR 4, P.O. Box 203
Sewell 08080

Helene Fuld School of Nursing
832 Brunswick Ave.
Trenton 08638

Helene Fuld School of Nursing in
Camden County
Mount Ephraim and Atlantic Aves.
Camden 08104

Holy Name Hospital School of Nursing
690 Teaneck Rd.
Teaneck 07666

Mercer County Community College
1200 Old Trenton Rd.
Trenton 08690

Mercer Medical Center School of Nursing
446 Bellevue Ave., P.O. Box 1658
Trenton 08607

Mountainside Hospital School of Nursing
Bay and Highland Aves.
Montclair 07042

Muhlenberg Regional Medical
Center-School of Nursing
Park Ave. and Randolph Rd.
Plainfield 07061

Ocean County College
College Dr.
Toms River 08753

Our Lady of Lourdes School of Nursing
1565 Vesper Blvd.
Camden 08103

Passaic County Community College
College Blvd.
Paterson 07509

Raritan Valley Community College
P.O. Box 3300
Somerville 08876

Saint Francis Medical Center School of
Nursing
601 Hamilton Ave.
Trenton 08629

Union County College
1033 Springfield Ave.
Cranford 07016

NEW MEXICO

Albuquerque Technical-Vocational
Institute
525 Buena Vista SE
Albuquerque 87106

Clovis Community College
417 Schepps Blvd.
Clovis 88101

Eastern New Mexico University-Roswell
Campus
52 University Blvd., P.O. Box 6000
Roswell 88202

New Mexico Junior College
5317 Lovington Hwy.
Hobbs 88240

New Mexico State
University-Alamogordo
P.O. Box 477
Alamogordo 88310

New Mexico State University-Carlsbad
1500 University Dr.
Carlsbad 88220

New Mexico State University-Main
Campus
Department 3Z, P.O. Box 30001
Las Cruces 88003

San Juan College
4601 College Blvd.
Farmington 87402

University of New Mexico-Gallup Branch
200 College Rd.
Gallup 87301

NEW YORK

Adirondack Community College
Bay Rd.
Queensbury 12804

Arnot-Ogden Medical Center School of
Nursing
600 Roe Ave.
Elmira 14905

Broome Community College
P.O. Box 1017
Binghamton 13902

Catholic Medical Center School of
Nursing
89-15 Woodhaven Blvd.
Woodhaven 11421

Cayuga County Community College
Franklin St.
Auburn 13021

Clinton Community College
RR 3, P.O. Box 8A
Plattsburgh 12901

Cochran School of Nursing
967 North Broadway, Andrus Pavillion,
Saint John's Riverside Hospital
Yonkers 10701

Columbia-Greene Community College
P.O. Box 1000
Hudson 12534

Corning Community College
Spencer Hill
Corning 14830

Crouse Irving Memorial Hospital School
of Nursing
736 Irving Ave.
Syracuse 13210

CUNY Borough of Manhattan
Community College
199 Chambers St.
New York 10007

CUNY Bronx Community College
West 181st St. & University Ave.
Bronx 10453

CUNY College of Staten Island
2800 Victory Blvd.
Staten Island 10314

CUNY Kingsborough Community
College
2001 Oriental Blvd.
Brooklyn 11235

CUNY La Guardia Community College
31-10 Thomson Ave.
Long Island City 11101

CUNY New York City Technical College
300 Jay St.
Brooklyn 11201

CUNY Queensborough Community
College
56th Ave. & Springfield Blvd.
New York 11364

Dorothea Hopfer School of
Nursing-Mount Vernon Hospital
53 Valentine St.
Mount Vernon 10550

Dutchess Community College
Pendell Rd.
Poughkeepsie 12601

Ellis Hospital School of Nursing
1101 Nott St.
Schenectady 12308

Erie Community College-City Campus
121 Ellicott St.
Buffalo 14203

Erie Community College-North Campus
Main St. and Youngs Rd.
Williamsville 14221

Finger Lakes Community College
4355 Lake Shore Dr.
Canandaigua 14424

Fulton-Montgomery Community College
2805 State Hwy. 67
Johnstown 12095

Genesee Community College
One College Rd.
Batavia 14020

Helene Fuld School of Nursing
1879 Madison Ave.
New York 10035

Hudson Valley Community College
80 Vandenburgh Ave.
Troy 12180

Iona College
715 North Ave.
New Rochelle 10801

Jamestown Community College
525 Falconer St.
Jamestown 14701

Jefferson Community College
Outer Coffeen St.
Watertown 13601

Long Island College Hospital School of
Nursing
397 Hicks St.
Brooklyn 11201

Maria College of Albany
700 New Scotland Ave.
Albany 12208

Millard Fillmore Hospital School of
Nursing
Three Gates Circle
Buffalo 14209

Mohawk Valley Community College
1101 Sherman Dr.
Utica 13501

Monroe Community College
1000 East Henrietta Rd.
Rochester 14623

Nassau Community College
One Education Dr.
Garden City 11530

Niagara County Community College
3111 Saunders Settlement Rd.
Sanborn 14132

North Country Community College
20 Winona Ave., P.O. Box 89
Saranac Lake 12983

Onondaga Community College
Rte. 173
Syracuse 13215

Orange County Community College
115 South St.
Middletown 10940

Pace University-Pleasantville Briarcliff
Campus
Bedford Rd.
Pleasantville 10570

Phillips Beth Israel School of Nursing
310 East 22nd St.
New York 10010

Regents College, University of the State
of New York
1450 Western Ave.
Albany 12203

Rockland Community College
145 College Rd.
Suffern 10901

Russell Sage College-Main Campus
45 Ferry St.
Troy 12180

Saint Elizabeth Hospital School of
Nursing
2215 Genessee St.
Utica 13501

Saint Joseph's Hospital Health Center
School of Nursing
206 Prospect Ave.
Syracuse 13203

Saint Vincent's Hospital School of
Nursing
27 Christopher St.
New York 10014

Samaritan Hospital School of Nursing
2215 Burdett Ave.
Troy 12180

Sisters of Charity Hospital School of
Nursing
2157 Main St.
Buffalo 14214

St. Vincent's Medical Center of
Richmond-School of Nursing
Two Gridley Ave.
Staten Island 10303

Suffolk County Community
College-Ammerman Campus
533 College Rd.
Selden 11784

Suffolk County Community
College-Western Campus
Crooked Hill Rd.
Brentwood 11717

Sullivan County Community College
Le Roy Rd., P.O. Box 4002
Loch Sheldrake 12759-4002

SUNY College of Technology &
Agriculture at Morrisville
Morrisville 13408

SUNY College of Technology at Alfred
Alfred 14802

SUNY College of Technology at Canton
Canton 13617

SUNY College of Technology at Delhi
Delhi 13753

SUNY College of Technology at
Farmingdale
Melville Rd.
Farmingdale 11735

SUNY Ulster County Community College
Cottekill Rd.
Stone Ridge 12484

SUNY Westchester Commmunity College
75 Grasslands Rd.
Valhalla 10595

Tompkins-Cortland Community College
170 North St.
Dryden 13053

Trocaire College
110 Red Jacket Pkwy.
Buffalo 14220

NORTH CAROLINA

Alamance Community College
P.O. Box 8000
Graham 27253

Asheville Buncombe Technical
Community College
340 Victoria Rd.
Asheville 28801

Beaufort County Community College
P.O. Box 1069
Washington 27889

Caldwell Community College and
Technical Institute
P.O. Box 600
Lenoir 28645

Cape Fear Community College
411 North Front St.
Wilmington 28401

Catawba Valley Community College
2550 Hwy. 70 SE
Hickory 28602-0699

Central Carolina Community College
1105 Kelly Dr.
Sanford 27330

Central Piedmont Community College
P.O. Box 35009
Charlotte 28235

College of the Albemarle
1208 North Road St., P.O. Box 2327
Elizabeth City 27906-2327

Craven Community College
800 College Ct.
New Bern 28562

Davidson County Community College
P.O. Box 1287
Lexington 27293

Durham Technical Community College
1637 Lawson St.
Durham 27703

Edgecombe Community College
2009 West Wilson St.
Tarboro 27886

Fayetteville Technical Community
College
2201 Hull Rd.
Fayetteville 28303

Forsyth Technical Community College
2100 Silas Creek Pkwy.
Winston-Salem 27103

Gardner-Webb College
P.O. Box 997
Boiling Springs 28017

Gaston College
Hwy. 321
Dallas 28034

Guilford Technical Community College
P.O. Box 309
Jamestown 27282

Halifax Community College
P.O. Drawer 809
Weldon 27890

James Sprunt Community College
P.O. Box 398
Kenansville 28349

Johnston Community College
P.O. Box 2350
Smithfield 27577-2350

Louise Harkey School of
Nursing-Cabarrus Memorial Hospital
920 North Church St.
Concord 28025

Mayland Community College
P.O. Box 547
Spruce Pine 28777

Mercy School of Nursing
1921 Vail Ave.
Charlotte 28207

Mitchell Community College
500 West Broad
Statesville 28677

Nash Community College
P.O. Box 7488
Rocky Mount 27804

Piedmont Community College
P.O. Box 1197
Roxboro 27573

Pitt Community College
Hwy. 11 S, P.O. Drawer 7007
Greenville 27835-7007

Presbyterian Hospital
1901 East Fifth St.
Charlotte 28233

Randolph Community College
P.O. Box 1009
Asheboro 27204

Robeson Community College
P.O. Box 1420
Lumberton 28359

Rockingham Community College
P.O. Box 38
Wentworth 27375-0038

Rowan-Cabarrus Community College
P.O. Box 1595
Salisbury 28145-1595

Sampson Community College
P.O. Box 318
Clinton 28328

Sandhills Community College
2200 Airport Rd.
Pinehurst 28374

Southeastern Community College
P.O. Box 151
Whiteville 28472

Stanly Community College
141 College Dr.
Albemarle 28001

Surry Community College
South Main St.
Dobson 27017-0304

Vance-Granville Community College
State Rd. 1126, P.O. Box 917
Henderson 27536

Wake Technical Community College
9101 Fayetteville Rd.
Raleigh 27603-5696

Watts School of Nursing
3643 North Roxboro St.
Durham 27704-2763

Wayne Community College
P.O. Box 8002
Goldsboro 27533-8002

Western Piedmont Community College
1001 Burkemont Ave.
Morganton 28655-9978

Wilson Technical Community College
902 Herring Ave.
Wilson 27893

OHIO

Ashtabula County Joint Vocational
School
1565 Rte. 167
Jefferson 44047

Aultman Hospital School of Nursing
2600 Sixth St. SW
Canton 44710-1797

Belmont Technical College
120 Fox Shannon Place
Saint Clairsville 43950

Central Ohio Technical College
1179 University Dr.
Newark 43055-1767

Christ Hospital School of Nursing
2139 Auburn Ave.
Cincinnati 45219

Cincinnati Technical College
3520 Central Pkwy.
Cincinnati 45223

Clark State Community College
570 East Leffel Ln.
Springfield 45505

Columbus State Community College
550 East Spring St., P.O. Box 1609
Columbus 43216

Community Hospital School of Nursing
330 South Burnett Rd.
Springfield 45505

Cuyahoga Community College District
700 Carnegie Ave.
Cleveland 44115-2878

Edison State Community College
1973 Edison Dr.
Piqua 45356

Fairview General Hospital School of
Nursing
18101 Lorain Ave.
Cleveland 44111

Good Samaritan Hospital School of
Nursing
375 Dixmyth Ave.
Cincinnati 45220

Hocking Technical College
3301 Hocking Pkwy.
Nelsonville 45764

Kent State University-Ashtabula
Regional Campus
3325 West 13th St.
Ashtabula 44004

Kent State University-East Liverpool
Regional Campus
400 East Fourth St.
East Liverpool 43920

Kettering College of Medical Arts
3737 Southern Blvd.
Kettering 45429-1299

Knox County Career Center
306 Martinsburg Rd.
Mount Vernon 43050

Lakeland Community College
7700 Clocktower Dr.
Mentor 44060-7594

Lima Technical College
4240 Campus Dr.
Lima 45804

Lorain County Community College
1005 North Abbe Rd.
Elyria 44035

Mansfield General Hospital School of
Nursing
335 Glessner Ave.
Mansfield 44903-2265

Marion Technical College
1467 Mount Vernon Ave.
Marion 43302-5694

Mercy School of Nursing
2238 Jefferson Ave.
Toledo 43624

Meridia Huron School of Nursing
13951 Terrace Rd.
Cleveland 44112-4399

Metrohealth Medical Center School of
Nursing
1803 Valentine Ave.
Cleveland 44109

Miami University-Oxford Campus
Oxford 45056

North Central Technical College
2441 Kenwood Circle, P.O. Box 698
Mansfield 44901

Northwest Technical College
22-600 South Rte. 34 & Rte. 1, P.O. Box
246A
Archbold 43502-9990

Ohio University-Zanesville Branch
1425 Newark Rd.
Zanesville 43701

Ohio Valley Hospital School of Nursing
One Ross Park
Steubenville 43952

Owens Technical College
30335 Oregon Rd., P.O. Box 10000
Toledo 43699-1947

Providence Hospital School of Nursing
1912 Hayes Ave.
Sandusky 44870-4788

Queen City Vocational Center
425 Ezzard Charles Dr.
Cincinnati 45203

Saint Elizabeth Hospital Medical Center
School of Nursing
1044 Belmont Ave., P.O. Box 1790
Youngstown 44501-1790

Saint Thomas Medical Center School of
Nursing
41 Arch St.
Akron 44304

Saint Vincent Medical Center School of
Nursing
2201 Cherry St.
Toledo 43608-2603

Shawnee State University
940 Second St.
Portsmouth 45662

Sinclair Community College
444 West Third St.
Dayton 45402

Southern State Community College
200 Hobart Dr.
Hillsboro 45133

University of Cincinnati-Raymond
Walters College
9555 Plainfield Rd.
Blue Ash 45236

University of Rio Grande
North College St.
Rio Grande 45674

University of Toledo
2801 West Bancroft
Toledo 43606

Xavier University
3800 Victory Pkwy.
Cincinnati 45207-1092

OKLAHOMA

Bacone College
2299 Old Bacome Rd.
Muskogee 74403-1597

Cameron University
2800 Gore Blvd.
Lawton 73505

Carl Albert State College
1507 South McKenna
Poteau 74953-5208

Connors State College
Rte. 1, P.O. Box 1000
Warner 74469

Eastern Oklahoma State College
1301 West Main St.
Wilburton 74578

Murray State College
1100 South Murray
Tishomingo 73460

Northeastern Oklahoma Agricultural and
Mechanical College
200 Eye St. NE
Miami 74354

Northern Oklahoma College
P.O. Box 310
Tonkawa 74653

Oklahoma City Community College
7777 South May Ave.
Oklahoma City 73159

Oklahoma State University-Oklahoma
City
900 North Portland
Oklahoma City 73107

Pontotoc Skill Development Center
601 West 33rd
Ada 74820

Redland Community College
1300 South Country Club Rd., P.O. Box
370
El Reno 73036

Rogers State College
Will Rogers and College Hill
Claremore 74017

Rose State College
6420 Southeast 15th
Midwest City 73110

Seminole Junior College
P.O. Box 351
Seminole 74868

Tulsa Junior College
6111 East Skelly Dr.
Tulsa 74135

OREGON

Blue Mountain Community College
P.O. Box 100
Pendleton 97801

Central Oregon Community College
2600 Northwest College Way
Bend 97701

Chemeketa Community College
P.O. Box 14007
Salem 97309-7070

Clackamas Community College
19600 Molalla Ave.
Oregon City 97045

Clatsop Community College
1653 Jerome St.
Astoria 97103

Lane Community College
4000 East 30th Ave.
Eugene 97405

Linn-Benton Community College
6500 Southwest Pacific Blvd.
Albany 97321

Mount Hood Community College
26000 Southeast Stark St.
Gresham 97030

Portland Community College
P.O. Box 19000
Portland 97280-0990

Rogue Community College
3345 Redwood Hwy.
Grants Pass 97527

Southwestern Oregon Community
College
1988 Newmark Ave.
Coos Bay 97420

Umpqua Community College
P.O. Box 967
Roseburg 97470

PENNSYLVANIA

Abington Memorial Hospital School of
Nursing
1942 Horace Ave.
Abington 19001

Altoona Hospital School of Nursing
620 Howard Ave.
Altoona 16601-4899

Alvernia College
400 Bernardine St.
Reading 19607

Brandywine Hospital School of Nursing
Rte. 30 Bypass
Coatesville 19320

Bucks County Community College
Swamp Rd.
Newtown 18940

Butler County Community College
College Dr. Oak Hills
Butler 16003-1203

Chester County Hospital School of
Nursing
701 East Marshall St.
West Chester 19380

Citizens General Hospital School of
Nursing
651 Fourth Ave.
New Kensington 15068

Clarion University of Pennsylvania
Clarion 16214

Community College of Allegheny County
800 Allegheny Ave.
Pittsburgh 15233-1895

Community College of Beaver County
One Campus Dr.
Monaca 15061

Community College of Philadelphia
1700 Spring Garden St.
Philadelphia 19130

Delaware County Community College
901 South Media Line Rd.
Media 19063

Episcopal Hospital-School of Nursing
100 East Lehigh Ave.
Philadelphia 19125-1098

Gwynedd-Mercy College
Sumneytown Pike
Gwynedd Valley 19437

Hahnemann University
Broad and Vine
Philadelphia 19102

Harrisburg Area Community
College-Harrisburg Campus
One Hacc Dr.
Harrisburg 17110

Jameson Memorial Hospital
1211 Wilmington Ave.
New Castle 16105-2595

Lancaster General Hospital-Education
and Training
555 North Duke St.
Lancaster 17603

Lehigh County Community College
4525 Education Park Dr.
Schnecksville 18078-2598

Lock Haven University
North Fairview St.
Lock Haven 17745

Louise Suydam McClintic School of
Nursing
105 Zeta Dr.
Pittsburgh 15238-2811

Luzerne County Community College
1333 South Prospect St.
Nanticoke 18634

Mercer County Area Vocational
Technical School
P.O. Box 152
Mercer 16137-0152

Montgomery County Community College
340 Dekalb Pike
Blue Bell 19422

Mount Aloysius College
One College Dr.
Cresson 16630-1999

Northampton County Area Community
College
3835 Green Pond Rd.
Bethlehem 18017

Northeastern Hospital School of Nursing
2301 East Allegheny Ave. S
Philadelphia 19134

Pennsylvania College of Technology
One College Ave.
Williamsport 17701

Pennsylvania State University-Main
Campus
201 Old Main
University Park 16802

Pottsville Hospital
Washington and Jackson St.
Pottsville 17901

Reading Area Community College
P.O. Box 1706
Reading 19603

Roxborough Memorial Hospital
5800 Ridge Ave.
Philadelphia 19128

Saint Francis Hospital School of Nursing
1100 South Mercer St.
New Castle 16101

Saint Luke's Hospital School of Nursing
801 Ostrum
Bethlehem 18015

Saint Vincent Health Center
232 West 25th St.
Erie 16544

Sewickley Valley Hospital School of
Nursing
Blackburn Rd.
Sewickley 15143

Shadyside Hospital School of Nursing
5230 Centre Ave.
Pittsburgh 15232

Sharon Regional Health System School
of Nursing
740 East State St.
Sharon 16146

University of Pittsburgh-Bradford
Campus
300 Campus Dr.
Bradford 16701

Washington Hospital School of Nursing
155 Wilson Ave.
Washington 15301

Western Pennsylvania Hospital School of
Nursing
4900 Friendship Ave.
Pittsburgh 15224

Westmoreland County Community
College
Youngwood 15697-1895

RHODE ISLAND

Community College of Rhode Island
400 East Ave.
Warwick 02886-1805

Saint Joseph Hospital School of Nursing
200 High Service Ave.
North Providence 02904

SOUTH CAROLINA

Florence-Darlington Technical College
P.O. Box 100548
Florence 29501-0548

Greenville Technical College
Station B, P.O. Box 5616
Greenville 29606-5616

Midlands Technical College
P.O. Box 2408
Columbia 29202

Orangeburg-Calhoun Technical College
3250 Saint Matthew's Rd.
Orangeburg 29115

Piedmont Technical College
P.O. Drawer 1467
Greenwood 29648

Tri-County Technical College
P.O. Box 587
Pendleton 29670

Trident Technical College
P.O. Box 118067
Charleston 29423-8067

University of South Carolina at Aiken
171 University Pkwy.
Aiken 29801

University of South Carolina at Coastal
Carolina
P.O. Box 1954
Myrtle Beach 29577

University of South Carolina at
Spartanburg
800 University Way
Spartanburg 29303

SOUTH DAKOTA

Dakota Wesleyan University
1200 West University Ave.
Mitchell 57301-4398

Huron University
333 Ninth St. SW
Huron 57350

Presentation College
1500 North Main
Aberdeen 57401

University of South Dakota
414 East Clark St.
Vermillion 57069-2390

TENNESSEE

Baptist Memorial Hospital School of
Nursing
999 Monroe Ave.
Memphis 38104

Chattanooga State Technical Community
College
4501 Amnicola Hwy.
Chattanooga 37406

Cleveland State Community College
P.O. Box 3570
Cleveland 37320-3570

Columbia State Community College
P.O. Box 1315
Columbia 38401

Dyersburg State Community College
1516 Nichols Ave.
Dyersburg 38024

East Tennessee State University
P.O. Box 70716
Johnson City 37614

Fort Sanders School of Nursing
1915 White Ave.
Knoxville 37916

Jackson State Community College
2046 North Pkwy.
Jackson 38301

Lincoln Memorial University
Cumberland Gap Pkwy.
Harrogate 37752

Methodist Hospital School of Nursing
251 South Claybrook
Memphis 38104

Motlow State Community College
P.O. Box 88100
Tullahoma 37388-8100

Roane State Community College
Patton Ln.
Harriman 37748

Saint Joseph Hospital School of Nursing
204 Overton Ave.
Memphis 38105

Shelby State Community College
P.O. Box 40568
Memphis 38174-0568

Southern College of Seventh-Day
Adventists
4881 Taylor Circle, P.O. Box 370
Collegedale 37315-0370

Tennessee State University
3500 John Merritt Blvd.
Nashville 37209-1561

Union University
Hwy. 45 Bypass
Jackson 38305-9901

Walters State Community College
500 South Davy Crockett Pkwy.
Morristown 37813-6899

TEXAS

Alvin Community College
3110 Mustang Rd.
Alvin 77511

Amarillo College
P.O. Box 447
Amarillo 79178

Angelina College
P.O. Box 1768
Lufkin 75902-1768

Angelo State University
2601 West Ave. N
San Angelo 76901

Austin Community College
5930 Middle Fiskville Rd.
Austin 78752

Baptist Memorial Hospital
System-Institute of Health Education
111 Dallas St.
San Antonio 78205

Blinn College
902 College Ave.
Brenham 77833

Central Texas College
P.O. Box 1800
Killeen 76540-9990

Chenier
6300 Richmond
Houston 77057

College of the Mainland
1200 Amburn Rd.
Texas City 77591

Collin County Community College
2200 West University
McKinney 75070

Cooke County College
1525 West California
Gainesville 76240

Del Mar College
101 Baldwin
Corpus Christi 78404-3897

El Centro College
Main and Lamar
Dallas 75202

El Paso Community College
P.O. Box 20500
El Paso 79998

Frank Phillips College
P.O. Box 5118
Borger 79008-5118

Galveston College
4015 Ave. Q
Galveston 77550

Grayson County College
6101 Grayson Dr.
Denison 75020

Houston Baptist University
7502 Fondren Rd.
Houston 77074

Houston Community College System
22 Waugh Dr., P.O. Box 7849
Houston 77270-7849

Howard County Junior College District
1001 Birdwell Ln.
Big Spring 79720

John Peter Smith Hospital
1500 South Main St.
Fort Worth 76104

Kilgore College
1100 Broadway
Kilgore 75662-3299

Lamar University-Beaumont
4400 Mlk, P.O. Box 10001
Beaumont 77710

Lamar University-Orange
410 Front St.
Orange 77630

Laredo Junior College
West End Washington St.
Laredo 78040

Lee College
511 South Whiting St.
Baytown 77520-4703

McLennan Community College
1400 College Dr.
Waco 76708

Midland College
3600 North Garfield
Midland 79705

Navarro College
3200 West Seventh
Corsicana 75110

North Harris Montgomery Community
College District
250 North Sam Houston Pkwy. E
Houston 77060

Odessa College
201 West University
Odessa 79764

Paris Junior College
2400 Clarksville St.
Paris 75460

PCI Health Training Center
8101 John Carpenter Fwy.
Dallas 75247

San Antonio College
1300 San Pedro Ave.
San Antonio 78284

San Jacinto College-Central Campus
8060 Spencer Hwy.
Pasadena 77505

South Plains College
1401 College Ave.
Levelland 79336

Southwest Texas Junior College
2401 Garner Field Rd.
Uvalde 78801

Southwestern Adventist College
P.O. Box 567
Keene 76059

Tarrant County Junior College District
1500 Houston St.
Fort Worth 76102

Texarkana College
2500 North Robison Rd.
Texarkana 75501

Texas Southmost College
80 Fort Brown
Brownsville 78520

Trinity Valley Community College
500 South Prairieville
Athens 75751

Tyler County Hospital School of Nursing
1100 West Bluff
Woodville 75979

Tyler Junior College
P.O. Box 9020
Tyler 75711

The University of Texas-Pan American at
Edinburg
1201 West University Dr.
Edinburg 78539

Victoria College
2200 East Red River
Victoria 77901

Wharton County Junior College
911 Boling Hwy.
Wharton 77488

UTAH

Salt Lake Community College
P.O. Box 30808
Salt Lake City 84130

Utah Valley Community College
800 West 1200 South
Orem 84058

Weber State University
3750 Harrison Blvd.
Ogden 84408

VERMONT

Fanny Allen School of Practical Nursing
29 Ethan Allen Ave.
Colchester 05446-3339

Norwich University
Northfield 05663

University of Vermont and State
Agricultural College
South Prospect, 223 Waterman Building
Burlington 05405-0160

VIRGINIA

Community Hospital of Roanoke Valley
College of Health Sciences
P.O. Box 13186
Roanoke 24031-3186

Dabney S Lancaster Community College
P.O. Box 1000
Clifton Forge 24422-1000

Danville Community College
1008 South Main St.
Danville 24541

De Paul Medical Center School of
Nursing
150 Kingsley Ln.
Norfolk 23505

Germanna Community College
P.O. Box 339
Locust Grove 22508

J Sargeant Reynolds Community College
P.O. Box 85622
Richmond 23285-5622

John Tyler Community College
13101 Jefferson Davis Hwy.
Chester 23831-5399

Memorial Hospital School of Nursing
142 South Main St.
Danville 24541

Mountain Empire Community College
P.O. Drawer 700
Big Stone Gap 24219

Norfolk State University
2401 Corprew Ave.
Norfolk 23504

Northern Virginia Community College
4001 Wakefield Chapel Rd.
Annandale 22003

Patrick Henry Community College
P.O. Box 5311
Martinsville 24115-5311

Piedmont Virginia Community College
Rte. 6, P.O. Box 1
Charlottesville 22902

Rappahannock Community College
Glenns Campus, P.O. Box 287
Glenns 23149

Sentara Norfolk General Hospital School
of Nursing
600 Gresham Dr.
Norfolk 23507

Shenandoah University
1460 University Dr.
Winchester 22601

Southwest Virginia Community College
P.O. Box SVCC
Richlands 24641

Thomas Nelson Community College
P.O. Box 9407
Hampton 23670

Tidewater Community College
Rte. 135
Portsmouth 23703

Tidewater Technical
616 Denbigh Blvd.
Newport News 23602

Virginia Highlands Community College
P.O. Box 828
Abingdon 24210

Virginia Western Community College
3095 Colonial Ave.
Roanoke 24015

Wytheville Community College
1000 East Main St.
Wytheville 24382

WASHINGTON

Bellevue Community College
3000 Landerholm Circle SE
Bellevue 98007-6484

Clark College
1800 East McLoughlin Blvd.
Vancouver 98663

Columbia Basin College
2600 North 20th Ave.
Pasco 99301

Everett Community College
801 Wetmore Ave.
Everett 98201

Grays Harbor College
1620 Edward P Smith Dr.
Aberdeen 98520

Highline Community College
P.O. Box 98000
Des Moines 98198-9800

Lower Columbia College
P.O. Box 3010
Longview 98632

Olympic College
1600 Chester Ave.
Bremerton 98310-1699

Seattle Central Community College
1701 Broadway
Seattle 98122

Shoreline Community College
16101 Greenwood Ave. N
Seattle 98133

Skagit Valley College
2405 College Way
Mount Vernon 98273

South Puget Sound Community College
2011 Mottman Rd. SW
Olympia 98512

Spokane Community College
North 1810 Greene Ave.
Spokane 99207

Tacoma Community College
5900 South 12th St.
Tacoma 98465

Walla Walla Community College
500 Tausick Way
Walla Walla 99362

Wenatchee Valley College
1300 Fifth St.
Wenatchee 98801

Yakima Valley Community College
P.O. Box 1647
Yakima 98907

WEST VIRGINIA

Bluefield State College
219 Rock St.
Bluefield 24701

Cabell County Vocational Technical
Center
1035 Norway Ave.
Huntington 25705

Davis and Elkins College
100 Campus Dr.
Elkins 26241-3996

Fairmont State College
1201 Locust Ave.
Fairmont 26554

Saint Mary's Hospital School of Nursing
2900 First Ave.
Huntington 25702

Shepherd College
King St., Ikenberry Hall
Shepherdstown 25443

Southern West Virginia Community
College
P.O. Box 2900
Logan 25601

The University of Charleston
2300 MacCorkle Ave. SE
Charleston 25304

West Virginia Northern Community
College
College Square
Wheeling 26003

West Virginia University at Parkersburg
Rte. 5, P.O. Box 167A
Parkersburg 26101

WISCONSIN

Blackhawk Technical College
P.O. Box 5009
Janesville 53547

Chippewa Valley Technical College
620 West Clairemont Ave.
Eau Claire 54701

Fox Valley Technical College
1825 North Bluemound Dr.
Appleton 54913-2277

Gateway Technical College
3520 30th Ave.
Kenosha 53144-1690

Lakeshore Vocational Training and Adult
Education System District
1290 North Ave.
Cleveland 53015

Milwaukee Area Technical College
700 West State St.
Milwaukee 53233

Milwaukee County Medical Complex
School of Nursing
1304 South 70th St.
West Allis 53214-3153

Nicolet Vocational Training and Adult
Education System District
P.O. Box 518
Rhinelander 54501

North Central Technical College
1000 Campus Dr.
Wausau 54401-1899

Northeast Wisconsin Technical College
2740 West Mason St., P.O. Box 19042
Green Bay 54307-9042

Southwest Wisconsin Technical College
Hwy. 18 E
Fennimore 53809

Waukesha County Technical College
800 Main St.
Pewaukee 53072

Western Wisconsin Technical College
304 North Sixth St., P.O. Box 908
La Crosse 54602-0908

Wisconsin Area Vocational Training and
Adult Education System-Moraine Park
235 North National Ave., P.O. Box 1940
Fond Du Lac 54936-1940

Wisconsin Area Vocational Training and
Adult Education System District
Number Four
3550 Anderson St.
Madison 53704

Wisconsin Indianhead Technical College
505 Pine Ridge Dr., P.O. Box 10B
Shell Lake 54871

WYOMING

Casper College
125 College Dr.
Casper 82601

Central Wyoming College
2660 Peck Ave.
Riverton 82501

Laramie County Community College
1400 East College Dr.
Cheyenne 82007

Northwest Community College
231 West Sixth St.
Powell 82435

Sheridan College
P.O. Box 1500
Sheridan 82801

Western Wyoming Community College
P.O. Box 428
Rock Springs 82902

Respiratory Technology

ALABAMA

George C Wallace State Community
College-Hanceville
801 Main St. NW, P.O. Box 2000
Hanceville 35077-2000

University of Alabama at Birmingham
UAB MJH 107 2010
Birmingham 35294-2010

ARIZONA

Apollo College-Phoenix, Inc.
8503 North 27th Ave.
Phoenix 85051

Apollo College-Tri City, Inc.
630 West Southern Ave.
Mesa 85210

Gateway Community College
108 North 40th St.
Phoenix 85034

Long Medical Institute
4126 North Black Canyon Hwy.
Phoenix 85017

Pima Community College
2202 West Anklam Rd.
Tucson 85709-0001

ARKANSAS

Arkansas Valley Technical Institute
Hwy. 23 N, P.O. Box 506
Ozark 72949

Black River Technical College
Hwy. 304, P.O. Box 468
Pocahontas 72455

Pulaski Technical College
3000 West Scenic Dr.
North Little Rock 72118

Red River Technical College
P.O. Box 140
Hope 71801

University of Arkansas for Medical
Sciences
4301 West Markham
Little Rock 72205

CALIFORNIA

California College for Health Science
222 West 24th St.
National City 91950

California Paramedic and Technical
College
4550 La Sierra Ave.
Riverside 92505

California Paramedic and Technical
College
3745 Long Beach Blvd.
Long Beach 90807

Concorde Career Institute
4150 Lankershim Blvd.
North Hollywood 91602

Concorde Career Institute
1290 North First St.
San Jose 95112

Crafton Hills College
11711 Sand Canyon Rd.
Yucaipa 92399-1799

El Camino College
16007 Crenshaw Blvd.
Torrance 90506

Foothill College
12345 El Monte Rd.
Los Altos Hills 94022

Grossmont College
8800 Grossmont College Dr.
El Cajon 92020

Hacienda La Puente Unified School
District-Valley Vocational Center
15959 East Gale Ave.
La Puente 91749

Modesto Junior College
435 College Ave.
Modesto 95350-9977

Napa Valley College
2277 Napa Vallejo Hwy.
Napa 94558

San Joaquin Valley College
201 New Stine Rd.
Bakersfield 93309

San Joaquin Valley College
8400 West Mineral King Ave.
Visalia 93291

Simi Valley Adult School
3192 Los Angeles Ave.
Simi Valley 93065

Victor Valley College
18422 Bear Valley Rd.
Victorville 92392-9699

COLORADO

Front Range Community College
3645 West 112th Ave.
Westminster 80030

FLORIDA

ATI Health Education Center
1395 Northwest 167th St.
Miami 33169

Daytona Beach Community College
1200 Volusia Ave.
Daytona Beach 32114

Flagler Career Institute
3225 University Blvd. S
Jacksonville 32216

Manatee Community College
5840 26th St. W
Bradenton 34207

Miami-Dade Community College
300 Northeast Second Ave.
Miami 33132

Palm Beach Community College
4200 Congress Ave.
Lake Worth 33461

GEORGIA

Augusta Technical Institute
3116 Deans Bridge Rd.
Augusta 30906

HAWAII

Kapiolani Community College
4303 Diamond Head Rd.
Honolulu 96816

IDAHO

Boise State University
1910 University Dr.
Boise 83725

ILLINOIS

Belleville Area College
2500 Carlyle Rd.
Belleville 62221

College of Du Page
Lambert Rd. and 22nd St.
Glen Ellyn 60137

Illinois Central College
One College Dr.
East Peoria 61635

Moraine Valley Community College
10900 South 88th Ave.
Palos Hills 60465-0937

Rock Valley College
3301 North Mulford Rd.
Rockford 61114

Saint John's Hospital School of
Respiratory Therapy
800 East Carpenter
Springfield 62769

Triton College
2000 Fifth Ave.
River Grove 60171

INDIANA

Indiana Vocational Technical
College-Central Indiana
One West 26th St.
Indianapolis 46206-1763

Indiana Vocational Technical
College-Northeast
3800 North Anthony Blvd.
Fort Wayne 46805

KANSAS

Seward County Community College
P.O. Box 1137
Liberal 67905-1137

Washburn University of Topeka
1700 College Ave.
Topeka 66621

KENTUCKY

Harry Sparks Area Vocational Education
P.O. Box 275
Mount Vernon 40456

Kentucky Department for Adult &
Technical Education-Central Kentucky
SVTS
104 Vo Tech Rd.
Lexington 40510

Kentucky Technical-Bowling Green
State Vocational Technical School
1845 Loop Dr., P.O. Box 6000
Bowling Green 42101

Kentucky Technical-Rowan State
Vocational Technical School
100 Vo-Tech Dr.
Morehead 40351

LOUISIANA

Bossier Parish Community College
2719 Airline Dr. N
Bossier City 71111

Delgado Community College
615 City Park Ave.
New Orleans 70119

Southeastern Louisiana University
100 West Dakota
Hammond 70402

West Jefferson Technical Institute
475 Manhattan Blvd.
Harvey 70058

MICHIGAN

Macomb Community College
14500 Twelve Mile Rd.
Warren 48093-3896

MINNESOTA

Northwest Technical College-East Grand
Forks
Hwy. 220 N
East Grand Forks 56721

MISSISSIPPI

Hinds Community College-Raymond
Campus
Raymond 39154

Mississippi Gulf Coast Community
College
Central Office, P.O. Box 67
Perkinston 39573

University of Mississippi Medical Center
2500 North State St.
Jackson 39216

MISSOURI

Hannibal Area Vocational Technical
School
4550 McMasters Ave.
Hannibal 63401

MONTANA

Great Falls Vocational Technical Center
2100 16th Ave. S
Great Falls 59405

NEBRASKA

Metropolitan Community College Area
P.O. Box 3777
Omaha 68103

NEW JERSEY

Gloucester County College
Tanyard Rd. & RR 4, P.O. Box 203
Sewell 08080

University of Medicine and Dentistry of
New Jersey
30 Bergen St.
Newark 07107

NEW YORK

CUNY Borough of Manhattan
Community College
199 Chambers St.
New York 10007

NYU Medical Center Allied Health
Education
342 East 26th St.
New York 10010

Onondaga Community College
Rte. 173
Syracuse 13215

NORTH CAROLINA

Carteret Community College
3505 Arendell St.
Morehead City 28557

Durham Technical Community College
1637 Lawson St.
Durham 27703

Edgecombe Community College
2009 West Wilson St.
Tarboro 27886

Stanly Community College
141 College Dr.
Albemarle 28001

OHIO

Columbus State Community College
550 East Spring St., P.O. Box 1609
Columbus 43216

Lima Technical College
4240 Campus Dr.
Lima 45804

University of Toledo
2801 West Bancroft
Toledo 43606

OKLAHOMA

Francis Tuttle Area Vocational-Technical
Center
12777 North Rockwell Ave.
Oklahoma City 73142-2789

OREGON

Apollo College-Portland, Inc.
2600 Southeast 98th Ave.
Portland 97266

PENNSYLVANIA

Lehigh County Community College
4525 Education Park Dr.
Schnecksville 18078-2598

SOUTH CAROLINA

Greenville Technical College
Station B, P.O. Box 5616
Greenville 29606-5616

Midlands Technical College
P.O. Box 2408
Columbia 29202

Spartanburg Technical College
Hwy. I-85, P.O. Drawer 4386
Spartanburg 29305

TENNESSEE

Memphis Area Vocational-Technical
School
550 Alabama Ave.
Memphis 38105-3799

Roane State Community College
Patton Ln.
Harriman 37748

TEXAS

Alvin Community College
3110 Mustang Rd.
Alvin 77511

El Centro College
Main and Lamar
Dallas 75202

Houston Community College System
22 Waugh Dr., P.O. Box 7849
Houston 77270-7849

North Harris Montgomery Community
College District
250 North Sam Houston Pkwy. E
Houston 77060

Saint Philip's College
2111 Nevada St.
San Antonio 78203

San Jacinto College-Central Campus
8060 Spencer Hwy.
Pasadena 77505

Southwest Texas State University
601 University Dr.
San Marcos 78666

Temple Junior College
2600 South First St.
Temple 76504-7435

Texas Southmost College
80 Fort Brown
Brownsville 78520

Tyler Junior College
P.O. Box 9020
Tyler 75711

UTAH

Weber State University
3750 Harrison Blvd.
Ogden 84408

VIRGINIA

Northern Virginia Community College
4001 Wakefield Chapel Rd.
Annandale 22003

WASHINGTON

Tacoma Community College
5900 South 12th St.
Tacoma 98465

WEST VIRGINIA

West Virginia Northern Community
College
College Square
Wheeling 26003

WYOMING

Western Wyoming Community College
P.O. Box 428
Rock Springs 82902

Surgical Technology

ALABAMA

Community College of the Air Force
Maxwell Air Force Base
Montgomery 36112

ARIZONA

The Bryman School
4343 North 16th St.
Phoenix 85016

CALIFORNIA

California Paramedic and Technical
College
3745 Long Beach Blvd.
Long Beach 90807

Institute of Business and Medical
Technology
75-110 Saint Charles Place
Palm Desert 92260

Newbridge College
700 El Camino Real
Tustin 92680

COLORADO

Concorde Career Institute
770 Grant St.
Denver 80203

FLORIDA

Sheridan Vocational Center
5400 West Sheridan St.
Hollywood 33021

ILLINOIS

Swedish American Hospital School of
Surgical Technology
1400 Charles St.
Rockford 61104-1257

KENTUCKY

Kentucky Department for Adult &
Technical Education-Central Kentucky
SVTS
104 Vo Tech Rd.
Lexington 40510

Kentucky Technical-Jefferson State
Vocational Technical School
727 West Chestnut
Louisville 40203

LOUISIANA

Delgado Community College
615 City Park Ave.
New Orleans 70119

MASSACHUSETTS

New England Baptist Hospital School of
Nursing
220 Fisher Ave.
Boston 02120

Quincy College
34 Coddington St.
Quincy 02169

MICHIGAN

Lansing Community College
419 North Capitol Ave.
Lansing 48901-7210

MINNESOTA

Minnesota Riverland Technical
College-Rochester Campus
1926 College View Rd. SE
Rochester 55904

Northwest Technical College-East Grand
Forks
Hwy. 220 N
East Grand Forks 56721

Saint Cloud Technical College
1540 Northway Dr.
Saint Cloud 56303

MISSISSIPPI

Itawamba Community College
602 West Hill St.
Fulton 38843

PENNSYLVANIA

Delaware County Community College
901 South Media Line Rd.
Media 19063

Mount Aloysius College
One College Dr.
Cresson 16630-1999

Saint Francis Medical Center School of
Nursing
400 45th St.
Pittsburgh 15201

Wilkes-Barre General Hospital-School of
Medical Technology
North River and Auburn
Wilkes-Barre 18764

SOUTH CAROLINA

Midlands Technical College
P.O. Box 2408
Columbia 29202

York Technical College
452 South Anderson Rd.
Rock Hill 29730

TENNESSEE

Aquinas Junior College
4210 Harding Rd.
Nashville 37205

Knoxville State Area
Vocational-Technical School
1100 Liberty St.
Knoxville 37919

Memphis Area Vocational-Technical
School
550 Alabama Ave.
Memphis 38105-3799

TEXAS

Houston Community College System
22 Waugh Dr., P.O. Box 7849
Houston 77270-7849

San Antonio College of Medical and
Dental Assistants
5280 Medical Dr.
San Antonio 78229

South Plains College
1401 College Ave.
Levelland 79336

Temple Junior College
2600 South First St.
Temple 76504-7435

Texas State Technical College-Harlingen
Campus
2424 Boxwood
Harlingen 78550-3697

VIRGINIA

NNPS RRMC School of Surgical
Technology
12420 Warwick Blvd.
Newport News 23606

WASHINGTON

Seattle Central Community College
1701 Broadway
Seattle 98122

WISCONSIN

Northeast Wisconsin Technical College
2740 West Mason St., P.O. Box 19042
Green Bay 54307-9042

Veterinarian's Assistant

ARIZONA

Long Medical Institute
4126 North Black Canyon Hwy.
Phoenix 85017

Pima Medical Institute
3350 East Grant Rd.
Tucson 85716

CALIFORNIA

San Diego Mesa College
7250 Mesa College Dr.
San Diego 92111-4998

Yuba College
2088 North Beale Rd.
Marysville 95901

COLORADO

Bel-Rea Institute of Animal Technology
1681 South Dayton St.
Denver 80231

FLORIDA

Saint Petersburg Junior College
P.O. Box 13489
Saint Petersburg 33733

IDAHO

American Institute of Health Technology,
Inc.
6600 Emerald
Boise 83704

ILLINOIS

Parkland College
2400 West Bradley Ave.
Champaign 61821

KANSAS

Colby Community College
1255 South Range
Colby 67701

MINNESOTA

Duluth Business University, Inc.
412 West Superior St.
Duluth 55802

Globe College of Business
175 Fifth St. E, P.O. Box 60
Saint Paul 55101-2901

MISSOURI

Maple Woods Community College
2601 Northeast Barry Rd.
Kansas City 64156

Midwest Institute for Medical Assistants
112 West Jefferson
Kirkwood 63122

NEVADA

Professional Careers
3305 Spring Mountain Rd.
Las Vegas 89120

NEW YORK

SUNY College of Technology at Canton
Canton 13617

SUNY College of Technology at Delhi
Delhi 13753

SUNY College of Technology at
Farmingdale
Melville Rd.
Farmingdale 11735

NORTH CAROLINA

Central Carolina Community College
1105 Kelly Dr.
Sanford 27330

OHIO

Columbus State Community College
550 East Spring St., P.O. Box 1609
Columbus 43216

PENNSYLVANIA

Allied Medical Careers, Inc.
2901 Pittston Ave.
Scranton 18505

Allied Medical Careers, Inc.
104 Woodward Hill Rd.
Edwardsville 18704

Median School of Allied Health Careers
125 Seventh St.
Pittsburgh 15222-3400

TEXAS

North Harris Montgomery Community
College District
250 North Sam Houston Pkwy. E
Houston 77060

WASHINGTON

Pima Medical Institute
1627 Eastlake Ave. E
Seattle 98102

Index

All jobs mentioned in this volume are listed and cross-referenced in the index. Some main entries appear in all capital letters; these relate to jobs that have separate occupational profiles. For example, ACUPUNCTURIST, ADMITTING CLERK, AIDS COUNSELOR, and so on are profiles in this volume. Main entries that are not capitalized refer either to jobs that do not have a separate profile, but for which information is given, or to relevant career topics.

Under some capitalized entries there is a section entitled "Profile includes." This lists jobs that are mentioned in the main-entry profile. So, in the case of ADMITTING CLERK, a job that is included in the profile is Admitting officer.

Some main entries are followed by a list of related job profiles. These appear in parentheses after the page numbers on which they can be found. For instance, in the BIOMEDICAL EQUIPMENT TECHNICIAN profile, a related job that is profiled in this volume is (Dialysis technician).

Photographic Credits